Key Concepts in Theatre/Drama Education

Key Concepts in Theatre/Drama Education

Edited by

Shifra Schonmann
University of Haifa, Israel

SENSE PUBLISHERS
ROTTERDAM/BOSTON/TAIPEI

A C.I.P. record for this book is available from the Library of Congress.

ISBN: 978-94-6091-330-3 (paperback)
ISBN: 978-94-6091-331-0 (hardback)
ISBN: 978-94-6091-332-7 (e-book)

Published by: Sense Publishers,
P.O. Box 21858,
3001 AW Rotterdam,
The Netherlands
https://www.sensepublishers.com

Printed on acid-free paper

TABLE OF CONTENTS

TABLE OF CONTENTS

Section X: Ways of Research and Methodology

Closing

ACKNOWLEDGMENT AS A NOTE OF PREFACE

Firstly, my thanks go to Lynn Fels, the language editor of this volume. With care, wisdom and dedication, she helped shape the language of those of us whose mother tongue is not English. She skillfully engaged with all entries, building on her knowledge in the field of theatre drama education. Her professionalism in editing enhanced the quality of this book, and I am in her debt.

Secondly, my thanks go to Menachem Schonmann, who edited the typescript intelligently, imaginatively, and with meticulous attention to details.

Thirdly, my thanks go to SENSEPUBLISHERS, who gave me the chance to undertake this project. Special thanks go to Michel Lokhorst, for believing in my idea of an evolving book, and supporting its production gently and without stress. He proffered a contract when there was only a raw idea of creating community of researchers, without specified writers nor well- defined issues in advance. I intended to choose the key concepts by heading a process of interactive discussion among the various contributors, attempting to push the boundaries of the ways in which we think about theatre/drama education possibilities. I deeply appreciate SENSEPUBLISHERS's support of this project, and am grateful for this invaluable opportunity.

Lastly, a bouquet of thanks goes to the sixty authors who shared their wisdom, care and enthusiasm in open peer-reviews, intelligent discussions, and the exchange of ideas that resulted in the bright and interesting entries that follow. Their belief in me, support and encouragement all the way through, until this book was finally completed, was a steady rainbow shining in the sky of the emerging key concepts. We present here the fruit of our accomplishment, a book expanding our vision of the possibilities of theatre/drama education.

This book is dedicated with gratitude to the sixty authors for making it all possible, for making it all meaningful and worthwhile.

Shifra Schonmann
June 2010

OPENING

SHIFRA SCHONMANN

1. AN IDENTITY CARD IN THE MAKING

Key Concepts in Theatre/Drama Education

Keywords: knowledge, constructing knowledge, professional identity, key concepts, modes of knowing

Reading a book is the most impressive game that people have yet invented maintains Wislawa Szymborska in the preface to her book, *Nonrequired Reading* (2002). I would like to echo her words by considering the idea of writing and asserting that **writing a book** is a similarly impressive activity created by people seeking to enjoy themselves. It is a demanding enterprise that entails concentration, dedication, restraint and patience. It demands creativity with thoughts that soar freely as well as utterances that are sensibly controlled. It is an activity that serves as a womb for the birth of the human spirit. With this thought in mind, I approached a number of the sixty authors now participating in this book; I was hoping my colleagues would join me in a journey of writing to convey the spirit of the times in our field of theatre/drama education.

What would happen, I asked them, if we wrote a book on theatre/drama education through an organic process of identifying, creating and engaging a community of scholars willing to share their wisdom and knowledge in an open process of negotiating meaning? In this process, I proposed, authors could choose the topic that they wanted to discuss, circulate it among all the participants, offer their comments and develop dialogues that would continue up to the point when each author felt that his or her entry was ready for publication.

Everything that I wanted to know on theatre/drama education is dispersed among many journals, books and reports but I could not find one volume that aims to convey the zeitgeist of the field. This is why this book is so needed.

I soon realized that if we wanted to compile a substantial body of knowledge in the field, we needed to propose different epistemological rules with which all participants agreed in order to set out on an intellectual journey together while not knowing exactly what or who we would meet along the way. What would be included? Who would participate? And how and when would it end?

Here it is: the story of a flow, a process, how this book was created and why, **a new way** of constructing knowledge as well as its merits and some of its problems. This exposure of how we created the book is an integral part of the game that Wislawa Szymborska mentions. Our process in writing the book is innovative in the sense that the list of the authors participating in this volume and the resulting entries developed in an organic, cumulative fashion.

S. Schonmann (ed.), Key Concepts in Theatre/Drama Education, 3–9.

I admit that the image of writing a book as a journey of adventure is a conventional one and thus might be seen as too simplistic; however, it contains one clear truth that helps to clarify the process underlying this project. It is an exciting, intellectual enterprise which contains a balance between searching and finding, between dialogue and defining, between closeness and detachment. This book, *Key Concepts in Theatre/Drama Education*, is a journey across three fields of scholarship: theatre, education and modes of knowing.

Constructing a list of contributors via a network was the first step toward defining a community of researchers in the field and it is a kind of study in itself. Identifying potential contributors through networking gives us a good idea of who is "out there", who is concerned, and who has an interest in developing the field in this way now. I approached only a few of the writers and then asked each one of them to suggest five other people who he or she considered to be good scholars, people with something interesting to say. The individual could be a well-known figure in the field or a PhD student, or a new researcher whose work is outstanding. I wanted the book to give voice to old and young, novice and expert and to include as many ideas as we could think of collectively. I regard it as a matter of great importance to open the door to young researchers so that they can be involved in a project portraying the present state of the field and its future. I wanted our project to be true and authentic, not bound to any pre-determined topic as is so often the case in our conferences, in our research books and in the special issues appearing in a journal.

Everything started with my first letter to participants sent on 12th March, 2009 which explains the raison d'etre of the book which then evolved:

Dear colleague and friend,
I have the pleasure to invite you to join me in an intellectual adventure and to be one of a group of scholars who wish to contribute to a new book entitled:
Key Concepts in Theatre/Drama Education
Why did I say "intellectual adventure"? What would be new in the concept of the book?
It will be new in the way in which the book will be developed and thus new in its scope and its content.
Key Concepts in Theatre/Drama Education, for which I have a signed contract with SENSE PUBLISHERS, is now ready to get started.
I have decided to compile this book, as I believe that there is no contemporary resource to convey the core, and the scope, as well as the developments and the intricacies of our field. Such a book, I believe, cannot be written by only one author or even by two or three. It should be written by a large number of scholars, in order to present a comprehensive picture.

By 14th April, 2009, I had received from my colleagues an evolving list of 140 names. The many encouraging, cheering and helpful replies indicated that there was a real "thirst" in the field to explore a wide range of topics. Forty-three colleagues who immediately sent positive and enthusiastic responses started the project rolling. An eclectic list of various topics was generated which served as an excellent starting point; its beauty lies in its significant number, variety, and mixture of ideas. However our real work began as we entered Stage Two and Stage Three of the project when everyone was asked to comment on the list of contributors and on the list of topics, and to commit to writing on the topic that he or she had chosen. By August 12th 2009 entries had begun to flow in and were distributed to all participants for their helpful comments.

This process of open peer reviewing encouraged an in-depth dialogue among most of the participants, and improved the quality of the writing of those who were actively involved.

Our process of reviewing, revising the entries and developing dialogues until the whole draft was completed proved to be a dynamic and productive process. The dialogues with one another added a layer of depth to our professional knowledge and to our identity as theatre/drama educators. Fourteen months from its start, the manuscript is now ready for publication. Such a process of constructing knowledge needed time to ripen, to evolve; it required more time from some contributors than from others.

The idea of creating a book in an "evolutionary way" came from my experience with the in-depth form of communication that one can find on internet websites (such as Web logs or form internet sites). It was also inspired by the easy access that Google offers its users. Each topic can and often does lead to others. Our process of reviewing entries confirmed my belief that constructing knowledge through transparent negotiated meaning making is the next step that we need to take while editing our journals, compiling new books, and/or reviewing projects. As we develop knowledge in our field, we need to join the third great Cultural Revolution, the revolution of constructing knowledge by evolving transparent peer reviews through constructive open-access dialogues. I recommend this approach as opposed to the generally accepted practice in the academic world that gives rise to closed hidden reviews, difficult access to publication, and limited dialogue during the process. This shared approach of knowledge creation and dissemination is in direct opposition to that of oversight by a small and powerful group that more often than not controls knowledge and its dissemination.

I propose that "Key Concepts for Theatre/Drama Education" is an innovative book not only because of its new and fundamental concept of writing a book through collaborative networking and open-peer review and meaning-making involving the participation of a wide group of scholars who have shared in an ongoing process, but also because - until now - no collection of key concepts or anything similar has been published in the field of theatre/drama education and, as I suggested earlier, our relatively young field of knowledge needs to be examined in the light of ideas which today's scholars consider significant. The length of each topic was determined in advance. Each entry contains around two thousand words. The book is designed to be a basic companion for every researcher, student, drama-teacher or any other scholar who wants to know the basic and important concepts that make the field solid and prominent in the sphere of Arts Education.

Of course, there are pros and cons to such an endeavor, and most of these were discussed in the comments that authors put forward while the entries of the book were evolving. When, because of our time limit, I announced the closing of the list of contributors, it included almost two hundred potential participants. Then there was a long process of elimination; there were those who did not answer the follow-up call for entries, and there were those who could not participate because of their over-loaded timetable. We finalized the list with seventy participants who agreed to take part in this project. Six then dropped out, perhaps because they received from me a letter along the following lines:

> *I read your entry with great curiosity. It is interesting and you are probably doing some great work. Unfortunately the way in which you present your wonderful experience is not close enough to theatre/drama education as a few colleagues have already written to you and this book is not intended to present one's own work per se... If you would like to go on working on your entry, please do so... please consider the comments you have received by dialoguing with your critics... Please read the letter that I sent recently to all participants... and let me know how you want to take it from here.*
> *All the best,*
>
> *Shifra*

Sixty-four entries remained and were circulated among all participants. Toward the end of the process, however, a few contributors could not make our final deadline, leaving us with fifty-seven entries.

Why am I bothering you with this account? First of all, it is to answer those who may not see the names of those whom they recommended to take part in the book. Secondly, it is to show the vital and problematic aspects of creating a virtual community of scholars who truly want to share, to negotiate, to give of their time and their minds to cultivating the field. In a relatively short time we captured the moment and assembled an inspiring group of participants who were fully committed to the standards and the processes we underwent over ten months of negotiation. The authors are from various countries and different cultures all of which entail a wide spectrum of subjects and voices. We ended with sixty contributors and fifty-seven entries (five were written by more than one author and two were written by the same author). Research was conducted in North and South America, Europe, Asia, Africa, New Zealand and Australia. Readers will find helpful viewpoints and valuable judgments within the framework of key concepts. The achievement of this project is that it clearly shows that we, as drama/theatre educators and researchers have created our own language with its own grammar and lucid syntax that we can appreciate and from which, via our entries, we can extract a profound discourse.

Furthermore, when I say that our endeavor proposes a new way of constructing knowledge, it is in the sense that the topics and concepts highlighted are the results of the authors' own initiatives. Each contributor could choose to write about what he or she sees as an important issue in the field, an issue that he or she knows intimately and wants to share from his or her viewpoint. Thus we have a real sense of what the key concepts are in the field at this point of time according to sixty scholars in the field as defined by their contribution. Some participants were concerned that with an open process such as this we would be in danger of receiving several articles on the same topics from a number of contributors or that we might end up in a state of chaos as regards issues and research approaches. The truth is that either way could be grounds for re-evaluation. If many researchers had chosen the same topic, it could expose a focal point to be analyzed and then lead to ways to open the field to further investigation. If chaos had occurred, then probably a new order (in the sense of a new meaning) would have been created. Order out of chaos is a well-known phenomenon that we expect from any state of chaos. The fact was that we received no identical suggestions but we did receive a variety of topics, terms and concepts. In addition, as mentioned before, more often than not, authors chose their favorite topic and this fact demonstrates that we do have an inner grammar that enables us to be different and yet belong to the same field.

The evolving list proved to be successful. If one analyzes the topics one can learn about a variety of multi-layered, colorful interesting issues; some of these are new and some are conventional, some provocative and some traditional - an intriguing **rainbow of thoughts**.

Of course some topics are "missing" but this is not the point since the nature of a collective book, an anthology or any other sort of edited book has to be shaped by decisions and preferences according to a set of criteria. In our project the topics convey the knowledge of a large body of scholars who depict what interests them; and thus collectively we express what is occurring in the field, what its scope of interest is and what its ways of research are. The issues also reflect the trends, images and the observations that a large body of researchers consider to be essential. I see this as a considerable achievement. There are, of course, other well-known scholars who could not participate but from my negotiations with some of them I can conclude that their topics would have gone along the same line of thought with those that we already have. **Entries cover inter-dependent topics on teaching and learning, aesthetics and ethics, curricula and history, culture and community, various populations and their needs, theatre for young people, digital technology, narrative and pedagogy, research methods, Shakespeare and Brecht, other various modes of theatre and the education of theatre teachers.**

When we hold a book in our hands we feel free. Free to decide what is important, what is of less value, what raises our curiosity and what does not. Only the readers themselves can decide how to navigate between the entries, how to listen to the arguments, whether to accept or refuse individual ideas. However, a road map can be created by looking at the keywords supplied by each of the authors below the title of each entry.

Yet pivotal questions still resonate in each of the six steps upon which this book was constructed. Some are Jeanne Klein's questions which she asked back in April, 2009.

In a short essay, "Key Questions to Key Concepts," she asked: *Why this book? Why does the international field of theatre and drama education feel the need to define its "key concepts"–for whom and to what end?* Furthermore, she asked:

How shall forty-three researchers {at that time} agree upon interpretations of definitions from self-selected concepts separated into clustered categories of childhood's mimetic knowledge? The answers to these bristly questions had already

SHIFRA SCHONMANN

been given in my first letter to participants, in March, but Klein took my answers to new heights echoing the basic question behind every epistemological attempt to create definitions. Yet it is not the intention of this project to define or to unify ideas, rather we seek to convey a clear description of who we are by mapping the field on the basis of fifty-seven entries, aiming to stimulate our thoughts and give us a taste of what the field encompasses in this point of time.

In the spirit of Szymborska I can say that writing is a game that no other activity can offer. I wanted the authors of this book to feel free, to enjoy the game, like children playing in a sandbox; that is to say, to create a space where authors could play with ideas and make new links, destroy some old opinions, and open windows to see new buildings of the mind. Playing with ideas - like playing with sand - means that one allows the self the freedom of mind, the flow of thought, to detach from the occasionally "frozen" rules of what we know as academic writing and allow ourselves as writers and scholars to enjoy new rules of mind and spirit which, in a relaxed playful way, elevates wisdom, creativity and self criticism.

Closing Remarks

At the beginning of the twentieth century, "as if" games were seen as a playful way for developing creative resources of the child; the practices of those engaged in drama education was defined by the work of Cook (1917), and later, by Ward, Slade and Way, during the middle of the 1920s to the 1960s, through 'Creative Dramatics'. Over time, a large group of individuals, mainly teachers, inspired by drama and theatre, identified with the educational movement of 'learning by doing' and the 'activity method' and their professional identity matched their ideological stance.

New inspiring practices of drama education were developed by leaders such as Dorothy Heathcote and Gavin Bolton in the 1970s who opened the field up to *acting out, acting in classroom drama, drama behaviors, drama for learning, and mantle of the expert*. Later, toward the end of the 1980s, the era of "stars" and "leaders" faded away. Never the less on their heels came quite a few 'newcomers' whose work was stimulating; the field expanded embracing ideas focusing mainly on variations of *process drama* and then of *applied drama*. When we come to the present, as this project illustrates, there are a multitude of voices within the field, whose work is informed by different identities, approaches, theories, practices, and ambitions.

Examining the scope of scholars and their entries in this book we could ask: *Who are we? What binds us together as a solid group of researchers and practitioners?*

The question of identity did not trouble many researchers in the past: we did the work, as each one of us saw fit. Over the years, there have been many moments, especially at conferences, when it seemed that gaps were becoming visible, cracks were being heard and questions were demanding answers. The questions included:

How can professional identity be created? Do we need leaders? Is developing the field possible without leaders? What are the themes that should concern us and in which contexts? What kind of research do we need to develop? What is the motivation to go on? What is the theoretical space in which we are working? Do we have boundaries? Do we need boundaries? What for? How can a field of know-ledge crystallize identity? What is meant by "professional identity"? Is there room for crystallizing personal identity along with crystallizing professional identity? Are they synchronic processes? What is the place of artists in the community? What is the place of social workers? Teachers? Researchers?

Embodied within all these questions is the concern, the genesis of our project: *What is the **present** role of theatre/drama education? What is the **future** of our field?*

By reading the fifty-seven entries written by sixty authors I believe my colleagues and readers will find focused and engaging ideas that they can explore and/or bring into practice, ideas they will be able to continue to 'play with'.

The critical task now is to keep on evolving the heart of the work contained within the individual entries, to associate these believes and stands, theories and practices with the abundant wisdom and experience that we already have in the field and to take them further over the rainbow, identity cards still in the making.

REFERENCES

Cook, H. C. (1917). *The play way.* London: Heinemann.
Szymborska, W. (2002). *Nonrequired Reading: Prose Pieces.* New York: Harcourt.

Shifra Schonmann *is Associate Professor at the University of Haifa, Israel, where she holds chair of TYA. Specialises in aesthetic education, theatre/drama education, teacher education & curriculum.*

SECTION I: LEARNING, TEACHING, CURRICULA AND TEACHER EDUCATION

JOHN O'TOOLE

2. EMMA'S DILEMMA

The Challenge for Teacher Education in Drama

Keywords: teacher education, drama teaching, theatre, process drama

Drama Education in Australia

This month, I am supervising a student, 'Emma', now in her fourth year of a pre-service Early Childhood degree, who is very keen on drama. I work in a faculty with a considerable reputation for drama education (from long before I arrived), where the first specialist drama teachers in Australia were trained forty years ago, even before there was a formal curriculum for them to teach! Drama is core curriculum from early childhood to tertiary entrance, part of the key learning area of The Arts in schools in all States, and in our forthcoming National Curriculum. Most States have established specialist drama teacher training courses, at least for secondary education. The Australian Curriculum Authority senior project officer for arts can state confidently, that "many of us stand strong and successfully in schools... because... we have had quality specialist teachers to teach us [and we] enjoy the status that comes with good curriculum and being valued" (Wise, 2008). Like our colleagues worldwide, we draw from the mature and still-growing bank of both scholarship and practical textbooks, journals and internet resources available to everybody, both from overseas, and from our considerable pool of home-grown expertise. There's no shortage of top-level resources now available to drama teachers via the touch of a button or the Amazons shopping basket.

Emma's Problem

Now let me tell you about Emma. She has had little prior experience of drama (*But didn't I say drama is a fully established core curriculum area?*). Emma's enthusiasm comes from the eighteen hours of drama workshops provided as her whole drama training. (*She was lucky; had she enrolled this year, she would have had only twelve hours. This in turn is twelve hours more than many other teacher education courses offer.*). As the only way to do more, she chose a practicum- based research project using drama with her assigned preschool class. Her supervisory teacher has no drama training or experience (*More doubts, eh...?*) and was reluctant to make time for it with her class. However, finally she has found a 'literacy' task for Emma: to teach these pre-schoolers to recognise how dramatic script is laid out differently on a page from discursive prose. This is in preparation for a future task - after

S. Schonmann (ed.), Key Concepts in Theatre/Drama Education, 13–17.

Emma has gone - when the children will be given a script written by the teacher to learn and publicly perform. These are pre-schoolers. Emma's eighteen hour training has been in structuring dramatic play in the classroom. She is finding the project very problematic, and so am I.

Educating Teachers

This chapter is part opinion piece, part jeremiad and mainly a lot of questions, grouped round three crucial interrogatives. I will attempt to answer the first two, based about equally on research - most of which I don't have space to quote - and on my privileged but bumpy experience of over thirty years engaged in teacher education. I invite you to accompany your reading with your own answers, or dispute mine, according to your context.

1. What do teachers need to teach drama?
The needs differ according to the teachers and their context. *Early childhood teachers and care workers*, I believe, need skills in managing and shaping dramatic play, understanding the relationships of drama to all the arts and play, and to learning. They don't need to learn to teach script recognition, or scripts.

 Primary teachers need those skills too, and also dramatic pedagogy across the curriculum including process drama, playmaking, and student-centred performance work, and in making use of theatre for young audiences. That's for all primary teachers, really; more of the same and deeper, for those few specialists and drama resource teachers who do exist.

 Secondary, post-secondary and adult drama teachers need all the above, plus knowledge and skill in making formal performance and theatre in multiple styles, teaching acting and production skills, teaching dramatic history, genre and background, and managing formal curricula & syllabuses.

 All other (non-drama) secondary and post-secondary teachers right across the curriculum need just the basic skill and confidence to use dramatic pedagogy in their specialist area/s, and understand the role of drama in the school context.

 Teachers and trainers of dramatic artists need not just to know and teach their speciality, but also how to cultivate their students' broader understanding of their context, and articulacy and advocacy skills. Given the shifting nature of contemporary theatre contexts and where their graduates will ply their trade, some at least need to teach artistic pedagogy, along with some basic knowledge of complementary skills for artists in residence and applied theatre, like directing, devising and scriptwriting, and arts administration.

2. Where can they get it?
In a nutshell, before they start or on the job.

 Pre-service education can include specialist four-year drama teacher education, usually mainly aimed at preparing secondary teachers. A common alternative is an undergraduate degree in drama or theatre, followed by a post-graduate education qualification. Those initial degrees range from conservatory-style artist-training, through broader practice-based study, to wholly theoretical Theatre Studies; the post-graduate study may or may not include a drama teaching component.

In addition or instead, teachers may rely on in-service training. This too may be specialist post-graduate university or technical college courses (*But those are rare*). They may attend professional development (PD) workshops, conferences and courses, run by their education authority (*Quite rare too*), a theatre company, the local drama teachers' association, or a specialist teacher in their own school as part of in-house PD. If they are lucky, they might get in-class PD from a local drama advisory teacher (*Rare as hen's teeth, these days*) or an artist-in-residence. Research (eg. Ball, 1985) suggests this might be potentially the richest form of training, with the expert and teacher co-planning, the expert demonstrating, the two co-teaching and then the teacher flying solo with the expert's ongoing support. Apart from that, the teacher can rely on the mass of on-line and print-based packs, text-books and teacher-resources, which, like Wikipedia, is a cornucopia, but caveat emptor, and the buyer by definition often does not yet have sufficient discrimination to beware the rotten fruit. This goes for the PD courses, too.

3. Questions and more questions
Let's start from the top down, as the questions become progressively more problematic.

Are artist-trainers responding to the needs of artists who also work as teachers or community educators?
The evidence is equivocal: the last few years have certainly seen considerable growth of new courses in applied theatre. On the other hand, my own observation of the marquee Australian artist-training establishments backs up Ross Prior's research (2004) that they see themselves training not teaching, and exclusively producing highly-trained specialists for the conventional theatre and film industries. This was highlighted here a few weeks ago by a protest at the Victorian College of the Arts mainly against introducing a 25% component of 'breadth studies' into the under-graduate performance degrees. Oscar-winning actor Geoffrey Rush was quoted throughout the media and on Youtube, saying "I always advise that you must train, train, not study - train." There is some irony here, as Rush himself completed a generalist Bachelor of Arts before he undertook actor- training, post-graduate. How-ever, his traditionalist stance gives me further questions about what is really needed, since in less renowned days he successfully ran a theatre-in-education company.

Are specialist drama teachers, secondary or primary, being given that rich, broad and deep knowledge identified in my answer to question 1?
The evidence is even more equivocal. This book gives a shining example of skilled secondary teaching; much contemporary Australian research documents exceptional secondary practice; I see a lot of very good secondary teachers in action. However, some states no longer have secondary drama teacher education; in many other courses the time available to teach drama education practice and pedagogy is shrinking, even if the courses aren't - especially in the pre-service post-graduate courses. And to contrast with Wise's and my own optimistic picture, one expert among us who spent a decade writing and implementing a national drama curriculum now questions despairingly whether drama should even be a curriculum subject, as

he constantly watches examples of bad practice (O'Connor, 2008), reinforcing the finding of the global compendium of arts education research (Bamford, 2005, p. 12), that bad arts teaching is worse than no arts teaching at all.

What is the story for generalist teachers - secondary, primary and pre-school?
When I started in teacher education, there were (almost) no Australian pre-service specialist drama courses for teachers, other than private organisations for speech-and-drama, like Trinity College, where the dedicated - and mostly well-heeled - got some kind of training. However, drama flourished in teachers' colleges, with a dozen full-time lecturers in three departments in medium-sized Brisbane alone, catering to primary and secondary teachers - usually under the guise of 'communication' or 'speech and drama'. From these units, over the next twenty years, emerged the specialist drama teacher education courses. Their original purpose was very different: to give would-be teachers - secondary as well as primary - the articulacy, confidence, oracy and performance skills necessary to be a good classroom teacher. Their existence was in my experience uncontested and valued by the institution and our colleagues. In the three years of their training, students did a lot more class workshop practice then - up to twenty-five hours a week (and we taught many more hours, too). So in their courses they all did at least a semester or two of drama, and could also choose drama major studies and electives. There was equal or more time for music and visual arts; early childhood and primary people often did just as much dance. Where are these courses now? They morphed into drama specialist courses or they died. As generalist courses, at best they withered into the six, twelve or eighteen hours of today: stricken by the simultaneous intellectualising of teacher-education, the crowding in of new generic imperatives such as inclusive education and research, and the savage cost-cutting that has been a feature of Australian education since 1990.

How can we revive in pre-service education the respect for practice of those days?
Is it in the very contemporary concentration on internships and intensive immersion in schools themselves - 'clinical practice', we call it (our Dean was a medic) - where students get lots of time observing and teaching in schools? It's potentially rich, in theory. However, where do we find the supervisory teachers who have the skills themselves to teach their apprentices? Emma is one of those new-breed immersion students, and look at her predicament.

How then can we give those students and teachers who start with a drama deficit from their own education at least the basic skills and confidence to get started?
Is the answer, perhaps, to concentrate our resources on specialists and in-service - training specialist drama teachers to work with classroom teachers developing their drama skills, pedagogy and confidence? I have seen it work wonderfully. But I have also seen the drama specialist become a one-person ghetto, teaching every class its half-hour a week of drama, while the class teachers get on with their marking elsewhere. This is a dilemma much fought-over in music, where the jury is still out, too. Another factor to note from music, which may or may not apply to drama: a colleague researching excellence in primary music teaching has found that the best primary music specialists tend to come from good generalist teachers with a love of music, rather than from trained music graduates (Jeanneret, 2009).

Straws in the wind for me, that I should have researched years ago, are two sets of graduate statistics I saw, twenty years apart, which showed that the drama graduates had scored far higher overall graduation results than any of their other colleagues. Is it just my impression, too, that drama teachers and lecturers are represented well above their numbers in excellence-in-teaching awards? Does drama bestow a significant pedagogical advantage? If so, it's a powerful argument to persuade education faculties to reopen their doors to us and make us the core providers that we were all those years ago.

But only if we get visible: and largely, we're not. If we were, those few in-service post-graduate courses which do exist would have people turning up in droves, instead of often struggling for numbers. How can we establish a culture of drama awareness in the schools sufficient to establish effective PD and the demand for drama-trained graduates? Do we have to do more listening ourselves and be more responsive to our colleagues, to find out not just what they want which we think we can supply, but what they have got that we ourselves could do with? When we're selling such a good product ourselves, it's hard to be humble, isn't it?

The education systems, too: how can we encourage them to be more inclined to make the arts and drama a priority in their PD and advisory services, as well as their demands for what their pre-service graduates come equipped with? How can we get the schools, the systems and our own faculty leaders to look beyond the relentless focus on literacy and numeracy standards? How can we get their masters in government to look beyond those narrow standards?

And why, given the wonderful progress and achievements that we have some-how made in drama education both in practice and in scholarship, are we still asking these questions fifty years after drama started to become established in schools, and forty years after teachers began to be trained in drama?

REFERENCES

Ball, S. J. (1985). *The Brisbane south region drama project.* Evaluation Report. Brisbane: Queensland Department of Education.

Bamford, A. (2005). *The wow factor: Global research compendium on the impact of the arts in education.* New York: Waxmann.

Jeanneret, N., & Robinson, P. (2009). *Excellence in primary school music.* Research Report. Melbourne: Department of Education and Early Childhood Development.

O'Connor, P. (2008, April). *Keynote: National drama international conference.* St Aidan's College, University of Durham.

Prior, R. (2004). *Characterising actor-trainers' understanding of their practice in Australian and English drama schools.* Unpublished Ph.D Thesis: Griffith University, Brisbane.

Wise, J. (2008). Extract from email posted on drama queensland internal e-group. Quoted (in full, pp. 206–207). In J. O'Toole, M. Stinson, & T. Moore, (Eds.), (2009). *Drama and curriculum: A giant at the door.* Amsterdam: Springer.

John O'Toole is Hon. Professorial Fellow at the University of Melbourne and a community playwright. Formerly foundation Chair of Arts Education at the University of Melbourne, Professor of Drama Education at Griffith University.

SHARON WAHL

3. LEARNING TO TEACH BY TREADING THE BOARDS

Keywords: teacher education, acting process, theatre

It has been said that no actor can act in a vacuum (Stanislavsky, 1925). I believe that the same is true for teaching. Imbedded within the act of teaching is a community of support, a foundation of skills and dispositions that have been fostered by training and previous experiences and an environment shaped by the interactions of teachers and students. How can the theatre play a formative role in educating pre-service educators as they struggle to find their own effective and engaging teaching styles?

"First you Must Learn to Know Who you are." Uta Hagen

The issue of identity is central to an actor's work in the theatre. As Hagen (1973) and others have stated, you cannot begin to create a new character until you are fully aware of your own understandings, attitudes and beliefs. As an actor, it is important to have a strong sense of self; this fuels your search for the articulation of other theatrical selves. As I have moved between the worlds of acting and teaching I have discovered that my work on the stage has directly influenced my work as a teacher.

If I'm going to build a character for the stage that has any basis in reality, I must first be aware of what I bring to the role. My prejudices, peccadilloes and preferences must be clear to me, so that I may choose the attributes that best contribute to the character. The importance of self-awareness is also fundamental to teaching. Maxine Greene (1995) speaks of it this way:

> To be yourself is to be in the process of creating a self, an identity. If it were not a process, it would not be a surprise. The surprise comes along with becoming different consciously different as one finds ways of acting on envisaged possibility. It comes along with hearing different words and music, seeing from unaccustomed angles, realizing that the world perceived from one place is not the world (p. 20).

In many pre-service teacher education programs in British Columbia, Canada, significant time is spent in the discussion and development of a personal philosophy of education. Students are encouraged to explore and develop their philosophy in order to make sense of the actions and decisions they will make later in their professional careers. You cannot create such a philosophy without first being aware of what is important to you and what shapes your understandings. This increased understanding of self helps these new teachers to identify their own biases and agendas that they bring into the classroom. William Hare (1993) speaks of this process as being crucial to developing a teaching practice that has the potential to be open and flexible. Deborah Britzman (1995) sees teaching and learning as also having a vulnerable quality. She speaks of teaching as a means of coming to terms with the power to shape young identities and their views of the world. And that once given this encounter, the teacher is also in the process of becoming. The theatrical disposition toward a critical self-analysis in preparation for creating a character is a useful starting point from which new teachers can examine their own unstated agendas and understandings as they struggle to form the beginnings of their individual teaching philosophies.

As an actor, I spend a considerable amount of time researching the context and background of a character. In order to build a realistic and engaging performance, I need to understand the world in which the character lived, the influences on her life, the societal nuances that surrounded her. I believe that the most effective teachers also devote time and energy to understanding the context in which they teach. They see their students not as isolated individuals, but as part of the larger community that includes family and neighborhood connections. This understanding of the bigger context is explored by a number of educational writers. Paulo Freire (1970) talks about the importance of authenticating the cultural context of the classroom. Michael Fullan (1998) speaks of the need for teachers to understand the societal context in which they teach. "It is through this (societal) understanding that new beliefs and understandings are formed." (p. 76). There is an implicit acknowledgement here, that new beliefs and understandings are necessary for dynamic and responsive teaching. Beginning teachers need to become aware of the cultural and sociological contexts of their classrooms. Although they are often preoccupied with obtaining what they consider to be the "bag of tricks" or the "manual" for teaching, it is our new teachers who must bring about what Maxine Greene (1995) calls "The responsibility to bring renewal to the conversation, to do what we can to include within it the voices of the long silent or unheard in this country" (p. 56). The theatrical process used to develop a character on stage can be explored with pre-service teachers in an effort to more fully understand the "characters" of their students.

One of the strongest correlations between the art of acting and the development of a particular teaching style comes with a look at the performance aspect of both. There is a presumption that it is the artistry of the actor that determines the response of the audience. This artistry is informed by the elements discussed above, but it is in the interaction and engagement of the audience that artistry turns into a truly affective performance. The creation of a theatrical space where students play an active role in the creation of the curriculum (both lived and content driven) is inherent in process Drama and in the give and take of improvisational Theatre. John Dewey (1934) spoke 75 years ago about the importance of student engagement and educational theorists have been saying something similar ever since. So if it is the interaction (as defined in a dialogical or reciprocal relationship) between teacher and learner that is crucial, why are more teachers not training for mastery of this connection?

Seymour Sarason (1999) draws some compelling examples from performance artists to illustrate the ways in which teacher preparation colleges are failing their students. He sees the actor's primary responsibility as the engagement of emotions and the instruction of their audiences, and he believes the teacher's role to be similar. Unfortunately, Sarason believes that teachers are victims of their training in that they are taught only to instruct and not to engage. It is in the emotional engagement of the students, that true learning happens and that (according to Sarason) is the art of teaching. Sarason makes a valid point about the inadequacy of some teacher training programs Some of us do endeavor to educate new teachers to connect with and motivate their students, to encourage them to be co-creators of their curriculum, but the realities of the current educational infra-structure, make such engagements difficult if not, in some cases, impossible. Students are often motivated and excited by the relevance and interconnectedness of a number of curricular areas but cross-disciplinary teaching collaborations can be difficult to create. Societal expectations also make deviations from the norm more challenging. Emphasis on standardized testing, expectations of parents and antiquated admission requirements from post secondary institutions combine to dictate the curriculum for pre-service teachers and limit the time available for student experimentation and risk taking.

Audiences expect to "feel" something when they go to the theatre. Should students not have similar expectations about school? Shirley Steinberg (Kincheloe & Steinberg, 1995) talks about student expectations regarding school as having three stages: the first stage is to keep the student occupied until the second stage; the second stage is where workbooks and drills rule; and the third stage is to keep students off the streets and out of trouble until they are old enough to be responsible. This is a very sad, and I feel, often accurate, depiction of the current educational system and about as far from the excitement and engagement of the theatre as you can get. How can we provide pre-service teachers with the experience of creating environments for their students that motivate and stimulate the emotions? Developing a teacher disposition for risk taking, experimentation, collaborative engagement (all key elements of theatrical work) is supported by many educational scholars including Eisner (1985), Greene (1995) and Gardner (1991).

The sense of theatrical teamwork that I've experienced in the theatre is also present in the teaching profession. As an actor, I work with a myriad of professionals in a number of relationships in order to produce a play. The director, stage manager, lighting and set designer, the stage crew, and front of house staff are all integral components of the final product. Just as actors cannot act in a vacuum, teachers cannot teach in isolation. The efficacy of collaborative teaching opportunities has been documented by a number of researchers (Schmoker, 1996; Fullan, 1991; Dufour & Eaker, 1998). The research shows that teachers who are provided with the infra-structure which allows for teacher, parent and support staff collaboration, develop a quality of teaching that goes beyond the norm.

Pre-service teachers must be given strategies to combat the isolationism commonly found in schools. As mentioned earlier, post secondary institutions do little to provide collaborative opportunities for cross-disciplinary work. It would go a long way to encouraging a change in the current discipline based infrastructure, if new teachers had substantive experience in working together with colleagues.

If pre-service teachers are to develop a teaching style that incorporates some of the elements articulated by the educators cited and which parallels the dramatic process previously identified, they might begin with a clear understanding of their own identities and the factors that influence their decisions. While on campus, opportunities should be given for students to work together collegially and across disciplines to develop curricula that will engage and motivate students.

The development of a community of learners where a safe environment is provided for risk taking and for supporting each other's efforts is important and theatre activities provide an excellent venue for such explorations. Theatre artists such as Judith Thompson (2003) and John O'Toole (1995) speak about ways in which they have incorporated elements of their own theatrical practice into their classrooms. Both of these educators speak to the importance of allowing time for the development of students' skills and encouraging time in that place of ambiguity in order to experience mastery over the notion of having to "be in control." During student practica, a substantive look at the students and the community in which they teach would help these new teachers to determine a direction in which to develop engaging and meaningful curriculum.

Pre-service teachers should be exposed to the rigour and discipline of the professionalism of teaching, and be encouraged to search for new and different ways in which to practice their craft. The theatre, with its own set of expectations and emotional engagements, provides a rich source of inspiration for educators of pre-service teachers.

REFERENCES

Britzman, D. (1995). *In thirteen questions: Reframing education's conversation.* New York: Peter Lang.
Dewey, J. (1934). *Art as experience.* New York: Minton, Balch.
Dufour, R., & Eaker, R. (1998). *Professional learning communities at work.* Bloomington, IN: NES.
Eisner, E. (1985). *The educational imagination.* New York: MacMillan.
Freire, P. (1970). *Pedagogy of the oppressed.* New York: Herder & Herder.
Fullan, M. (1991). *The new meaning of educational change.* New York: Teachers College Press.
Gardner, H. (1991). *The unschooled mind.* New York: Basic.
Greene, M. (1995). *Releasing the imagination.* San Francisco: Jossey-Bass.
Hagen, U. (1973). *Respect for acting.* New York: Macmillan.
Hare, W. (1993). *What makes a good teacher.* Ontario: Althouse.
Kincheloe, J., & Steinberg, S. (1995). *Thirteen questions: Reframing education's conversation.* New York: Peter Lang.
O'Toole, J. (1995). The rude charms of drama. In P. Taylor (Ed.), *Selected readings in drama and theatre education.* Brisbane: NADIE Publications.
Sarason, S. (1999). *Teaching as a performing art.* New York: Teachers College Press.
Schmoker, M. (1996). Results: *The key to continuous school improvement.* Virginia, VA: ASCD.
Stanislavski, K. S. (1925). *My life in art.* New York: Viking.
Thompson, J. (2003). *"I will tear you to pieces": The classroom as theatre. As cited in How theatre educates: Convergences & counterpoints.* Toronto: University of Toronto Press.

Sharon Wahl *is a professional actor and teaches Performing Arts at Vancouver Island University. Her research interests include Theatre, Teacher and International Education.*

AUD BERGGRAF SÆBØ

4. THE RELATIONSHIP BETWEEN THE INDIVIDUAL AND THE COLLECTIVE LEARNING PROCESS IN DRAMA

Keywords: learning process, collective learning, the creative subject, socio-constructivist pedagogy, phenomenology, learning experiences

The individual and collective aspects in the learning process will always be present at the same time in the classroom in drama in education. The individual aspect is represented by the individual student's or teacher's experiences and perspectives, while the collective aspect is represented by the community that the students and the teacher create together. This collective aspect is all the experiences that the students and the teacher have in common in the same social and cultural context of the classroom.

DRAMA, PHENOMENOLOGY AND SOCIO-CONSTRUCTIVISM

The field of drama, as we know it from the beginning of last century and until to day, is first and foremost connected to a student- activated pedagogy with an inextricable foundation in progressive pedagogy (Schonmann, 2007). Progressive pedagogy is founded in a socio-constructivistic concept of knowledge and learning that grew out of phenomenology (Fuglsang & Olsen, 2004; Steinsholt & Løvlie, 2004). Phenomenology arises as a human science in protest to all the fact-based, realism science and as a protest against the view of science that argues that knowledge is already given in our objective world. On the contrary, phenomenology argues that knowledge is constructed by the subject in a subjective process of meaning making to understanding the world (Fuglsang & Olsen, 2004).

Phenomenology is concerned with how a phenomena, whether it is an object, a case or a social relation, stands forth and is experienced by the human being in the process of meaning making. The premise for human knowing is our living in the world as interpreting and meaning making creatures (Heidegger, 2001), and a central concept in phenomenology is consequently "the creative subject". The parallel between phenomenological science and socio-constructivism is obvious, since both argue that it is the creative subject who constructs knowledge, and that it is the interaction between the subject and the subject's social and cultural lifeworld that is the basis for the meaning making.

THE IMPORTANCE OF EXPERIENCES IN THE LEARNING PROCESS

In phenomenology, it is the bodily experiences of the human being that is the basis for making meaning of the world and it is through conscious cognitive processes

S. Schonmann (ed.), Key Concepts in Theatre/Drama Education, 23–27.

that understanding is constructed. That is why it is the human being's direct and concrete experiences with a phenomena, i.e. that the phenomena is experienced in a first person perspective, that is the premise for understanding/knowing (Zahavi, 2004). But the human being lives in a social world, in a specific social and cultural context that decides the frames for understanding. In drama this phenomenological basis first and foremost means that each student's individual potential in the learning process is dependant on the possibilities available to him or her to create or construct his or her own experiences while working with the subject matter content.

Gadamer (1997) distinguishes between experience as reconstruction and experience as construction. Experience as reconstruction is to experience once more something that we already have experienced and which consequently already is a part of our previous knowing. Typically, these experiences confirm our expectations, whether it is to give the correct answer to the teacher's question or to remember the teacher's instruction. Experience as construction is to make new experiences; experiences that are not yet confirmed as part of our lifeworld, and that consequently will stand as a protest, objection or contrast to our previous experiences. When a new experience is made, that is to say constructed by the subject, it will enter into and be included in the person's lifeworld of experiences. It is this creative experience that Gadamer says is the premise and basis for the construction of understanding.

THE INDIVIDUAL AND COLLECTIVE LEARNING PROCESS

The individual perspective emphasizes the importance that each individual have the opportunity to be creative and construct new experiences in the process of meaning making. To address the individual aspect of the learning process in drama implies that the focus of the drama work is on the students' individual, embodied, and constructive experiences with the subject matter content. However the creative subject does not live alone, he or she lives together with other human beings within a social and cultural context. In phenomenology the social is understood as inter-subjectivity; as relationship between human beings that share a common social lifeworld (Rendtorff, 2004). In the classroom the teacher and the students share a social lifeworld. The social or collective aspect of the learning process is included in drama when the students are organised in smaller or larger groups, and engaged in a process teacher-structured drama or working together more or less independently on their own. My question is how the emphasis on the creative/constructive human being is to be understood in relation to both the individual and collective aspect in the process of meaning making in drama.

As an example, I will refer to a process drama conducted with a grade four class (Sæbø, 2009) about Tore who has no friends because he does not play football. The teacher begins by showing a picture of Tore on the overhead projector, and gives a short introduction to Tore and his problem. In so doing she creates a collective context for the first drama activity. The students are asked to walk around the class-room as if they are in the schoolyard. She encourages them to act as if they are a student who does not have anyone else to be together with. "You really want to have somebody to be together with, but you do not dare to contact anyone," she says.

With these impulses, each of the students constructs, on the basis of their previous experiences, a new experience while improvising in a fictional context. The individual aspect happens according to how each of the students interprets the fictional and common situation that was the starting point for the improvisation. Each student presents the subject matter content "to be an outsider", and at the same time each student constructs individual new experiences through the improvisation. According to Husserl this is to be understood so that the phenomena, "to be an outsider" is presented on a high level of possibility for meaning-making (Zahavi, 2004).

Even though individual creative work is central in the situation above, the collective aspect of the learning process is definitely present. This is expressed by the fact that the students' individual constructions of experience occur within the collective context that the teacher provides for the improvisation i.e. the story of Tore, and in the non-verbal community that is created as everyone joins into the shared fictional situation in the schoolyard. This community will nevertheless be experienced differently according to the each student's individual and previous experiences.

The process drama continues as the students create tableaux that show how they think Tore experiences the breaks between classes. The collective aspect here emerges as students negotiate how they want to create their tableau. Each student must be willing to contribute ideas, while at the same time remaining open to the possibility that their idea may become an impulse for the development of a collective idea, or may be revised and turned around, or even rejected in the inter-subjective inter-action of the group. The result, for this grade four class, were powerful expressions about bullying created by the students through their tableaux. That success might be an expression of the collective aspect of the learning process, where all individual impulses were tested out in the inter-subjective community in each group and included in the collective drama work of the creation of a group tableau. According to phenomenology, it is the interactions between the students' individual construction of experiences and those experiences created through the inter-subjective interactions that construct the students' collective understanding, which are expressed, in this example, by each group through their tableaux.

Gadamer (1997; 2003) is concerned about dialogue as an existential meeting where each participant must dare to put his or her understanding "at stake". In the inter-subjective interactions in drama, dialogue needs to be characterised by an openness that helps each participant to be freely inspired by others to discuss their own and each other's ideas to create, in this situation, a common tableau. On the other side, the tableau may also be a result of the fact that one student in the group had an idea about how the group could create a tableau, and that this idea was accepted by the others without discussion. In that case, it is an open question to what degree the final tableau is an expression of the collective learning process of the group.

In this process drama, the students' engagement increased through the experiences that they constructed in the process of meaning making, especially when the students met the teacher in role as Tore's teacher Linn in a "hot seat". The teacher pretends/acts as if she knew nothing about how Tore experiences the breaks and that everyone in the class were good friends. The students' individual learning process here is a phenomenological experience as a result of their emotional understanding of Tore's situation. This emotional understanding is created by the quality of interaction between the individual and collective aspects in the learning process, in the process of meaning making. The students choose to join in, ask confronting questions, and try to draw Linn's attention to Tore's situation at school. Each student makes an existential choice to participate and that choice demands creative courage, which Gadamer calls putting one's own understanding "at stake". The students' questions and the teacher's answers construct the collective content of the play. Those students who choose not to take verbal part in the interrogation may participate communally by contributing their creative empathy and non-verbal embodied expression to the fictional situation. If this happens, the collective aspect in the learning and meaning making process is strengthened.

The above example shows that the learning process in drama is subject to the students' individual and collective participation as they create their own experiences in relation to the subject matter content. These possibilities for learning are determined by the level of meaning making engaged in through embodied and aesthetic concretizing. The students' learning process in drama first and foremost is dependant on how the teacher structures and presents the subject matter content with the primary focus on enhancing student opportunities for meaning making and interactions between the individual and the collective in the drama.

SUMMING UP

The relationship between individual and collective aspects of the learning need to be further researched in drama. My research shows that the individual aspect of the learning process in drama is important, because it is the individual person who constructs his or her understanding through a conscious, phenomenological, meaning-making process. But this does not at all mean that students construct their meaning-making independent of the social and collective worlds in which they live. The focus on the individual aspect is important, because all meaning making would be meaningless without a meaning-making subject. However, it is when the collective aspect in the learning process is recognized, that drama can be seen to function as a collective process actively promoting learning for individual students. As shown above, the content of the play is constructed within collective meaning making processes. Individual and collective aspects of the learning process are reciprocally dependent on each other, but it is the quality of the collective learning process that decides the quality of the individual learning process in drama.

REFERENCES

Fuglsang, L., & Olsen, P. B. (2004). Introduktion. In I. L. Fuglsang & P. B. Olsen (red.), *Videnskapbsteori i samfunnsvidenskaberne* (2 utg., s. 7–51). Roskilde: Roskilde Universitetsforlag.

Gadamer, H.-G. (1997). *Sanning och metod/Truth and method*. Göteborg: Daidalos.

Gadamer, H.-G. (2003). *Forståelsens filosofi*. Oslo: Cappelen.

Heidegger, M. (2001). Forståelse og utlegning fra Væren og tid. In I. S. Lægreid & T. Skorgen (red.), *Hermeneutisk lesebok: Spartacus*.

Rendtorff, J. D. (2004). Fenomenologien og dens betydning/Phenomenology and its meaning. In I L. Fuglsang & P. B. Olsen (red.), *Videnskabsteori i samfunnsvidenskaberne. På tværs av fagkulturer og paradigmer* (s. 277–308). Frederiksberg: Roskilde Universitetsforlag.

Schonmann, S. (2007). Reflection from an Israel Point of View. I. L. Bresler (red.), *International handbook of research in arts education* (Vol. 16, s. 65–66). Dordrecht: Springer.

Steinsholt, K., & Løvlie, L. (2004). *Pedagogikkens mange ansikter/ All the faces of pedagogy.* Oslo: Universitetsforlaget.

Sæbø, A. B. (2009). *Drama og elevaktiv læring. En studie av hvordan drama svarer på undervisnings- og læringsprosessens didaktiske utfordringer/Drama and student active learning. A study of how drama responds to the didactical challenges of the teaching and learning process.* NTNU, Trondheim.

Zahavi, D. (2004). *Fænomenologi/ Phenomenology.* Fredriksberg: Roskildes Universitetsforlag.

Aud Berggraf Sæbø, PhD, *is a teacher educator and researcher in drama/theatre at the University of Stavanger, Norway. She has published textbooks, research reports and articles.*

JULIE DUNN

5. CHILD-STRUCTURED SOCIO-DRAMATIC PLAY AND THE DRAMA EDUCATOR

What's Our Role?

Keywords: dramatic play, playwright function, metacommunication, imagination

Spencer (2003, p. 3) warns us that, "imagination shrivels and shrinks if it is not nourished by the negotiations that occur between different dimensions of reality" and while drama educators have been keen advocates for, and facilitators of, the type of adult-structured drama experiences that offer children opportunities to explore these spaces, far less attention has been paid to the development of children's imaginations, creativity and dramatic skills via child-structured dramatic play. This is especially the case for children in formal primary school settings, with Hadley (2002, p. 11) suggesting that play has become "ghettoised" within kindergarten and entry classrooms, out of the reach of older children for whom it is positioned as the binary opposite of work. This situation exists in spite of current efforts aimed at building a "creative class" (Florida, 2002, 2005), for play has become marginalized in these discussions, replaced by discourses focused on the development of creative products that can readily be assessed and shared.

However, for a growing number of writers from within the field of drama and beyond (Guss, 2005a; Hadley, 2002; Lobman, 2003; Lofdahl, 2005; Sawyer, 2006), child-structured, socio-dramatic play is being recognized as a key form of dramatic improvisation, which Sawyer (2006), in particular, believes leads to the development of "group genius" or "collaborative creativity". These authors, and others, recognise that within this form, participants must work together to create shared dramatic worlds. These dramatic worlds, like those created by drama teachers *for* children, allow participants to become "other" or be "elsewhere", exploring alternatives beyond the actual worlds they inhabit in their everyday lives. However, in both contexts, it is the successful manipulation of the elements of drama which enables their creation.

O'Neill (1995) believes that all forms of dramatic activity depend on the temporary acceptance of an illusion, while Goffman (1974) has described this process as a "conspiracy". He refers to audience members in the theatre as "collaborators in unreality" and suggests that they actively engage in a process of "playful unknowing-ness" (p. 135). Within dramatic play however, players must not only become collaborators in an unreality created for them, they must simultaneously create it, doing this by adopting the concurrent roles of actor, playwright and audience, guided only by a set of unwritten rules which although not explicitly stated, nevertheless help provide the structuring guidelines that are needed for play to be successful.

S. Schonmann (ed.), Key Concepts in Theatre/Drama Education, 29–33.

For this reason, "child-structured dramatic play" is a more appropriate term than the more commonly used "unstructured dramatic play", for as O'Neill (1995) suggests, within all improvised texts, the participants are engaged in a text creation process that, while spontaneous and oral, still requires the structuring services of a playwright. She reminds us (p. 24) that improvised texts are not prior documents, but rather, "animating currents" to which the participants submit and that in submitting to this current, each participant assumes at least part of the playwright function, doing this from *within* the event. O'Neill's argument is that each time a player offers an action or fragment of dialogue, they are applying a playwright function, for their moment by moment contributions are spontaneously building the dramatic play text. Indeed, even when a player chooses to remain completely still and silent in response to the action, they may in fact be adopting a playwright function.

Building upon O'Neill's initial application of this term, I have elsewhere identified and described four playwright functions (Dunn, 2003) used within improvised forms of drama, with each of these having a different impact upon the collaboratively generated play or improvised drama episode. These functions include the narrative, intervening, reinforcing and reviewing playwright functions which should not be thought of as being in any way fixed or pre-determined, or indeed understood as a way of labeling individual players. Rather, they should be understood as being fluid, shifting rapidly from one player to the next in a spontaneous attempt at structuring the action.

The narrative playwright function is by far the most commonly used of these four functions, for here the offerings continue the planned or current line of action, creating dialogue and action that simply falls into line with the existing direction of the text. By contrast, the intervening playwright function provides textual innovations that are aimed at either subtly or radically changing the direction of any text. These changes are however crucial for the survival of a play episode, for without them tension can easily be lost, with the result being that players become bored and the text repetitive. However, not all ideas offered by the intervening playwright will be useful or accepted by co-players and when offered may be ignored. To be included, the reinforcing playwright function is required, with players signalling through their words or actions acceptance of the intervention. In this way, the reinforcing playwright function ensures that new "What's up?" factors are woven into the text. This support generally means that the text will now follow this new direction, with the narrative playwright function being used once again to keep the text flowing along this revised pathway. Finally, the reviewing function is used by players as means of calling the group together in order to review what has happened in the text thus far. Without these reviewing moments, coherence can be lost, but this function is the one used least within young children's play.

Applied via the use of a range of implicit and explicit meta-communicative strategies, which are the signals that are used to regulate the emergence of the drama, these playwright functions are, of course, not overtly understood by the players, but nevertheless, operate in conjunction with the dramatic elements to keep the action moving and all players engaged in the spontaneously developing action.

For some children, the structuring of dramatic play using these functions and strategies comes easily, with Creaser (1989) famously adapting Fein's (1987) use of the term "master player" to describe these children as "master dramatists". For others however, this manipulation does not come so easily, and whilst they may understand the unwritten rules of play, they are unable to generate play experiences that are engaging or satisfying.

What then is the role of the adult, and in particular, within formal educational contexts, the role of the teacher? How can we support the unique opportunities inherent within child-structured play without transforming it into adult-structured drama? Should the support be offered before, during or after the play, and if during, what form should this direct intervention take?

In terms of pre-play support, one appropriate approach involves introducing children to aesthetically charged materials that might serve to stimulate play. Here play may develop as the result of exposure to high quality stories (told or read), visits to the theatre or other real-world spaces, or additionally, by engaging the children in adult-structured drama. Of course, experiences such as these may or may not result in play, but when children's imaginations are opened up and expanded in these ways, play is always a possibility. Indeed, the teacher who provides these opportunities may never be aware of the play that this material generates, for some children may choose the privacy of their own homes to become a "cocoon" for play (Sobel, 1993), with the permissions needed to make their play more public being unavailable.

The next step for the teacher who is keen to support play, might be to create a shared understanding of the roles, situations, tasks and materials relevant to the materials presented or experiences offered. This shared understanding is needed so that players are able to collaborate in the construction of shared dramatic worlds. This shared understanding can once again be achieved through the application of a range of adult-structured drama strategies, with teacher-in-role being one of the most significant of these. Here the teacher not only introduces some of the roles possible within the play, but is also able to model context appropriate language, symbolism and the use of space.

Such modelling is especially necessary where the potential play contexts include fantasy worlds far beyond the experience of children's lives—fantasy worlds like Magic Carpet Tour Offices (Dunn, 2008), Giantologist Headquarters (O'Toole & Dunn, 2002), or Dream-maker kitchens (Dunn & Stinson, 2002). In each of these examples, the teacher's support via structured drama was critical to the establishment of shared play opportunities—giving players and their imaginations the stimulation needed to get ideas flowing, before stepping back to provide a space for the children's creativity to develop through child-structured experiences.

At times, this play, once generated, will continue without any further need for adult involvement. However, more often, it will slow and eventually die unless there is a continued injection of tension. O'Toole (1992) adopts Ryle's metaphor of dispositional flow and emotional 'eddies' to describe the nature of tension as "boulders in a stream", with these boulders slowing down the action and preventing it from reaching resolution too rapidly or easily. O'Toole goes on to note (p. 134) that within the dramatic narratives of very young children, resolutions are swiftly achieved, but that as children mature, satisfaction will not be present unless the characters in their narratives "experience vicissitudes" and "feel sufficient frustrations for the resolution to accrue significance as an event". Players may therefore need to be supported in generating tensions within their play, and while "master dramatists" are quite capable of generating these on their own, other children may need support and scaffolding in order to develop an understanding of this aspect of play. Such learner scaffolding should begin the process of developing what Guss (2005b) calls dramatic intelligence, with the teacher's use of the co-player role being one highly effective means of achieving this provision.

The purpose of such co-player interventions are however critical, for as Rogers & Evans (2007, p. 163) point out, play benefits most from those styles of intervention that "extend and rejuvenate rather than constrain and frustrate". Drama educators, in particular, have to be careful to ensure that their dramatic structuring skills and aptitude for improvisation do not result in the players being disempowered through teacher intervention.

To walk this fine line between support and dominance, co-player roles must be chosen that are not only relevant to the specific dramatic world the children have created, but also have a status level (high, medium or low) that meets the needs of both the context and the individual children playing. Adults also need to time their entry, observing the action closely prior to joining the children in order to ensure that their contribution is still needed. Play texts move rapidly and if the children have already re-generated the play for themselves, intervention may not be needed. Finally, and most importantly, the teacher must decide how they want to influence the text, making a decision about the kind of offering they will make once they enter the play frame. Do they, for example, want to support the current direction of the text (narrative function), change it radically (intervening function), or simply offer support for a textual direction offered by one of the children but not taken up by the group (reinforcing function)?

For adults who want to support the development of children's imaginations and creativity within child-structured play contexts, an understanding of these playwright functions might be highly useful, accompanied by an ability to actively apply a range of metacommunicative strategies. In addition, if as Hadley (2002) argues, older children need to play in the company of adults who are playfully disposed, adults in general and drama educators in particular, will also need to re-connect with their own sense of playfulness—a quality that the pressures of curriculum, literacy and testing regimes may have dulled. Finally, if these teachers are to be of real use to the children they work/play with, they will also need to develop a renewed respect for play as an authentic and valid form of improvisation, acknowledging that to be a successful player, complex structuring and collaboration skills are required. Drama teachers can support the development of some of these skills within adult-structured experiences, but when it comes to the development of collaborative creativity, there are few mediums that offer as much to children of all ages as child-structured play.

REFERENCES

Creaser, B. (1989). An examination of the four-year-old master dramatist. *International Journal of Early Childhood Education, 21*, 55–68.

Dunn, J. (2003). Enhancing dramatic activities in the early childhood years. In S. Wright (Ed.), *The arts, young children and learning* (pp. 211–229). Boston: Allyn and Bacon.

Dunn, J. (2008). Play, drama and literacy in the early years. In J. Marsh & E. Hallet (Eds.), *Desirable literacies: Approaches to language and literacy in the early years* (pp. 162–182). London: Paul Chapman.

Dunn, J., & Stinson, M. (2002). *The dream-maker*. Brisbane: Queensland Studies Authority.

Fein, G. (1987). Pretend play in childhood: An integrative view. *Child Development, 52*, 1095–1118.

Florida, R. (2002). *The rise of the creative class*. Christchurch, New Zealand: Hazard Press.

Florida, R. (2005). *Cities and the creative class*. New York: Routledge.

Goffman, E. (1974). *Frame analysis: An essay on the organization of experience*. New York: Harper and Row Publishers.

Guss, F. (2005a). Reconceptualizing play: Aesthetic self-definitions. *Early Childhood, 6*(3), 233–243.

Guss, F. (2005b). Dramatic playing beyond the theory of multiple intelligences. *Research in Drama Education, 10*(1), 43–54.

Hadley, E. (2002). Playful disruptions. *Early Years, 22*(1), 9–17.

Lobman, C. (2003). What should we create today? Improvisational teaching in play-based classrooms. *Early Years, 23*(2), 132–142.

Lofdahl, A. (2005). 'The funeral': A study of children's shared meaning-making and its developmental significance. *Early Years, 25*(1), 5–16.

O'Neill, C. (1995). *Drama worlds: A framework for process drama*. Portsmouth, England: Heinemann.

O'Toole, J. (1992). *The process of drama: Negotiating art and meaning*. London: Routledge.

O'Toole, J., & Dunn, J. (2002). *Pretending to learn: Helping children learn through drama*. Frenchs Forest, NSW: Pearson Education.

Rogers, S., & Evans, J. (2007). Rethinking role play in the reception class. *Educational Research, 49*(2), 153–167.

Sawyer, R. K. (2006). *Explaining creativity: The science of human innovation*. Oxford: Oxford University Press.

Sobel, D. (1993). *Children's special places*. Arizona, AZ: Zephyr Press.

Spencer, M. (2003). What more needs saying about imagination? *Journal of Adolescent and Adult Literacy, 47*(1), 106–113.

Julie Dunn is a Senior Lecturer within the Faculty of Education, Griffith University, Australia where she teaches within the Applied Theatre and Drama Education programs.

BOGUSIA MATUSIAK-VARLEY

6. DEVELOPING PUPILS' LEARNING THROUGH THE USE OF MANTLE OF THE EXPERT

Keywords: learning, life skills, mantle of the expert

It has been both a pleasure and a privilege to have been involved with the development of Mantle of the Expert since 1991 when Dorothy Heathcote ran the Mary Morgan Project (see Archives A series, Birmingham City University) at Cape Primary School in Smethwick, West Midlands. Over 19 years have passed since then I have watched the system develop and grow from strength to strength. It is now recognised as a major vehicle to teach the curriculum in a highly creative and meaningful manner. Mantle of the Expert has a significant impact on the types of learning experienced by pupils as it provides opportunities for pupils to not only acquire academic know-ledge but also the skills needed for the world of work. Lave (1988) states that know-ledge needs to be presented in authentic contexts, setting and situations that would normally involve that knowledge. He argues the case that social interaction and collaboration are essential components of situated learning, pupils become involved in a 'community of practice' which embodies certain beliefs and behaviours to be acquired. As a novice moves from the periphery of a community to its centre, he or she becomes more active and engaged within the culture and eventually assumes the role of an expert. Never has the time been more appropriate than now to focus on implementing this method of pedagogy as globally, the media informs us that students are not ready to cope with demands of the work place (Onyekakeyah, 2009).

The Mantle of the Expert approach to teaching and learning is dramatic enquiry using theatre skills in the 'as if' mode of working within or across curriculum programmes. There is always an enterprise to be run, a client who needs help with a job to be executed by the pupils. Pupils grow into expertise by executing tasks carefully structured by the teacher and through these they take on the mantle of 'those in the know'. The emphasis is on undertaking the necessary tasks to make the enterprise a success and to serve the ever increasing demands of the clients. Pupils carry out their curriculum tasks with an increased sense of responsibility because they have accepted the fiction of working in an enterprise that places a demand on their emerging expertise. Learning manifests itself in qualitative undertakings of independent enquiry. The teacher fuels learning by placing ever-increasing demands on task execution from the perspective of the client. This dramatic tension contributes to the bonding of the group as collectively they are responsible for delivering the goods. The 'them and us' situation provides the necessary tensions to bring about effective learning. Through the skilful intervention

S. Schonmann (ed.), Key Concepts in Theatre/Drama Education, 35–38.

and planning of teacher, pupils undertake a range of different tasks which are engineered jointly by the needs of the curriculum and by the teacher's thorough analysis of pupils' next steps of learning.

The updated National Curriculum (2010) reorganises the programmes of learning into six areas including understanding the arts that places Mantle of the Expert in a much sought after position of creative curriculum planning. The recent legislative emphasis of ensuring that the principles of the Every Child Matters agenda: Enjoying and Achieving, Being Healthy, Staying Safe, Making a Positive Contribution, Achieving Economic Well-being, are fully implemented in schools, adds further weight to the efficiency of this dramatic system in preparing pupils for future employment.

If we accept that the main purpose of education is to prepare pupils for life emotionally, socially and academically, then we cannot underestimate the power of using Dorothy Heathcote's Mantle of the Expert as a powerful learning tool to ensure that all pupils are ready to cope with the challenges employment offers. What better way is there of exploring the 'as if' world of work than through participating in a Mantle of the Expert project? This approach to learning is further characterised by offering 'service to society'. Pupils are taught that their fictional enterprise can provide innovative solutions to a wide range of consumer demands. Helping society, developing responsible and ethical practices, being led by values-based leadership built upon the tradition and history of an enterprise empower pupils to develop their emerging skills of providing quality customer care. Whether they are running a zoo, an animal sanctuary, a museum or a shoe factory, the needs of the client become the real impetus for learning. 'Learning is a process where knowledge is presented to use, then shaped through understanding, discussion and reflection' (Freire, 1987).

Pupils' personal development and well-being are at the core of learning in Mantle of the Expert. Pupils develop skills of rigour and responsibility because task execution 'matters' as through careful guidance from the teacher, pupils are given opportunities to identify, organise, plan and allocate resources needed for effective working. They set goals, prepare and follow schedules and, above all, learn how to adapt to change (a prerequisite for a successful working environment). Pupils learn how to deliver on time, working within given time constraints, and develop concerns about quality. They acquire, evaluate, organise, interpret and communicate information whilst researching independently or participating in group tasks. It is the quality and range of teacher-pupil interactions which impact on pupils' learning and enables them to develop an ever increasing repertoire of knowledge, skills and understanding that puts them in good stead for future employability.

A significant aspect of their learning is related to developing interpersonal skills. Pupils participate in teams, learn from and teach one another, exercise leadership by taking initiative and problem solving, communicate their ideas to justify their courses of action, persuade and convince others and responsibly challenge existing procedures and policies. Above all, pupils are introduced through the carefully crafted fiction, to negotiate, take on other's viewpoints and resolve divergent interests. Their learning transcends normal classroom practice because the teacher, through the perceived demands of the client, can engender a sense of urgency. This enables pupils to gain a deeper understanding of the world of systems procedures and accountability understanding how complex organisations work and how employees struggle to fit their own needs around the demands of the client. This is priceless learning within the security of a classroom environment and gives pupils the opportunity to understand how organisations function.

Skilful teacher interventions, brought about by the needs of the client, are the key to successful learning in Mantle of the Expert. Scaffolding exercises to encourage the participation of wide ranging needs of pupils where individual instructional modifications are made to ensure inclusive practices guarantee success for all. Co-operative learning groups pool knowledge and skills to complete tasks which must be executed to the best of pupils' ability. Teacher modelling and demonstrating, coupled with performance feedback and opportunities to improve on previous best performance then demonstrating the knowledge to others enable the pupils to develop self confidence, high self-esteem and a feeling of success. While there is no magic formulae for motivating students, the creative teacher can encourage student investment in learning in ways that do not require use of formal reward systems. Learning matters because academic requirements are related to real world situations. (the enterprise has to fulfil the needs of the client). The client becomes the audience. Pupils know that their work will be accepted or rejected (modifications might have to be made at the insistence of the client). This external validation fuels pupils' desire to 'get it right' and motivation becomes intrinsic.

Participating in a Mantle of the Expert approach to learning enables pupils to develop their thinking skills. Creative thinking in collaboration with others requires the generating of new ideas to be used when problem solving and implementing an agreed plan of action (Lipman et al., 1980). Pupils learn how to collaboratively make decisions by generating alternatives, considering risks and evaluating the best course of action to undertake. Their reasoning skills improve when they discover the relationships between different groups within the fictitious enterprise and understand that the drive for a common purpose overcomes any personal reservations that they might have. The group develops as a community of enquiry every time a demand is being placed by the client. Collaborative dialogue, disagreement, respectful listening and following a train of thought prepare pupils for achieving economic well-being. Care, respect, safety and co-operation are the cornerstones of reaching for under-standing meaning, truth and exploration of reasoned values. The ability to assimilate complex, often conflicting, data to simultaneously adopt different perspectives on a subject encourages the pupils to see the part (the enterprise) and the whole (task execution) at the same time. It invites pupils to see interconnectedness and to value alternative perspectives.

This collaborative approach to learning is based upon Dorothy Heathcote's paradigm of 'Child as a Crucible, you and I keep stirring knowledge together' (Heston, 1993). In this paradigm, both teacher and child stir the learning experience together thus creating transformation. In Friere's (1987) terms, "it is a dialogue with pupils which resolves the teacher taught contradiction. Teachers and pupils often reverse their roles as they engage in the democratic dialogue of authentic classroom praxis. Liberating education consists of acts of cognition not transferrals of information" (p. 42).

REFERENCES

Freire, P. (1987). *Pedagogy of the oppressed* (M. B. Ramos, Trans.). New York: Continuum.

Heston, S. (1993). *The Dorothy Heathcote archive.* (A Ph.D thesis).

Lave, J. (1988). *Cognition in practice: Mind, mathematics, and culture in everyday life.* Cambridge, UK: Cambridge University Press.

Lipman, M., Sharp, A. M., & Oscanyan, F. S. (1980). *Philosophy in the classroom.* Philadelphia: Temple University Press.

National Curriculum Primary Handbook. (2010, February). QCDA Onyekakeyah, L. (2009). *The Guardian*, Lagos, August 11.

Bogusia Matusiak-Varley *is an international trainer, key note speaker, educational inspector and executive coach. She is director of both Top Quality Marque and Incyte Limited.*

DEBRA MCLAUCHLAN

7. WHAT MAKES A GREAT HIGH SCHOOL DRAMA TEACHER?

Keywords: high school drama, student perceptions, student motivation, drama pedagogy, teacher characteristics and behavior

Many university drama education scholars began their careers as secondary school drama/theatre teachers; several, myself included, have chronicled their own teacher-as-researcher experiences with teenagers (e.g., Gallagher, 2000; Gonzalez, 1999; Gonzalez, Cantu, & Gonzalez, 2006; Hatton, 2001, 2003, 2004; McLauchlan, 2000, 2008; Owens, 2000; Yassa, 1999). From the different perspective of non-participant observer, I recently visited six drama classrooms in four publically funded secondary schools, with the aim of eliciting viewpoints about studying drama from students hitherto unknown to me. This article summarizes my discoveries about teen-agers' motivations to study drama and opinions related to effective drama pedagogy.

The sites I visited included three Grade 9 (students aged 14–15) and three Grade 12 (students aged 17–18) drama classrooms from a medium-sized, predominantly Caucasian, public school board in Ontario, Canada. Teachers in these classrooms are all highly respected educators, viewed by their principals as excellent drama teachers. In addition to teaching drama as part of the curriculum, all offer extra-curricular or co-curricular drama programs at their schools.

After preliminary conversations with the teachers involved, I visited each class-room on three occasions. On the first visit, I explained to the students my interest in hearing their opinions about high school drama; observed them at work in their class; and distributed an information package about the study, including appropriate consent forms. During the second visit, students began class by engaging in regular classroom activities, while I observed, and then completed a questionnaire that probed their perceptions of studying drama. The questionnaire included a demographic section (e.g., gender, age, grade), a 12-item checklist section (e.g., Check Yes or No to the following statements: My parent(s) encouraged me to take drama this year; I am involved in drama activities outside of class), and a 12-item short-answer section (e.g., Why did you decide to take drama this year? What did you expect to learn in drama this year?). At the end of class, students willing to be audio-taped for an interview placed their names in a jar, from which two girls' and two boys' names from each class were selected at random. I conducted the interviews during my third visit, which also included a pizza lunch for the entire class. In total, I inter-viewed 24 students (six Grade 9 boys; six Grade 9 girls; five Grade 12 boys; seven Grade 12 girls) for approximately half an hour each. Both questionnaire and inter-view results remained confidential and anonymous, and teachers were not informed

S. Schonmann (ed.), Key Concepts in Theatre/Drama Education, 39–44.

of individual student responses or opinions. All quotations in this article are drawn directly from either questionnaire or interview responses.

FACTORS MOTIVATING GRADE 9 STUDENTS TO STUDY DRAMA

In Ontario secondary schools (Grades 9–12), drama is an optional subject that some students select in Grade 9 only, some select throughout high school, and some never select at all. As a requirement for graduation, students must complete one arts credit in drama, music, visual arts, or comprehensive arts.

In the schools I visited, Grade 9 students selected drama as their compulsory arts credit for diverse reasons. For both boys and girls, elementary school experiences provided a positive incentive ("We had [drama] in Grade 7 and 8 and I enjoyed the activities"; "I was always in the school plays in elementary school, and I was told that I was good"). As a negative inducement, some students, both boys and girls, sought to avoid either music or visual arts ("I'm not really good with art and music isn't my thing either"; "I wasn't really interested in the art and music thing."). Some parents had encouraged students of both genders to study drama as a means of overcoming shyness.

Overall, boys offered a wider range of reasons for taking drama than girls. Several viewed it as a potentially easy and/or fun credit; some hoped to improve their expressive/communication skills; some were interested in drama's physically active components; a few sought a safe outlet for expressing feelings/emotions. Girls tended to select drama based on either curiosity or interest, as well as recommendations from friends and/or family about course content or the teacher's reputation.

FACTORS MOTIVATING SENIOR STUDENTS TO STUDY
DRAMA THROUGHOUT HIGH SCHOOL

Grade 12 (senior) drama courses in the schools I visited emphasized the production and public performance of scripts, either collaboratively created by students or professionally written. Four major factors motivated students to study drama at the senior level. In order of frequency, these include: (a) the opportunity to work with peers of similar interests, (b) the teacher, (c) the thrill of performing for a public audience, and (d) the drama classroom's unique opportunities (e.g., "I can be myself and at the same time be someone else"; "It's a place for me to express myself in a fun way").

Senior students consistently described the drama classroom as a place of emotional safety; several referred to classmates as a surrogate family or emotional oasis. Many suggested that the drama room differs from most classrooms because it is a space where student opinions are encouraged, supported, and valued. All viewed their teachers as essential components of a positive classroom environment.

In fact, many placed so much emphasis on the teacher's role that I decided to look more closely at drama pedagogy as a factor related to student motivation and retention in drama classrooms.

WHAT MAKES A GREAT HIGH SCHOOL DRAMA TEACHER?

Students in both Grades 9 and 12 strongly viewed teacher behavior as a crucial determinant of their high school drama experience. Their opinions clustered into ten characteristics of effective drama pedagogy, which together suggest a conceptual blueprint of exemplary instructional practice. Some characteristics refer to knowledge; some, to procedural skills and techniques; others imply affective or perhaps personality traits. Affective characteristics combined a passion for teaching drama, an abiding interest in teenagers, and a propensity to trust and listen with acceptance and open-mindedness.

Students believed that great drama teachers exude passion for their jobs. "They really have to love what they do." "The teacher has to have the right enthusiasm." The teachers' passion infectiously motivates their classes. "[The teacher] has to bring the stuff to the table; he's gotta [sic] basically make it look good and make us want to learn."

Along with passion for their subject area, great drama teachers also display keen interest in teenagers' concerns and abilities. They "relate well to teenagers" and "get where we're coming from." "The teacher knows [us] and what [we] can do." "[A great drama teacher] gives us work that relates to who we are and what we do." One senior male student identified the teacher's interest in student enjoyment as a primary aspect of great drama pedagogy: "The most important duties of [a great] drama teacher would have to be, I guess, assigning [appropriate] work to us and making sure we're enjoying it and still learning at the same time."

Students believed that great drama teachers listen to, accept, and respect teenagers' opinions. They explicitly instruct their students on the importance of listening in drama classrooms, and model respectful collaborative behavior. "[Our teacher] encourages us to listen to each other, and teaches us how to give constructive criticism." "[Our teacher] always brings his thoughts [to a discussion], but he isn't aggressive about it. If we have an idea, he listens and tries to add it on."

Students value and learn from their teachers' trust. Genuine displays of teacher trust motivate teenagers not only to behave maturely and responsibly, but also to complete tasks with minimal supervision and maximum effort. Great drama teachers both rely on students' decision-making capabilities and demonstrate faith in the goodness of their intentions, thus encouraging students to accept responsibility for their actions. "My [drama] teacher gives us a lot of independent options." "For our major production, we had a student director, and the teacher let him make really important decisions."

Students entwined notions of teachers' subject-specific knowledge and generic pedagogical skills. They expected their teachers to know and teach them about drama; at the same time, they valued teacher readiness to learn and work with teenagers. Students repeatedly stated that great drama teachers willingly display the vulnerability of not knowing all the answers and eagerly share in joint classroom tasks. "The teacher doesn't give the impression that she already knows [everything]. She learns with us." "Our teacher helped paint sets [for our class production] and typed up the program." "The teacher wrote scenes with us."

Students expected their drama teachers to provide the classroom with structure and stability. Predictable routines and procedures, from the students' perspective, not only promote a sense of security and class community, but also encourage teenagers to generate valuable ideas from within an orderly atmosphere of familiarity. Grade 9 coursework usually involves students working in groups on specific drama techniques, and then showing their work to their teacher and peers. Every Grade 9 student I interviewed indicated that structured routines anchor their diverse classroom experiences. For example, many recalled ritualistic beginnings and endings to their drama class.

Although Grade 12 offers a greater range of class activity than Grade 9, senior students also described the structured routines of a typical drama class. For example,

> A typical day is, you arrive on time and then there is usually a warm-up exercise - get everyone up there with the class - and then we start on theories or we have different scenarios we have to create in different forms, and then usually at the end of the day we do an improve game, and then we do it all again the next day. (School A respondent)

> We all come together in our energy circle, have a focus exercise, and get straight down to work....We brainstorm, hash out ideas. Then we all come together and share our ideas and then come to, like, general consensus. Then we start improvising scenes. (School B respondent)

According to the students I interviewed, great drama teachers directly impart know-ledge and actively "teach us a lot." At the same time, by inviting creative freedom within structured boundaries, they encourage students to follow idiosyncratic learning paths. "[The teacher] gives us an outline, and then we create from it and work with it, and make it our own." "[The teacher] won't tell you exactly what to do...You kinda hafta [sic] find your own [way] within yourself." As projects and activities progress, teachers ensure that students are supportively challenged, focused, and on task. "If you're scared, that's fine, the teacher will encourage you." "[Our teacher] pushes you to do well, and it helps you shoot out your energy." "If someone is [off-task], the teacher will take care of it fast and not let it get too bad."

Great drama teachers encourage students to develop a productive class-wide community that is focused on achievement. One way they achieve this aim is by ensuring that peers work throughout the course with all classmates, and not only self-selected friends. Students suggested various ways that teachers devise group membership; regardless of grouping techniques used, students would rather work in teacher-assigned groups than always with the same clique. "It's better that the teacher picks groups for us because then we can learn to work with different people instead of the same ones all the time." "It's not like everyone's just separated off into different groups that are always together, and we're less likely to goof around."

A final trait of exemplary drama pedagogy from the students' viewpoint is a lack of perceived teacher comparison among classmates according to innate theatrical talent. Rather than focus on natural performance ability as a standard of accomplishment, great drama teachers weave individualized and ongoing student assessment into every component of the learning tasks assigned. "[Our teacher] is not really judging someone on talent, on how good they are. [Our teacher] is judging them [sic] on constantly improving." "To get good marks in drama, it's not just about [talent] or brains or how well you can write stuff down on paper. It's how much you are willing to test your limits and how much you are willing to go above and beyond." Student assessment in the classrooms of great drama teachers focuses on a range of components beyond performance skills and factual memorization. Students are encouraged, for example, to formulate and justify artistic opinions and choices. "It's not about if you get a wrong answer on, like, a math test and then you get a bad mark....It's more abstract...as long as you express yourself in such a way that you believe is important to you, then if you have a great teacher, you get a mark for it." Great drama teachers thus procedurally rely on ongoing student assessment as a teaching, learning, and motivational tool.

SUMMARY: WHAT LESSONS DO STUDENTS' OPINIONS TEACH?

The teacher is a major factor in motivating students to study drama throughout high school. Successful drama pedagogy involves a complex weaving of teacher knowledge, skills, and affect. Although great drama teachers may differ in individual teaching styles and specific learning activity choices, they share both strong curriculum knowledge and common approaches to structuring, recognizing, and assessing student work. Most importantly, great drama teachers seem capable of balancing what might appear as opposites. For example, they display robust content knowledge of drama as a subject while simultaneously functioning as co-learners in the classroom. They provide structure and predictability, while at the same time offering freedom of choice and prudent opportunities for risk taking and creativity. They treat students fairly and respectfully, but also assess achievement on individual rather than normative measures of growth. Perhaps most importantly, great drama teachers consistently display a passion for and commitment to both the art form of drama and the teenagers who study it.

REFERENCES

Gallagher, K. (2000). Interrupting "Truths", Engaging perspectives, and enlarging the concept of "Human" in classroom drama. *Youth Theatre Journal, 14*, 13–25.

Gonzalez, J. (1999). Directing high school theatre: The impact of student-empowerment strategies and unconventional staging techniques on actors, director, and audience. *Youth Theatre Journal, 13*, 4–21.

Gonzalez, J., Cantu, R., & Gonzalez, A. (2006). Staging whiteness: Possibilities for resistance and revelation in A High School Production of Simply Maria, or, The American Dream. *Youth Theatre Journal, 20*, 124–139.

Hatton, C. (2001). A girls' own project: Subjectivity and transformation in girls' drama. *NJ (Drama Australia), 25*(1), 21–30.

Hatton, C. (2003). Backyards and borderlands: Some reflections on researching the travels of adolescent girls doing drama. *Research in Drama Education, 8*(2), 140–156.

Hatton, C. (2004). On the edge of realities: Drama, learning, and adolescent girls. *NJ (Drama Australia), 28*(1), 88–103.

McLauchlan, D. (2000). Collaborative creativity in a high school drama class. *Youth Theatre Journal, 15*, 42–58.

McLauchlan, D. (2008). Factors constraining teacher choices of material for high school actors. *Applied Theatre Research, 9.*

Owens, D. (2000). Gendered experiences in the drama classroom. *NJ (Drama Australia), 24*(1), 53–60.

Yassa, N. (1999). High school involvement in creative drama. *Research in Drama Education, 4*(1), 37–49.

***Debra McLauchlan**, Associate Professor, teaches drama education at Brock University, Canada. Research interests include secondary school drama, drama teacher education, and TYA.*

SECTION II: AESTHETICS AND ETHICS

JANINKA GREENWOOD

8. AESTHETIC LEARNING, AND LEARNING THROUGH THE AESTHETIC

Keywords: aesthetic, learning, complexity, drama, theatre

The aesthetic is at the heart of all our work in theatre and drama, yet it remains a term that eludes definition, and perhaps rightly so. The art of drama and theatre is complex, culturally situated, and forever renegotiating the expectations and boundaries of previous work. That which excites or moves us in the art is also complex, culturally situated, and escaping definition through words. But because it eludes firm definition does not mean it is not important to consider, describe, and attempt to understand, particularly so because as teachers and community workers we often talk about 'aesthetic learning' as something that is not only particular to the arts in education but also of significant value.

The discussion that follows briefly reviews some of the influential ways that the concept of aesthetics has been addressed, and proposes a consideration of complexity theorising as a way of engaging with the concept. It then turns to learning: distinguishing between learning about the aesthetic, learning through aesthetic experience, and something further that we might call 'aesthetic learning".

A [TO Z] IS FOR AESTHETIC

Abbs' influential body of writings addresses aesthetics within the context of arts education. He describes (1987, p. 85) aesthetics as "a distinct category of under-standing... a mode of sensuous knowing, [a response] that is cognitive in nature". His approach may be aligned with that of Dewey (1934) who talks about perception as a complex interaction between the watcher and the watched, and explains that an art work acquires its aesthetic meaning through the active contemplation of the viewer; and with that of Eisner (2002) who addresses art as "a way of knowing". All three writers emphasise the experiential, the subjective and the socially-constructed aspects of the aesthetic.

In a wider framework, Kant (1790/2000) proposes that beauty exists not as a property of an artwork but in the consciousness of pleasure that results from free play between imagination and understanding. Habermas (in Lyotard, 1992) and Giroux (1988) critique and problematise positivist concepts of beauty and pleasure within the aesthetic. Foucault (in Rabinow, 1984) reframes aesthetics in terms of life and discusses the need to live life as a work of art. Feminist theorists (such as Callaghan, 1995; Kruger, 1995) add an activist political dimension to the discussion stressing the importance of women-centred epistemologies and marginalised theatre

S. Schonmann (ed.), Key Concepts in Theatre/Drama Education, 47–52.

practices. My own work in intercultural theatre (2002; 2006) has explored the importance of cultural values and culturally located repertoires of symbols, images and experiences.

The embedded theory of various theatre practitioners also points to a range of considerations of the aesthetic. Stanislavski's work leads us to see the aesthetic in terms of authenticity in the representation of experience and society. Brecht expects us to add an awareness of the social impact of the craft we see on stage. Artaud's work demands a consideration of the passionate, violent and 'unacceptable' aspects of the human condition. In Grotowski's practice the aesthetic is explored in terms of physicality, the tension of the group, and, in his later work, interdependence with breath.

A body of contemporary theorists (such as Hagendoorn, 2005; Ramachandran & Rogers-Ramachandran, 2006) focus on neuroaesthetics, conceptualising the relationship between neurological pathways and aesthetic response. In these terms the feelings an individual might experience when watching dance are the product of a myriad sensory, cognitive and emotional brain processes. The processes are not accidental but neurologically coded. Their neuroaesthetic models might be construed as a challenge to the propositions of Abbs, Dewey and Eisner, or, in the context of possible further knowledge of how the brain works, they might simply offer a neurological map of such perception, inquiry and reflection.

An extensive range of other writings could be considered alongside those I have cited to further illustrate the multi-faceted and sometimes contradictory discussion about the nature of the aesthetic. So does that multiplicity of dimensions and complexity need be a problem for us as drama educators?

COMPLEXITY THINKING AND THE AESTHETIC

It may be useful to take a non-normative, fluid and multi-faceted approach to the aesthetic, acknowledging it as a complex (rather than complicated) and dynamic concept. Analogies to aspects of complexity theory - particularly those of emergence, wholeness, multiplicity, tolerance of dichotomy and tension - offer the opportunity to investigate component elements of the aesthetic without a need to reduce, enumerate or align the elements that suggest complication. The complexity theorists (among them (Waldrop, 1992; Byrne, 1998; Davis, Sumara, & Luce- Kapler, 2000; Richardson 2005) have largely come from science and mathematics but have adapted complexity thinking to engage with social sciences, education and business management. Adapting such an approach allows us to teach our students that aesthetics is a complex system of semiotics, responses and meanings, at the same time as we select particular frames to explore for particular purposes.

AN ILLUSTRATIVE EXAMPLE

For the purpose of illustration let's take the example of a particular dance performance by a group of older Bhutanese women on Refugee Day. How might a teacher prepare students to engage with the dance? And understand the contextual situatedness of aesthetic responses?

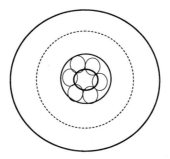

The diagram above suggests a number of frames of reference within which an aesthetic response might be located. The inner circle represents the dance itself as it was passed down in Bhutan: a dynamic of symbols, movements, flows that have evolved over time to evoke particular sensual, emotive, intellectual and spiritual responses from those who are accustomed to them. The next circle represents the way this group of women engage with the dance and its traditional meanings: individually and as a group. The dotted circle represents the way the group offers this dance to this audience: one made up both of a significant number of their own community and of strangers to their culture. The outer circle represents the way the group offers the dance within the new country, which is at once their exile and their new home.

Each of the frames carries different triggers for emotional response and meaning. And of course each evokes a corresponding set of frames through which the different communities in the audience might respond.

If the teacher's students were not themselves immigrants they might need guidance through any one of these frames in the same way as through a foreign language. But what if the students were the group of Bhutanese young people who performed later in the same programme? How would they respond to the performance as a whole? To each of the frames?

Within the scaffold of complexity, a number of other frames might have been selected. While it might not be practicable, or even possible, to examine the aesthetics of the dance across the totality of the frameworks, and it is probably useful to select one or more as a platform for learning, it is important to remember, and to teach, that each frame of engagement is just part of a greater whole.

LEARNING ABOUT AND THROUGH THE AESTHETIC

The selection of frames relates to the kind of learning we hope to provoke. When we talk about the aesthetic and learning, we talk about three quite different, though possibly interrelating, things: learning about the aesthetic, learning through aesthetic experience, and a kind of learning that is not predominantly intellectual but that is located in the body: that is visceral, emotional and intuitive. All are important in drama in education.

In terms of the frames discussed above, learning about the aesthetic might occur practically in terms of studying and learning the movements and signing of the traditional dance. It might also occur at the conceptual level in studying the over-lapping frames and interpreting how the aesthetic might reshape itself within each of them.

Learning through the aesthetic might occur in a number of ways. Students might learn about cultural difference, community, the history of Bhutan, or a number of other not essentially aesthetic topics through the aesthetic experience of engaging with Refugee Day - itself a piece of public theatre in Schechner terms (1993). Perhaps if they had the chance to learn the dance with some of the women they might learn about disorientation and cultural isolation through their own physical and emotional responses as well as developing a conceptual understanding. Or, like the group of young Bhutanese dancers they might learn their place in history, their loss and their community's aspiration at some visceral level that both precedes and exceeds conceptual understanding through the aesthetic experience of participation.

It is these last two examples that might be called aesthetic learning.
And any combination of the three might occur together.

FRAMES WITHIN CURRENT LITERATURE OF DRAMA EDUCATION

Contemporary literature of drama and theatre in education contains discussions of the aesthetic with a wide range of points of focus, as the following small selection shows. However, one or more of the above kinds of relationships between learning and aesthetics are considered in all of them. For example, Jackson (2005, p. 110) examines the inscription of the audience into the play as the means for creating a dialogic encounter that is at the heart of theatre as a learning medium. While a primary focus is learning through the aesthetic, he speaks to the importance of learning about the aesthetic and to the heightened impact of learning when it is aesthetic as well as discursive.

Neelands (2004) distinguishes between "intra-aesthetic approaches in pedagogy" which give primacy to "students' artistic and technical skill development" and which are a practical skill based form of learning about the aesthetic, and para-aesthetic approaches which are intended to "develop a broad range of social and cultural learning', which focus on learning through the aesthetic (p. 50). However, in what he describes as the "collision of actualities/realities/fictionalities between the stage and the social space" aesthetic learning about "the sense of instability between what has been, what is and what might be" (p. 53) potentially occurs.

O'Toole (2009, p. 127) refers to "drama as an art-form" as "the aesthetic/cognitive", exploring a way of knowing that is protean and potentially truthful. While he acknowledges the value of learning about and through the aesthetic, it is the potential power of aesthetic learning that he is most concerned with. Ostern (2007, p. 244) takes a broad popular cultural view of aesthetics when she contends that young people today "live in a highly aestheticised world", where they form their identities "in a symbiotic relationship to the mobile and the internet" which develops their "artistic competence". Is this generation then learning aesthetically much of the time? Bundy (2005) talks about the three key characteristics of the experience of aesthetic engagement: "animation, connection and heightened awareness" (p. 2).

Her article focuses on the occurrence of such engagement by children and on ways of talking to children about such experience. When read against Ostern's article it might pose a framework for considering whether exposure to an 'aestheticised world' automatically leads to aesthetic engagement.

THE IMPORTANCE OF AESTHETIC LEARNING

Finally the question needs to be asked whether there is further value in aesthetic learning than in using the art forms and the aesthetic experience for other forms of behavioural or conceptual learning.

It gives us experience, both embodied through our participation and empathetic through exploring another's world. It allows us to absorb a multiplicity of new stimuli, cognitive and visceral, that we can unpack and play with. It permits ambiguity, incompleteness, contradiction and complexity, and provides a means to express these without reducing them. And perhaps more.

Brecht's *Caucasian Chalk Circle* provides an example. His prologue to the play offers the entire discursive argument: that property needs to be considered and attributed according to a capacity for improving the well-being of the people as a whole. But the student who participates in performance of the play, as audience or actor (or as spect-actor in a process drama around it), has the opportunity to emerge with more than a Marxist analysis. (S)he is challenged to respond to Azdak as sycophant, thief, survivor, as well as hero. (S)he may cringe at Grusha's naivety, as well as rejoice in her courage and generosity. (S)he may soar on the wings of epic narrative, as well as crash with interruptions to action. (S)he can catch his or her breath in nervousness and let it out in relief. And perhaps more.

REFERENCES

Abbs, P. (1987). Towards a Coherent arts aesthetic. In P. Abbs (Ed.), *Living powers: The arts in education* (pp. 9–65). London & New York: The Falmer Press.

Bundy, P. (2005). Asking the right questions: Accessing children's experience of aesthetic engagement. *Applied Theatre Researcher, 6,* Article 12.

Byrne, D. (1998). *Complexity theory and the social sciences: An introduction.* London & New York: Routledge.

Callaghan, D. (1995). The aesthetics of marginality: The theatre of Joan Littlewood and Buzz Goodbody. In K. Laughlin & C. Schuler (Eds.), *Theatre and feminist aesthetics.* London: Associated Presses.

Davis, B., Sumara, D., & Luce-Kapler, R. (2000). *Engaging minds: Learning and teaching in a complex world.* New York: Routledge.

Dewey, J. (1934). *Art as experience.* New York: Minton, Balch & Co.

Eisner, E. W. (2002). *The arts and the creation of mind.* New Haven, CT: Yale University Press.

Giroux, H. (1988). Teachers as intellectuals: *Towards a critical pedagogy of learning.* Granby, MA: Bergin & Garvey.

Greenwood, J., & Wilson, A. (2006). *Te Mauri Pakeaka: A Journey into the Third Space.* Auckland: Auckland University Press.

Greenwood, J. (2002). *History of bicultural theatre: Mapping the Terrain.* Christchurch: Christchurch College of Education Press.

Hagendoorn, I. G. (2005). Dance perception and the brain. In S. McKechnie & R. Grove (Eds.), *Thinking in four dimensions.* Melbourne: Melbourne University Publishing.

Jackson, T. (2005). The dialogic and the aesthetic: Some reflections on theatre as a learning medium. *The Journal of Aesthetic Education, 39*(4), 104–118.

Kant, E. (1790/2000). *Critique of the power of judgement* (P. Guyer & E. Matthews, Trans.). New York: Cambridge University press.

Kruger, L. (1995). The dis-play's the thing: Gender, and public sphere in contemporary British drama. In K. Laughlin & C. Schuler (Eds.), *Theatre and feminist aesthetics*. London: Associated Presses.

Lyotard, J. (1992). *The postmodern explained to children*. Sydney: Power Publication.

Neelands, J. (2004). Miracles are happening: Beyond the rhetoric of transformation in the western traditions of drama education. *Research in Drama Education, 9*(1), 47–56.

O'Toole, J. (2009). The three pillars of art. In J. O'Toole, M. Stinson, & T. Moore (Eds.), *Drama and curriculum*. Netherlands: Springer.

Ostern, A.-L. (2007). The future of arts education: A European perspective. *Journal of Artistic and Creative Education, 1*(1), 222–248.

Rabinow, P. (1984). *The foucault reader*. New York: Pantheon Books.

Ramachandran, V., & Rogers-Ramachandran, D. (2006, October). The neurology of aesthetics. *Scientific American Mind*.

Richardson, K. (Ed.). (2005). *Managing organisational complexity: Philosophy, theory and application*. Greenwick: Information Age Publishing.

Schechner, R. (1993). *The future of ritual*. New York: Routledge.

Waldrop, M. (1992). *Complexity: The emerging science at the edge of order and chaos*. New York: Simon and Schuster.

Janinka Greenwood *is Associate Professor at the University of Canterbury, New Zealand, works in interconnecting fields of drama and learning as a teacher, researcher and writer.*

AMY CORDILEONE

9. NEGOTIATING AESTHETICS AND CULTURE

Keywords: distance, space, culture, drama, ambiguity, aesthetics

Aesthetics as a discourse is fraught with structural ambivalence. But, many of the tensions rooted in the philosophical discipline have metamorphosed into tenets of aesthetic education. The concepts with which scholars violently wrestle in academic arenas, classroom teachers and teaching artists embrace as central to their work with young people. Aesthetic education is recognized as set apart from other modes of teaching and learning by its central focus on interweaving knowledge, intuition, and experience in core subjects of study, through the manipulation of various artistic media, including those pertaining to visual arts, musical forms, language arts, and kinesthetic explorations, like dance or theatre (Eisner, 2002; Greene, 2001). Immanuel Kant theorized aesthetic assessment as disinterested valuation of a universal bent, existing just outside of one's merely cognitive and merely intuitive faculties. Kant's Critique of Judgment (1952) originally published in 1790, posits that human assessments fall into two distinct categories, reflective and determinant (determinative). Aesthetic evaluation is reflective in nature, a process that affords individuals the opportunity to personally rectify any number of unknowns. Beyond the nomination of reflection as a criterion for aesthetic response, Kant's articulations on the subject are highly praised, and widely contested, making his theories of aesthetics (addressed with brevity and simplicity here) fodder for over two centuries of polemics. In particular, three areas of discord within the field of aesthetics resound as specifically relevant to aesthetic education—the relationship of cognition to intuition, negotiations of sensus particularis in light of sensus communis, and the hegemonic implications of a dominant cultural aesthetic.

Kant claims disinterestedness as key to aesthetic evaluation of an object. The subject of much academic reflection, disinterestedness continues to lure scholars into debate. Meanwhile aesthetic educators, especially in the field of drama, have engaged the concept as integral to our explorations. Taking the term to mean, as Edward Bullough describes, the "psychical distance" placed between an object and oneself, disinterestedness is precisely what drama educators use to safely invest students in dramatic worlds. Whether these are worlds of the play, or of the study, Bullough states that functions of distance are,

> ... not simple, but highly complex. It has a negative, inhibitory aspect—the cutting-out of the practical side of things, and of our practical attitude to them—and a positive side—the elaboration of the experience on the new basis created by the inhibitory action of the Distance. (1973, p. 371)

S. Schonmann (ed.), Key Concepts in Theatre/Drama Education, 53–57.

This stepping back, as it were, affords educators more than safe entry into exploration, it supports the building of bridges between cognition and intuition. The dramatic strategy of going in and out of role is a cogent example of disinterestedness in action. As young people step into the shoes of others, or maintain their personae amidst altered realities, and subsequently return to their previous states, use of psychical distance (stabilized by the continued observation of the drama, even as one becomes a participant) creates an ideal playground for exploration, experimentation, postulation, and reconstruction (O'Neill, 1995).

In adhering to Kant's aesthetic moments, the disinterested stance is perhaps what gives license to the notion of universality, the feeling of a shared aesthetic judgment that renders said judgment as true for all of mankind, termed sensus communis (1952). Under scrutiny, the theory of sensus communis has politicized aesthetics due to the perceived emotional lure of an aesthetic experience, which could easily be manipulated for the purposes of propagating doctrine among the masses (Castronovo, 2007; van Binsbergen, 2002). Across the spectrum, from Aristotelian catharsis to revolution, the shadow of manipulation affiliated with a sensus communis has spurred scholars to proffer a postmodern alternative, sensus particularis (van Binsbergen, 2002). Sensus particularis mounts the platform from the position of the individual whose nuanced history, beliefs, and background cannot be divorced from her ways of knowing the world. Allowing that the process of socialization into any context is part of the scaffold of one's perceptions, the introduction of the sensus particularis to this dialogue posits an individual's aesthetic valuations as no exception. Interestingly, though scholars may champion one point of reference over another, aesthetic educators have found value in walking the tightrope between the two notions. Once again, a dramatic structure lends us a very practical illustration. Boal's Forum Theatre model situates members of the audience as spect-actors (1979). Spect-actors "... leave the privacy of the audience, enter the dramatic world, and transform the dramatic action" (O'Neill, 1995, p. 119). This transformation does not happen once, but over and over again, with multiple spect-actors determining the outcome of the theatrical, or aesthetic, experience. For the duration of the piece, the audience as a unit, though disrupted by shifts in constitution, remains intact. It cannot lose either the functions of the spectator or those of the actor. Were that to happen, the very essence of the work would be destroyed, its aesthetic would cease to exist. Forum Theatre depends upon the joint endeavors of the sensus communis and the sensus particularis. The two notions are not polarized, but fused.

Maxine Greene conceives one's role as learner to be synonymous with that of interpreter and re-interpreter. Exploring the ideologies of our predecessors, we "... make sense, all kinds of sense, but we make the culture's symbol systems our own" (2001, p. 6). For aesthetic educators, this notion becomes increasingly complex as one negotiates 21st-century learning communities. The heterogeneity of most class-rooms demands interrogation of aesthetic forms, aesthetic judgments, and on the most basic level, the very theorization of aesthetics. The studied practice of evaluating works of art is one source of contention. Layered onto this are the questions - how is a work of art determined as such, and who delimits the criteria. If educators can agree that the word 'aesthetic' functions as an adjective apart from the noun 'aesthetics', which primarily pertains to scholarship, then as an eclectic group of teachers and learners we must investigate the moments in which we have been attuned to aesthetic experiences (Blocker, 2001). This exposure might happen in the home, a cultural center, the work or play place, in fact these experiences can happen anywhere. We must then determine to what degree the experiences were actually composed of aesthetic elements. Western traditions of artistic achievement, most importantly the notion of 'art for art's sake', often belie the multifarious nature of those things typified as artistically engaging (Blocker, 2001). As educators we must probe rigid aesthetic categories, pushing toward a fluidity that will allow, for instance, something to exist as both aesthetic and socially functional. In northern Uganda, male adolescents of the Acholi tribe study spear tactics specific to war through a dance called the Otole. As a unit, the young men learn and perform the dance for weeks, working with found objects as representations of a spear and shield. This culminates in a public presentation of the dance, during which each young man is individually assessed. A panel of elders determines which of the men will then rise through the ranks to become a warrior, thereby receiving his first real spear and shield (Okot, 2008). To define the Otole by the principles of Western aesthetics would be erroneous, though an Acholi would clearly enter the experience of the dance with a personal and culturally developed aesthetic, or artistic, sensibility. This notion problematizes the introduction and use of, for lack of a better term, art forms in the classroom, especially as works or concepts are delineated as 'art', and then objectified for the purposes of assessment.

Aesthetic educators must wrestle with this tension devoid of any goals toward acculturation or classification. In the same way that a universal aesthetic has the potential to undermine authentic human response and social action, the formalization of culture often assumes the hegemonic dynamics of one particular class, thereby directing individuals and/or groups to limited articulations of self, as determined by those in power (Castronovo, 2007; Yúdice, 2007). Educators must resist the temptation to "... act as 'brokers' of otherness" (Cruikshank, 1994 cited in Yúdice, 2007). Rather, our responsibilities lie in the direction of continued reframing. Educators are called to critically examine the materials that students are expected to read/reread, the mode through which the community is asked to explore, the desired outcome of such activity, and the underlying principles or beliefs that could incite a particular line of inquiry. On the other hand, it is not the aesthetic educator's responsibility, nor would it be ethically sound, to alleviate given contexts of their historicity. To do so would be detrimental to the learning community's under-standing(s) of their, albeit unstable, positionality. Drama educators possess the unusual ability to facilitate the delicate negotiations of multiple perspectives through the creation of alternate realities in which young people can question, experience, act out against, and explore the ramifications of their choices on simulated terrain. Though one cannot create truly neutral space, engaging with these tensions gives creative resistance due diligence, through the continued rewriting of the social contract. This is integral to the production process. Production does not here refer to theatre making, rather it refers to the re- imagining of contexts and constructions, determining what one sees as fixed and what is fluid, and from there projecting alternative viewpoints. This is juxtaposed with reproduction, in which elements of one's specific knowledge go untested and are therefore perpetuated as social, moral, intellectual, spiritual, artistic, and/or cultural fixities. Whatever the probing art form, the key element is imaginative commitment. Aesthetic education values both the imaginative process and product, and in doing so supports participants as they push boundaries and exercise new freedoms. "Imagination gives us images of the possible that provide a platform for seeing the actual, and by seeing the actual freshly, we can do something about creating what lies beyond it" (Eisner, 2002, p. 4).

In its attempts to engage the whole learner through the blending of culture, cognition, creation, and reflection, an aesthetic education allows participants (including the facilitator) to question the world around them. Additionally, perhaps more importantly, it encourages individuals to self-assess, to be critical of ways in which they perform their various capacities. Drama as a medium of exploration has the added benefit of revisiting and revising. Though no dramatic moment can be absolutely recreated, the essence of the experience can indeed exist in multiple incarnations with relative ease. This particular characteristic of drama provides the unique opportunity to rehearse alternatives and possible outcomes, perhaps elongating the journey from the private to public sphere, perhaps easing social actors into real world playing spaces.

There are an incredible number of practical benefits to inclusion of artistic exploration in the core curriculum. Learners whose foremost intelligences lie on the margins of contemporary teaching and learning methods are given the opportunity to deeply investigate the world in atypical fashion, and those participants most comfortable with traditional models of schooling are challenged to take risks in developing new relationships to what they know and understand. Talents can be revealed and celebrated. New skills are nurtured. Historical trajectory is illuminated through holistic exploration of political, social, and artistic movements/ counter-movements. These are but few of the many justifications for interdisciplinary exploration of aesthetic experiences in education. But despite clear and traceable evidence of the benefits inherent in this pedagogy, it remains a very dangerous model, as it threatens to upend the typically heteronormative, sovereign institutions that patrol the distribution of knowledge. Education as determined by standards, examinations, and the functionality of factoids leaves little room for exploration on even basic artistic, cultural, and/or psychosocial levels. This places the onus of synthesis on a typically unarmed individual, one who has not necessarily been taught to be untaught, as it were, to question the information and perspectives being distributed. The innate power of such "critical potential" is the double-edged sword of aesthetic education (Yúdice, 2007, p. 76). But this tension, this precarious position, cannot dissuade us from walking the roads of ambiguity with young people. Rather, we must use this contested space, as we have used contested spaces before, to spur us on to critical awareness and action.

REFERENCES

van Binsbergen, W. (2002). *Sensus communis or sensus particularis*. Retrieved from http://www. shikanda.net/general/gen3/kant_afrika.htm

Blocker, H. G. (2001). Non-western aesthetics as a colonial invention. *Journal of Aesthetic Education, 35*(4), 3–13.

Boal, A. (1979). *Theatre of the oppressed* (C. A. & M. L. McBride, Trans.). London: Pluto Press.

Bullough, E. (1973). Psychical distance. In M. Rader (Ed.), *A modern book of aesthetics*. New York: Holt, Rinehart and Winston.

Castronovo, R. (2007). Aesthetics. In B. Burgett & G. Hendler (Eds.), *Keywords in American cultural studies*. New York: New York University Press.

Eisner, E. (2002). *The arts and the creation of the mind*. New Haven, CT: Yale University Press.

Greene, M. (2001). *Variations on a blue guitar: The Lincoln Center lectures on aesthetic education*. New York: Teachers College Press.

Kant, I. (1952). *The critique of judgment* (J. C. Meredith, Trans.). London, UK: Oxford University Press. (Original work published in 1790).

Okot, N. (2008). *Acholi culture and customs*. MPEG. Gulu, Uganda: Invisible Children Uganda.

O'Neill, C. (1995). Drama worlds: A framework for process Drama. Portsmouth, NH: Heinemann.

Yúdice, G. (2007). Culture. In B. Burgett & G. Hendler (Eds.), *Keywords in American cultural studies*. New York: New York University Press.

Amy Cordileone holds a PhD in Educational Theatre from NYU. She is a theatre practitioner, activist, and international educator, working primarily in the United States and northern Uganda.

ANNA-LENA ØSTERN

10. TRANSFORMATION

Keywords: transformation, transportation, transduction, aesthetic doubling, autopoetic feedback loop

I start the analysis regarding the concept *transformation* by referring to anthropologists studying communities with rituals that aimed at transformation of the participants. When Victor Turner in 1969 published *The Ritual Process*, he had had a long period of experiences, of which, especially living with the Ndembu, from 1950 to 1954, brought him to a rich ethnographic reportage. In The Ritual Process he extended the analytic framework of Arnold van Gennep (1909), produced more than fifty years ago. Roger D. Abrahams (1995) writes about this extended analytic framework mentioning the ritual progression in three steps (separation from the everyday flow of activities, a passage through a threshold state into a ritual world, where the structures of everyday life are both elaborated and challenged, and a reentry into the world of everyday life).

The *symbolic cultural dimensions* of *both simple and complex societies*, the notion of *liminality and communitas*, which were central in Turner's cultural perspective, gave tools for observations of altered states of being. In performance studies the notion of transformation has been studied extensively by, among others, Richard Schechner. *Between Theater & Anthropology* (Schechner, 1985) contains a foreword by Victor Turner, which is informative. Turner writes that one big difference between anthropologists and performance directors is that the former observes, but the latter interferes. Turner describes his meeting with Schechner:

> My own self was now presented with an experimentalist in performing. I learned from him that all performance is "restored behavior", that the fire of meaning breaks out from rubbing together the hard and soft firesticks of the past (usually embodied in traditional images, forms and meanings) and present of social and individual experience.

Schechner (1985, p. 116) writes about the theatrical reality marked as "nonordinary—for special use only". He introduces the concept transportation and suggests that not every single performance brings about a transformation:

> Thus each separate performance is a transportation, ending about where it began, while a series of transportation performances can achieve a transformation./.../ Transformation performances are clearly evidenced in initiation rites, whose very purpose it is to transform people from one status or social identity to another. (op. cit., pp. 126f)

S. Schonmann (ed.), Key Concepts in Theatre/Drama Education, 59–63.

Schechner further elaborates the notion of the spectators' role in transformation performances. He mentions that the role of the audience is often participative (op. cit. 132). Also the audience is part of the transportation and transformation. The thought that not only the performer but also the audience is affected by the transformative power of performance is brought into Erika Fischer-Lichte's (2008) discussion about the performance as an art event.

She approaches the concept transformative aiming at a description of a new aesthetics for performance. Of special interest for the analysis in this entry is the notion *autopoetic feedback loop*. Fischer-Lichte (2008, pp. 38–39) identifies a continually operating feedback loop provided in any performance event by the ongoing interactions of performers and audience. In her analysis the notion of presence is brought to the centre of attention. She also underlines the importance of corporeality in the emergence of a new aesthetics of performance with a transformative power.

In this first section of the entry I have traced the central dimension of the concept transformation back to rituals, and how this notion is developed by performance artists and theorists.

In the next section of this concept analysis I will dwell further on the concept transformation as applied in educational drama and theatre. Helene Nicholson makes a clear reference to Schechner's notion transportation when she questions the use of transformation in applied drama:

> If applied drama is socially transformative, is it explicit what kind of society is envisioned? If the motive is individual or personal transformation, is this something which is done to the participants, with them, or by them? Whose values and interests does the transformation serve? Seen in this light, the idea of transportation suggests greater scope for creativity and unpredictability than that of transformation. /.../ It is about travelling into another world, often fictional, which offers both new ways of seeing and different ways of looking at the familiar. (Nicholson, 2005, pp. 12f)

Nicholson points to a central debate within the field of drama and theatre education about the possible outcomes of drama education as change in understanding of a phenomenon, as an insight into the human condition. The debate has, for instance, been about learning in general compared with learning in the arts. One dominant expression of all learning is change.

John Dewey in *Art as Experience* (1934/1980) has made an attempt to outline an aesthetic theory which builds upon transformation of interaction into experience. He writes:

> Experience is the result, the sign, and the reward of that interaction of organism and environment which, when it is carried to the full is a transformation of interaction into participation and communication. (op.cit., p. 22)

Dewey is interested in the playful attitude in transformations in the production of a piece of art: "In art, the playful attitude becomes interest in the transformation of material to serve the purpose of a developing experience." (op. cit., p. 279). Transformative aesthetic theory describes the aesthetic product as an ongoing interactive process. This dialogical elaboration is transformative when an emotional experience or an everyday experience, that is, a sensuous impression, is transformed through poetic elaboration in an art form into an aesthetic experience.

Inkeri Sava (1994) has further developed the description of an artistic learning process. She has made a cyclical model starting from an impulse as point of departure for a series of transformations towards the final product. This productive aesthetics, containing transformations of form in order to produce meaning, can be recognized in drama and theatre educational work. Sava concludes her description of the cycles in an artistic learning process as a series of transformations, which lead to change. She mentions three types of changes: quantitative change, qualitative change and finally structural change. Increased knowledge about the theme and form elaborated is quantitative change. Qualitative change is the change in understanding of a phenomenon. Structural change is a more fundamental change in the way a person understands herself, others, the environment, society, or some aspect of the world.

In Jack Mezirow's (2000) outline of a transformative theory of learning (regarding adult learners), a starting point is described as a disorienting dilemma, a crisis, when the learner experiences that the frames of reference might be wrong, based on socio-cultural distortions, or there is a piece missing. This might lead to a sudden process, or a slowly evolving process of transformation, where objective or subjective (or both) re-framing of the frame of reference is happening. This process involves critical thinking as well as affective involvement. The transformation leads to actions, changes in focus, and eventually new habits of mind.

As a conclusion of the analysis of the meaning potential of the concept trans-formation in education, I have brought critical pedagogy and transformative aesthetic theory into a dialogue, which shows that both claim that learning processes of a certain type (involving affective as well as cognitive dimensions) lead to a change of understanding or to new habits of mind. The productive aspect is underlined in the description of transformations in every phase of an artistic learning process emanating in an expression. To encourage transformations and to reflect upon the transformations of form might be one way to qualify the supervision of artistic learning processes in education.

In the final section of this concept analysis I will turn the focus on literature and literacy. Wolfgang Iser (1978) describes the reader's encounter with a fictive text as a developing competence in making an aesthetic doubling. Iser's theory of aesthetic reception describes the meeting between the text of the author and the reader as an active creation from the reader, a reader response to the author's text. In the author text there are gaps and blanks, empty spaces, which the reader fills out with his interpretations. Fictive or aesthetic reading is characterized by a special competence: not only decoding letter by letter but by interpreting the sub- text, reading between and beyond the lines, catching up with threads planted earlier in the text and making new interpretations when new information about the characters is given.

In a devised piece of theatre, in a process drama and in other genres of drama in education this aesthetic doubling implies a transformation of real time to fictive time, real space to fictive space, constructing a character or role, and building a plot. In this process the students use the signs of theatre in order to create an expression. This is done through a series of transformations, explorations and discussions about intention and meaning (Østern, 2009). In multimodal literacy theory the simultaneous use of different modes in expression forms a cluster of meanings for the student to express and receive.

Gunther Kress in *Literacy in the New Media Age* shows how new media will change the theories about meaning, language and learning (Kress, 2003, p. 168). Multimodality implies the (simultaneous) use of different types of semiotic signs in a communication, for instance visual signs like images, graphs and film; corporeal signs like dance, drama, gesture and mime; auditive signs like music and sounds; and finally printed or written signs. Kress writes about how this new literacy challenges traditional understanding of rationality, like rationality should be only of one kind, or that rationality and affect are separated from each other. He writes that the concepts will be much more open:

> There will be much more open notions, which bring materiality, bodyliness, sensuality and affect into the centre of attention together with rationality and cognition - or challenge the distinctions between such categories. (Kress, 2003, p. 169)

Kress underlines that when written text and image are integrated, there is continuously produced theory about how meaning is constructed, but the meaning is constantly changing. Kress and Theo van Leeuwen (2001, p. 39) introduce the concept transformation in order to describe shifts within one mode, and transduction to describe shifts across modes. They assume that all shifts within a mode or across modes of representation have effect on inner resources which "constantly reshape (transform) the subjectivity of the child."

The affordances offered by literature and multimodal theory are focused upon the active role of the reader, and definitely on a wide definition of text, including performative modes. Thus to the theoretical load of the concept transformation can be added semiotic resources within modes as well as across modes of expression. These semiotic resources are means a learner uses in the construction of meaning for instance in the production of drama.

Conclusion

In this concept analysis I have made a close reading of what transformation might imply in four different contexts. The concept can be applied on the transformation of a person's identity in ritual. Repeated transportations in performance might end up in a transformation that affects as well performer as audience. The transformative aesthetic theory has a focus on the productive process in art, and this process consists of a series of transformations. Of special relevance for supervising artistic processes in drama and theatre education is the notion of aesthetic doubling of time, space, role and plot as transformations. Finally multimodal literacy as a complex competence was introduced. The emerging theory of meaning produced by transformations of semiotic signs or as a transduction across modes of expression was looked upon as one further contribution to the analysis of the concept transformation as a cultural tool informing artistic learning processes.

REFERENCES

Abrahams, R. D. (1995). Foreword to the Aldine paperback edition. In V. Turner (Ed.), *The ritual process: Structure and anti-structure* (pp. v–xii). New York: Aldine de Gruyer.

Dewey, J. (1980*). Art as experience.* New York: Perigree Books. (First published in 1934.)

Fischer-Lichte, E. (2008). *The transformative power of performance* (S. I. Jain, Transl. from German). New York: Routledge. (Orig. publ. 2004)

Gennep, A. van (1909). *The rites of passage* (M. B. Vizedom & G. L. Caffee, Trans.). London: Routledge and Keagan Paul.

Iser, W. (1978). *The act of reading.* Baltimore: John Hopkins University Press.

Kress, G., & van Leeuwen, T. (2001). *Multimodal discourse: The modes and media of contemporary communication.* London: Hodder Education.

Kress, G. (2003). *Literacy in the new media age.* Oxon: Routledge.

Mezirow, J., & Associates. (2000). *Learning as transformation. Critical perspectives on a theory in progress.* San Fransisco: John Wiley & Sons.

Nicholson, H. (2005). *Applied Drama: The gift of theatre.* New York: Palgrave MacMillan.

Turner, V. (1995). *The ritual process: Structure and anti-structure.* New York: Aldine de Gruyer. (First published in 1969.)

Sava, I. (1994). Den Konstnärliga Inlärningsprocessen. [The artistic learning process] In I. Porna & P. Väyrynen (Eds.), *Handbok för Grundundervisningen i konst* (pp. 35–61). Helsinki: Kunnallisliitto.

Schechner, R. (1985*). Between theater & anthropology.* Philadelphia: University of Pennsylvania Press.

Østern, A.-L. (2009). Beyond the dance of life. *Applied Theatre Research Journal, 10* (Online journal).

Anna-Lena Østern is professor of arts education at the university of Trondheim, Norway NTNU. She is scientific leader of a national graduate school for teacher education in Norway.

STIG A. ERIKSSON

11. DISTANCING

Keywords: distancing, Verfremdung, ostranenie, estrangement, making strange, alienation

A main source for this entry is my doctoral thesis *Distancing at Close Range. Investigating the Significance of Distancing in Drama Education* (Eriksson, 2009).

Distancing as a Multifaceted Concept

Etymologically, *distance* comes from the Latin *distāntia*: 'standing apart', hence meanings of separation, distance, remoteness, difference, diversity. In daily life people or objects can be 'placed at a distance', 'made to appear distant', 'kept distant from', or 'outrun'. In figurative speech distance expresses degrees of remoteness, as in 'ideal disjunction, mental separation'. In interpersonal relations distance signifies detachment in interaction, 'keeping and knowing one's distance', or simply an aloof or deferential attitude. In psychology it designates reactions for escaping engaging, in therapy and special education it is technique used to help with building identity and communication through symbols and referential language. In combat sports distancing is a technical terminus for the appropriate selection of distance between oneself and a combatant throughout an encounter. In dramatic art distancing may designate an aesthetic principle, delineating the boundaries of fiction and reality through the mental faculty referred to as psychic distance (Bullough), or it can be a description of a poetics, including uses of stylistic devices, such as rhetoric figures or distancing effects (Shklovsky, Brecht, Heathcote).

Three Significant Meaning Connotations of Distancing in Drama Education

Of particular relevance to drama education are the following basic conceptions of the term: (a) Protection, (b) aesthetic principle, (c) poetic device. The first conception represents a didactic[1] orientation that has to do with creating a protective dramatic fiction (Bolton, 1984, p. 128). The second represents an aesthetic-philosophical orientation that has to do with distancing as an aesthetic principle in art (Bullough, 1957/1912). The third represents a poetic orientation that has to do with artistic devices for exploring and learning through dramatic fiction (Brecht, 2003/1930).

(a) Distancing as protection from 'the real' - a psychological aspect of distancing - has a prominent position in drama education literature as a safeguarding strategy in the drama classroom. The issues explored in the drama can be distanced, and therefore experienced as less threatening, by keeping the action at one (protected) remove from real-life situations. (b) Distancing understood as an aesthetic principle - an ontological aspect of distancing - is closely related to the awareness of fiction in drama, and thus to fiction as protection as well. Distancing is seen as a generic principle in art and that it exerts itself, to a lesser or greater degree, in all dramatic contexts. An awareness of degree in distancing, expressed as over-distance, under-distance and distance-limit is helpful to explain the dynamics available in drama education traditions and schools of theatre in relation to distancing - figure 1. (c) The purposeful use of distancing as an artistic device for obtaining a critical look at the drama experience - an epistemological aspect of distancing - implies the act of making transparent, or of breaking illusion. Resources for realizing distancing on this level are *distancing devices*.

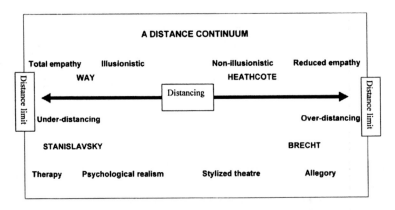

Figure 1. Distance continuum (Eriksson, 2009, p. 45).

Estrangement

Distancing devices are artistic means purposely activated to provide exposure and reflection. They involve a meaning making orientation concerned with a critical look at habitual "givens" and with an intention of promoting change; in society, in schools, in individual lives, in everyday routines. A significant reference for breaking up habitual perception by distancing is the concept of *making strange*. It is characterized by the intention of seeing anew, finding new meanings, opening up novel insights:

> [Estrangement is a] process of becoming strange or making strange - in a narrow sense by artistic procedures - which dissolve the customary contexts of representation and meaning, opening up new perceptions and possibilities of cognition (Primavesi, 2005, p. 377) (my translation).

A main proponent associated with this stance is Bertolt Brecht, who productively drew on a number of distancing traditions and gradually subsumed them under one integrative concept: *Verfremdung*. Another promoter of distancing is Victor

Shklovsky, from whose concept *ostranenie* Brecht received impulses for his coinage of the word Verfremdung[2]. A third intermediary of distancing as estrangement is Dorothy Heathcote, whose theory and practice exhibit significant traits of distancing from all the three orientations mentioned above, and not the least from Primavesi's definition of estrangement just quoted. Estrangement represents an important perspective in the didactics of Heathcote's drama pedagogy and is an important meaning making factor in drama education.

Main Theoretical References

The theory base of distancing comprises formalist theory connected to Shklovsky (1988/1917), and epic theatre theory connected to Brecht (1963a; 1963b; 1963c). However, a lineage of the notion of distancing can be traced in literary and rhetoric theory from Aristotle (*Poetics*, p. 30; *Rhetoric*, part III, p. 207), via Hegel (1807, ch. 9:92) and Diderot (1883, p. 7), to Coleridge (1817, ch XIV, p. 145), Shelley (1821/1840, p. 42) and Novalis (1799/1846, part 3, p. 236). Helmers makes a distinction between distancing in a broad versus narrow meaning (Helmers 1984, pp. 26–29). *Distancing in a broad sense* denotes all poetic uses of estrangement with an intention of making the ordinary strange in such a way that the attention of the recipient is awakened and reflection promoted. *Distancing in a narrow sense* denotes poetic uses of estrangement with the particular intention of practising social criticism and expressing a dissenting opinion of the existing social conditions (Brecht). Distancing is also associated with the poetic device of irony[3]. Theory and practice reflections by Brecht (1963a/1937) and German learning-play practitioners (Steinweg, 2005/1995), theory and practice reflections by Heathcote (1980), supplied by Nordic and Anglo-American-Australian drama education theory, offer examples of uses of distancing in drama education.

Shklovsky

The Russian formalists considered it a task of the literary avant-garde to resurrect the faculty of conscious experience of "the world", by de-familiarization of habitual perception, i.e. by representing well-known phenomena in new and unaccustomed ways. Human perception is susceptible to the lethargic effect of automatization and routine: "If we start to examine the general laws of perception, we see that as perception becomes habitual, it becomes automatic" (Shklovsky, 1988/1917, p. 19). Habitualization of thought and reflection needs opposition, otherwise life is reckoned as nothing: "Habitualization devours works, clothes, furniture, one's wife, and the fear of war" (op.cit., p. 20). Shklovsky finds in poetic language the antidote against automatization of perception. It becomes Shklovsky's thesis that the task of art is to free perception from senseless reproduction of objects and events, to restore fresh perception: "Art exists that one may recover the sensation of life; it exists to make one feel things, to make the stone *stony*. The purpose of art is to impart the sensation of things as they are perceived and not as they are known" (ibid.). The key concept to enhance perception poetically is distancing, in the sense of making strange[4]. In Shklovsky criticism an understanding of *priem ostranenie* as the device of *making strange* is the most common. But the word priem also entails procedure, which gives it a quality of process rather than technique, which is of interest in relation to how the making strange concept can be used in drama pedagogic contexts.

Brecht

Verfremdung is frequently put on par with *epic theatre*. Brecht sees epic theatre as a theatre of actuality and a theatre of education (Brecht, 2001a)[5]. Few aspects of Brecht's work have received more attention in the literature than *Verfremdung*. It is a most central concept and a programmatic principle underpinning Brecht's entire theory and practice - including the Lehrstück genre: "One thing is common between Lehrstück and epic theatre: the use of *Verfremdung*. The more thoroughly one investigates the language and structure of Brecht's poetry, the more clearly it reveals itself as the governing principle" (Grimm, 1972, p. 72) (my translation). The following quotations of how Brecht defines Verfremdung illustrate what this governing principle amounts to. The notion of estrangement is dominant. The interpretative keywords are mine:

> One was looking for a kind of presentation, by which the familiar could become conspicuous, the habitual amazing. Common events should appear strange, and much which seemed natural should be recognized as artificial (Brecht, 1963b, p. 196) (my translation).
> **Keywords: To make the familiar strange, to recognize what is false.**

> Estranging an event or a character means first of all stripping the event of its self-evident, familiar, obvious quality and creating a sense of astonishment and curiosity about them (Brecht, 1963c, p. 101) (my translation).
> **Keywords: To de-mask the self-evident of an event, to raise curiosity.**

> The new alienations[6] are only designed to free socially-conditioned phenomena from that stamp of familiarity which protects them against our grasp today (Brecht, 2001c, p. 192).
> **Keywords: To make social structures transparent, to understand the known anew.**

In Brecht there is a commitment to apply estrangement as a means for promoting societal change. Brecht's artistic and educational philosophy is unmistakably rooted in Marxist thought, and his project is political. He is "radically engaged with social, political and cultural processes, convinced that the world needs change and that we can change it" (Kuhn & Giles, 2003, p. 1). The epic theatre and the device of distancing are significant ingredients in this process. Estrangement's dynamic relevance to education seems obvious. Its political potential for change does not weaken its importance in drama education - rather, it strengthens it.

Heathcote

The term distancing in the process drama literature is dominantly associated with protection[7]. This is the case in Heathcote as well, but many of Heathcote's central concepts, like *framing*[8], the *self-spectator*, poetic *distortion* and all her *conventions* (or *depictions*) can be regarded as poetic distancing devices. Heathcote's educational philosophy, and her use of language, is pervaded by the notion of estrangement: "One of the ways I use often is to create a bizarre/noticeable procreation so that no one can miss it - it can intrude' on their[9] vision/their space" (Heathcote, 1984, p. 154). Significantly, Heathcote's dominant teaching strategy amounts to enabling the ordinary to become fabulous (Eriksson, 2009, p. 128). The philosophy embedded in the following Heathcote-quote is both Shklovskian and Brechtian at the same time:

All I do believe in was present all the time I taught:

1. Slowing matters down (though not necessarily seeming so to children) - sometimes slow seems fast, within the context and the strategy. I slow so that some "stumbling upon authenticity" be achieved.
2. Removing the situation when I could from prejudicial view, so as to enable a new view without the burden of an old label which prevents re- view.
3. Creating the experience and the reflection side by side.
4. Working within the framework of that which is dramatic, structuring so that thought and action arise and follow through thinking and acting from within" (Heathcote, 1976, p. 21).

It is pertinent to an understanding of Heathcote's work to realize that all her foundational strategies are strategies of distancing. Her political aim is not out-spokenly concerned with societal change, but she is aiming at creating change in participants' understanding, and changes in the ways learning takes place in classrooms. She does that essentially through the poetic-didactic device of distancing.

In Conclusion

Distancing continues to have an important relevance to present day developments in the field of drama education. Today's schooling seems increasingly focussed on expedience and delivering, and less concerned with exploration, reflection and encouragement for facilitating change. A dynamic alternative, distancing offers a means of stimulating critical reflection through amazement, curiosity and surprise – which is a mark of scientific performance. Distancing is also a contribution to the rekindling of a more socially oriented drama teaching. It provides parameters within which themes and issues can be safely explored artistically, critically and educationally, and with a commitment for change. The current growth in applied drama/theatre, the challenges and opportunities presented by the Internet and new media, the relationship and interaction between drama education and performance arts, the concept of being 'betwixt and between', the idea of postdramatic theatre – these are all extended perspectives through which distancing can be applied, and researched.

NOTES

[1] The terms *didactic* and *didactics* are used here as pedagogical terms. Even though not commonly used like this in English, the terms are widely used in the Nordic countries and in many parts of Europe to designate the interplay of theory and practice in education, i.e. the connection between preparation, selection of content/form and realization in teaching.

[2] The terms *Verfremdung* and *ostranenie* both essentially carry the meaning of *making strange*. Etymologically, *strange* comes from the Old French *estrange*, meaning 'external', 'foreign', 'alien'. In Latin it is *extraneus*, with the additional meaning 'without', 'outside', 'who comes from outside'. In Italian the etymological version of strange is *strano*, which seems to be a related form to the Russian *strannost*', meaning 'strangeness', 'fremdness'. This element of foreignness, which seems to be the etymological dominant, has evident connotations with the Old English word *fremede* or *fremde* and the Old High German word *framadi* or *fremidi* - in a later form *fremd* - meaning 'foreign', 'strange' or 'unfamiliar', which can also contain the quality of being unfriendly; hence *fremdly* becomes 'strangely' or 'unkindly', and *fremdness* becomes 'strangeness' or 'coldness'.

[3] Romantic irony is usually a device in which an illusion is created and then deliberately interrupted. In its playing with a fiction/reality distinction, Romantic irony can be said to have the quality of a distancing device.

[4] I find the following two exemplifications by Brecht of what estrangement amounts to, strikingly similar to those cited by Shklovsky above. Brecht explains: "To see one's mother as a man's wife one needs an A-effect" and: "If one sees one's teacher hounded by the bailiffs an A-effect occurs" (Brecht, 2001b, p. 144).

[5] The emphasis on education fused with entertainment is repeated in the essays "The German Drama: pre-Hitler [1935], "The Street Scene" [1938] and "On Experimental Theatre" [1939].

[6] Several critics have pointed out that the choice to translate Verfremdung by alienation, or A-effect, has been unfortunate, because alienation/A-effect carries with it inopportune overtones of feeling alienated or subjected to something "off-putting" (Willett, 1984, p. 221; Wright, 1989, p. 19).

[7] I consulted 39 English-language drama education publications from the period 1974 to 2005 and found that distancing and protection are frequently regarded as similar notions, mostly connected to the concepts of dramatic fiction, the make-belief, the imagination and the relationships of fiction/not-fiction. References to distancing as a poetic device, like estrangement, are noticeably less encountered (Eriksson, 2009, p. 36.).

[8] See the entry of Kari Mjaaland Heggstad in the present publication.

[9] In this case mentally handicapped people. However, that does not invalidate the typicality of the strategy.

REFERENCES

Aristotle. (1987). *Poetics* (R. Janko, Trans.). Indianapolis, IN: Hackett Publishing.

Aristotle. (2006). *Retorikk [Rhetoric]* (T. Eide, Trans. to Norwegian). Oslo: Vidarforlaget.

Bolton, G. (1984). *Drama as education: An argument for placing drama at the centre of the curriculum.* London: Longman.

Brecht, B. (1963a/1937). Zur Theorie des Lehrstücks. *Schriften zum Theater*, b. 4, 78–80. Frankfurt am Main: Suhrkamp.

Brecht, B. (1963b/1936). Episches theater, Entfremdung. *Schriften zum Theater*, b. 3, 196–197. Frankfurt am Main: Suhrkamp.

Brecht, B. (1963c/1939). Über Experimentelles Theater. *Schriften zum Theater*, b. 3, 79–106. Frankfurt am Main: Suhrkamp.

Brecht, B. (2001a/1936). Theatre for pleasure or theatre for instruction. In J. Willett (Ed. & Trans.). Brecht on theatre: *The development of an aesthetic* (pp. 69–76). London: Methuen.

Brecht, B. (2001b/1940). Short description of a new technique of acting which produces an alienation effect. In J. Willett (Ed. & Trans.). *Brecht on theatre: The development of an aesthetic* (pp. 136–147). London: Methuen.

Brecht, B. (2001c/1948). A short organum for the theatre. In J. Willett (Ed. & Trans.). *Brecht on theatre: The development of an aesthetic* (pp. 179–205). London: Methuen.

Brecht, B. (2003/1930). Theory of pedagogies. In T. Kuhn & S. Giles (Eds.), *Brecht on art & politics* (pp. 88–89). London: Methuen.

Bullough, E. (1957/1912). 'Psychical distance' as a factor in art and an aesthetic principle. In E. M. Wilkinson (Ed.), *Aesthetics: Lectures and essays by Edward Bullough* (pp. 91–130). London: Bowes & Bowes.

Coleridge, S. T. (1817). *Biographia literaria; or biographical sketches of my literary life and opinions.* London: William Clowes. Retrieved August 29, 2009, from http://www.archive.org/stream/biographia litera00coleuoft#page/145/mode/1up

Diderot, D. (1883). *The paradox of acting* (W. H. Pollock, Trans.). London: Chatto & Windus.

Eriksson, S. A. (2009). *Distancing at close range. Investigating the significance of distancing in drama education.* Doctoral thesis. Vaasa: Åbo Academy University.

Grimm, R. (1972/1959). *Bertolt Brecht: Die Struktur seines Werkes.* Nürnberg: Verlag Hans Carl.

Heathcote, D. (1976). Of these seeds becoming. In R. B. Schuman (Ed.), *Educational drama for today's schools* (pp. 1–40). New York: Scarecrow Press.

Heathcote, D. (1980). Drama as context. Dorothy Heathcote. In B. Myra (Ed.), *NATE papers in education.* Aberdeen University Press.

Heathcote, D. (1984). Considerations when working with mentally handicapped people. In L. Johnson & C. O'Neill (Eds.), *Dorothy heathcote: Collected writings on education and drama* (pp. 154–155). London: Hutchinson.

Hegel, G. W. F. (1807). Preface: On scientific knowledge (J. B. Baillie, Trans.). *In Hegel's The phenomenology of mind.* Retrieved October 21, 2008, from http://www.class.uidaho.edu/mickelsen/texts/ Hegel%20Phen/hegel_phen_preface.htm

Helmers, H. (Ed.). (1984). *Verfremdung in der Literatur.* Darmstadt: Wissenschaftliche Buchgesellschaft.

Kuhn, T., & Giles, S. (Eds.). (2003). *Brecht on art and politics.* London: Methuen.

Novalis. (1799/1846). *Novalis Schriften.* Dritter Theil. (T. Ludwig & E. v. Bülow Eds.). Berlin: Verlag von G. Reimer. Retrieved August 29, 2009, from http://books.google.com/books?id=dXkTAA AAYAAJ&pg=PP3&dq=novalis+schriften&lr=#v=one page&q=&f=false

Primavesi, P. (2005). Verfremdung. In E. Fischer-Lichte, D. Kolesch, & M. Warstat (Eds.), *Metzler Lexikon Theatertheorie* (pp. 377–379). Stuttgart: Verlag J. B. Metzler.

Shelley, P. B. (1821/1840). A defence of poetry. In C. W. Eliot (Ed.), *The harvard classics: The shelves of fiction*, XXVII. English Essays: Sidney to Macauly. New York: Bartleby. Retrieved February 14, 2009, from http://www.bartleby.com/27/23.html

Shklovsky, V. (1988/1917). Art as technique (L. T. Lemon & M. J. Reis,Trans.). In D. Lodge (Ed.), *Modern criticism and theory: A reader* (pp. 16–30). London: Longman.

Steinweg, R. (2005/1995). *Lehrstück und Episches Theater: Brechts Theorie und die Theaterpädagogische Praxis.* Frankfurt am Main: Brandes & Apsel.

Willett, J. (1984). *Brecht in context: Comparative approaches.* London: Methuen.

Wright, E. (1989). *Postmodern brecht: A re-presentation.* London: Routledge.

Stig A. Eriksson *is Associate Professor in drama education. His research interests are the history of the development of drama education, political theatre and process drama.*

VIVIANA NICOLETA FERRARI

12. ETHICS IN THEATRE/DRAMA EDUCATION

Keywords: aesthetics, ethics, creativity, assessment, history

The past decade has witnessed a growing emphasis upon creativity and innovation as a way to promote economic and social development. For example, a recent study prepared for the European Commission by KEA European Affairs (2009), which echoed similar studies in the US, UK, and Australia, called upon the Arts to assist in developing economic competition and social innovation and upon artists to train future generations to be creative, imaginative, and inventive. Although studies of the ability of the Arts to enhance competition and innovation are important, instrumental uses of the Arts must occur within the context of a deep, historically grounded understanding of the Arts. This requires consideration not only of the instrumental functions of Art, and the technical skills required to create art, but also of how education in, and through, the Arts promotes human flourishing.

A focus upon the instrumental functions of art increases the risk that the Arts – and arts education – will be primarily understood and evaluated in terms of economic utility at the expense of such valuable but non-utilitarian qualities as "appreciation of beauty, love and wisdom, noble sense of purpose, [and] cultivated imagination" (Armstrong, 2009, p. 76). Education in the Arts involves cultivating the innate human impulse towards mastery of the self, particularly the expression of the self in the context or presence of others, and the distinctively human intentionality that under-girds this mastery; specifically, the cultivation of the sense of *taste* that undergirds *good judgment* (Gadamer, 1960; Galimberti, 1987; Sennett, 2008).

Beside these general concerns related to all artistic education, specifically within the field of applied drama and theatre in education, there is still tension between the instrumental and the artistic-aesthetic functions (e.g. Schonmann, 2005). Schonmann argues that the majority of roles that theatre and drama have in education today point towards roles in sociology, psychology and communications – "by-products", than to roles in aesthesis. Thus, Schonmann observes, by "cutting ourselves off from our artistic-aesthetic roots, there is the risk of losing the basis for our justification" (p. 35) and calls for "another proportion (balance)" between the artistic-aesthetic function (aesthetic intention primary) and the instrumental function (aesthetic intention secondary) (p. 31).

The main question that arises is where can arts education look in order to find an "another proportion" between the artistic-aesthetic function and the instrumental function in arts education and more specifically in theatre and drama education, in order to address responsibly the pedagogical requests. This voice will consider a possible answer that stands in viewing the ethicality implicit in theatre and drama

S. Schonmann (ed.), Key Concepts in Theatre/Drama Education, 73–77.

as a dimension that permeates and acts as a connecting tissues (a whole) in between the multiple parts that compose the dynamic educational phenomenon at hand, and thus reconsider the tensions expressed above.

ETHICS – HARMONIOUS PROPORTIONS

The ethicality of education in, and through, the arts, particularly drama and theatre, is manifest in the fact that dramatic acts are frequently social – and thus intrinsically ethical – acts that involve the recognition of, attendance to, and synchronization with others. As Heikkinen (2003) suggests, theatre and drama in education develops a dramatic arena for ethical dialogue. The ethicality of aesthetic and artistic education is, however, often tacit, which has profound implications for the conception, content and practice of responsible pedagogy. In part due to art's craftsmanship component that is passed on orally from master to apprentice, in part due to how the aesthetics construct is generally used by cognitively dominated education; impasse generated in the dissociation of mind from body (Martin-Smith, 2005).

Gardner (1999) calls for philosophically-minded focus in education on *truth*, *beauty* and the *good*, with the aim of activating the student's capacity to grasp complex and subtle ideas and to make sound judgements and decisions by developing a "righting mechanism" (p. 249). These elements can express their full educational power if grasped at their origin that can be traced back to Greek thought, to the ethics of measure as harmonious proportions of the Pythagoreans and to Plato's "the supreme measure of all things" (Reale, 2004, p. 245). Posed on these bases Aristotle created the ethics of *mesotes* – the Doctrine of Means, treated in *Nicomachean Ethics*; and it stands for: a relative "due and right proportion" which should be observed in all our actions (e.g. Armstrong, 1947; J. Armstrong, 2009; Gadamer, 1960). In Gadamer's view, the ethics of *mesotes* may be intended as an "ethics of good taste"; good taste intended here as the peak of moral judgment, a construct that comprises reference to the act of comprehension. Kant subsequently in *Critique of Pure Reason* restrained the field of good taste to a judgment on beauty and thus inaugurated the transcendental justification of the aesthetical conscience (Gadamer, 1960), and divaricated further the distance in between the subjective and the objective.

Although the subsequent historical delimitation of the aesthetics as a construct, the art form maintained, through a particular sense of proportion, in its generative structure unity of the concepts of truth, beauty and the good. It may be argued that the pedagogical value of arts education is within the aesthetical dimension that is an integral part of ethics. This profound ethical component is the point of reference for quality assessment of the interrelations within the work of art as well as the intercurrent interrelations within the artistic, pedagogical and social dimension. With this ethical perspective in mind, we are compelled to agree with Schonmann's (2005) statement, that of the three interrelated orientations in theatre and drama education today, the *artistic-aesthetics*, the *pedagogical-educational*, and the *sociological-cultural*, the artistic-aesthetic dimension is the core from which both pedagogical and cultural aspects spring (p. 38).

Moreover, it is important to observe that the widely diffused dichotomic vision between instrumental and aesthetic functions of the arts is limitative, that at a practical level it obnubilates the educative value of the artwork itself. To view art education within the two polarities obscures the role of education, in and through the arts, in the larger pedagogical project of cultivating an individual's personhood and ethical sensibility, for at least three reasons. Firstly, there can be no authentic separation between arts and education as the pedagogical elements reside in the constitutive details of the art form itself. Secondly, the art form (and its interpretation) is a manifestation of reason (a cognitive process) produced by one's creativity, which is in turn an essential function of the mind that incorporates both emotionality and logic (Ferrari, 2005). Thirdly, one-sided perspectives on the instrumental or on the aesthetic functions of arts in education are theoretical artifices (constructs), which at operational (pragmatic) level can create an artificial gap that can obscure (take away attention from) the main element that connects arts, education and society – the work or art itself. It is in my belief that if art educators educate through art, it is within the art form and the artwork that one must find the trigger towards authentic knowledge transfer without losing sight of all the elements at play.

It was posited earlier that instrumental uses of the arts must occur in the context of a deep, historically grounded understanding of the meaning and multiple functions of art. The next two sections of this entry offer sketches of how art has functioned – instrumentally and aesthetically – in different historical periods to cultivate the intuition, imagination, and ethical sensibilities of individuals. What is most instructive, perhaps, is the manner in which art was intended conceptually and used to effect a transformation in these cognitive and moral characteristics of individuals not only in different periods but with a diverse perspective that consequently points to diverse communicative outcomes in between the dimensions of art, artists, and education (the first) and education and aspects of art (the second).

THE WORK OF ART

In the Middle Ages the artists were Art's servants. What made it Art was the fact that the work was imbued not with fleeting personal sentiments, but rather with what were understood to be enduring sentiments of humanity – those of belonging, love, hope, despair, betrayal, and longing. These works were crafted with great care, respect, tenacity and sufferance. Walking the path of Art creation – intuition and *techne* – meant (and means) that the creator, as well as the interpreter (performer or spectator), ought to force one-self to see his or her own weaknesses and courageously confront them, as well as "learn the indispensable proportions" (Ionesco & Pronko, 1959, p. 5). Only through such a profound ethical experience could the creator capture the essence of humanity and express it with sympathy and compassion. Art only gave (and gives) herself to those who emptied the self of the 'I' and enabled the 'Ideal' to enter, through the act of contemplation. In so doing, an inner transformation was effected in the mind and character of the individual interpreter and the memory store of humanity – our cultural heritage – was created and promulgated. The imaginative act of recapitulating universal sentiments through contemplation suggests that the interpreter not only become mindful of her connection with an imagined community of other living people, but also of her connection with those of the unknown past and future. In other words, such acts of imagination and reflection collapsed the temporal, spatial and social distance that normally delineates one from the other; a sentiment powerfully expressed by Barba (2002, p. 14):

> We were not alone. The theatre became the place in which the living could meet the nonliving, the ancestors-reformers who had crossed the desert... that is our way of breathing... The living are incapable of noticing all the details, but the nonliving accept the details and relish the personal temperature that has forged them in alternate layers of light and darkness... My true spectators have been absences that are forcefully present, most of them nonliving: not only the dead, but also those not yet born.

FROM "ETHICAL DRAMA" TO CHILD-CENTRED THEATRE/DRAMA IN EDUCATION

Before the societal aims of the twentieth century, theatre/drama in education already had secondary to artistic aims, such as the "ethical theatre" used by the Jesuits since the 1551 for over two hundred years in order to promote faith and moral judgment. The intuition behind the praxis was expressed in the idea that live theatre was like a basic training school for life – the repeatable form enacted as a preview of the moral dilemmas that students would encounter later in life (Levy, 1997). Redington (1983) traces the child-centred concept in education to J. J. Rousseau. The idea become a construct in the hands of pedagogues such as Fröbel (1782–1852), guided by the principle that education should lead the child to observe and think for him or herself rather than just being the recipient of knowledge. Similarly, Dewey "believed that 'learning by doing' was a 'consummatory' experience for the learner; it was dramatic, dialogical, and felt" (Martin-Smith, 2005, p. 3).

The social utility construct grew with Slade (1954), who focused his attention on the relationship between drama and the natural play activity of the child, and Way (1967), for whom drama education was a separate entity from theatre arts. Improvisation and playing-out psychologically significant situations were some of the new pedagogical approaches. During the 1970s, Theatre in Education (TIE) became a complex structure involving myriad methods, each one tailored to specific educational programs not only for the school environment. The ideas of psychologists such as Piaget, Bruner, Vygotsky were incorporated into the methodologies, as were seminal ideas from Brecht's theatre. Brecht shifted the user's attention from the poetics of drama to its structure. Consistent with this, Bolton in Gavin Bolton: Selected Writings (Davis & Lawrence, 1986) writes: "the learner's focal awareness must be on the activity itself and not on the 'things' to be learned" (p. 81).

CONCLUSION

The basic thesis advanced here is that education in and through arts, generally, and drama and theatre, in particular, is an intrinsically ethical practice. A historical reconsideration of the elements that compose an art education event observed through an ethical perspective, would enlarge the artistic educational panorama and thus allow for new ways to revaluate the *artistic-aesthetics*, the *pedagogical-educational*, and the *sociological-cultural* orientations within theatre and drama education towards finding ad hoc artistic educational proportions for each pedagogical necessity.

ACKNOWLEDGMENTS

I would like to thank Prof. Samuel Leong, Prof. John O'Toole, Prof. Shifra Schonmann, and Dr. Samuel G. Wilson for their support in reviewing the numerous versions of this manuscript.

REFERENCES

Armstrong, A. H. (1947/1968). *An introduction to ancient philosophy*. London: Methuen & Co.
Armstrong, J. (2009). *In search of civilization*. London: Allen Lane, Penguin Group.
Barba, E. (2002). The essence of theatre. *The Tulane Drama Review, 46*(3), 12–30.
Davis, D., & Lawrence, C. (Eds.). (1986). *Gavin Bolton: Selected writings*. London: Longman.
Ferrari, V. (2005). *L'insegnamento Pianistico di Vincenzo Vitale*. University of Bologna: Unpublished Dissertation.
Gadamer, H. G. (1960/2004). *Wahrheit und Methode* (G. Vattimo, Trans. Verità e Metodo). Milan: Bompiani.
Galimberti, U. (1987/1993). *Gli Equivoci dell'anima*. Milano: Feltrinelli.
Gardner, H. (1999/2000). *The disciplined mind*. New York: Penguin Group.
Heikkinen, H. (2003). *Special interest fields of drama, theatre and education: The IDEA dialogue*. Finland: University of Jyväskylä.
Ionesco, E., & Pronko, L. C. (1959). Discovering the theatre. The Tulane Drama Review, 4(1), 3–18. KEA
European Affairs. (2009). *The impact of culture on creativity*. Retrieved from http://ec.europa.eu/culture/news/news2234_en.htm
Levy, J. (1997). Theatre and moral education. *Journal of Aesthetic Education, 31*(3), 65–75.
Martin-Smith, A. (2005). Setting the stage for a dialogue: Aesthetics in drama and theatre education. *Journal of Aesthetic Education, 31*(4), 3–11.
Reale, G. (2004/2006). *Platone e L'Accademia Antica*. Milan: Bompiani.
Redington, C. (1983). *Can theatre teach?: An historical and evaluative analysis of theatre in education*. Oxford: Pergamon Press.
Schonmann, S. (2005). "Master" versus "Servant": Contradictions in drama and theatre education. *Journal of Aesthetic Education, 39*(4), 31–39.
Sennett, R. (2008/2009). *The craftsman*. London: Penguin Group.
Slade, P. (1954). *Child drama*. London: London University Press.
Way, B. (1967). *Development through drama*. London: Longmans.

Viviana Nicoleta Ferrari *is a pianist and musicologist. Finalising PhD in Education (University of Melbourne). Has interest and lectures in various fields within the humanistic area.*

SECTION III: IDENTITY, CULTURE AND COMMUNITY

BETHANY NELSON

13. POWER AND COMMUNITY IN DRAMA

Keywords: multiculturalism, power, community, playmaking, process drama, in–role

Schools do not simply reflect the problems of the larger society, they perpetuate them. Schools are designed to create citizens, fill market needs, and generally replicate the socioeconomic divisions represented by the student population and in society as a whole (Apple, 1995). Consequently, students of color and the urban poor experience the same oppression and lack of substantial opportunities for advancement in schools that are reflected in wider society. They attend schools that are under-resourced and prepare them to fill the same lower socio-economic slots occupied by the members of their communities (Fine and Weis, 2003; Apple, 1995; Ladson-Billings, 1994). Further, "young people who are subjugated by oppressive social, economic and cultural forces are denied any real sense of agency and lack a capacity to act on and change their world" (McInerney, 2009, p. 28).

Educational theorists agree that the development of identity is a critical task of schooling, schooling which should disrupt socially imposed constructs around race, class, gender, sexuality, and traditional power roles. By utilizing curriculum, pedagogy, and structural dynamics that integrate opportunities for students to think critically, explore multiple perspectives, experiment with a range of identities and presentations of the self, and draw connections between the oppression they experience in their lives and larger social dynamics, students in schools will be better prepared to participate in redefining themselves and the society of which they are a part (McInerney, 2009; Gallagher, 2007; Fine and Weis, 2003; Freire, 1993). Further, theorists on culturally relevant teaching agree on the importance of the establishment of community as a necessary factor for facilitating school success for urban students of color (Ladson-Billings, 1994). Reflecting a communal orientation characteristic of the home cultures of many urban students generates a sense of belonging for individual students, and allows them to scaffold new learning on familiar group dynamics.

Through drama, we can create communities of learners engaged in a collective struggle against the status quo. Process Drama, in-role drama, and playmaking are optimal tools for facilitating the development of community among students and between students and teachers, exploring unequal power dynamics, and practicing various forms of power. For the purposes of the following discussion, process drama refers to drama work that utilizes a variety of drama and theatre conventions, in which "the conventions selected are mainly concerned with the processes of theatre as a means of developing understanding about both human experience and theatre itself" (Neelands & Goode, 1990, p. 5). In-role drama refers to work in which students in role as experts, stakeholders or problem-solvers are confronted with a

S. Schonmann (ed.), Key Concepts in Theatre/Drama Education, 81–85.

real or fictitious problem and are asked to question, debate, discuss, consider, and come to a resolution of that problem. Playmaking refers to the use of a variety of drama/theatre techniques to develop original performance work with students which emphasizes the exploration of their ideas and realities with the goal of developing their voices and visions of the world and bringing them to a broader audience.

DRAMA AND COMMUNITY

The fact that drama is an effective way to build community is nearly a truism in the field, and practitioners point to the way that the fictional community of drama situations fosters the development of real community among participants. In previous research on the effects of drama on classroom community, there is compelling evidence that drama structures facilitate a sense of collaboration between teachers and students, and within the peer group (Gallagher, 2007; Manley and O'Neill, 1997; Neelands & Goode, 1990).

> The dramatic arts have a unique capacity to create an experience of community. The collaborative processes of the drama classroom can provide a powerful opportunity to enhance young people's need for belonging and purpose. (Cahill, 2002, p. 21)

Community is characterized by caring relationships, high expectation messages and opportunities for meaningful participation and contribution (Cahill, 2002). Further, the development of trust, among students and between students and teachers, is identified as a critical element in the establishment of community.

Playmaking, in-role, and process drama facilitate the development of classroom community. In these approaches, the focus is on group roles and group activities, in which students become responsible for and to each other. For example, in in-role drama, students work collaboratively to gain an understanding of a situation and explore and implement possible solutions. In playmaking, students share their ideas and life experiences and work together to bring them into effective dramatic action. In process drama work, the teacher often works alongside the students, taking role or serving as a coach and facilitator, and guiding the students' exploration of the topic rather than mandating their learning, facilitating a sense of collaboration between teacher and students. In the process of working collaboratively toward a common goal, hearing others and being heard about issues that are of consequence to them, classroom community builds.

DRAMA AND POWER

"Power is always in and around classrooms." (Foucault, in Fine et al, 2000; Fine & Weis, 2003, p. 125). Power, and the reinforcement of White, middle-class power in particular, are apparent in curriculum, tracking, the racial and class make-up of the staff, faculty, and administration of schools, and in the buildings themselves (Gallagher, 2007; Fine and Weis, 2003; Ladson-Billings, 1994). Students of color are often denied access to power in schools, and lack a sense of agency in settings when they "have little power over their learning, when learning has little relevance to their lives and aspirations, or when they are devalued or marginalized" (McInerney, 2009, p. 24). The literature detailing studies of power discusses at length the profound effects that power has on every aspect of human functioning (Keltner, Gruenfeld, & Anderson, 2003). Facilitating student understanding of unequal power dynamics, creating curriculum that brings students' knowledge and capabilities into the classroom, and giving students the opportunity to explore ideas about power and practice the skills underlying the acquisition and exercise of power are key to creating culturally relevant schooling in which students can develop a sense of agency. Process drama, in-role drama, and playmaking are ideally suited to this task.

There are two primary ways in which these forms of drama are effective in creating culturally relevant curriculum about power. The first is content. Drama curriculum can be used to teach specifically about race, the history of non- dominant cultures, the literature of people of color, unequal power dynamics, etc. Drama curriculum offers a variety of process drama lessons that directly address the experiences of non-dominant groups, including lessons on racism, the Civil Rights Movement, Jim Crow Laws, etc. which invite students from both the dominant and non-dominant cultures to step inside the experiences of people of color (Manley and O'Neill, 1997; Neelands & Goode, 1990). In a recent playmaking experience in an under-resourced urban setting, high school students explored their ideas about power and powerlessness, and performed their play for an audience of both dominant and non-dominant group members. The students' understandings of societal power dynamics developed as they explored their own experiences through the process of playmaking, and they shared their insights with the audience. In-role drama is a flexible tool for presenting a variety of situations that both engage students and offer them the opportunity to experiment with solutions to complex problems. When students, in role as attorneys, inform their client that utilizing unpaid homeless workers to run her organic grape farm is a form of slavery, they are both coming to an understanding of the unequal power dynamics involved in the situation and developing their own abilities to utilize decision-making and power in directing the outcome of the situation.

Secondly, the structure of process drama, in-role drama, and playmaking curriculum facilitates the exploration and practice of power, regardless of the content being studied. In the safety and community of the drama situation, students have time to strategize, consider options, and experiment with solutions. Students can experiment with a variety of powerful roles, adopting the language and register appropriate to those roles. Most important, students can begin to see themselves as agents of change as they develop inquiry, analysis, and negotiation skills that are the foundations of social action.

No consideration of the connection between drama and power would be complete without mentioning Boal, whose work offers structures for exploring oppression in very direct and powerful ways, bringing the life experiences of the students into the classroom (Boal, 2002).

BETHANY NELSON

DRAMA, COMMUNITY, AND POWER

Recent research conducted with five classes of urban high school students of color in Massachusetts suggests a complex relationship between drama, community and power, and offers an exciting direction for further research into the use of drama for facilitating school success for students of color and the urban poor. In a series of studies which utilized Boal structures, process drama, and playmaking to explore and develop students' understandings of, and ability to utilize, power, results suggest that community is a source of power for urban students that positively affected their performance in the classroom (Nelson, 2009). Students in the studies demonstrated a wide range of academic capabilities, literacy levels, and special needs. However, their academic performance in the drama classes was uniformly competent, standing in contrast to their performance in other classes. Why?

Psychology tells us that power has profound effects on all aspects of human functioning, and is a tool for personal growth and social transformation (Keltner, Gruenfeld, & Anderson, 2003). Further, the development of a Sense of Community, as defined by belonging, connectedness, influence, fulfillment of needs, and the importance of both having power and recognizing it is acknowledged as a critical factor for psychological wellness. Finally, power stimulates action, and communal power orientation characterizes individuals who use their power for the communal good rather than their personal good (Chen, Lee-Chai, & Bargh, 2001). These constructs provide a foundation for considering the effect of community and power on the function of the students who participated in these studies and offer a possible explanation for their improved performance in the drama classes relative to their performance as students in other contexts.

Students in all groups demonstrated a strong sense of community socially and in the drama work, regularly making choices that were in the best interests of the group rather than any one individual. This was demonstrated in their negotiation of ideas for tableaux and scenes and a notable degree of shared leadership and lack of conflict in making decisions in small groups. Students reported feeling a strong sense of community in the classes not experienced in the wider school environment. They explored ideas about power and wielded power in the classroom with sophistication and authority.

In interview, the students identified helping roles as those that made them feel most powerful. The examples offered by the students shared several features, including 1) a sense of being an important part of the function of a system, 2) having a higher degree of knowledge or competence than others in the situation, and 3) a moral imperative to contribute to the situation as a result of that competence. Students reported feeling powerful in the drama classes.

When students felt powerful within their community in drama class, it enabled them to act more effectively as students, both individually and as a group. If, as seems indicated in these studies, community is a source of power for urban students of color, the community-rich environment of the drama class is uniquely well-positioned to facilitate the development of a sense of agency and a capacity to act on and change their world. Further research on the specific effects of different forms of drama on the formation of community and the support of communal power orientation seems like a logical next step. Then, using the community established through drama as a model, how can we better foster community in schools to facilitate the school success of this population?

REFERENCES

Apple, M. (1995). *Education and power* (2nd ed.). New York: Routledge.

Boal, A. (2002). *Games for actors and non-actors.* New York: Routledge.

Chen, S., Lee-Chai, A. Y., & Bargh, J. A. (2001). Relationship orientation as a moderator of the effects of social power [Electronic version]. *Journal of Personality and Social Psychology, 80,* 173–187.

Cahill, H. (2002). Teaching for community: Empowerment through drama. *Melbourne Studies in Education, 43*(2), 12–25.

Fine, M., Anand, B., Jordan, C., & Sherman, D. (2000). Before the bleach gets us all. In L. Weis & M. Fine (Eds.), *Construction sites* (pp. 161–179). New York: Teachers College Press.

Fine, M., & Weis, L. (2003). *Silenced voices and extraordinary conversations: Re-imagining schools.* New York: Teachers College Press.

Freire, P. (1993). *Pedagogy of the oppressed.* London: Penguin Books.

Gallagher, K. (2007). *The theatre of urban: Youth and schooling in dangerous times.* Toronto: University of Toronto Press.

Keltner, D., Gruenfeld, D. H., & Anderson, C. (2003). Power, approach, and inhibition [Electronic version]. *Psychological Review, 110,* 265–284.

Ladson-Billings, G. (1994). *The dreamkeepers: Successful teachers of African American children.* San Francisco: Jossey-Bass.

Manley, A., & O'Neill, C. (1997). *Dreamseekers: Creative approaches to the African-American heritage.* Portsmouth: Heinemann.

McInerney, P. (2009). Toward a critical pedagogy of engagement for alienated youth: Insights from Freire and school-based research. *Critical Studies in Education, 50*(1), 23–35.

Neelands, J., & Goode, T. (Eds.). (1990). *Structuring drama work: A handbook of available forms in theatre and drama.* Cambridge: Cambridge University Press.

Nelson, B. (2009). Beyond belonging: The relationship between community and power for urban students of color. *Drama Research: International Journal of Drama in Education, 1,* 60–74.

Bethany Nelson *is a faculty member at Emerson College in Boston, MA. She specializes in the use of Applied Theatre and Drama with urban students.*

DAN BARON COHEN

14. TOWARDS A PEDAGOGY OF TRANSFORMANCE

Keywords: performance, dialogic pedagogy, intercultural sustainable community, transformation

STAGE PRESENCE

When I am asked in Brazil where are you from? I pause for a split second. This question is asking more than just where I live. It is beginning the age-old process of identification on meeting to discover what we seem to have in common and whether our differences might threaten this community. It is interpreting whether we have any living histories or desires whose 'chance' meeting might unknowingly and even unintentionally provoke a dangerous confrontation in the space where we have crossed paths. For the histories or imagined futures that link nations, classes, genders, races and generations - and how their effects accumulate, overlap, confront, disperse and return - are lived or imagined by and through individuals and their communities in real places and through real everyday objects.

For this reason, no place or object is just made up of the three objective dimensions of its physical form. Its form also contains the two subjective and potentially dangerous dimensions of memory and imagination - their histories, and their imagined futures - that can be 'seen' in its spaces, surfaces and depths, depending upon who is interpreting their presence. My focussed gaze - my curiosity, desire to see, the knowledges I bring to this interpretation and all that has shaped my receptivity-constitutes my aesthetic power.

This aesthetic power is clearly always culturally shaped, but it is not just formed. It is forming. We can imagine, give form to something that is not real and real at the same time. The theatre, most obviously, is based and depends upon this aesthetic power which transforms the real into fiction and the fictitious into the real. The more people who agree to focus their aesthetic power on the same space, the more powerful this collectively focused space becomes. Through their aesthetic power they can transform a physical space into an aesthetic space which in turn, depending on how it is focused, transforms anyone who walks into it. Just by imagining the gaze of others, looking out and within simultaneously, a person can step onto this stage and transform his/her 'performance'.

INTIMATE AND PUBLIC DIALOGUE

People have always had to be alert in moving between communities, particularly those with unresolved, dangerous living histories. No matter where we are from, if

S. Schonmann (ed.), Key Concepts in Theatre/Drama Education, 87–91.

we do not have this performance-sensitivity to the dialogic effects of our presence, we may well unintentionally provoke a fatal confrontation. This 'performance sensitivity' or stage-presence, however intuitive or professional, is what we identify in all the 'actors' we notice in our lives. It is more commonly misunderstood in its negative form of shyness and over-sensitivity to 'being in public', a self-protective performance based on direct or inherited memory of how the focused power of a public space was once abused. For these reasons, we need to demystify theatre to democratize the performance of power.

THE DIALOGIC TRIANGLE

Most Brazilians are curious to know about everyday life in Wales and London. They want to use this rare opportunity not just to check or extend their knowledge, but to see themselves and their world through my eyes. This is part of their silent, intimate dialogue. As the stranger, I am expected to identify myself. I do so and then return the question to sense the threshold where we have met.

As soon as my question has left my lips, another fractional pause and set of silent intimate dialogues have been activated. Within seconds, we have inverted roles and I am learning about the person before me and about myself, and we are establishing not just a dialogue between two stories, but the possibility of a shared dialogic story in the future. In seconds, we have focussed and transformed the aesthetic space between us into an intercultural stage of reflection, interpretation and performance, to include two different stories, two different kinds of performance, and two different kinds of interpretation and expectation.

In just one brief dialogue, we have transformed an existing space into a complex stage of simultaneous rehearsal, interactive performance, spectating and self-spectating. And through the way in which we use this space, we can quickly and profoundly sense and judge our equality or inequality. How we re-cognize this first relation depends upon how we understand the relationship between our stories. But in this first interactive drama of identification, we have both summoned up our pasts to imagine a series of possible futures to create a place of possible dialogue, community, decision-making and agreement - even if that agreement is that it should be our last! If this drama of three interacting dialogues occurs between just two people, imagine the dialogic potential and activity of a space full of people!

COLONIZATION: THE MUTILATION OF INTIMATE DIALOGUE

But what if we have inherited lost and/or destroyed histories? What if we have inherited only fragmented, confused, contradictory or condemning colonial histories that engender self-doubt, self-disrespect, self-loathing and self-effacing self-representation? How can we build this drama of identification and community, or participate in its construction as equals? Without knowing ourselves, without under-standing and decolonizing the histories that we carry within mindful-body - our language, our gestures and our corporal memory - our capacity to question and transform the 'cultural reflexes' in our everyday performances let alone to resist the seductive performance of others, is radically weakened.

DECOLONIZATION: THE REBUILDING OF INTIMATE DIALOGUE

Wales. Canada. But now I live here in Brazil. I have given my public response. But in spaces of proven solidarity, care, sensitivity and principle, I can tell my more intimate stories. I can speak of the cracked, torn and bleached photos of my great uncles and aunts from Poland who perished in the ovens of industrialized destruction that left a thirst for justice and a silent cry for the right to remember in the names and gestures of those who witnessed from afar, that I inherited. And excavating even deeper still, I can tell the story of an early childhood that tiptoed round a profoundly disabled sister whose silent helplessness unknowingly formed her siblings into activists, scientists, doctors and artists of the emotions.

I resisted both stories for decades, for paradoxically different but ultimately identical reasons. The larger racial story nurtured a deep respect and ache for human freedom, but in self-subjugating, self-ghettoizing and self-valorizing memory to thousands of years of persecution and resistance. My relationship to my sister more wordlessly nurtured emotional responsibility and care towards the helpless, at the expense of my personal needs. Both stories in the populist and careless mouth of the playground and imperial post-war street corner became the means of mocking our Welsh and Canadian class difference. And because they were so intimately a part of my identity, both intimate stories found refuge behind the more public, more lucid, more detached and more masculine barricades of nationality and class.

I learned to tell these intimate stories through the courage of friends in Manchester, Derry, Rhondda, Palestine and Africa whose communities had also been ruthlessly and calculatedly denied the right to memory, language or self-knowledge. I could see in their eyes why they hid their intimate unspeakable stories of colonial self-hatred and violent inarticulate emotional and sexual self-pity behind proud and articulate anti-colonial street murals and anti-imperialist banners of protest. They could not bear the agony of being judged by their own for the cruel contradictions within their own compulsive subjectivity, and could not bear the torture of their own self-judgement. But gradually, during the years that we worked together, their intimate stories silently became metaphors for mine, and mine for theirs. And we discovered a fascinating fact of performance: in learning to tell our intimate stories in public, we simultaneously had to hear and learn to tell them to ourselves. By breaking our silence in an intimate space of principled but empathetic solidarity where we could reflect analytically and creatively, not defensively and dogmatically about the politics of our subjectivity, we were able to find the voice and the courage to break our silence in a space of judgement.

As we learned to tell these intimate stories, we began to understand why we need to see what we have internalized within our immunized self to avoid reproducing our oppressors within our own subjectivity. We began to understand how victims of any holocaust can become tyrannical and ruthless human rights' advocates and developed dialogic techniques to illuminate our structures of feeling; and we learned to integrate this intimate inter-subjective dimension into the larger project of social transformation.

As I came to understand the archeology of the mindful-body and contradictions that lay on the threshold between my determined present and self-determined future, I came to see how their emotional and psychological force could continue to structure my feelings, gestures and needs, and necessarily touch and influence the lives and performances of others. I realized that as a community-based 'performing arts educator', I had a responsibility both to re-cognize the motivational power of my humanity and understand its 'performance effects', particularly if I hoped to learn the skills and praxis of a new community-based subjectivity.

This is how I explain what motivates and animates my reflexive-empathetic solidarity with any person or people struggling to tell their story to create a new identity. But it also explains my commitment to illuminating the subjective effects of not knowing or denying this intimate history, and to understanding their significance in the quest for democracy and self-determination. The psycho- emotional illnesses 'caused' by amnesia, cultural dislocation, lack of self-confidence, lack of self-esteem, lack of self-knowledge and lack of self-acceptance not only deny the possibility of interrupting the desire for affirmation that dialectically locks victim and violator into the abusive co-dependent cycle that characterizes all authoritarian relationships; it also explains the disability to say 'no', the justice-seeking desire for centre-stage, the (consequent) tendency to assume excessive responsibility, the (consequent) dis-ability to organize time, the relentless cry of (self)accusation and consequent inability to listen, and the chronic disability to perceive how the personal is present in every reading of the world, which characterizes all victim cultures. Of course, inexperience in coordinating time and responsibility, and (impoverished) resources exacerbate these difficulties. But these factors tend to be turned into the key causes by victim cultures to rationalize and disown responsibility for their deaf and compulsive performance practice, an understandable but tell-tale reflex to blame rather than to re-cognize the intolerable possibility of complicity in any continuing suffering.

This is the fundamental link between storytelling and self-determination. I often ask myself when I am most acutely uncertain how to read a culture that is not my own, or any individual I am working with: do I as an 'outsider' have any right to participate in other people's struggles? This uncertainty is no less present in my 'own culture' or 'community'. We are all outsiders to others. But the question is fundamental. It is what inhibits any authoritarian desire to 'conscientize' others and generates the necessary self-doubt and need to question that ensures permanent questioning and learning.

However we tell our story - whether we have to borrow the courage or techniques of other storytellers to tell it, whether we have to smuggle it into another time and place to tell it, whether we have to tell it in the margins or the silences of other people's stories, whether we have to conceal it within other people's narratives or even between the teeth in their smile, whether we have to lie and cheat to tell it or bend it almost beyond recognition to match it with the world - tell it we must, at least to ourselves. For storytelling is how we try to know and recognize ourselves.

We could say storytelling is the way the world's history is revealed in our actions, or that our intimate stories enable us to clarify our part and responsibility in the shared histories we are making. We could say storytelling is the act of closing one story to enable another to begin, or the act of maintaining a story as open and incomplete to extend it into the future. However we choose to see and define it, storytelling is much more than the mere telling of stories. It is an intervention in a shared living history that contributes to the definition of the present and the making of the future, an act of 'making sense' through the making of a story for the first time or making it differently from the last time, the aesthetic space of making history. For this reason, the dialogic performance of storying is inseparable from the understanding and making of democracy. We should judge our cultural and educational institutions by the extent to which we share and nurture these performance skills, in practice.

REFERENCES

Baron Cohen, D. (2005). Towards a performance-based pedagogy of self-determination. In J. Crowther, V. Galloway, & I. Martin (Eds.), *Popular education: Engaging the academy* (pp. 192–203). Leicester: NIACE (National Institute of Adult Continuing Education).

Baron Cohen, D. (1999). Listening to the silences: Defining the language and the place of a New Ireland. In S. Brewster (Ed.), *Ireland in proximities* (pp. 173–188). London: Routledge.

Boal, A. (1994). *The rainbow of desire: The Boal method of theatre and therapy.* London: Routledge.

Freire, P., & Macedo, D. (1987). *Literacy: Reading the word and the world.* London: Routledge.

Freire, P., & Shor, I. (1987). *Medo e Ousadia: o cotidiano do professor.* Rio de Janeiro: Paz e Terra.

Fromm, E. (1997). *The fear of freedom.* London: Routledge.

Kershaw, B. (1999). *The radical in performance.* London: Routledge.

Thiong'o, N. Wa. (1993). *Moving the centre.* London: Heinemann.

Thiong'o, N. Wa. (1982). *Decolonising the mind.* London: Heinemann.

Dan Baron Cohen *is President of IDEA and WAAE, a community arts educator whose international projects advocate for teacher education and sustainable development through a new arts-based paradigm of education.*

SANJOY GANGULY

15. THEATRE IS HOPE, THEATRE IS FREEDOM

Keywords: oneness, freedom, relation, optimism and argument

I would like to explain briefly why I have chosen to write about democracy, transformation and theatre. Art is a social metaphor because art is a human creation; any creation is essentially the expression of an idea. Theatre theorist and director, Augsto Boal writes, "Theatre is the first human invention and also the invention which paves the way for all other inventions and discoveries" (Boal, 1995, p. 188).

Human beings seek information by being spectators of the wonderful nature around them, and like theatre spectators, humans hunger for information. To search for more information through spectatorship is a human need. This need for information inspired human beings and the art of making came into being. The practice of art made our hands free and as a consequence, labour was born.

The search for information has been an intellectual need from the beginning of civilisation. Human beings started acquiring new information from the wider vision which they obtained as a result of freeing their hands. The positive conflict between two sets of information produced knowledge that was necessary and responsible for the advancement of the human civilisation.

Development is dialectical, a product of dynamic thought and making. Initially, both the intellectual journey and the cultivation of applied art and fine arts, like sculpting, was owned and practiced by people by and large. Unfortunately with the progress of modern society the intellectual and the artistic need of large populations of people began to be neglected. Society became divided along class lines and the artistic and intellectual world became eliticised.

The eliticisation of art and intellect has dehumanised human society. Every human being is essentially intellectual. Vivekananda said, "Education is the manifestation of the perfection already in Man" (Vivekananda, 1987, vol. 1, p. 410). The problem is that people are not aware of this perfection. That is precisely the reason why art was eliticised. Therefore we need art which can make visible this perfection which is normally invisible.

Making thought a doctrine is the kind of religiosity which can be found within the political culture of the political parties and can also be found in the modern development philosophy which looks at participation from the perspective of the developers rather than the developed. It is dogma that prevents us from accepting the dynamic nature of thought, inhibits us from accepting positive conflict, makes us the prisoners of our ideology.

In the political culture nowadays, rational citizenship is not the demand of modern democracy as it is run by political parties which seek to produce blind followers. Non-party activism (pressure groups) carried out by NGOs also promotes the culture

S. Schonmann (ed.), Key Concepts in Theatre/Drama Education, 93–98.

of blind following. For them of course the agenda is not to acquire state power. But fundamentally their actions turn out very often no different. Theatre is seen as a support service to a political action, not politics in itself. Politics outside parties is based on economics. Development activities do not consider the need for the kind of intellectual space and endeavor that poor people require, as if they only need bread, clothes, and shelter.

The absence of the cultivation of art prevents people from discovering their talents and expressing what matters. Without a political venue for voice, people are disempowered and by making people feel inferior (or threatened), the social system can introduce a culture of silence. Therefore, as a means to democratise politics, we need theatre, we need art. Boal has said,

> "I believe that all the truly revolutionary theatrical groups should transfer to the people the means of production in the theatre so that people themselves may utilise them, The theatre is a weapon and it is the people who should wield it." (Boal, 1979, p. 122.)

Positive conflict can produce thoughts whereas negative conflict cannot. The art of argument is not to win against the other. Nobody actually wins as a result of an argument, only truth wins. We argue in order to discover the truth. There is a certain animalistic aspect in a dogmatic nature; it instigates violence. Thought is thoughtless when it does not allow conflict, thought becomes doctrine, something unchangeable and not the philosophy which is changeable.

Freedom is the product of a relationship. That is the reason why civil society evolved from human thought. Theatre is essentially a construction of relationship, a relationship between actors and spectators and between us and ourselves. Theatre creates freedom, theatre is freedom.

Theatre of the Oppressed and Forum Theatre:

The foundation of Theatre of the Oppressed is based on the true concept of democracy where human beings are seen from a respectable point of view. Boal has said, "*Equally the human being is a rational creature, it knows things, it is capable of thinking, of understanding, and of making mistakes. Every human being is capable of thinking, of understanding, and of making mistakes.*" (Boal, 1995, p. 30). Boal did not say this as theory; he has learned from the people as a democratic political practice.

One very interesting dimension here is that theatre is seen as a method of introspection. The method makes the actors their own spectator. In the process a person experiences both the actor and the spectator in him. By being so an individual discovers his/ her potentials and also the dichotomy inside. An oppressed individual can very well be an oppressor. An oppressed agricultural worker sometimes acts as an oppressor in his family, sometimes he beats his wife, gets drunk, neglects the children in the family etc. By being the spectator of his own actor sometimes an individual experiences the conflict between the human being and the inhuman personality he has. Thus he can humanise himself, which is essentially a spiritual experience.[1]

The actor also here makes theatre. The group I belong to is called Jana Sanskriti Centre for Theatre of the Oppressed. Here we script plays instead of playing the script. While scripting plays actors become spectators of their own reality. They identify Oppressors, Oppressed, passive oppressors, etc. Also the play-making process includes the scope to understand the ideology of the oppressor and the same applies to the oppressed character. So in the workshop the actors - who should come from the oppressed community - script the intellectual power which resides in them. Scripting plays become scripting power. This is how the process of democratising politics starts. The individual analyzes society from his own perspective, as well as that of others. Such is the collective effort of scripting a play.

In Forum Theatre an event of oppression or torture is enacted. Here facts are the only material for drama. Fiction has no role to play in such theatre. Actors on stage enact an event where the distinction between the oppressor and the oppressed is clearly marked. Boal projects a concrete situation in order to motivate the audience to find out ways of ending this oppression. There is no place for passive spectators in Boal's theatre. Here spectator becomes 'spect*actor*'.

Forum Theatre is a theatrical game in which a problem is shown in an unsolved form, to which the audience, against spect-actors, is invited to suggest and enact solution. The problem is always the symptom of an oppression, and generally involves visible oppressors and a protagonist who is oppressed. In its purest form, both actors and spect-actors will be people who are victims of the oppression under consideration; that is why they are able to offer alternative solutions, because they themselves are personally acquainted with the oppression. After one showing of the scene, which is known as 'the model' (it can be a full-length play), it is shown again slightly speeded up, and follows exactly the same course until a member of the audience shouts 'Stop!', takes the place of the protagonist and tries to defeat the oppressors.

The game is a forum of contest between spect-actors trying to bring the play to a different end (in which the cycle of oppression is broken) and actors ostensibly making very possible effort to bring it to its original end (in which the oppressed is beaten and the oppressors are triumphant). The proceedings are presided over by a figure called the 'joker', whose function is to ensure the smooth running of the game and teach the audience the rules; however, like all the participants in Forum Theatre, the joker can be replaced if the spect-actors do not think he or she is doing a fair job, and virtually any of the 'rules' of the game can be changed if the audience wants. Many different solutions are enacted in the course of a single forum - the result is a pooling of knowledge, tactics and experience, and at the same time what Boal calls a 'rehearsal for reality'. (Boal, 1992, p. xxiv - Translators' introduction to the first edition).

In India, Jana Sanskriti is the only exponent of Forum Theatre in which members of the theatre team select, construct, and narrate a social problem from their daily life. With artistic direction this play is taken to an audience who must now find a solution to the problem. Passive spectators them become engaged spect-actors. Spect-actors come on stage to enact the solutions they have thought of, debating with trained activists on the feasibility of the solutions suggested. Thus individuals publicly engage in tacking a problem that has thus far provoked the most profound cultural silence and acceptance. This exercise gradually suggests the possibilities for liberation from that oppression in real life. Over the years we have seen that the experience of 'spect-acting has motivated people to be active outside theatre as well.

In many cases in our villages we have seen oppressive husbands have become humanised by watching our plays related to patriarchy. It is necessary to note that Jana Sanskriti has been performing plays on patriarchy in the same large area for the last decade. Jana Sanskriti believes in continuity and consistency. Theatre teams are located in the villages, the members of the team are from the villages. Actors and spectators know each other well. Throughout the year these theatre teams address various oppressions through Forum Theatre. The issues vary from place to place, but issues related to patriarchy are common for all 30 teams in West Bengal.

When we started our group in 1985, we had no women in the team. Women were not allowed to participate in artistic work; now we have women acting in all our teams. In Jana Sanskriti, the largest Forum Theatre group in the world as acknowledged by Boal there are now 50% women actors. Considering the strong presence of patriarchy in the village society in India, it is a revolution indeed. But we continuously talked about it, discussed it with the people through Forum plays for many years, and this has now resulted in families becoming democratised. We have succeeded to a large extent in the villages where we have been in the last ten years.

Politics is not about dividing one into two. It is the opposite: it is to bring two into one where every one is present with his/her own dignity and differences if there are any. In Forum Theatre argumentative space is created. Diversified opinions play with each other, the stage gets extended. The debate here unifies people, actors and spectators come together, learn together, feel together, rationalise the situation shown in the play together. They construct a relationship based on a respectful attitude to each other. This is how theatre here democratises politics.

I have mentioned earlier that information we receive from elsewhere and information we get from spectators often conflicts and produces a thesis which is a basis for change. A Forum play appears to the spectators as a piece of information which conflicts with the information stored as an experience in the mind of the actors and spectators. Here actors and spectators are engaged in a collective action which also leads to an introspective action. While acting collectively they deal with a local form of an oppression, which is the manifestation of a much more macro level of oppression. For example a scene of domestic violence involves a couple or a family. But after a certain time it often takes actors and spectators to a rational journey where they understand patriarchy. The journey here starts from dealing with an experience and continues toward making theories, it moves from effect to the cause of an oppression. In this intellectual journey actors and spectators experience the intellectual growth to what I can call internal transformation. This internal transformation inspire actors and spectators to become active citizens in real life. Acting continues outside the stage in the form of action where people are not blind followers of any political force, they become rational social engineers, they act to transform the oppressive reality, an external transformation. Boal described his theatre as rehearsal of revolution, but in a true sense his theatre is an act of total transformation, which includes revolution both internal and external.

Participation; the very word is being used narrowly nowadays. To see people as implementers is the objective there, but "Theatre as Politics"[2] can create an opportunity for people to become policy makers. Let's be optimistic about it and let's try to understand the scope of theatre beyond performing art.

Conclusion

Theatre is a space for introspection and collective action. A space where politics in the form of a collective action is complemented by spirituality in the form of introspection. Theatre is all about the construction of relationship, therefore audience here demands respect from the artists. Unfortunately, very often artists think of themselves as either stars or intellectually superior to the spectators. A respectful attitude towards spectators is created through the connection between our head and heart. A theoretical belief is not enough, a positive emotion is also required. Politics comes from the head and spirituality comes from the heart. They need to be connected. The lack of this connection is the reason some kinds of theatre are losing their audience. Theatre with the kind of attitude of actors I have described creates a truly democratic space. A space which allows debate and argument, makes us social critic and at the same time optimistic. Theatre creates hope, theatre is hope.

NOTES

[1] In many cases in our villages we have seen oppressive husbands have become humanised by watching our plays related to patriarchy. It is necessary to note that Jana Sanskriti has been performing plays on patriarchy in the same large area for the last decade. Jana Sanskriti believes in continuity and consistency. Theatre teams are located in the villages, the members of the team are from the villages. Actors and spectators know each other well. Throughout the year these theatre teams address various oppressions through Forum Theatre. The issues vary from place to place, but issues related to patriarchy are common for all 30 teams in West Bengal. When we started our group in 1985, we had no women in the team. Women were not allowed to participate in artistic work; now we have women acting in all our teams. In Jana Sanskriti, the largest Forum Theatre group in the world as acknowledged by Boal there are now 50% women actors. Considering the strong presence of patriarchy in the village society in India, it is a revolution indeed. But we continuously talked about it, discussed it with the people through Forum plays for many years, and this has now resulted in families becoming democratised. We have succeeded to a large extent in the villages where we have been in the last ten years.

[2] Boal (1998) in his book Legislative Theatre has said this on the question of political theatre. (p. 16).

REFERENCES

Boal, A. (1979). *Theatre of the oppressed*. London: Pluto.

Boal, A. (1992*). Games for actors and non actors* (A. Jackson, Trans.). London: Routledge.

Boal, A. (1995). *The rainbow of desire: The boal method of theatre and therapy*. London: Routledge.

SANJOY GANGULY

Boal, A. (1998). *Legislative theatre*. London: Routledge.
Vivekananda, S. (1987). *The complete works of Swami Vivekananda*. Kolkata: Reflect Publisher.

Sanjoy Ganguly *is Founder and Director of Jana Sanskriti, as well as being Artistic Director of the Jana Sanskriti Centre for Theatre of the Oppressed in Calcutta.*

MARGRET LEPP

16. DRAMA FOR CONFLICT MANAGEMENT
DRACON INTERNATIONAL

Keywords: conflict handling, conflict management, interdisciplinary and comparative action research, adolescents in schools, DRACON

"DRACON is an interdisciplinary and comparative action research project aimed at improving conflict handling among adolescent school children by using the medium of educational drama" (DRACON International, 2005 rev. 2007, p. 13). DRACON was initiated in 1994 by a Swedish industrial consultant, Mr. J. Andersson, with the idea of joining the two academic and practical fields of drama and conflict resolution. Collaboration with Malaysia began in May 1994 at a meeting in Kuala Lumpur in Malaysia, involving Swedish conflict researchers and Malaysian drama specialists. At an international meeting in January 1996, in Aldinga, Australia, it was decided to extend the Swedish-Malaysian research cooperation with two Australian teams. DRACON International was born!

The fundamental hypothesis in this project is that drama can be an effective way to learn conflict handling. The importance of learning conflict competence through one's own experience (experiential learning) rather than through books or lectures is in focus. However, the learning situation needs to be structured by a trained facilitator. Educational drama can be a way of structuring and processing the experiences of conflicts. Through re-enactment or role-play the participants access a more meaningful experience of the conflict, including thoughts, feelings and body experiences. *Educational drama* within the field of drama was chosen and *mediation* from the field of conflict management. Both these fields emphasise voluntary participation in a group process, under the guidance of a trained facilitator (drama pedagogue or mediator).

The Aim

The purpose of the research has been to develop new methods to teach conflict management, focussing on young adolescents in schools. The school was chosen as a strategic arena for learning, practicing and spreading conflict competence. Teenagers often find it difficult to handle their own conflicts. The field studies were primarily focused on students age 13–16 years in selected schools, and secondarily focused on teachers and school counsellors. The main purpose of DRACON has been to "develop an integrated programme using conflict management as the theory and practice, and drama as the pedagogy in order to empower students through an integrated, school-based programme to manage their own conflict experiences in all aspects of their lives" (Bagshaw, Burton, Grünbaum, Lepp, Löfgren, Malm, & O'Toole, 2005, rev. 2007, p. 422).

S. Schonmann (ed.), Key Concepts in Theatre/Drama Education, 99–104.

Eight overall research questions have been in focus throughout the DRACON project. These question might give the reader a guide to the field of interest and knowledge:

1. "What are the most common types of conflicts among adolescents? How do they perceive their conflicts and how do they behave in typical conflict situations?
2. How can adolescents explore their own conflicts through the medium of drama?
3. Can the development of relevant drama methods and programmes in schools improve adolescents' capacities for handling conflicts?
4. How resilient are these drama methods and programmes? Will they function under troublesome conditions, such as in "problem" classes, and in ethically divided schools?
5. Can the same or similar drama programmes be used for schoolteachers and counsellors to stimulate their participations as facilitators in the drama programmes?
6. Under what conditions and to what effect can the drama programmes be implemented in a whole school? Can they be taken over and run by the school itself and under what conditions?
7. What kind of observations/measurements can be developed for studying the long and short-term effects of drama programmes?
8. What are the effects of different backgrounds or contextual factors (national and ethnic cultures, school systems etc) on the design and outcome of the field studies?" (Bagshaw, Burton, Grünbaum, Lepp, Löfgren, Malm, & O'Toole, 2005, rev. 2007, p. 422–423).

The Research Design

Ethical issues and challenges that arose in the DRACON International project are discussed, for example responsibility and liability for a breach of ethics must be clearly spelled out at the beginning of a research project, within the context of relevant legislation and policies. Research that is interdisisciplinary or international, involves vulnerable participants or those who are legally underage, or where information is being shared and reported across professional and cultural boundaries, clear and shared ethical guidelines are essential (Bagshaw & Lepp, 2005).

Each DRACON team had specialists in two fields, drama and conflict resolution, both as researchers and as practitioners. More than 30 researchers and drama pedagogues have at different times been associated with the project. The core group consisted of 13 persons from four cooperating and independent teams:

- the Malaysian DRACON team: Latif Kamaluddin and Janet Pillai
- the South Australian DRACON team: Dale Bagshaw, Rosemary Nursey Bray and Ken Rigby
- the Brisbane DRACON team: Bruce Burton, John O'Toole and Anna Plunkett
- the Swedish DRACON team: Mats Friberg, Anita Grünbaum, Margret Lepp, Horst Löfgren and Birgitte Malm.

Several international workshops have been created, eight of them, the first in Aldinga 1996 and the last in Penang 2004. Most conferences have been held in

Penang, Malaysia. Between the international workshops and conferences, each DRACON team worked within their national team, related to different research focus, namely:
- the Malaysian DRACON team: Creative arts in conflict exploration
- the South Australian DRACON team: Adolescent conflicts and educational drama
- the Brisbane DRACON team: From DRACON to Cooling Conflicts focused on peer teaching to Acting Against Bullying.
- the Swedish DRACON team: Teenagers as third-party mediators.

Results and Implications

Numerous people from two disciplines and three countries have managed to work together on a complex research design for almost ten years (1996–2005) and have produced about 100 working papers plus a major international publication without a central budget. This is extraordinary. DRACON has included approximately 4000 students in surveys studies. A further 2500 students, 150 teachers and 20 school counsellors have participated in intensive drama programmes and 1300 students have experienced a Theatre in Education programme about conflict handling. One of the reasons for the success of the project is that the international research co-operation has been based on symmetry and carried out with great enthusiasm.

A short summary of the answers related to the above eight research questions are as follows:

1. Typical areas for conflicts are the family, schools and leisure time activities. Differences between girls and boys basic strategies for handling conflicts are described (Löfgren & Lepp, 2001) and the cultural distinctions between the participating countries concerning soliciting information from students.
2. In the end, it has been easy to get students interested in learning more about conflicts because drama combines playfulness with serious involvement in questions that affect every teenager.
3. The analysis of the study shows that students involved in the DRACON project have gained new knowledge and understanding on several levels; a social level, an aesthetic level and a cognitive level.
4. Both teachers and school counsellors can benefit from the same drama programmes. DRACON courses for teachers and counsellors have lasted about one week or less. However, it requires a certain amount of drama competence and knowledge of conflict theory to facilitate the DRACON programmes.
5. To be able to secure the success and resilience of the DRACON programme, certain conditions need to be fulfilled. Students voluntary participation, support from the school staff and parents, well-organised DRACON lessons and, if possible, a facilitator trained in both drama and conflict theories.
6. If the conditions described under question four are met, and the whole school supports one of the DRACON programmes, there might be a good chance to successfully involve a whole school.

7. Different forms of self-reported data, such as questionnaires, videos, diaries and questions requiring problem solving have been used. The use of journals as tools for drama research are further analyzed by Lepp and Bagshaw (2003). Observations of students during lessons and breaks were used as well as interviews with students and their teachers.

8. Many students expressed positive changes of attitude on cultural matters, including new insights into the experience of others, and a willingness to accommodate difference, a growing self-confidence in public, and a greater acceptance within the class or school group (DRACON International, 2005, rev. 2007).

Conclusions

To bridge the fields of drama and conflict management, has been an innovative and important move. Theories of conflict have provided the framework and given support to practical implementation through drama in schools. New competences need to be developed in order to cope with the global increase in aggressive behaviour among students in schools. Therefore, an integration of drama and conflict theories in teacher-training programmes is a pre-requisite in order to secure future implementation and stability of programmes such as DRACON. The school of tomorrow needs to focus on goals such as promoting conflict literacy, empathic competence, and respect for the individual and democratic values. The theories and practical experiences described in the book DRACON International can encourage and inspire others to realize the significance of empowering students to handle conflicts.

Related Research to DRACON

Research related to DRACON is still in process. For example, a book about managing bullying and conflict in schools by O'Toole, Burton, and Plunkett (2005) is the result of several years of action research. Other examples are two books were the Swedish DRACON programme is described, one in Swedish (Grünbaum & Lepp, 2005) and one in Danish (Grünbaum & Lepp, 2008). In 2001 (Norway) 2004 (Canada) and 2007 (Hong Kong) the Special Interest Group (SIG) in the field of Drama for World Peace at International Drama/Theatre and Education Association (IDEA) conferences were highlighted. The SIG chose to look at effective models that already existed to identify the strengths and weakness of using drama to manage conflict (Burton & Lepp, 2003).

Techniques developed during the DRACON research were also used to help adults who were dealing with the trauma of abuse they experienced as children in orphanages in Australia. *The Moving On* project was a three year research program conducted by Burton, Bundy and Bates (Bundy, 2006). In it, drama was used in conjunction with counselling to offer a safe environment for survivors of childhood institutional abuse to tell their stories without re-traumatisation, both in workshops and in public theatre performances.

Another project inspired by DRACON is the *Core Conflict Competency* coordinated by Morag Morrison, Bruce Burton and Margret Lepp. The aim is to construct a programme of teaching and learning in conflict management that will be applicable to graduate and undergraduate education in the field of Health Sciences, Teaching and Criminal Justice in three countries, Australia, UK and Sweden. Not directly inspired by DRACON but using drama for learning and empowerment from all over the world is described by (O'Toole & Lepp, 2000). Research projects in the field of Nursing education using drama for learning and reflection is explored by Lepp (2002) and Ekebergh, Lepp, and Dahlberg (2004).

DRACON also inspired to research about essential strategies for promoting effective collaboration and conflict resolution in international research projects. The results are:
- valuing diversity and developing cooperative goals
- engaging in self-reflection and reflexivity
- promoting collaborative dialogue
- taking time and developing trust (Bagshaw, Lepp, & Zorn, 2007).

REFERENCES

Bagshaw, D., Burton, B., Grünbaum, A., Lepp, M., Löfgren, H., Malm, G., et al. (2005, rev. 2007). Conclusions. In *DRACON international. Bridging the fields of drama and conflict management: Empowering students to handle conflicts through school-based programmes* (pp. 422–439). (Studia psychologica et paedagogica, series altera CLXX). Malmö: MUEP (Malmö University Electronic Publishing). Retrieved from http://dspace.mah.se/bitstream/2043/5975/1/drac06nov.pdf

Bagshaw, D., & Lepp, M. (2005). Ethical considerations in drama and conflict resolution research in Swedish and Australian schools. *Conflict Resolution Quarterly, 22*(3), 381–396.

Bagshaw, D., Lepp, M., & Zorn, C. R. (2007). International collaboration: Building teams and managing conflicts. *Conflict Resolution Quarterly, 24*(4), 433–446.

Bundy, P. (2006). Using drama in the counselling process: The moving on project. *Research in Drama Education, 11*(1), 7–18.

Burton, B., & Lepp, M. (2003). Playing against violence: Cooling conflicts. In. H. Heikkinen (Ed.), *Special interest fields of drama, theatre and education* (pp. 114–124). The IDEA dialogues, University of Jyväskylä, Department of Teacher Education: IDEA publications.

DRACON International: Empowering Students to Handle Conflicts through School-Based Programmes. (2005, rev. 2007). (Studia psychologica et paedagogica, series altera CLXX). Malmö: MUEP (Malmö University Electronic Publishing). Retrieved from http://dspace.mah.se/bitstream/2043/5975/1/drac06nov.pdf

Ekebergh, M., Lepp, M., & Dahlberg, K. (2004). Reflective learning with drama in nursing education: A Swedish attempt to overcome the theory praxis gap. *Nurse Education Today, 24*(8), 622–628.

Grünbaum, A., & Lepp, M. (2005). *DRACON I SKOLAN. Drama, Konflikthantering och Medling.* (DRACON in the School: Drama, Conflict Management and Mediation). Lund: Studentlitteratur.

Grünbaum, A., & Lepp, M. (2008). *DRACON I SKOLEN. Drama, Konflikthåntering och Maedling.* (DRACON in the School: Drama, Conflict Management and Mediation). Fredrikshavn: Dafolo.

Lepp, M. (2002). *Reflection of drama in nursing education in Sweden.* Applied Theatre Researcher (ATR). Brisbane, Australia: Griffith University. Retrieved from http: www.gu.edu.au/centre/atr

Lepp, M., & Bagshaw, D. (2003). Journals as a tool for learning and evaluation in drama and conflict research projects involving adolescents. *Nadie Journal (Drama Australia Journal), 27*(1), 55–67.

Löfgren, H., & Lepp, M. (2001). Students' basic strategies for handling conflicts: A study of grade 8 students in Sweden. In C. Day & D. van Wee (Eds.), *Education research in Europe* (pp. 383–396). Yearbook 2001. Leuven Apeldoorn: Garant Publisher.

O'Toole, J., Burton, B., & Plunkett, A. (2005). *Cooling conflict: A new approach to managing bullying and conflict in schools.* Pearson Education Australia.

O'Toole, J., & Lepp, M. (Eds.). (2000). *Drama for life: Stories of adult learning & empowerment.* Brisbane: PlayLab press.

Margret Lepp*, RN, RNT, PhD, Professor at the Institute of Health and Care Sciences, The Sahlgrenska Academy, University of Gothenburg, Sweden.*

BELARIE ZATZMAN

17. DRAMA EDUCATION AND MEMORY

Keywords: memory, history, witnessing, narrative, performance, identity, Holocaust

Mapping memory onto the landscape of drama and theatre education can help illuminate the diverse ways in which practices of memory are made manifest in a multiplicity of aesthetic forms across the discipline(s). Drama education has the capacity to situate participants between history and memory, offering a process for constructing and rehearsing our own identities among the narratives of others, present and past. "Contemporary research examining memory and memorial underscores the fact that in provoking history as an act of remembrance for a new generation, we are narrating a sense of self" (Zatzman, 2005, p. 95). How might the performance of memory invite youth to theorize their lives in performance as acts of retrieval? While not exhaustive, what follows here is a representative listing of practices of memory found in current drama and theatre education literature.

The study of memory in applied theatre contexts has been deftly articulated by Helen Nicholson who provides a comprehensive analysis of embodied practices of memory in her own work (2003); further, she positions the performance of memory as both political act and social justice response (2009). Drawing on a Foucauldian construction of counter-memory, Nicholson reminds us of the scope and promise of "re-locating memory" and asks us to consider "the different ways in which memories are shaped and reshaped performatively" (2009, p. 269). She highlights the significance of counter-memory insofar as it supports alternative voices, narratives of belonging, and the creation of community.

Drama/theatre practices that stage memory as a cultural archive of possibilities include documentary forms such as verbatim theatre/ theatre of witness/ theatre of testimony/ museum theatre/ site-specific performance and ethnographic theatre which focuses on, for example, health and theatre. These theatrical constructions may highlight remembering/forgetting and uncover traces of (self) representation in sometimes unexpected sites and documents (Kadar et al., 2005). Nora has suggested that any place, object, action, or condition is potentially a "realm of memory", in the recovery of identity (Nora & Kritzman, 1996). Drawing upon objects and archival traces as pre-texts for exploring memory can help to make visible performances of identity and to counter historical erasure. Interviews, documents and other ephemera, for example, can be shaped to re-inscribe events/issues/sites/ histories, in the present. The collecting of memories is (often) an inherent part of the gathering of data; a foundation from which to excavate textualized identities

S. Schonmann (ed.), Key Concepts in Theatre/Drama Education, 105–109.

and histories of individuals or communities. Anderson and Wilkinson (2007) describe a characteristic example of a verbatim theatre process:

> Memories, typically free from analysis, raw and vivid, were gathered through interviews. Hours of tapes were then transcribed, edited and frequently fed back into the community as a play by the same actors who first collected the stories, as a way of triangulating the data. The theatre projects that came out of this process represented a way of understanding a shared past, a traumatic present, a diversity of truths. (p. 156)

From the multiple subjectivities and geographies that identify diasporic communities of memory in performance (e.g., Foon's *New Canadian Kid*, 1989; Sher's *Under the Banyan Tree*, 2005; Roy's *Letters to my Grandma*, 2009), to issues of compassionate care in the resonant and alternative forms of scholarship that theatre offers to research in health (e.g., Holm et al., 2005), for example, memory is often situated as central to aesthetic explorations. Museum Theatre, using "theatre and theatrical techniques as a means of mediating knowledge and understanding in the context of museum education" (Jackson & Leahy, 2005, p. 304), not only unearths the memories and narratives held by objects, ephemera and collections (Bridal, 2004; Hughes et al., 2007), but also raises questions about whose voices/stories are heard in or are absent from museum spaces. Reminiscence Theatre (e.g., Schweizter, 2007; Wang, 2006), Playback Theatre (Dennis, 2008; Fox, 2009), and site-specific performance (Mackey, 2002). provide opportunities to "share thoughts, feelings, memories-stories" (Fox, 2009, p. 241). From facing difficult knowledge in the theatre of witness (e.g., Kaufman's *The Laramie Project*; Soans' *Arab-Israeli Cookbook*; McLeod's *The Shape of a Girl*) or theatre of testimony (e.g., Moving On Project, 2007; Linden's *I Have Before Me a Remarkable Document from a Young Lady from Rwanda*, 2003; Greig's *Dr. Korczak's Example*, 2004; Sher's *Hana's Suitcase*, 2006; Nottage's *Ruined*, 2009) to my own work in Holocaust Education, the pedagogical and aesthetic project of memory acts to unfix the past in an effort to inform the personal and public present, both critically and creatively.

In both formal and informal educational/community settings, participants need to know that "they themselves are located at the intersection of histories, memory space and artmaking" (Zatzman, 2003, p. 35). "We cross boundaries in drama work, both in and out of role, carrying memories from the other". As such, drama/theatre can signal both a form of witnessing (p. 35) and an "ethical responsibility that underpins this kind of work" (Stuart-Fisher, 2009, p. 110). With respect to the study of the Holocaust, witnessing is defined as receiving the obligation to re-tell, to re-perform testimony, enabling the staging of stories across fluid generational and temporal boundaries. From the outset, it is important to note that the shaping of memory is also mediated by an awareness of the very reasons for recalling particular histories. Thus, I am conscious of the necessity for artists and teachers to engage the lived experiences of participants in order to support their sense of agency and shared authority in the remembering and re-telling (Hatton, 2003; Zatzman, 2003). Further, when these "communities of memory" read the specific circumstances of their past against their present, the aesthetic practices they shape can serve to highlight shared concerns as well as productive differences.

Addressing the complexity of practices of memory, Hirsch (1997) identifies "post-memory" as the experience of "those who grow up dominated by narratives that preceded their birth, whose own belated stories are displaced by the stories of the previous generations" (pp. 22–23). Post-memory has also come to signify a "space of remembrance" in which empathy and imagining can actively carry us toward remembering the suffering of others. My own interest in memory, post-memory and memorial is back-shadowed by the Holocaust; and my work in Holocaust Education through the fine arts may be understood as a discrete representation of the performance of memory. However, while the context of my scholarship and art-making may be specific to my experience of [Jewish] identity, belonging and memory, it is also characteristic of the play of memory and history in the recovery of identity, broadly wrought. The performance of memory, the obligation to witnessing, and the representation(s) of narratives of identity have become critical to the designing of my arts education projects. Please find, below, an example of one project exploring memory/memorial with youth entitled "Wrapped in Grief" excerpted from "Staging History: Aesthetics and the Performance of Memory" (Zatzman, 2005).

"Wrapped in Grief" was produced with youth between the ages of twelve and sixteen years old. As a Holocaust memorial project, it was designed as a scaffolded pedagogy in which historical contexts became the foundation informing all of the exploration that followed. First, young people created tableaux to locate particular events during the Holocaust; for example, Kristallnacht (9–10 November 1938), the Warsaw Ghetto uprising (19 April-16 May 1943), the book burnings of 10 May 1933, and the White Rose movement (public demonstrations against the Nazi regime by a network of students and faculty in Germany, 1942–43). The second stage of this arts education project asked participants to work on the identification of loss in their own lives, in juxtaposition to the historical archive with which they had been presented. "Wrapped in Grief" culminated in the staging of a mise-en-scene of memory, in which the young people fashioned large-scale sculptures as an artifact of their experience of memorial.

David Booth's call to "continually remind ourselves of the complex and different contexts that allow us to enter the 'as if, what if' world" (2003, p. 17) is important in understanding that this research project was designed around the construction of specific historical contexts, with the intent of supporting thoughtful and critical improvisation, role-playing, art-making, as well as in and out of role writing about the Holocaust. The complexity of this undertaking lies in the recognition that we are working between spaces of documentation and the (im)possibility of knowing. In performing historical events, "Wrapped in Grief" bears witness through arts education, so that like the best curatorial practices, we, too, can [imagine as an act of public witness]. Indeed, Richard Courtney addressed "imagining" as "the fundamental operation of the aesthetic." (1982, pp. 158–59). In imagining within an aesthetic frame that claimed absence, impermanence, participation, and context, youth were invited to inscribe not only their questions but the boundaries of this work.

For example, in response to the historical context of the Warsaw Ghetto uprising, a young woman named Sam navigated these shifting boundaries and difficult questions as a part of her experience of the memory act itself. Moving back and forth across the threshold of intimacy and distance - in the shared authority of her post-memory relationship to the Holocaust - she wrote:

> I've learned that in order for the Warsaw ghetto uprising to take place, it was the women and children who had to put on that fearless face and risk their lives, so that the people of the ghetto could fight for theirs. I am a woman and yet, I am also a child. I am in that in-between stage, not yet a full woman and not yet done growing up. I have my whole life ahead of me. I dream about kissing boys, playing games with my friends, travelling, laughing. I can whine and pout and cry over spilt milk, but I am also mature and thoughtful, I want to heal the world, I can put on a brave face if necessary. I love to read and sing, and spin and spin and spin in the sunshine. Boom! The little girl is blown to bits trying to sneak a gun through a hole in the ghetto wall. Her childhood was taken away from her, STOLEN. I struggle to shed my childhood, I want to be an adult, I want to be responsible, I want to be appreciated. But that little girl, or little boy, they were forced to mature too fast. I scold myself. Why am I rushing, when they never got to live? When all they would dream about was to maybe be able to live another day. When their games became real life or death – deliver this gun into the ghetto wall or die. I am child, but I am also a young woman. I have a woman's shape, a woman's breasts. I can't help but think of those women, sitting on a train, bullets in their backpacks. Pretending not to be Jewish to help the resistance fighters. It is a mission of great importance. If she succeeds she has made a difference, however miniscule. What if she was caught? She would not just be killed. She would be raped, tortured, and then murdered. Or maybe they wouldn't even be nice enough to murder [her]. A woman, lying naked in the street, brutalized. Lying just outside the ghetto wall, trying to deliver ammo. A woman, with a woman's body. A body like mine. A woman just like me.

Sam, 16 years old (pp. 99–100).

REFERENCES

Anderson, M., & Wilkinson, L. (2007). A resurgence of verbatim theatre: Authenticity, empathy and transformation. *Australasian Drama Studies, 50*, 153–169.

Booth, D. (2003). Towards an understanding of theatre for education. In K. Gallagher & D. Booth (Eds.), *How theatre educates: Convergences and counterpoints with artists, scholars, and advocates* (pp. 14–22). Toronto: University of Toronto Press.

Bridal, T. (2004). *Exploring museum theatre*. Walnut Creek, CA: Alta Mira Press.

Courtney, R. (1982). *Re-play: Studies of human drama-in-education*. Toronto: OISE Press.

Dennis, R. (2008). Refugee performance: Aesthetic representation and accountability in playback theatre. *Research in Drama Education, 13*(2), 211–215.

Fox, J. (2009). Playback theatre in Burundi: Can theatre transcend the gap? In T. Prentki & S. Preston (Eds.), *Applied theatre reader* (pp. 241–248). New York: Routledge.

Hatton, C. (2003). Backyards and borderlands: Some reflections on researching the travels of adolescent girls doing drama. *Research in Drama Education, 8*(2), 139–156.

Hirsch, M. (1997). *Family frames: Photography, narrative and postmemory.* Cambridge, MA: Harvard University Press.

Holm, A. K., Lepp, M., & Ringsberg, K. (2005). Dementia: Involving patients in storytelling - a caring intervention. A pilot study. *Journal of Clinical Nursing, 14*(2), 256–263.

Hughes, C., Jackson, A., & Kidd, J. (2007). The role of theatre in museums and historic sites: Visitors, audiences, and learners. In L. Bresler (Ed.), *International handbook of research in arts education,* Part 1 (pp. 679–696). Dordrecht, The Netherlands: Springer.

Jackson, A., & Leahy, H. R. (2005). "Seeing it for real?" authenticity, theatre and learning in museums. *Research in Drama Education, 10*(3), 303–325.

Kadar, M., Warley, L., Perreault, J., & Egan, S. (Eds.). (2005). *Tracing the autobiographical.* Waterloo: Wilfrid Laurier University Press.

Mackey, S. (2002). Drama, landscape and memory: To be is to be in place. *Research in Drama Education, 7*(1), 139–156.

Nicholson, H. (2003). The performance of memory. *Drama Australia, 27*(2), 79–92.

Nicholson, H. (2009). Re-locating memory: Performance, reminiscence and communities of Diaspora. In T. Prentki & S. Preston (Eds.), *Applied theatre reader* (pp. 268–275). New York: Routledge.

Nora, P., & Kritzman, L. D. (Eds.). (1996). *Realms of memory: Rethinking the French Past. Volume 1: conflicts and divisions.* New York: Columbia University Press.

Schweitzer, P. (2007). *Reminiscence theatre: Making theatre from memories.* London: Jessica Kingsley Publishers.

Stuart-Fisher, A. (2009). Bearing witness: The position of theatre makers in the telling of Trauma. In T. Prentki & S. Preston (Eds.), *Applied theatre reader* (pp. 108–115). New York: Routledge.

Wang, W.-J. (2006). The subversive practices of reminiscence theatre in Taiwan. *Research in Drama Education, 11*(1), 77–87.

Zatzman, B. (2003). The monologue project: Drama as a form of witnessing. In K. Gallagher & D. Booth (Eds.), *How theatre educates: Convergences and counterpoints with artists, scholars, and advocates* (pp. 35–55). Toronto: University of Toronto Press.

Zatzman, B. (2005). Staging history: Aesthetics and the performance of memory. *Journal of Aesthetic Education, 39*(4), 95–103. (Special Issue: Aesthetics in Drama and Theatre Education)

Belarie Zatzman, *PhD, York University, Canada, focuses on issues of history, identity, narrative and memory in drama education. Her research also examines Holocaust education through the fine arts.*

PETER WRIGHT

18. AGENCY, INTERSUBJECTIVITY AND DRAMA EDUCATION

The Power to Be and Do More

Keywords: agency, intersubjectivity, drama education, applied theatre, young people, identity

Theories of agency have long been implicit in drama education and applied theatre where the focus is on the performative, action, and engagement. What the notion of agency foregrounds is the individual, choice, freedom, and intentionality; it speaks to being purposeful and having and taking control in one's life. However, agency can also be situated within the realm of self-interest where difference is individually measured and achieved; this being seen as some worse forms of new individualism defining living in the 21st Century (Elliott & du Gay, 2009). What is not as well understood is that agency also exits in relation to others with social bonds being a powerful way of knowing ourselves and attributing meaning. Intersubjectivity is a related concept that helps reveal how this process works, and the power that drama has in contributing to young people's meaning making and the way they construct learning identities. Consequently, this entry will describe notions of agency and intersubjectivity within drama and applied theatre as particular forms of personal, social and collective action where the social and personal are inextricably linked.

In addition, I describe how dramatic processes, forms and content link and develop meaning and identity, and where representations link events through symbolic means - drama being the dance between them. It is also important to understand that while drama education is traditionally thought of as occurring in schools, drama education and the cognate field of applied theatre also occurs in the 'third learning space' beyond school and family (Stevenson & Deasy, 2005). This entry then uses the understanding gained from each of these 'spaces' to help better understand drama practices across each.

One long-standing principle of drama has been the notion of active participation, or learning by doing. Many long-standing traditions of theory and practice have elaborated drama games and exercises, skill development, and forms to enact, hold and present these as active and participatory. In addition, the theories that have evolved from this praxis consequently have foregrounded notions of embodiment (Bresler, 2004), process (O'Toole, 1992), an increasing range of application (Prentki & Preston, 2009), and critical questions that unfold from this nexus (Nicholson, 2005). What the notion of agency foregrounds is the implied benefits that flow from this active participation and the "sensuous acts of meaning making" (Willis & Trondman, 2000, p. 9) that drama enables.

S. Schonmann (ed.), Key Concepts in Theatre/Drama Education, 111–115.

Agency can be understood to be an attribute of all living things and involves the capacity to effect change. What this might mean in terms of drama and young people is that drama practices, forms and structures enables individuals to become creative and active constructors of knowledge and so cultural producers rather than cultural consumers. This means that young people can be seen to be intentional and active in creating their identities rather than having things done to them as 'objects', or being passive receptors of external action. For example, certain groups of young people are often demonised and thought to be 'at risk' (Case, 2006). Implicit within this construction is an adult presumption or prescription of risk in an increasingly risk-averse world. Indeed, all young people can be thought of to be 'at-risk' as a consequence of their relative level of powerlessness within contemporary society. However, what this construction also fails to reveal is that young people are active with or without the intervention and observation of adults, and not always in ways that are deemed 'acceptable'. This is a disregard of young people's inherent desire to be engaged with their communities, as actors, change agents and knowers, as bearers of rights, and as citizens. One consequence of this form of labelling is punitive, restrictive and increasingly controlling societal responses. This response suggests convergent as opposed to divergent thinking where options are narrowed, confined and closed, rather than open and creative. It is the antithesis to the role that drama and creativity can play in education wherever that may occur.

Conversely, drama and notions of agency enables us to think of young people as being 'at promise' rather than 'at risk'. It is through drama, for example, that risk can be thought of as engaging and providing opportunities for growth and development - the 'hard fun' often associated with the arts (Borden, 2006). Drama develops participant's awareness and the capability of being social actors or agents in their own lives; importantly this implies both understanding one's own world representations, the way these are socially constructed, and the feelings that define one's own unique individuality.

Agency, however, is not completely individual, can be constrained in a variety of ways (Schaefer-McDaniel, 2004), nor always a good thing in and of itself. Unfettered agency, for example, can be construed as unencumbered selfishness or greed, this coming at the expense of others. Structures or systems can constrain these forms of rampant individualism and drama education is a powerful model of this notion in application. What is important about this contribution is that just as the forms that are created in drama and applied theatre are a consequence of the actions of those within it, participant's actions are shaped by the forms that are created. This means that awareness of self and others is developed conjointly and strengthened by the compelling aesthetic frame that drama provides.

Intersubjectivity, which arises out of interaction, is a notion that helps us better understand the impossibility of isolated individuality through foregrounding the social elaboration of subjectivity - in other words, agency at work. This can be understood as part of the ecology of drama education and applied theatre where social processes provide the checks and balances between being for self, and being for others. What intersubjectivity also reveals is the importance of relationships to the quality of the learning experience. Furthermore, intersubjectivity highlights the way that young people do not exist in isolation but are in interrelationship with, and embedded in, their communities.

While the conceptual terrain of intersubjectivity itself is contested (Crossley, 1996), what it does do is reveal how meanings and relationships are conjointly developed and how these are used to better understand social and cultural life; in this way being educational. For example, the development of empathy - or in drama terms 'stepping into another's shoes' - allows us to infer and experience the lives of others. In the same way, performing our own subjectivity presents it as being corrigible and enables us to have distance on it. This ability grows out of our own self-awareness as a reference point, that is, our own bodily presence and it is this self-awareness that allows us to infer the mental states of others. In other words, rationality is grounded in bodily experience and the embodied mind is intersubjectively constituted at its most fundamental levels. Consequently, our sense of self is inseparable from our recognition of others (Merleau-Ponty, 1964).

Donaldson (Hughes, Grieve, & Grieve, 1991) argues for a developmental 'map' of the human mind with four main modes - perception, action, thought, and emotion. What intersubjectivity does is to highlight how we first 'see' a situation through the feeling of bodily affect before we are deliberately rational about it, and emotions mark significance, what we care about; all in relation to others. Hence, we act towards others out of feelings first, principles come second. Thich Naht Hanh (1993) helpfully refers to this as 'inter-being', a process inherent in drama education. Drama practices, for example, enable us to experience and express emotion, and this ability enables us to see and understand it in others. What this means is that the actions, emotions and sensations experienced by the other become meaningful to us because we can share them. To put it differently, the *thinking* body intersubjectively comes from an awareness of the *acting* body; it is neural, somatic, and situated. Consequently agency and intersubjectivity are linked where drama practices provide the means and methods for these to be developed both brain and body alike.

Agency and intersubjectivity are threads running through drama pedagogy, each iteratively developing the other with benefits for participants. For example, in drama what begins as helplessness can become agency - where agency is understood to be both a state and a process. In addition, the social action that is a consequence combines both action and significance that enhances the life world and is often present in those who seek emancipatory change. Agency, consequently, as developed through drama can be thought of in activist terms. Drama education develops young people's capacities to investigate, evaluate, and ultimately act on issues they think are important; art has always served these purposes.

This capacity, intersubjectively constituted, is important because if young people are to actively participate in the future, they need to understand how the past shapes the present, and how an awareness of the present enables us to see possibilities for the future. This is a process that drama educators know well; for example, identification, action planning, collective action are critical to how community grapples with serious issues, and human experience - as developed through drama - is the site where this is felt and understood.

Agency and intersubjectivity, then, can be seen as core in understanding and responding to human experience. And human experience, as both the subject and object of drama, can be seen as accomplished through mutually constructing actions, interactions, and meanings as they emerge and are shared through action and symbol systems including language, sound, and movement. The capacity for understanding others then can be seen to be deeply rooted in the relational nature of action. For example, our social lives are largely determined by the way that we attribute agency to others through their actions, and recognise, understand, and respond appropriately to them. What drama foregrounds, and these two concepts reveal, is that the process is as important as the product and that art which inquires, provokes and expresses is possible from the collaboration of multiple positions.

Agency, in short can be thought of as *knowledge building* through drama and applied theatre employing both making and looking that is student-centred, -led, and -driven. Importantly these pedagogic processes are intersubjectively contextualised through the social and aesthetic so that individual perspectives are interwoven into shared understanding. What this foregrounds is that human agency is embedded and iteratively engaged in cultural understanding, change and diversity, and the practices of drama education as a social art purposefully develops each. Agency and intersubjectivity as strengthened through drama in this way then can become an antidote to despair and hopelessness many young people feel when faced with manifestations of globalisation, instability and change. For many people this can mean hope, understanding, social transformation, and an enriched way of seeing the world (Wright, 2009; Wright & Palmer, 2009).

Finally, a better understanding of agency and intersubjectivity enable us to see their power when thinking about a curriculum for the future. And a curriculum for the future is one based on the power of relationship, agency and intersubjectivity - in short a curriculum of communication (Kress, 2000). This curriculum of communication is one where culture is not merely reproduced, but actively made by those who imagine and create it. This means that young people can effectively participate in the world, have their thoughts and perceptions valued, actions count, and voices heard. In this sense, both community and personal control are developed through social participation that is drama's raison d'être, and where aesthetic understanding and experience inform new possibilities of thought and action - a search for something better.

REFERENCES

Borden, R. (2006). *Arts education research: A primer on findings, methodologies, and advocacy.* Washington, DC: Arts Education Partnership.

Bresler, L. (2004). *Knowing bodies, moving minds: Towards embodied teaching and learning.* Dordrecht: Kluwer.

Case, S. (2006). Young people 'At risk' of what? Challenging risk-focused early intervention as crime prevention. *Youth Justice, 6*(3), 171–179.

Crossley, N. (1996). *Intersubjectivity: The fabric of social becoming.* London: Sage.

Elliott, A., & du Gay, P. (Eds.). (2009). *Identity in question.* London: Sage.

Hanh, T. N. (1993). *Interbeing.* Berkeley, CA: Parallax Press.

Hughes, M., Grieve, R. B., & Grieve, R. (1991). *Understanding children: Essays in honour of Margaret Donaldson*. Oxford: Blackwell.

Kress, G. (2000). A curriculum for the future. *Cambridge Journal of Education, 30*(1), 133–126.

Merleau-Ponty, M. (1964). *The primacy of perception and other essays on phenomenological psychology, the philosophy of art, history and politics*. Evanston, IL: Northwestern University Press.

Nicholson, H. (2005). *Applied drama: Theatre and performance practices*. Basingstoke, Hampshire: Palgrave Macmillan.

O'Toole, J. (1992). *The process of drama*. London: Routledge.

Prentki, T., & Preston, S. (Eds.). (2009). *The applied theatre reader*. London: Routledge.

Schaefer-McDaniel, N. J. (2004). Conceptualising social capital among young people: Toward a new theory. Children, *Youth and Environments, 14*(1), 153–172.

Stevenson, L. M., & Deasy, R. (2005). Third space: *When learning matters*. Washington, DC: Arts Education Partnership.

Willis, P., & Trondman, M. (2000). Manifesto for ethnography. *Ethnography, 1*(1), 5–16.

Wright, P. R. (2009). *It's like thinking with both sides of your brain*. Murdoch: Murdoch University.

Wright, P. R., & Palmer, D. (2009). Big hART at John Northcott Estate: Community, Health and the Arts. *The UNESCO Observatory, Refereed E-Journal. Multi-Disciplinary Research in the Arts, 1*(4). Retrieved from http://www.abp.unimelb.edu.au/unesco/ejournal/vol-one-issue-four.html

Peter Wright is a Senior Lecturer in Arts Education and Research Methods, and Academic Chair, Research and Postgraduate Studies School of Education, Murdoch University, Perth, Western Australia.

SECTION IV: NARRATIVE AND PEDAGOGY

UTE PINKERT

19. THE CONCEPT OF THEATRE IN
THEATRE PEDAGOGY

Keywords: different perspectives, current discourse, skill and competence, aesthetic
experience, cultural practice

In an international context, the term "theatre pedagogy" may appear somewhat
awkward; however the term makes clear this subject's relation to the art form of
theatre and its central significance in terms of contemporary developments in
educational theatre here in Germany.

There are countless opinions regarding what theatre, or the art of acting, actually
does. As theatre scholar Andreas Kotte observes, on close inspection, there are hardly
any two people "who have a similar perception of theatre. (...) Theatre is used as a
label." (Kotte, 2005, p. 62) Thus, theatre audiences usually seek out the kind of
theatre they *prefer*. Theatre educators, on the other hand, who dedicate themselves to
imparting and/or working with theatre, are called upon to critically engage in a
professional way with their own and foreign concepts of theatre. Within the practice
of educational theatre, especially, when various concepts collide with each other, it
becomes clear how decisions made during working processes strongly depend upon
the perceptions and attitudes of all the participants concerned. Consciously or uncon-
sciously, in every pedagogical theatre project, worldviews, ideas of human nature,
and conceptions of theatre are communicated and, in the best cases, negotiated.

In the following, I will roughly sketch the current discourse in German-speaking
theatre pedagogy under the aspect of its understanding of "theatre" or "acting". I look
upon this essay as a contribution to the formation of a theory of theatre pedagogy,
which is presently expanding beyond the provisional "hyphenated" explanations
(theatre pedagogy as defined by the location of its enactment, or by its target group).
As my own position will also become apparent, I am not methodically concerned
with developing a valid concept of theatre on the basis of devaluing others; but
rather, with comprehending different perspectives on the central topic of pedagogical
theatre. This approach creates a premise for an understanding of the practical
consequences of these conceptions of theatre in our work.

1. The Practical Perspective - Theatre as Competence, Skill, and Craft

This perspective arises from a practical concern: How does one make good theatre?
What does this involve, and how may it be learned? In this view, theatre is not
questioned; instead, it appears as a given, traditional technique, in the sense of the
ancient Greek *téchne*, as a competence, skill, or craft. There are various perspectives
related to the assessment of the specific human predisposition toward (theatre)

S. Schonmann (ed.), Key Concepts in Theatre/Drama Education, 119–123.
© *2011 Sense Publishers. All rights reserved.*

acting that I will not address here. For no matter whether theatre acting is viewed as an anthropological constant, as a "liberation" from blockades and a "return" to "the natural ability to play"; or whether acting is seen as a kind of cultural technology, comparable to reading and writing, theatre is always considered to be a specific form of human *communication*, which enables individual expression and particular forms of social relationships. For the most part, both a anthropologically-aligned perspective (acting as an ability) as well as a cultural-technologically-aligned perspective (acting as a skill, a craft) refer to the institution of theatre in its historical forms, and represent a scripted and, above all, role-centered concept of theatre (Kotte, 2005, p. 64).

Even if in principle, the *téchne* of theatre may be learned by all people, within (German) practice there is still a clear distinction between "professionals" who are trained in these techniques within a formal educational setting, and "amateurs" who learn the craft of theatre in a non-formalized way. In Germany, formal theatre education is offered by specialists such as acting educators who are mostly located in theatre academies or university theatre departments. Non-formal training, or learning through working with other amateurs, is an area of theatre pedagogy primarily located in the sector of pedagogy or education rather than that of the arts. Despite a growing field of avant-garde forms of theatre/performance in which these differences become irrelevant, in Germany in the relationship between the professional and the amateur, a hierarchy related to *mastery* within the *téchne* of theatre still exists.

When theatre pedagogy broadly comprises of all kinds of theatre work with *non professional actors*, there arises the practical question of the delivery of inter-mediation/theatre education. Due in no small measure to the time-related and structural conditions of this theatre work, specialists of theatre pedagogy have developed various kinds of modularization. Depending on the context, theatre acting is conveyed for instance through certain stages (getting acquainted, training in expression, creation of characters, etc.); through certain "building blocks" (space, time, character) or through certain forms (theatre with masks, with shadows, with improvisation etc.).

If theatre acting as a field of educational practice comes under pressure to legitimize itself, as it has increasingly in recent years, this pragmatic classification of the téchne of theatre into individual, cumulatively learnable steps inevitably becomes related to particular (socially recognized) competencies. The resulting, increasingly-observed concentration upon social abilities (skills) can easily result in a transfer of emphasis, and some elements of the téchne of theatre then appear only as a *means* toward the construction of a socially competent personality.

2. The Educational Theory Perspective: Theatre as Subjective Experience

The driving motive behind this view is educational theory's explanation of theatre acting as a non-interchangeable (and therefore irreplaceable!) area of aesthetic education. Here, the attention is focused on the *relation* between theatre as an aesthetic product and process on the one side, and a subject (to be educated) on the other. This relation is described in the field of aesthetic education as *aesthetic experience.* The question here is: What aesthetic experiences might a subject have, when seeing or acting in theatre?

The relevant examination of this question to date comes from Ulrike Hentschel (Hentschel, 1996, p. 2000). According to her, the educational effects of subjective encounters with an art form cannot be described in general terms. Instead, they are grounded in the *media-specific* characteristics of that art form. Looking for the media-specific characteristics of theatre play, Ulrike Hentschel distances her search from all social processes during a theatre production and focuses on the process of *acting.* Within an educational theory perspective, theatre appears as the production of a second reality, within which the symbols of the first reality are used as "symbols of symbols" (Fischer-Lichte, 1997, p. 987). The specificity of the medium of theatre is grounded in the fact that here (in contrast to other art forms), "subject, object, and the medium of the creation cannot be separated from one another, (...) [but rather] the created object (remains) bound to the body of the creating subject" (Hentschel 2007, p. 7). So the players (and the audience also) are always acting simultaneously on two levels: on the level of symbol and meaning (referential) and on the level of the concrete physicality of the players (performative).

According to Hentschel, this experience of the *dual nature of theatrical communication,* identified as the awareness of difference, is "the central educational experience of theatre acting and -viewing" (Ibid.). The awareness of difference creates the conditions for aesthetic competence as an educational target in theatre pedagogy. Aesthetic competence is grounded in the experienced insight (within one's own body) and translated into the construction of realities - be they theatrical, media-based, or social - and the resulting ability to handle different representational forms, media, and intentions (ibid.). Furthermore, it may be expected that actors, through being required to act consciously within different levels of representation, develop an overall ability for balanced detachment and self-reflection.

The current academic discussion within German-speaking theatre pedagogy is essentially characterized by this question: To what degree does the awareness of difference still play a role, when current theatre practices are being applied within educational theatre work in which these practices make an issue of playing with different levels of reality, and test the boundaries between play and not-play (i.e. site-specific performance, autobiographical theatre)?

With this question, the participants in such projects come to be seen as self-forming subjects, and their presentation is studied primarily with a view toward whether, and in what way, the theatre processes and ambitions involved fulfills the purpose of enabling the players to consciously handle forms of representation. The intentions of the players, and their concerns, are thereby appreciated less for their (political, social, personal...) relevance, as for the quality of their aesthetic creation.

3. The Cultural Studies Perspective: Theatre as Cultural Practice

This concept of theatre exists in the context of trends in theatre arts toward the dissolution of boundaries within current culture; it has been scarcely elaborated so far in German theatre pedagogy.

In view of certain developments in current theatre which are marked by a dissolution of the understanding of roles (performance theatre, live art); by an abandonment of traditional hierarchical relations to theatrical symbols (post-dramatic theatre [Lehmann, 1999]); and by playing with the staging of everyday life (participatory, site-specific actions), the narrow conception of theatre as role- and text-centred is left behind. It has been replaced by a theatre conception that regards theatre as primarily performance (Fischer-Lichte, 2004, p. 42 et sqq). On that condition theatrical events appear to be a particular form of "cultural performances", and are structurally comparable to them (Singer on Fischer-Lichte, 1998, p. 12 et sqq.) As in other cultural performances (i.e., rituals, festivals, etc.), within theatrical events, the "self-conception and self-image" of a culture is formed (ibid.), and in this perspective, culture itself is thereby generated and manifested. As regards theatre pedagogy, the cultural self-image which becomes apparent in theatre performances is looked at from the aspect of its own production. In this way the relationships which determine the process itself are brought into focus: the relationship between players and their subjects, the relationships among the players themselves, and the relationship of the players to their audience.

The theatre concept that is most useful for observing these qualities of relationship does not begin with an assumption of particular characteristics. In reference to a relational understanding of theatricality (Münz, 1998; Kotte, 2005), theatre is conceived as a relational dimension, which exists in constant interaction with other cultural practices and events, and is changed by them. Theatre has decidedly influenced, and has been most influenced by, the practice of the theatricality of the everyday. From this perspective, the participants in theatre pedagogy projects appear to be not so much amateurs as experts, who have formed a particular "practical knowledge" (Bourdieu, 1987) of theatrical behavior patterns in their daily lives. When theatre educators ground their work in this expertise, especially in their work with marginalized groups, they move into a relationship of reciprocal exchange with the players. They consider themselves as learners, and in return, they make their practical theatre skills available, so that the players can become conscious of this "practical knowledge", and they can articulate it, reflect upon it and vary it.

In this perspective, the primary focus is on enabling the cultural participation of the respective participants. In order to realize this, the process as well as the product of pedagogical theatre work is observed in relation to the cultural practices and products of the surrounding culture (Pinkert, 2005).

Consequently, from a cultural studies perspective, theatre educators can consider themselves not only as experts for the art of theatre (see 1) and for educational processes (see 2). Moreover, they are required to engage themselves with cultural practices and images beyond the theatre, and with the underlying power relations and societal conditions that produce them. When this challenge meets with a progressive attitude, a broader concept of theatre and political involvement can be combined: "In part this suggests the necessity for cultural workers to develop dynamic, vibrant, politically engaged, and socially relevant projects in which the traditional binaries of margin/centre, unity/difference, local/national, and public/private can be reconstituted through more complex representations of identification, belonging, and community." (Giroux & Shannon, 1997, p. 8).

A preliminary conclusion: Theatre acting and –viewing is a competence/a technique/a craft; and it is the object of subjective experience, and it is a cultural practice. Each of these three means of understanding theatre has its history, its field of application and its consequences. So it makes absolute sense to apply the first concept of theatre in the area of amateur theatre; to pursue the awareness of difference in the setting of educational theatre in and outside of school; and to seek out cultural practices and meanings within applied drama (Nicholson, 2005) or theatre work in social areas (Koch et al., 2004). Beyond this, each concept of theatre holds a perspective with the potential to pose productive questions, depending on the respective interests and goals, in any pedagogical theatre practice.

REFERENCES

Bourdieu, P. (1987). Sozialer Sinn. Kritik der Theoretischen Vernunft. Frankfurt/Main: Suhrkamp.
Fischer-Lichte, E. (1997). Theater. In C. Wulf (Ed.), *Vom Menschen: Handbuch Historische Anthropologie* (pp. S. 985–996). Weinheim: Beltz.
Fischer-Lichte, E. (1998). Grenzgänge und Tauschhandel: Auf dem Wege zu einer Performativen Kultur. In E. Fischer-Lichte et al. (Ed.), *Theater seit den 60er Jahre: Grenzgänge der Neoavantgarde* (pp. 1–20). Tübingen, Basel: A. Francke.
Fischer-Lichte, E. (2004). *Ästhetik des Performativen.* Frankfurt/Main: Suhrkamp.
Giroux, H. A., & Shannon, P. (1997). *Education and cultural studies: Toward a performative practice.* New York and London: Routledge.
Hentschel, U. (1996). *Theaterspielen als Ästhetische Bildung: Über einen Beitrag Produktiven Künstlerischen Gestaltens zur Selbstbildung.* Weinheim: Beltz.
Hentschel, U. (2007). "...mit Schiller zur mehr social skills...?" Zur Rolle des Theaters im aktuellen Bildungsdiskurs. dramaturgie. *Zeitschrift der Dramaturgischen Gesellschaft, 1,* 5–9.
Koch, G., et al. (Eds.). (2004). *Theatre work in social fields.* Frankfurt/Main: Brandes und Apsel.
Kotte, A. (2005). *Theaterwissenschaft.* Köln Weimar Wien: Böhlau.
Lehmann, H.-T. (1999). *Postdramatisches theater.* Frankfurt/Main: Suhrkamp.
Münz, R. (1998). *Theatralität und Theater. Zur Historiographie von Theatralitätsgefügen.* Berlin: Schwarzkopf und Schwarzkopf.
Nicholson, H. (2005). *Applied drama.* New York: Routledge.
Pinkert, U. (2005). *Transformationen des Alltags. Theaterprojekte der Berliner Lehrstückpraxis und Live Art bei Forced Entertainment. Modelle, Konzepte und Verfahren kultureller Bildung.* Berlin. Strasburg. Milow: Schibri.

Ute Pinkert is a Dramaturge and Theatre Educator, since 2007 Professor for theatre pedagogy at University of the Arts Berlin, Germany.

MARIE-JEANNE MCNAUGHTON

20. RELATIONSHIPS IN EDUCATIONAL DRAMA

A Pedagogical Model

Keywords: pedagogy, holistic, partnership, issues-based learning, process

The pedagogical model proposed in this chapter has been developed as a result of the analysis of a wide range of data, gathered over a series of educational drama lessons with pupils aged 10–12 years in three Scottish Primary schools. The data comprised: interviews; observers' commentaries; pupils' evaluations; teachers' reflective journal entries and video recordings of the lessons. Close analysis of the data uncovered an overarching theme: that the nature of the relationships between the participants in drama lessons, and between the participants and the learning contexts, afforded a climate in which learning (in its widest sense) can take place.

Context

The drama lessons were based in narrative and story (Bruner, 2003): the stories of the people in the drama and the problems they faced (pollution, eviction, deforestation, disempowerment). The drama referred to here is issues-based, offering the learners, working both in and out of role, human dilemmas to explore and problems to solve. This was process drama, mainly improvised and employing a wide range of theatre-based strategies (Neelands & Goode, 2000). The strategy of teacher-in-role was central to the lessons, with the teacher adopting a range of stances from neutral to sympathetic or antipathetic.

Relationships in Educational Drama: The Model

The matrix (see Figure 1) sets out the elements pertaining to each of the four aspects of relationships that emerged from the analysis of the data from the lessons. It is offered both as a summary of the conclusions emerging from the research and as model for teachers and educators who are planning educational drama based on issues of human concern, for example, social or environmental issues. It is suggested that all four elements should be considered when planning, teaching and evaluating drama projects. The elements of the table are discussed in the following sub-sections.

S. Schonmann (ed.), Key Concepts in Theatre/Drama Education, 125–130.

Relationships in drama	Teaching and leaning strategies
The learners' relationships with the learning context	– Relevance of content/context – Shared learning intentions – Holistic, integrated learning – Range of activity modes – Peer assessment – Evaluative experiences – Sense of empowerment in tackling issues
All participants' relationships with the fictional context	– Story at the centre – Context building – Role building – Range of dramatic conventions – Empathy and affective engagement – Action experiences
The relationships between the learners	– Opportunities for collaboration – Sharing ideas/plans – Whole group participation – Sharing common goals – Supporting peer learning – Respect for self and others – Kinaesthetic engagement
The relationships between the teacher and the learners	– Transformative – Responsive and supportive of learning – Democratic – Values-based – Varied status within lessons – Shared reflection and evaluation

Figure 1. Relationships in educational drama: a pedagogical model for practice.

The Learners' Relationships with the Learning Context

When introducing drama lessons, the ways in which the contexts and content of the lessons are relevant to their interests and learning should be made explicit to the learners (Black & Williams, 1998). In order for the learners to engage with the learning context, it is important to introduce the drama in ways that acknowledged the learners as partners, with each other and with the teacher, in the learning processes. Sharing the learning intentions with the learners gives them status within the learning experience and allowed them to monitor and evaluate the learning processes (LTS, 2006).

The holistic, integrated nature of the learning experiences in drama allows learners opportunities to make connections across other areas of learning: the drama contexts can offer learners opportunities to draw, to write, to research the issues involved, and to present information and ideas in a range of formats. Within drama lessons the learners are afforded opportunities to engage in a range activities that provided them with opportunities to experience four of modes of learning: 'living through' concrete experiences; actively experimenting; planning and thinking; and reflecting on their actions and the action of others (Kolb, 1984). This variety of modes of learning allows learners to become engaged with and actively involved in their learning experiences.

During drama lessons, learners can be offered opportunities to assess the work of others and to share in the assessment and evaluation of their own learning. They can comment on ways in which the learning intentions matched the learning outcomes and on the value of the learning experience. The value of this was evidenced in the research in the learners' positive reflections and evaluations, and in the way they remained involved and self-monitoring during the lessons. In addition, within the fictional contexts of the drama, the characters were afforded many opportunities to take action to benefit their own lives and situations. This empowerment gave the learners as sense of achievement and resulted in affirming learning experiences.

The Participants' Relationships with the Fictional Context

The stories of the problems and issues faced by the characters are central to many dramas. These can provide meaningful contexts and real purposes for the learners' drama activities. The time taken to build and develop the fictional contexts allows the learners' knowledge and concepts of the issues to develop gradually during the lessons, and this helps them to construct their own understandings and meanings based on their experiences (Selly, 1999). The drama process also allows the learners opportunities to construct their characters and to begin to form an understanding of them. In dramatic encounters, employing a range of dramatic conventions, they make an effort to be 'true' to the representations of their characters. Importantly, unlike some more traditional teaching, the roles adopted by the teacher allow her to enter the fictional worlds and to share, with the learners, in the problems and dilemmas encountered there.

In drama, the learners are asked, metaphorically, to put themselves 'in others' shoes'. This allows the learners to sympathise and even to empathise with the characters and their situations. They are personally involved with the imaginary context and are able to identify with the characters that they have developed. The research data demonstrated the learners expressing concern for, and understanding of, the problems facing the characters in the drama story.

The range of dramatic conventions covers four aspects of dramatic action: context building, narrative, poetic and reflective (Neelands & Goode, 2000). This range is important as it offered opportunities for variety of responses: opportunities to look at the dramatic situations in different ways and from different perspectives. Within the unfolding story of the drama, the learners face a number of challenging, unfamiliar situations calling for carefully considered responses. *A Curriculum for Excellence* (SECRG, 2004) advises that pupils should have opportunities to "develop and demonstrate their creativity" and to "sustain their effort" (p. 12). Drama offers opportunities for both. Because of the wide range of theatre-based conventions employed, responses, both vocal and physical, are often creative. Learners are required to consciously sustain their roles within the drama. The post-drama evaluations provided evidence that the learners were aware of this: "You had to keep being your character or the drama wouldn't work."

Within the context of the drama story, learners can have opportunities to plan for and engage in actions that can have a positive effect on the fictional environment. Critical discussion can also allow them to take a stance and to express their concerns outside the fictional context. Thus, the "action experiences", central to citizenship and environmental education, (Laing & McNaughton, 2001, p. 177) can be part of the drama experience for the learners.

Relationships between the Learners

Central to the pedagogy of drama education, is the provision of opportunities for collaborative and co-operative learning. Within the drama lessons, the learners are able to work collaboratively in small and larger groups, and this can support individual and group learning. Skills in communicating and collaborating are practised and developed during these small-group sessions.

In addition to working in small groups, the building of the fictional communities within drama lessons allows the whole class to participate in the creation and development of the fictional context. Bolton (1998) describes each child's contribution to the "making" of *living through* drama as, "part of a collective enterprise, culturally determined in language and action" (p. 271). Both the 'real' class of learners (and their teacher) and the fictional communities share common goals. For the class, there is the goal of developing and maintaining the fictional context. For the fictional community, there is the goal of enhancing or sustaining an aspect of the environment in which they live. The research suggested that, because learners are engaged and focused, instances of disruption or inappropriate behaviour or responses are less likely to occur.

Educational drama usually begins with the negotiation of a drama contract in which all of the participants (teacher and learners) agree to 'work for the common good' (O'Toole, 1992). This enables whole-group trust to be built, with learners responding to and supporting each other's efforts and learning, both in and out of role. They are encouraged to react to and respond to each other while in role, offering advice or showing concern for other members of the community. Respect for others, and for one's self, central to citizenship education (LTS, 2002), is also central to drama education in, for example, turn-taking, listening, supporting each others' efforts to speak and act in role, and offering positive feedback. In my research, during interviews and in class discussion, learners commented that the drama had helped them to find out more about other learners in the class: that they had seen "another side" of some of their classmates and that "people worked together well".

Particular to drama is the physical and kinaesthetic aspect of the learners' experiences and relationships. Learners will often move together, and explore relationships though their physical proximity, posture and gesture. This, the evidence suggests, brings them closer as learners and as human beings and extends the 'languages' of learning (Nicholson, 1999).

The Relationships between the Teacher and the Learners

The teaching approaches commonly adopted in drama lessons often fit Sterling's (2001) model of a transformative approach to sustainable education: learners are supported in the construction of meaning from their experiences and allowed owner-ship of the learning context. The teacher is responsive and reactive to the learners' behaviour and ideas, rather than seeking to impose rigid lesson structures. Strategies to support learning and to create a positive classroom climate (Massey, 2003) included: providing opportunities for the learners to participate in decision-making; allowing then to think freely about and to express their views; allowing for different perspectives and views; and encouraging the learners to be active contributors to the class and to the fictional communities within the drama.

These strategies are predicated on a certain set of teacher values about the nature of teaching and learning (Hayward, 2007): that learning is a democratic process and that the teacher's role is to offer strategies that facilitate learning rather than imposing it. In drama, the attitudes and dispositions of the teacher in the education process are well-documented (Winston, 1998; Taylor, 2000): that a teacher should be open, flexible and approachable, but also should be fair and should ensure that there is a safe and secure working atmosphere in which learning can take place. These principles are communicated to the learners as part of the negotiation of the drama contract.

The participation in the drama, through teacher-in-role, allows the teacher opportunities to alter her status in relation to that of the learners; thus changing the nature of the relationship between them. Equal status and high status learners' roles enable the teacher to seek help and advice, to be interrogated, and to be ignored and defied: all relationships outside the normal classroom pupil-teacher dynamic (Bolton, 1998). These relationships, and the open sharing of reflections and evaluations between the teacher and the learners, are instrumental in allowing learning to take place. In my research, the learners' appreciation of the partnership between them and the teacher, developed during the drama lessons, was evidenced in unsolicited comments, both oral and in their evaluations, thanking the teachers for their work with them and saying that had enjoyed working in this way.

In conclusion, the research on which this chapter is based suggests that, when planning issues-based drama lessons, it might be useful for educators to be aware of the four aspects set out in the Relationships Model as discussed above.

REFERENCES

Black, P., & William, D. (1998). *Inside the black box*. London: King's College.
Bolton, G. (1998). *Acting in classroom drama: A critical analysis*. Stoke on Trent: Trentham Books.

MARIE-JEANNE MCNAUGHTON

Bruner, J. (2003). The narrative construction of reality. In M. Mateas & P. Sengers (Eds.), *Narrative intelligence*. Philadelphia: John Benjamins.

Hayward, L. (2007). Curriculum, pedagogies and assessment in Scotland: The quest for social justice 'Ah Kent Yir Faither'. *Assessment in Education*, 14(2), 251–268.

Kolb, D. (1984). *Experiential learning: Experience as the source of learning and development*. Englewood Cliffs, NJ: Prentice-Hall.

Laing, M., & McNaughton, M. J. (2001). Environmental education should take children further. *Scottish Educational Review*, 32(2), 168–179.

Learning and Teaching Scotland (LTS). (2002). *Education for citizenship in Scotland: A paper for discussion*. Dundee: Learning and Teaching Scotland.

Massey, I. (2003). *Rights respect and responsibilities: Children's rights to education in Hampshire*. Hampshire County Council website. Retrieved June 12, 2009, http://www3.hants.gov.uk/education/childrensrights/rrrthecase.htm

Neelands, J., & Goode, T. (2000). *Structuring drama work: A handbook of available forms in theatre and drama* (2nd ed.). Cambridge: Cambridge University Press.

Nicholson, H. (1999). Walking with shadows. In C. Lawrence (Ed.), *Canterbury keynotes* (pp. 37–44). London: National Drama.

O'Toole, J. (1992). *The process of drama: Negotiating art and meaning*. London: Routledge.

Scottish Executive Curriculum Review Group (SECRG). (2004). *A curriculum for excellence*. Edinburgh: Scottish Executive.

Selly, N. (1999). *The art of constructivist teaching in the primary school: A guide for students and teachers*. London: David Fulton Publishers.

Sterling, S. (2001). *Sustainable education: Revisionary learning and change*. Bristol: Schumacher Briefings.

Taylor, P. (2000). *The drama classroom: Action, reflection, transformation*. London: Routledge Falmer.

Winston, J. (1998). *Drama, narrative and moral education*. London: Falmer Press.

Marie-Jeanne McNaughton, Senior Lecturer in education at the University of Strathclyde, Glasgow. Her main areas of interest - educational drama, Sustainable Development/Global Citizenship Education and Scottish Storyline.

ANNE WESSELS

21. DEVISING AS PEDAGOGY

Keywords: devising, dialogue, silence, community, pedagogy

Devising, or in generic terms, playbuilding, in widespread use in classrooms and applied theatre settings, has much to offer democratic pedagogy. Often devising has aspired to build community and create cohesive ensembles but what may these aspirations mask and in what ways might they insist on sameness rather than difference? This is important to consider because if these goals of devising are not made explicit and examined critically, there is the danger that these collectively created projects, however well-intentioned, become vehicles of conformity. If devising, in its efforts to build community demands sameness at the expense of difference, the potential for democratic pedagogy is lost.

Govan, Nicholson and Normington (2007) define devising as "processes" and "creative strategies" that contribute to the generation of original performed work. (p. 7). This creation of new work that is responsive to local context and/or the particular interests of students using participatory practices fits with Edward Little's (2008) description of "cultural democracy" that is, "predicated on direct public participation in the creation of a living, responsive culture" (p. 158). Devising's social pedagogy requires a dialogical approach that includes negotiation and deliberation that are key components of active citizenship and democratic learning. Community-building that harmonizes the tensions between the individual and the larger community of the class has also been associated with devising. Adopting this rhetoric of 'community-building' and 'cohesive ensemble' however; may not be as innocuous as it might first appear. Iris Marion Young's political theory regarding community, theories of devising and theories of dialogue/silence and conflict will be explored to guide and develop this brief discussion of devising as a democratic pedagogy.

Iris Marion Young (1990) presents the problem of community by suggesting that they are not necessarily inclusive as, "unity or wholeness in discourse generates borders, dichotomies, and exclusions" (p. 301). Although critical of community, she does not offer individualism as the alternative. She stresses that the binary of the community vs. the individual is false because they share a common denial of difference, "liberal individualism denies difference by positing the self as a solid, self-sufficient entity, not defined by or in need of anything or anyone other than itself" (p. 307). Community also denies difference by seeing the subject in a "relation of unity composed by identification and symmetry among individuals within a totality" (p. 307). Both entities, community and the individual, deny difference and assume sameness. She cautions against the pull to reconceptualise community as composed of individuals because this still totalizes by reconciling difference.

S. Schonmann (ed.), Key Concepts in Theatre/Drama Education, 131–134.

According to Young (1990), minimizing difference is dangerous because, "the desire for mutual understanding and reciprocity underlying the ideal of community is similar to the desire for identification that underlies racial and ethnic chauvinism" (p. 311). Instead, using the city as model, she offers the vision of a "politics of difference" (p. 301). She appeals to institutions to resist the homogenization of community, "radical politics, moreover must develop discourse and institutions for bringing differently identified groups together without suppressing or sub-suming differences" (p. 320). So, in dispensing with community-building as one of the justifications for devising, how are more democratic pedagogical spaces created that resist conformity and facilitate Young's (1990) notion of "openness to unassimilated otherness"? (p. 319)

Devising depends on participation but, as Deidre Heddon and Jane Milling (2006) point out, participation is anything but simple. In examining the supposedly egalitarian structure of the collective in devising, they address the ways in which power can be masked to inhibit the contribution of some participants (p. 107). They describe the challenges of working collectively, "the struggle to develop a totally democratic form was painful and never wholly successful as hidden hierarchies established themselves; while devising in a community context was and continues to be affected by anxieties around the politics of participation" (p. 229). Some of the 'hidden hierarchies' affecting participation are linked to the complexities of dialogue/silence and conflict. Who is talking, who keeps quiet and for what reasons? What happens when someone says one thing and immediately says the opposite as a form of self-silencing? What conditions have created the silence and who might dare to speak in the face of taboos that have become accepted as normal? When should silence be respected and when should it be shaken up?

Nancy Fraser (1992) in response to the assumptions about dialogue that were made by Habermas, states that rational dialogue does not necessarily mean all will join in the conversation even if it is open to them. People may not feel that they have the skills to speak in the proscribed way that has become accepted by those who have had the opportunity to be schooled in rational discourse. Traditionally, rational discourse would have excluded women and people of lower socio- economic status without access to education. She suggests that dialogue, both the content and the ground rules for engagement, have to be negotiated (p. 215). The questions remain: dialogue for whom, on whose terms, playing by whose rules and for the benefit of whom? For devising then, unless the rules of engagement are negotiated, it does not necessarily follow that the results and processes will be any more democratic than other forms of theatre pedagogy.

Megan Boler (2005) writes about the "interdependencies of speaking, listening and silence" (p. xxiv). In describing the varieties of silence, she says silence, "can be voluntary and self-imposed, or it can be the result of external pressures and constraints; silence can be expressive, or it can be empty, unreadable; silence can be temporary, situational, or it can represent a consistent even pathological pattern; silence can signal withdrawal from a conversation, or it can be an indicator of attentive and thoughtful listening" (p. xxiv).

Huey Li Li (2005) calls for "recognition of the pedagogical merits of silence" (p. 70). She outlines how much liberatory education has tried to allow for the silenced to be heard but problematizes that notion by recognizing the agency of the silenced, "the silenced can be complicit in the cultural practice of their silences" (p. 78). On an institutional level, she suggests that curriculum has, until now, silenced all but the dominant language in dialogue. For devising to become a democratic pedagogy, there needs to be a serious consideration of these politically-charged aspects of silence and the privileging of speech.

Conflict, closely associated with speaking and staying quiet, is also a critical component of devising. Kathleen Gallagher (2007) stresses the importance of difference and conflict, "simply put, drama takes difference (and sometimes conflict) as its starting point rather than its challenge" (p. 88). She coins the phrase "pedagogies of conflict" as a way to describe fruitful but difficult work in drama (p. 140). Tracy Crossley (2006) addresses conflict in relation to devising specifically, and suggests that students may internalize the hidden message that a well–functioning group presents no disagreement. Individual members of a group may resist conflict because they are afraid to assert themselves for fear of appearing disruptive. As a result, the group succumbs to a 'groupthink' yielding less than dynamic results, "groupthink refers to the condition in which a group makes defective decisions through conformity pressures in order to avoid disagreement and reach quick compromises" (p. 37). To counter this, she suggests using improvisation to explore, through role play, the kinds of artistic conflict that benefit the devising of a play (p. 41).

Crossley (2006) also warns that the teacher can be complicit in this avoidance of conflict if he or she is, "uncomfortable in having his or her ideas and knowledge challenged" (p. 46). This analysis invites the teacher to examine personal attitudes regarding conflict so that it is encouraged and not silenced.

Another important form of silencing in the classroom has been documented by Angelina E. Castagno (2008) whose work, completed in Utah schools, examines censored talk about race. Her statistics show that overt talk about race is shut down very quickly by teachers and she uses the phrase "colormuteness" to describe this imposition of silence (p. 320). She suggests that this discomfort with these challenging conversations perpetuates a privileging of Whiteness because, "within a framework of Whiteness in which the status quo is desirable and beneficial, silence is truly golden. But within a framework of equity in which social justice and fairness are sought, silence is both indifference and highly problematic" (p. 330).

Gallagher (2007), writing about the inability to talk about race in schools, describes how so often the conversation becomes one of showing how we are so much more advanced in our thinking about race than our ancestors (p. 149). She suggests that this reflects "a 'new racism' which seems to effectively evade notions of race, racial injustice, equity and democracy" (p. 149).

Speaking and staying silent in the process of devising is complex but we need not lose sight of devising's social possibilities completely. As Nicholson (2005) suggests in her exploration of notions of community that move beyond those defined by locality or identity, there are the, "possibilities of positive social networks through drama" (p. 86). She describes a loose 'social network' that creates itself through bonds of friendship. This happens more or less by chance as people work together but it is not a 'community' that insists on cohesion and conformity.

Little (2008) suggests that the processes of devising reflect concern for the social collectivity by attempting to reveal relationships of power (p. 154). Devising may create performances that address imbalances of power and injustice but, at the same time, it has to remain cognizant of its own processes to ensure that they do not demand conformity at the expense of difference. The pedagogy of devising, in its aspiration to become part of a larger project of 'cultural democracy', invites space for conflict, difference and diversity, recognizing the subtle play of dialogue and silence.

REFERENCES

Boler, M. (2005). Editor's introduction: Troubling speech, Disturbing silence. In M. Boler (Ed.), *Democratic dialogue in education: Troubling speech and disturbing silence*. New York: Peter Lang.

Castagno, A. E. (2008). "I don't want to hear that!": Legitimating whiteness through silence in schools. *Anthropology and Education Quarterly*, 39(3), 314–333.

Crossley, T. (2006). Letting the Drama into group work: Using conflict constructively in performing arts group practice. *Arts and Humanities in Higher Education*, 5(33), 33–50.

Fraser, N. (1992). Rethinking the public sphere: A contribution to the critique of actually existing democracy. In F. Barker, P. Hulme, & M. Iverson (Eds.), *Postmodernism and the re-reading of modernity*. Manchester: Manchester University Press.

Gallagher, K. (2007). *The theatre of urban: Youth and schooling in dangerous times*. Toronto: University of Toronto Press.

Govan, E., Nicholson, H., & Normington, K. (2007). Making a performance: *Devising histories and contemporary practices*. New York: Routledge.

Heddon, D., & Milling, J. (2006). *Devising performance: A critical history*. New York: Palgrave Macmillan.

Huey, L. L. (2005). Rethinking silencing silences. In M. Boler (Ed.), *Democratic dialogue in education: Troubling speech and disturbing silence*. New York: Peter Lang.

Little, E. (2008). Towards a poetics of popular theatre: Directing and authorship in community-based work. In B. Barton (Ed.), *Collective creation, collaboration and devising*. Toronto: Playwrights Canada Press.

Nicholson, H. (2005). *Applied Drama: The gift of theatre*. Basingstoke, UK: Palgrave MacMillan.

Young, I. M. (1990). The ideal of community and the politics of difference. In L. Nicholson (Ed.), *Feminism postmodernism*. London: Routledge.

Anne Wessels *is a PhD student in the department of Curriculum Teaching and Learning at the Ontario Institute for Studies in Education at the University of Toronto, Canada.*

KATHRYN RICKETTS

22. UNTANGLING THE CULTURALLY UNSCRIPTED SELF THROUGH EMBODIED PRACTICES

Keywords: interdisciplinarity, embodiment, "ostraneine", un-silencing, poetic narratives

This paper addresses two interrelated parts of embodied pedagogy. One, the slippery slopes of global fluidity in relation to the 'learner' and two, my particular handling of embodied learning in relation to a consortium of scholars from Performance, Culture and Dance/Drama studies who acknowledge performance as a tool for cultivating an awareness of the culturally inscripted body. Globalization brings erasure of the distinct - the extinction of the heritage, the deletion of the local, the annihilation of the particular (Shapiro, 2008). In attempts to address multi-culturalism within this tension, we understand the need to recognize both the differences of humankind as well as the commonalities. I celebrate the interdisciplinarity of scholarship and its continued bridgework to other communities and creative practices in the quest to enrich the perspectives of naming 'self' in relation to 'other' and with this inquiry I submit that individual agency nests within a matrix of shared human truths.

I am a PhD candidate wrestling with 30 years of dance practice as fodder to articulate a politicized stance that dance can be a means to cultivate agency within displacement. Uncovering stories that have been silenced or hidden I trigger others' stories and thereby connections and interconnections which construct a scaffolding of compassion and empathy. This then becomes the foundation for agency of voice and collective amplitude of that voice through means other than an exclusively cognitive process.

I have termed this 'handler' Embodied Poetic Narrative.

I am referencing a brief sweep of scholars and their performative processes that illuminate the misunderstood leverage and impotence of traditional devices such as *text centered* and *speech centered* learning strategies. This survey of vibrant embodied methods that work from and through text evidences the potential to cultivate learning spaces steeped with the possibility of transformation, articulation, revelation, and empowerment. Their imaginative practices construct hybrid spaces containing both fiction and non-fictional discourses, allowing students to examine identity and place within their immediate social-political location.

Medina (2005), specializing in drama and literacy with marginalized children, believes that these constructed dynamic performative spaces are contested sites whereby students can better understand the political and social ideologies that shape their daily lives. Moreover, they begin to understand how they can employ a criticality within these forces allowing a shift from complacency to a location of potential agency and transformation.

S. Schonmann (ed.), Key Concepts in Theatre/Drama Education, 135–139.

To lay the foundation for this 'contested site', Conquergood (2002), considered one of the masters of Performance Studies, urges us to think about our notions of 'place' and how this has radically transformed our definitions of words such as 'local' or 'boundary'; "we now think of 'place' as a heavily trafficked intersection, a port of call and exchange instead of a circumscribed territory" (p. 145). Conquergood explains that we no longer have static points we would claim as our community - he uses words such as "leakage", "thin", "membranes", "retracted", "transitive" - all in service of the claim that the freneticism of migrations within globalization has created a fluidity which can transfer both to a rejuvenation and/or a stripping away of a traditional meaning-making process. Conquergood (2002) writes of this "transgressive travel between two different domains of knowledge" (p. 145) as a critical point in Performance Studies whereby the story - local, knowing, grounded in a collection of memories, stories and interactions - cuts across the map - which is objective knowledge, authorized and legitimized through texts. This process dissolves the notion of authorship within silos of self and proprietorship.

Story #1: Uncovering the stories, resuscitating the voice, igniting shared spaces of meaning making.

I performed a LUG, my research character, [solo improvistational performance with a 'Waiting for Godot' like character using artifacts concealed in a suitcase to tell stories of displacement] moving through space silently 'lugging' my suitcase as if it were my heart, my home, the ship of my arrival/departure and then manipulated the artifact within - an antique book, balancing it on the back of my neck, fingering the onion skin pages upside down , burying my face in the crease of its musty covers. It became a passport, the torah, a photo album. A scholar who witnessed this particular performance at a conference overseas approached me trembling. "I come from a family of holocaust survivors - you have just uncovered my family's story which has not been allowed to see the light of day. I will now return home and encourage our words to penetrate space - you have somehow given me the permission to do this."

Oh the honour of allowing stories to run through me like a blood stream which I extract from and allow to be embodied by another. A transfusion of meaning; embodied and assimilated within a new host of memories.

It was not my story - this LUG.

It was not his story.

It was a shared story.

I realize now, as I try to articulate what is distinctive to Embodied Poetic Narrative, that it is these shifting axis points that become critical in the manipulation of narrative as well as that of objects/artifacts and these shifts are critical to the story telling process. I am not reading the book - I am balancing it on the back of my neck. I am interested in disrupting the patterns of object/narrative by abstracting the handling of the objects, which in turn introduces new information within a story. To work with the poetics of the object, stripping it of preconceived notions of its meaning, emptying the container, peeling away the identifiers.

Marjorie Siegal (1995) speaks of this departure from privileging conventional containers of meaning making such as text and celebrates this shift from transmission of information in the learning space or as Freire (as cited in Siegal) would term, the *banking system*, claiming that students now need more than words for an optimum learning experience. Siegel attends to this by a process sourced through a semiotic concept of transferring meaning from one sign system to another - *transmediation* - which "highlights and intensifies the generative nature of meaning-making" (p. 455), calling upon the learner to construct a poetic syntax. These are dynamic spaces of learning where meanings are collectively constructed and connections are invited to emerge. In this way, Siegel writes of the traps within verbocentricity in the same way that Conquergood writes about the tyranny of textocentrism.

Shapiro (2008), voiced in both Woman's Studies and Dance Education, writes of dance as serving an important role in challenging one to imagine new formations of self in relation to the world. She claims that dance connects mind and body allowing one to re chart oneself into time and space.

Story #2: Shifting Leverages, Re-centering Self

I am conducting a workshop for a group of adults with mixed abilities. I am showing them how to listen kinesthetically to the 'other' by facing their partner, joining their hands and leaning back. They begin to play with a shared fulcrum, which is constantly travelling as they shift their weight to respond to or provoke each other. My partner has cerebral palsy and the axis in her body is ever changing - joining hands, I embark upon a dance I had never experienced - the level of deep listening entailed in navigating this ever shifting fulcrum in this partnership was astounding. It was like trying to catch a butterfly in a dark room.

What happens when our body centre shifts? - new leverages are created as we move with an object in foreign paths and if these shifts become constant then both images by association and these shifting leverages result in a re centering of oneself in relation to the world. This in turn brings new information to the same familiar body, objects, and history. This cannot be considered re-imagining oneself but moreover allows a new understanding of that which is intoned or tacit. Heathcote (1984) proposes that a shift in value occurs which balances fact constituted knowledge with meaning-making processes driven by individual curiosities and mindfulness.

Gallagher (2001), located in Drama Education and Pedagogy, invites a playful collective imagining of a story and calls attention to remembered histories while embracing current realities. Within this work, Gallagher begins to blur the distinction between non fiction and fiction as the players begin to recognize themselves in the stories and consequently begin to understand how their notions of self are manifest within a particular social construct.

Dorothy Heathcote (1984), considered one of the most important scholars in Drama Education, speaks of this collapse of time, space and distinction of consequence, affording us the opportunity to actually *see* the world opposed to merely recognizing it. To understand our location rather than merely accept it or as Mohanty (2003), Feminist Studies scholar writes, corporeality is a vessel containing the forces of

137

cultural discourses and must be recognized and understood within both *practices* and *strategies* not just within theories.

Story #3: Fractured Signifiers

I am working with a counselor/theater director who is also interested in exploring unconventional ways of developing script. He has brought a hockey stick as an emblem of self within a particular period in his life. He begins his story holding the stick with ease; an extension of his body - he sweeps around making imaginary slap shots on goals, and with power and control, he speaks of his father. He is telling me what he knows, I, however, am more interested in what he doesn't know, the space where discovery lives. I ask him to work with the stick, using any part of his body except his hands. The signifier becomes fractured as he begins to work with the properties of the stick. The stick brings another movement to his body and tone to his voice. I begin to hear another side of the same story - what was once power and control is transformed to a gentle inquiry and tender curiosity. With this comes a concert of emotions playing back and forth and inviting the participant into a place of unknowing; a place of discovery...

The fracturing of the signifier causes a rupture in the triangulation of story/action/object and allows new understandings to seep in. This is how the poetic comes into the object in relation to narrative, affording an entirely new reading. As a dancer I am constantly reading the world through movement and reading movement as sentences of meaning grammared and punctuated with all the nuances of shifting weight, leverages, and centers. We re-story ourselves in each telling and the world in turn stories us.

Shapiro invites the possibility of re-charting ourselves into time and space, Conquergood promotes a 'cutting across the map' of fact based knowledges, and Victor Shklovsky (as cited in Heathcote) writes of "ostraneine" or "that of making strange" (p. 127) - disrupting hegemonic 'educational' structures. This is the powerful juncture where I am left with suitcase in hand gazing at many intersecting tracks of theories and practices. In fact, literally, I have a suitcase in hand, donning my over-size overcoat and hat; as I perform my way through my research. I work within a triangulation of remembered stories, artifacts and movement. Embodied stories merge movement and words, and this fusion/collision invites the ambiguity of a location between accuracy, recollection, and resonance. These are stories of displace-ment, stories where fact and fiction meet like a horizon; continuous, fluid and without fixity. Some practitioners call this imagined stories - stories of the imagination - somehow, I say no.

I think that the imagination is a place where creative construction occurs and it is external to the swamps that hold our secrets. I visualize the imagination as a utopic location outside of the body, which we tether our ideas to and consequently gain a buoyancy of self. On the contrary, the silenced stories that exist and have existed through our lived experiences, lay far below, entangled in the swamps of ourselves, squinting with the mere mention of possible lightness of being. Imagine - if I were a therapist I would lower myself down into the swamp and we would conjure the escape plan together, but therapist, I am not...If I was merely interested in imaginative play I would suggest an effervescent location of new stories, constructed identities and playful renderings of self. However, I am interested in an intersticial space, a hybrid zone that synthesizes the best from all of these locations. I am curious to know if it is possible to 'un silence' the voice, to tell the stories that have not been named, but with craft and refinement honour the grace of time/distance and the aesthetics of selectivity. I am asking - can these stories be re configured and yet remain authentic? 'Handled' and yet bare? Uncovered and polished rather than decorated and accessorized?

I have outlined a few vibrant methods of using the body as a site for progressive and active problemetization and possible re articulation of self in relation to cultural displacement. I find myself gratefully flanked by the courage, vitality and clarity of a few of these scholars within this community of practice as I forge ahead articulating my particular corner - Embodied Poetic Narrative.

REFERENCES

Conquergood, D. (2002). Performance studies: Interventions and radical research. *The Drama Review, 46*, 145–156.

Gallagher, K. (2001). *Drama education in the lives of girls.* Toronto, Ontario: University of Toronto Press.

Heathcote, D. (1984). Material for significance. In D. Heathcote [L. Johnson & C. O' Neill (Eds.)] *Collected writings on education and drama* (pp. 114–137). Evanston, IL: Northwestern University Press.

Medina, C. (2005). *Critical performative literacies: Intersections among identities, social imaginations and discourses.* 55th Yearbook of the National Reading Conference.

Mohanty, C. T. (2003). *Feminism without borders: Decolonizing theory, practicing solidarity.* London, UK: Duke University Press.

Shapiro, S. B. (Ed.). (2008). *Dance in a world of change.* Champaign, IL: Human Kinetics.

Siegel, M. (1995). More than words: The power of transmediation for learning. *Canadian Journal of Education, 20*(4), 450–475.

Kathryn Ricketts, PhD candidate, S.F.U. Vancouver, Canada is researching and articulating Embodied Poetic Narratives as a means towards cultivating dynamic and empowering educative spaces.

DAN URIAN

23. DRAMA IN EDUCATION AS A THEATRE REPERTOIRE

Keywords: repertoire, theatrical genre, democracy, negotiating meaning

There have been a great many expectations from educational drama, particularly from the second half of the 20th century on, from the moment that it succeeded in freeing itself from the status of merely serving as a tool to teach the English language. Beginning from the 1950s, educational drama was seen as a potential universal panacea in education and instruction. An exaggerated expectation? Possibly. But such hopes are undoubtedly no different from similar hopes held for other means and methods of teaching such as instructional television, computers and audio-visual tools.

Educational drama has no established or agreed theory. Teachers and theoreticians (mainly teachers who have become theoreticians), define in various - even contrasting - ways, its aims, desired contents and strategies. Educational drama has tended to suffer in each generation from the "leading personality" syndrome, in which every generation has established an Oedipal relationship with the teacher whose footsteps it follows and whom it critiques. The increasing number of approaches is also attested to by the multiplicity of names, which are not necessarily all directed at the same purpose, such as "creative drama", "children's drama", "drama in schools" and "development through drama"".

Initially, these were plays for children or youth written to be performed as "classroom drama", and many references to them can be found, dating from when the educational system first began to keep records. Ken Robinson notes: "The use of drama in schools goes back as far as schooling itself." (Robinson, 1980, p. 141). One such example is *Wilhelm Meister*, an "autobiography" of Johann Wolfgang Goethe, who made the transition from puppet theatre to theatre, to the sorrow of his father, who saw the whole thing as a waste of time. Drama has also been an important part of the literature curriculum in many countries. However, recognition of drama as an active educational field, distinct and unique, only began in the 1940s, with Peter Slade and "child drama", aimed at an educational concept with the child at its centre. "Development through drama" was the next step, in which a dramatic program began to coalesce, aimed at assisting and supporting development of the child. This approach structured dramatic creativity as an organized process, beginning with relaxation techniques and ending in improvisation of dramatic situations (Way, 1973). In the 1970s attention was diverted by Gavin Bolton and Dorothy Heathcote, from the "child at the centre" concept back to the 1920's approach of Harriet Finlay-Johnson, who had attempted to teach many subjects by

S. Schonmann (ed.), Key Concepts in Theatre/Drama Education, 141–145.

means of dramatic activity (Bolton, 1984, 11–3). From the 1990s on one can discern a move back towards the consideration of educational drama, which is also making its return in productions of school plays. The change, which has been noted by David Hornbrook, reveals a compromise between the two approaches: that which emphasizes the emotional nature of the dramatic undertaking and its contribution to the emotional development of those who attempt it; and that which sees educational drama as a tool for teaching various subjects, or even as a cognitive channel for innovative thought and studies.

The literature engaging with the theory of educational drama has three main components:

1. The majority of theoreticians relate to those who came before them, and agree in general with their approach while arguing over certain points (Hornbrook, 1985, 346–58).
2. The majority also seek some point of theoretical support: Slade bases his approach on progressive theories in education; Brian Way supports his contentions with developmental psychology; Bolton seeks a foundation in the theories of Lev Vygotsky and others; Hornbrook is influenced by cultural theories and frequently cites Roland Barthes, Clifford Geertz and Pierre Bourdieu.
3. The majority of publications on educational drama feature a full or partial description of practical experience. These descriptions are generally used to illustrate and reinforce the theoretical claims. Most of these texts are not perceived as important in themselves, and certainly not related to as theatrical activities, but as examples of recommended activity or cited to illustrate a particular contention.

While Slade, Way, Heathcote, Bolton and Hornbrook all offer different approaches to educational drama, this does not necessitate following one to the exclusion of all else. Quite the opposite. Each of them offers a repertoire of dramatic activity which may suit a teacher for a particular class (Fleming, 1995, p. 27). The contextual adoption of a choice of different approaches and texts, or combinations, is the teacher's concern. The *repertoire* of exercises, activities and plays is therefore of great importance, constituting a rich and varied source of possibilities.

The question of a theatre's repertoire contents, i.e. what can be considered a theatrical text, is bound up with the attitude to "high" culture and "popular" or "fringe" culture. In general, theatre research tends to deal with theatre as "high" culture. This approach usually includes the plays staged by the public [establishment] theatres, but does not touch upon the "fringe" plays - fringe theatre, stand-up comedy, commercial theatre, musicals, entertainment shows, community theatre, educational theatre, and appearances by religious preachers as performers. In recent decades, there has been a move, albeit as yet insignificant, from discussion of the "professional" theatre towards an examination of non-canonical and non-mainstream plays. (Schechner, 1993).

I believe educational drama to be a *theatrical genre*. This follows the increasing tendency in contemporary theatrical thinking (particularly performance) to expand the repertoire of "suitable" texts. These now include texts only given legitimacy in the 1980s, such as performances by community theatres. Plays or shows created in schools are still not considered worthy of theatrical discussion. Nonetheless, the school play, when staged professionally, can indeed be the subject of such discourse. The two following examples illustrate the possible relationship that can obtain between educational drama and the theatre repertoire. The first is a teaching experience of the subject of democracy and the second is a youth play, *Clouds over Samaria*, on the conflict between Jews and Palestinians.

These are two examples of a dramatic activity that can be performed anew within different theatrical frameworks. A detailed study of these examples can offer a basis for changes within such frameworks, just as a study of a production that has won great acclaim and documentation provides a basis for additional theatrical interpretations.

Bolton first visited Israel in 1984, election year, in which Meir Kahane and his Kach party (a radical fascist movement) were elected to the Israeli parliament. The Israeli Ministry of Education and other bodies, fearing that Israeli democracy was becoming endangered, set in motion a great many study programs relating to the subject of democracy. However, while many of these programs were well-written and fascinating indeed, I believe that they all had the same problem in common: they missed the point! The designers of these programs forgot - or perhaps simply failed to take their target audience of students sufficiently into account - the simple question: How does it concern me? Why should I study the composition of the Israeli parliament? Or the role of the High Court? These programs simply provided information, but without finding a way to motivate the students to *want* to study the issue of democracy.

Bolton provided an answer to stimulating an interest in democracy by providing an exercise for Israeli drama teachers using a dramatic text which he himself had written and in which he participated. I "borrowed" this text and was thus able to experience it for myself many times later on with my students. Bolton's central situation was that of a visit to a mental hospital, which was in effect a prison in a totalitarian state. The activity divided the class into a number of groups, creating "families": a son who was an inmate, warders, and visitors (family members) who want to get a message through to the prisoner, while the warders do not allow it. Several of the participants were left shocked by the event. Within a short period of time they had experienced life in a totalitarian state.

Using such an exercise as a starting point for a study program on the subject of education for democracy gives the program a far greater chance of success. Such activity teaches the students, who undergo the experience of life in a totalitarian state, that the alternative to democracy is truly frightening. In this way *personal* motivation to study the subject of democracy is achieved, as well as an understanding of the tools of government which enable preservation of freedom of the individual.

David Steinberg has worked for six years in a Tel Aviv high school as coordinator for the theatre courses. Steinberg has a professional approach to teaching theatre and he plans the instruction in such a way as to achieve professional results. He customarily writes the end-of-year play himself, as the culminating project of the course. During the writing and editing, Steinberg involves his students in the process. Because the plays are political in nature, the accompanying discussions fuel the work and also help to balance somewhat his own personal political stance, which does not always reflect that of all his students. This is a process which O'Toole termed "negotiating meaning". (O'Toole, 1992, pp. 223–227). Steinberg raises issues which are subject to pointed ideological and political controversy in Israel. He himself holds radical views ("left-wing" in the Israeli political jargon); while some of his students take an opposite position. The writing, editing and rehearsals of the play constitute a process of discussion and clarification of all these issues.

The second example is that of my own school's "professional" theatre performance, which departs from the repertoire of dramatic activities and integrates easily into the theatrical repertoire.

Clouds over Samaria (1994) is about the peace agreements with the Palestinians, also known as the Oslo accords. The play's world is populated with representatives of most of the groups involved in the political procedures: religious settlers from the occupied territories, local Palestinians and those who have dispersed elsewhere, and Israelis from areas bordering the Green Line (Israeli border prior to 1967) who object to the settlements. The debate which accompanied the writing, editing and directing of the play mitigated the perspective of all the participants, as expressed in the play itself. The settlers in the play included those who were ready for a business partnership with the Palestinians; among the Palestinians were fighters willing to lay down their weapons; and the Israelis bordering the Green Line included those who understood both the plight of the settlers and the desire of the Palestinians for independence. Nevertheless, this was not an optimistic text fostering the illusion of a swift and easy solution, such as the "co-existence" plays staged in Israel in the 1970s. (Urian, 1997, pp. 26–27). The play ends in the murder of the rebellious Palestinian, who has laid down his weapon, by other Palestinians who object to conciliation. This murder puts an end, at least on stage, to any chance of peace.

The play was staged by high-school students; amateurs whose theatrical training is incomplete. The play's reception was nonetheless extraordinary, interesting and instructive. It was taken up by a theatre producer who enabled its production at the Festival of Experimental Theatre in Akko. The framework of the Akko festival conferred the status of "worthy" upon the play. The Educational Television network filmed the play and broadcast it following signing of the Oslo accords between Israel and the Palestinians, accompanying it with a study program dealing with the peace process. *Clouds over Samaria* is an interesting example of a working process which refutes any conciliation that denies or diminishes the ideological-educational influence of the theatre. Throughout the run of the play a discussion took place between the radical-left-wing playwright-director and his class of youngsters, some of whom held right-wing views, and others of whom were totally indifferent to political matters. A concomitant study of the play and of the views initially held by the students, revealed important changes in perspective experienced by the young actors.

The stock of interesting dramatic texts which could be transferred from teacher to teacher, or from one school drama director to another, is not a particularly large one. This is hardly surprising. The total number of interesting and important plays within the entire world theatrical repertoire is also not large; and recent years have shown an increasingly restricted choice of dramatic texts. Writing successful drama requires great talent. Just as the theatre has a repertoire of "successful" plays, so too does educational drama possess such a repertoire; but one which still needs documenting.

The possible tension between the "contextuality" of these texts and their possible influence in the area of "inter-textuality" (Kershaw, 1992, pp. 246–251) dissolves when, for example, a play originating in Israel is staged in Ireland. Plays about the Israeli-Palestinian dispute, such as *Clouds over Samaria*, or about other conflicts between different groups, may, following adaptation, prove to be equally suitable for many other countries and societies, even for those whose disputes may not be quite as severe or as violent as the Israeli-Palestinian one. And the opposite is also true. A Shakespearean play such as *Macbeth*, with the craving for power at its centre, is still a very realistic play in many countries.

REFERENCES

Bolton, G. (1984). *Drama as education*. Burnt Mill, Harlow, Essex, UK: Longman.

Fleming, M. (1995). *Starting drama teaching*. London: David Fulton Publishers.

Hornbrook, D. (1985). Drama, education and the politics of change: Part one. *New Theatre Quarterly, 1*(4), 346–358.

Kershaw, B. (1992). *The politics of performance*. London: Routledge.

O'Toole, J. (1992). *Process of drama*. London: Routledge.

Robinson, K. (1980). Drama, theatre and social reality. In K. Robinson (Ed.), *Exploring theatre and education* (pp. 141–175). London: Heinemann.

Schechner, R. (1993). *The future of ritual: Writings on culture and performance* (Chapter 3 - The Street is the Stage pp. 45–93). London: Routledge.

Urian, D. (1997). *The Arab in Israeli drama and theatre* (N. Paz, Trans.). London: Routledge, Harwood Academic.

Way, B. (1973). *Development through drama*. Atlantics Highlands, NJ: Humanities Press.

Dan Urian *is Associate Professor in the Theatre Department at Tel Aviv University. His research interests are Sociology of the Theatre, Drama in Education, Israeli Theatre and Television Drama.*

CAROLE MILLER AND JULIANA SAXTON

24. STORY DRAMA STRUCTURES

'Recipes' for Success

Keywords: classroom drama, pedagogy, language arts, embodied learning, narrative

Twenty-five years ago, drama innovator Gavin Bolton (1984) recognised the power of embodied narrative when he argued for placing drama at the centre of the curriculum. Rather than seeing literacy practices as discrete competencies unconnected to students' lives outside school, Bolton, together with Dorothy Heathcote (2003), uses drama to cross disciplines and subject areas. They create learning contexts in which students use their literacy skills in multi-modalities immersed in situations that demand their participation. It is this "apprenticeship into the very specific forms of [social] languages and literacies represented inside and outside the classroom" (Hawkins, 2004, p. 17) that makes drama such a rich pedagogy.

Our own work in drama and theatre education has been steeped in conversation about pedagogy and how we can assist in the development of teachers and learners. No matter what or whom we are teaching, drama is always an integral component of our classroom practice; story drama structures evolved out of that need to help pre-service teachers to become confident and competent users of drama across the curriculum. In story drama structures, there are two fictional worlds, the one provided by the story text and the one created by the drama participants who "play" within the context of that story and who reframe those worlds to reflect their own thoughts and actions. The bridge between the fictional world and the real world of the students' everyday experiences is built through the variety of strategies, themselves bridges of access, as they only work when they are experienced, shared and undertaken by the whole class.

According to David Booth (2005), a *story drama* is "improvised role play stimulated by a story" (p. 8). *Dramatic structure* refers to a narrative in which the whole may be divided into parts. In *story drama structures* (Miller & Saxton, 2004), we use the improvisational nature of classroom drama allied to a narrative. That narrative, for our work, is drawn from children's picture books where the illustrations often play a significant means of engaging with the text.

Childrens' picture books are a part of the language arts program from early years through to teacher education programs and so young teachers are familiar with and comfortable using them in the classroom. Drama, on the other hand, is frequently a mandated component of the curriculum but not an area with which many teachers are experienced. Marrying the dis-ease of drama with the comfort

S. Schonmann (ed.), Key Concepts in Theatre/Drama Education, 147–151.

of a known curriculum component was a natural approach. The structures serve teachers as complete frameworks of organization and are laid out as a series of parts (or activities) that provide teachers with specific directions as to the grouping, the strategy, the administration (requirements) and the focus. The teacher "talk" that follows serves as the facilitation of the strategy and is written out in action language: direct speech that will result in student action. Fundamental to each activity are questions and reflection. The former engenders wider thinking and opportunities for personal and generalized application, the latter for considering what has happened in the action. At the meaning level they serve to uncover the possibilities of where to go next. One of the challenges for effective drama is building coherence achieved through the linking of strategies. In story drama structures, the links are clearly demonstrated, often through teacher narration, moving the story forward while deepening meaning ("In the next bit of work, you will need to hold on to those new thoughts and perspectives to help you make some important decisions.") The initial suggestion of Key Question and Statements offers possible themes and opportunities to enable reflection that moves from the particulars of the story to the more universal issues that the story addresses.

Through the use of drama and picture books, our pre-service teachers begin to understand how the structures provide a powerful means of integrating curriculum as each story acts as a lens into the human condition whether it be historical, social or personal. Stories that serve as the contexts for drama structures should connect in some way both to mandated curriculum and the "hidden" curriculum of social and cultural learning that Howard Gardner (1999) cites as a most significant part of a curriculum (p. 113). Good stories, writes Katherine Paterson, stretch children's imaginations and "help them make sense of their own lives," while at the same time, "encourag[ing] them to reach out toward people whose lives are quite different from their own" (Ewing, Miller, & Saxton, 2008, p. 122).

To illustrate, here are the introductory notes and initial three activities from "Now, write!" a story drama structure based on *The Composition*, written by Antonio Skármeta and illustrated by Alphonso Ruano.

Why Did We Choose this Story?

− This is adult-themed story told from the perspective of a child.
− The story personalizes the struggle that all oppressed people experience under a dictatorship.
− By setting the story in another country and another culture, the story provides the distance that allows us examine issues of bullying.
− The story provides an interdisciplinary approach to social studies and the hidden curriculum of ethical behaviour.
− The illustrations provide rich opportunities for interpretation and perspective-taking. There is a great deal of non-verbal text to be read and many spaces for the imagination to roam.
− *The Composition* was the winner of the Américus Book Award and the Jane Adams Award for the best picture book promoting peace and social justice.

Key Understandings and Questions:

- There are many ways to use power for control.
- When does it become important to get involved?
- How is it that dictatorships are able to thrive?
- What drives the decision to take a stand?
- What causes someone to remain a bystander?

---

1. What Pedro wrote   *2 minutes*

Grouping:	**Whole class**
Strategy:	**Reading aloud**
Administration:	**A copy of Pedro's composition**
Focus:	**To enter the story**

Teacher: The story we are going to be working with today takes place many thousands of miles away from where we live and our experiences. Yet it is about things with which we are all familiar. I'd like you to listen carefully to a short excerpt. Its words are the ones out of which we will begin our work

Teacher reads Pedro's composition on the second last page of the text.

Teacher: Would it be helpful if I read it again?
Teacher responds accordingly.

---

2. Seeing the world that Pedro inhabits   *10 minutes*

Grouping:	**The size of the groups depends upon the group skills of your students; with senior students use 4 groups; with younger students use 6 groups.**
Strategy:	**Tableaux**
Administration:	**One copy of the composition per group**
Focus:	**To see the world that Pedro inhabits**

Teacher: Please get into groups of equal numbers. There will be two groups of As and two groups of Bs [and two groups of Cs].

                    Each group will be creating a tableau based on Pedro's composition. Each group will have a partner group that will be using the same instructions. The tasks are going to require you to work with great imagination because you will be using your skills of interpretation.

                    Each group will present their interpretation through a still picture or tableau.

                    Everyone must be in the tableau and it should incorporate as many ideas as you can. Some of those ideas may seem contradictory. In drama, often that is where we learn the most.

Teacher: Both group As, please stand. From the words of Pedro's composition, what does his writing tell you about his life at home with his family? Using everyone, create a tableau of how this family spends time together.

Both group Bs, please stand. What does Pedro's writing tell you about his school and school culture? Your tableau will show what kind of classroom we would see.

[Both group Cs, please stand. What does Pedro's composition tell you about the kinds of teachers who would give this assignment? What might we see that would tell us something about those teachers?]

For older students or larger classes, you may substitute/include,

Both group Ds, please stand. In what kind of a society might Pedro's story take place? What words would you use to describe that society and how would you depict them in a tableau?

Teacher: You have three minutes to generate your ideas and explore them. Try not to spend a lot of time talking. Get up on your feet as soon as you can because that is a good way to stimulate your thinking.

Before moving on to the next strategy, it is helpful to rehearse the tableaux to make sure that the students are clear about what they are depicting, as the next strategy requires that they hold on to their ideas while adding to them in another way.

Teacher: Let's just have a little rehearsal. Everyone ready? I am going to count down from three and by the end you should be in your tableau. Hold it for a count of three and, on the last count of three, slowly relax. [They do]

Quickly make any adjustments. [They do]

Keep those ideas in mind, as they are important to helping us understand Pedro's life more fully.

Helen Nicholson (2008) tells us that "the combination of action and reflection that characterizes the most inventive teaching encourages students to discover how meanings are made through the playfulness of theatre making" (p. 108) but that "playfulness" is exactly what it is that makes theatre so threatening for those teachers without experience in it. How, then, to provide access to theatre-making experiences? Novice cooks have turned to recipe books for as long as they have been published and, for young brides, the cookbook was a treasured wedding gift. It allowed us to see what the dish would look like, what we needed to buy at the grocery store, how much time we would require, and so on; it gave us the confidence to go beyond scrambled eggs. It also, and this is important, gave us the confidence to experiment with recipes we had already conquered and, upon occasion, to invent something new. In any profession, we rely on clear guidelines to give us the way to begin and, in our experience, our student teachers and generalist teachers need that kind of support.

There has long been a concern with "teacher scripts"—and for good reasons—but as tightly structured as the drama is for the teacher, it is an open structure for the students, inviting them to become co-creators in their own version of the story. Student responses are not a part of the structure because the context of the story determines their responses and are always dependent on the experiences they bring with them to the drama. Holden (1994) points out that, "[a]s often as we do the 'same' drama, every drama is different, regardless of whether the same stimulus and/ or starting point are used each time. Each drama is created by a particular group, in a particular school, at a particular time" (p. 9). After ten years of piloting, feedback has been strongly positive, not only from our teachers who share their students' favourite stories with their own story drama structures but, also, from our colleagues in the arts and language arts who tell us that they are using the structures as teaching resources.

In drama, we have the opportunity to draw our students' attention to what they are listening to with their eyes and seeing with their ears—that is the dramatic action: the accumulation of movement and meanings; the action that lies underneath the words and the doing. Stimulated by a feeling engagement and entertained by curiosity, students working in a story drama structure find themselves practicing their selves in new roles and in new lights in a possible world suggested by the story but owned and operated by them.

REFERENCES

Bolton, G. (1984). *Drama as education: An argument for placing drama at the centre of the curriculum.* Essex, UK: Longman.

Bolton, G. (2003). *Dorothy Heathcote's story: The biography of a remarkable drama teacher.* Staffordshire, UK: Trentham Books.

Booth, D. (2005). *Story drama: Creating stories through role-playing, improvising and reading aloud.* Markham, ON: Pembroke.

Ewing, R., Miller, C., & Saxton, J. (2008). Drama and contemporary picture books in the middle years. In M. Anderson, J. Hughes, & J. Manuel (Eds.), *Drama and English teaching: Imagination, action and engagement* (pp. 121–135). Sydney, NSW: Oxford.

Gardner, H. (1999). *The disciplined mind: What all students should understand.* New York: Simon & Schuster.

Hawkins, M. R. (2004). Researching English language and literacy development in schools. *Educational Researcher*, 33(3), 14–25.

Holden, J. (1994). Fear of flying. *Broadsheet:* The Journal for Drama in Education, 10(3), 2–12.

Miller, C., & Saxton, J. (2004). *Into the story: Language in action through drama.* Portsmouth, NH: Heinemann.

Nicholson, H. (2008). Narrative, drama and the English classroom. In M. Anderson, J. Hughes, & J. Manuel (Eds.), *Drama and English teaching: Imagination, action and engagement* (pp. 104–120). Sydney, NSW, Australia: Oxford.

Carole Miller, Associate Professor in the Department of Curriculum & Instruction, Faculty of Education, University of Victoria; internationally recognized scholar/ practitioner and writer.

Juliana Saxton, Professor Emeritus, Department of Theatre, University of Victoria; scholar//practitioner; author of Applied Theatre: International Case Studies and Challenges for Practice.

HELI AALTONEN

25. SELKIE STORIES AS AN EXAMPLE OF ECOSOPHICAL STORYTELLING

Keywords: storytelling, ecology, ecosophical storytelling, sustainable development, selkie stories

I will first briefly present the connection between storytelling and ecology. Then I will suggest that the writings of Raymond Williams, Arne Naess and Suzanne Langer offer valuable theoretical foundations for this theme. Thirdly, I will discuss selkie/ seal people stories as an example of ecosophical storytelling, where the human-animal relationship is explored. I propose that the main focus in ecosophical story-telling is to bridge gaps between humans and other life forms by telling connecting stories, which awaken feelings and make a transformational change in the human—non-human/environment relationship by challenging humans' structures of feeling. According to Anthony Nanson (2005, pp. 25–26), change occurs by creating a sense of connection: "an emotional investment in the locality where the storytelling takes place, so that people will care what happens to it." This emotional investment is created by working with the symbols of feeling, arts, and on this occasion, oral storytelling.

STORYTELLING REVIVAL

Storytelling is truly interactive, a real time mode of communication which reaches small audiences, local communities. Before scripted communication modes, which began in 3100 BC, storytelling has been the only mode of communication linking individuals to the community and to the environment. Stories are narratives, which Donald Smith, leader of the Scottish Storytelling Centre, defines as follows:

> Narrative is a way of ordering our experience and understanding: a follows b follows c, though somehow d may be fitted in as well. The story involves active agents, which will and desire and do, as well as the world of nature and impersonal forces or circumstances which may limit or produce action. The narrative does not convey random discrete units of experience but a pattern that connects people, events and places. There is a sequence of linked happenings through time. (Smith, 2001, p. 1)

Other life forms are not able to argue with humans about story structures, plots or content of stories, because narrative thinking is unique to humans; and yet narratives are embodied within life forms, the changing of seasons, the lay of the land. Storytelling has a significant educational value, because it unlocks a world of

S. Schonmann (ed.), Key Concepts in Theatre/Drama Education, 153–158.

metaphors and imagination. Fictive stories open spaces for reflection, abstract thinking, and offer us a narrative distance to make meaning of real life events. Fairytales and myths are like theoretical perspectives which we can use to explore lived experiences.

Human communication modes developed from scripts to print, through wired electronics to wireless electronics and today, in many cases, digital (Rantanen, 2005, p. 26). This global media development in multiple modes of human communication caused many people in the 1960s to ask whose stories are being told, and is one of the key reasons that a counter-cultural storytelling revival movement started in that time. The emergence of counter-cultural storytelling may be described as a movement from global to local and the intention, in many cases, has been to empower people to find their own stories, create communities and re- construct relationships to their own, personal lived experiences in a specific culture-historical location (Zipes, 1995; 2004).

A union between storytelling and ecology may take place in many different contexts. Michael Wilson (2006, p. 9) connects different forms of storytelling in his model called "the performance continuum." On the one side of the continuum are characteristics for conversation; low intensity, informal, subconscious, low risk and low rewards. On the other side are characteristics for cultural performance; high intensity, formal, conscious, high risk and high rewards. In this way he links storytelling and theatrical performance, and does not want to claim that they are divided from each other. Canonized traditional fairytales offer raw material to re-construct new stories and interpretations around lived experiences and up-dated scientific facts about living nature and other species.

ECOLOGICAL ACTIVISM, GLOBAL CITIZENSHIP AND EDUCATION FOR SUSTAINABLE FUTURE

When the first satellite photographs of the planet Earth were sent fifty years ago from the US satellite Explorer 6, our way of perception changed profoundly. Planet Earth was seen for the first time from a distance. Seeing the blue, living Globe in limitless space made people worry about the material limits of the Earth. The starting point of ecological activism is tightly connected with space exploration and global media development. Stories about our relation to home life are now in transition as we witness the white polar areas getting smaller and smaller, and environmental destruction has become visible in satellite photographs.

The word ecology is derived from the Greek –oikos, meaning 'household' and –logia, meaning 'study of.' According to Arne Næss (1991, p. 36), ecology can be explained as "the interdisciplinary scientific study of the living conditions of organisms in interaction with each other and with the surroundings, organic as well as inorganic."

At the moment there is an urgent need to find effective methods for promoting environmental education and sustainable development, because it seems that the facts of environmental reports alone do not cause people to change their way of living. The Grand Narrative of Human Rights needs to be updated with situated, site-specific connecting stories where sustainable development, the values of biological diversity and ecological limits of human activity are taken seriously. Such stories are necessarily linked with the concepts of 'ecological', 'global' and 'environmental citizenship.' Environmental citizenship, according to James Connelly (2006, p. 63), is "characterized not by rights but by the self-imposed duties of the citizen."

I will now briefly present three different philosophical foundations which are interrelated with each other and illuminate the key concept behind ecosophical storytelling.

PHILOSOPHICAL BASIS OF ECOSOPHICAL STORYTELLING

The concept 'ecosophical storytelling' is inspired by Arne Næss' (1991) deep eco-logical thinking. Næss (1991, p. 35–67) explores different philosophical approaches to studying ecology. He explains that ecosophy is a position of philosophy that concentrates on human relations to nature. According to Næss, "ecosophy becomes *a philosophical world-view or system inspired by the conditions of life in the eco-sphere*" (1991, p. 38). All is related to everything and from that it follows that in ecosophical thinking humans, plants and animals are "intimately interconnected" (ibid.) to each other.

In reality, many people feel themselves disconnected and lost. The environmental reports demand urgent action to arrest climate change, but governmental and inter-national decisions are made following the dominant narrative called 'economic progress.' Global media which generally represent the ideology of global companies do not have an ecosophical world view. Political and economic decision makers behave as if there were no material limits on this globe.

'Structure of feeling' is a concept invented by cultural materialist Raymond Williams (2001/1977). According to Williams, the structures of feeling, our social past, ideology, world view and cultural prejudices, as well as language use, have been constructed through social interaction and influenced by material elements such as the environment we live in and/or other species we encounter. This means that language use and the stories we tell about our relationship to nature and the animals around us may be influenced by our social past and are not accurate any more.

Connecting, life nurturing stories need to be told in order to change humans' relational separation from other life forms. The basic elements of myth are called 'life symbols' by Susanne Langer (1942/1996, p. 171). Myths are archaic and the symbols of myths are trans-cultural. Myth and fairytale telling reaches beyond the rational, realistic universe, and guides us to navigate into the unknown, mysterious territories of unconsciousness and sources of life and death. Langer points out that art is a language of feelings. Beautiful connecting stories touch feelings and awaken emotional investment.

Jack Zipes (2004, p. 3) points out "the utopian tendency of storytelling: turning the world upside down." He cites the philosopher Ernst Bloch, who argues that all art "contains images of hope" (ibid.). Storytelling is a way to re-build bridges between individuals and community from individuals to community and on that bridge the structures of feeling about animals and environment are re-constructed and re-evaluated.

TELLING SEAL PEOPLE STORIES IN THE SCOTTISH SEABIRD CENTRE

One example of ecosophical storytelling is my own storytelling experience with seal people stories. The theoretical foundation of Williams, Næss and Langer is exemplified here.

In Arctic areas and the northern hemisphere seals and humans have a long shared history and seals have been essential to all human existence in these areas. Climate and marine ecological changes and human hunting of the seals has had drastic influences on seal populations. During the last 60 years, 90% of the oceans' seal populations have disappeared. Nowadays, the seal is an illuminating symbol for the ecological activist movement. It is a truly global citizen and crosses national borders. Seals cannot change their breeding places to relocate to territories where they are protected.

In the Scottish Seabird Centre it has been possible to celebrate the return of grey seals every autumn. They come to the Isle of May to breed. On the island, there are 'live streaming web cameras,' and people visiting the Seabird Centre can see the seal mothers with their pups from a close distance. They become connected with real seals in the seals' own environment without disturbing them. The visitors are connected on a material level to the animals, which is essential in Williams' theory of structures of feelings.

At the Scottish Seabird Centre, I told the seal people stories of Duncan Williamson (1992) to the visitors of the Centre. Seal people or 'selkie' stories are known among the Gaelic speaking people on the Scottish and Irish islands, as well as in Iceland and Faroe Islands. Tom Muir clarifies the meaning of selkies in the Orkney folklore:

> It was thought that seals, called selkies in Orkney, had the power to take human form during certain times of the tide. There were two different stories about how selkie folk came into being. One was that they were angels that had been cast out of heaven for some unknown offence. The crime was not so bad as to see them being sent to hell, but they were forced to live as seals in the sea. The other version is that they were the souls of the people who had drowned. Some said that it was only suicides who turned into seals. Both stories agree that they had the power to throw away their skin and dance in human form at certain times of the tide. The selkie folk were thought to be very lovely looking, hence the young man's desire to carry away the selkie girl as his bride. (Muir, 1998, p. XV)

John M. MacAulay (1998) suggests that these stories may have a connection with the Sea-Sami people who were probably ocean paddlers who had travelled a long way from the Norwegian coasts in kayaks covered with seal skins. In selkie stories metamorphosis functions as a characteristic theme. Selkie stories affect on the deep level. They are healing with life power and energy. At the same time, there is an aspect of grief and loss. It is not so easy to change and transform. It requires courage to live in two worlds and experience a true exchange of love. The stories which I told were not scientific descriptions of the grey seal, but were stories from folklore where fictive and real elements were blurred. They were told in the form of a myth or fairytale and allowed listeners to take a step back and enter into a metaphoric world of life symbols. Such stories are symbols of feeling, as Langer (1942/1996) points out in her philosophical writing. Transformation stories, where non-humans are sometimes humans and humans are sometimes non-humans, connect us to other living species, which is the most important aspect in ecosophical thinking.

"RE-ENCHANTING NATURE..." ADDITIONAL RESOURCES

Ecological storytelling encourages us to believe in utopian hope. Storytellers connect us by telling stories of our home life, believing that the structures of feeling and social past can be changed by telling connecting, loving and caring stories about the interrelatedness between environment, other life forms and humans. There are number of valuable web sites which illuminate this emerging field of storytelling. Teaching and learning for a sustainable future: a multimedia teacher education program by UNESCO (2006) has a good web site which presents many stories and educational methods to work with storytelling. Ron Donaldson (2009) has collected "Top 50 Storytelling and Sustainability websites." Included on these websites is a valuable resource of literature. The RSA Arts and Ecology Centre also provides several lists of books recommend by artists and activists of the field. Many story-tellers have their own websites, such as, for example, a group called *Fire Springs* (2009) from Wales. They published their "Ecobardic Manifesto" in 2008. They propose that creative artists should start to use five 'ecobardic' principles. One of them concerns "re-enchanting nature and existence as filled with significance." This is one of the most important tasks of ecological storytelling, to create significance for non-human life forms and in such a way work for a sustainable future. A related area to ecological storytelling is site- specific art, and ecology and theatre, which, for example Baz Kershaw (2007) has written extensively about.

REFERENCES

Connelly, J. (2006). The virtues of environmental citizenship. In A. Dobson & D. Bell (Eds.), *Environmental citizenship* (pp. 49–74). Cambridge: The MIT Press.

Donaldson, R. (2009). *The ecology of knowledge*. Retrieved November 10, 2009, from http://rondon.wordpress.com/2008/10/15/top-50-storytelling-and-sustainability-websites/

Fire Springs. (2009). *Words Woven on the loom of life*. Retrieved November 10, 2009, from http://www.firesprings.org.uk/

Kershaw, B. (2007). *Theatre ecology: Environments and performance events*. Cambridge: University Press.

Langer, S. (1942/1996). *Philosophy in a new key: A study in the symbolism of reason, rite and art*. Cambridge, MA: Harvard University Press.

MacAulay, J. M. (1998). *Seal-folk and ocean paddlers*. Cambridge: The White Horse Press.

Muir, T. (1998). *The Mermaid Bride and other Orkney folk tales*. Orkney: The Orcadian Limited.

Næss, A. (1991). *Ecology, community and lifestyle* (D. Rothenberg, Trans. and ed.). Cambridge: Cambridge University Press.

Nanson, A. (2005). *Storytelling and ecology: Reconnecting people and nature through oral narrative.* Pontypridd: University of Glamorgan Press.

Rantanen, T. (2005). *The media and globalization.* Thousand Oaks, CA: Sage.

RSA Arts and Ecology Centre. (2009). *Art for social change.* Retrieved November 10, 2009, from http://www.rsaartsandecology.org.uk/about-us

Smith, D. (2001). *Storytelling Scotland: A nation in narrative.* Edingburgh: Polygon.

UNESCO. (2006). *Teaching and learning for a sustainable future: A multimedia teacher education program.* Retrieved July 30, 2009 from http://www.unesco.org/education/tlsf/

Williams, R. (2001). Structure of feeling: Raymond Williams from Marxism and literature (1977). In C. Counsell & L. Wolf (Eds.), *Performance analysis: An introductory course book* (pp. 193–199). London: Routledge.

Williamson, D. (1992). *Tales of the seal people.* Edingburgh: Canongate Press.

Wilson, M. (2006). *Storytelling and theatre.* New York: Palgrave Macmillan.

Zipes, J. (1995). *Creative storytelling: Building community, changing lives.* New York: Routledge.

Zipes, J. (2004). *Speaking out: Storytelling and creative drama for children.* New York & London: Routledge.

***Heli Aaltonen**, PhD, is Associate Professor in Drama and Theatre Department Institute of Art and Media Studies, Norwegian University of Science and Technology (NTNU).*

CHEELA F K CHILALA

26. THE AFRICAN NARRATIVE TALE AS A TOOL OF EDUCATION

Keywords: narrative, kalulu, education, greed, dramatisation, HIV/AIDS

The African narrative tale has its origins in the African oral traditions. Before the coming of western colonialism and civilisation, African traditional art forms were used as tools for educating people of a particular society, especially children and youths. The art forms were used to transmit information on history and belief systems. As Mwansa (1999, p. 7) argues, African traditional art forms were used as 'techniques for teaching eloquence, games and sharpening young brains'.

The African narrative tale, which may also be referred to as the oral narrative or folk tale, is one of the most significant traditional art forms whose effectiveness as a tool for educating children and young people can not be overemphasised. This is because the animal characters in the stories, such as the hare (known in Zambia as Kalulu), the tortoise and the hyena 'represent human attributes' (Mwansa, 1999, p. 3).

The narratives tend to teach good morals through the interaction of the animal and or human characters who represent and mirror a variety of human forms of behaviour. The stories could also be used to teach 'aspects of family and tribal history' (Mwansa, 1999, p. 30), including greed, jealousy, selfishness and selfless-ness, honesty and dishonesty, love and hatred, among others. Kalulu, in the Zambian oral narratives, is always the trickster hero, the clever animal who outsmarts other animals, including the bigger ones.

Through the narrative tales, children and youth are taught how to behave and how not to behave. Usually it is Kalulu who is used to teach the positive lessons, while the negative ones are usually taught through Kalulu's antitheses or enemies such as the hyena. For example, in most Zambian folk tales Kalulu manipulates, tricks, abuses and outsmarts the hyena.

The trickster hero tends to be a small animal whose lack of brawn is compensated for with brains. Thus, for example, while Zambia has the hare (Kalulu), some parts of West Africa have the tortoise, both small animals. The trickster hero wins fights or conflicts through trickery and manipulation of circumstances rather than physical strength. In addition, the trickster hero tends to have the capacity to study and understand the character of other animals, especially the ones it interacts with most often. It is able to identify their strengths and weaknesses. Hence it is able to manipulate and defeat them.

Thus, for example, Kalulu is aware of hyena's weaknesses, which include greed and blind ambition. In one folk tale, Kalulu develops a habit of stealing maize cobs

S. Schonmann (ed.), Key Concepts in Theatre/Drama Education, 159–162.

from the farms of villagers. Unaware of whom the culprit is, the villagers set a trap. As fate would have it, Kalulu's foot gets caught in the trap. He fails to free himself and waits for his fate.

Fortunately for him, hyena comes by and, unaware of the circumstances behind Kalulu's predicament, asks Kalulu what is going on. In response, Kalulu claims the villagers have captured him in order to force him to become their chief—a responsibility he is unwilling to take up.

Blinded by greed and selfish ambition, hyena offers to take Kalulu's place. Kalulu 'obliges', and hyena frees him. Then Kalulu lets hyena put his foot in the trap and walks to freedom, leaving hyena defenceless. When the villagers come, hyena is shocked when they attack him instead of making him their chief. His pleas for mercy fall on deaf ears.

Such a story teaches children and youth not to be greedy or to have unholy ambition. The use of the story to put the message across is more effective than using a more direct means, which can be boring.

African oral narratives are delivered by storytellers with the capacity to dramatise the story. As a matter of fact there is no other way to narrate an African folk tale than to dramatise it. The storyteller has to assume the roles of the various animals in the tale, changing from one character to another.

In this regard, therefore, the African folk tale has some dramatic elements, and these can be exploited for educational purposes. In using folk tales as an educational tool, or as drama in education, some adjustments have to be made to the traditional approach.

The first adjustment is that, instead of the story being told by one person, the storyteller, others are involved. By way of narration and dramatisation, within the school context, the folk tale can be adapted for use as a play to be performed by a number of children or young people. Secondly, the final product can be developed using the methods of process drama, with the teacher and the children working together.

Narrative tales may be use in three ways: first, to teach the same moral lessons as in the original tale; two, to teach new lessons perhaps more relevant to contemporary times, problems and needs. For example, it is possible to adapt a traditional African tale and use it for HIV/AIDS advocacy, or for disseminating information on children's rights.

For example, the folk tale outlined earlier, about Kalulu and the hyena, may be used to teach about the dangers of HIV/AIDS, with the possibility of hyena becoming chief representing the desire for pleasure—in this case sexual pleasure—which would then lead to one being trapped by the virus and then being destroyed when full-blown AIDS sets in. A foolish person would, like the hyena, end up in trouble, while a wise person, like Kalulu, would realise the danger of their actions and find a way of escape from the consequences of HIV/AIDS.

The third possibility is where the original tale is told, perhaps by one storyteller, or enacted through process drama. The performance is followed by an in-depth discussion of the story and the lesson or lessons it seeks to teach. A link is established between the lessons and the characters used to teach them. In the end, it should be possible to determine which character is clever or wise, and which character is foolish or unwise and therefore vulnerable to the dangers of life. Next, a play can be developed through process drama or what some scholars and practitioners prefer to call creative dramatics. Goldberg (1974, p. 8) explains that in this kind of process the main goal is not the aesthetic of the performance. Rather, the focus is on the 'development of the child's personality'.

It is here that process drama and traditional African narrative tales meet - the need to develop the personality of the child - for both art forms seek to enrich the child's knowledge and abilities. 'Thus, while the narrative tale is a traditional form of enhancing child development and drama in education is a modern form, the two are not necessarily mutually exclusive. On the contrary, the two methods can be mutually beneficial; they can be blended effectively and harmoniously.

Blending traditional African art forms and western art forms is neither new nor un-African. Wole Soyinka, the renowned Nigerian playwright and Nobel Prize winner, is famous for his experimental theatre in which he mixes traditional African forms of art, customs and religion, with western conventions of drama. The product is a hybrid product of high quality which can be appreciated by both Africans and non-Africans.

Soyinka's eclectic work does not escape the attention of Schipper (1982, p. 136), who says of the man: 'Into his work he has integrated most facets of the African experience. Between the poles of tradition and change he searches for essential human values, which he tries to make universally recognisable from an African perspective.'

Schipper draws our attention to the fact that the 'facets of African experience' are due to Soyinka's 'deep roots in Yoruba culture' (1982, p. 138). Hence his plays are characterised by a courageous blending of western technique and African traditional art manifesting itself in the form of traditional music, songs, and dance.

Soyinka also has a tendency to draw Yoruba religion into the fabric of his plays, as in his adaptation of Euripides' play, 'The Bacchae'. Similarly, 'The Strong Breed', 'A Dance of the Forest' and 'Death of the King's Horseman' are based, in part, on Yoruba religious practice. In these works Soyinka generally seeks 'to build a bridge between the philosophy of the West and the Yoruba religion and cosmology' (Ford, 1983, p. 339).

Like Soyinka, Chinua Achebe, also a Nigerian writer, blends western writing conventions and Igbo traditions to produce a masterpiece in the form of the novel 'Things Fall Apart', first published in English in 1958, but now translated into a number of languages around the world. Ford (1983, p. 330) says of Achebe: '...one of his greatest achievements was the creation of a staple prose style which while incorporating African usages and thought patterns is fluent, lucid—and impeccably good English'.

An approach that blends western conventions of drama and African narrative tales is therefore not only welcome but workable. This is especially so in contemporary Africa where, due to the dynamics of social change and the influence of western civilisation African children and youth are exposed to foreign ways of life.

One of the effects of constant change is that some traditional art forms have lost the strong link they once had to African children and youth. The narrative tale has not been spared: it is a generally ignored art form in the urban areas, although it is still alive in the rural areas.

The use of the narrative tale as a form of process drama, therefore, has an appeal for both rural and urban children and youth in Africa. For the rural dweller, it is an opportunity to learn something about western conventions of drama, while for the urban dweller it is an opportunity to connect with the traditional art forms.

African narrative tales tend to be rich in traditional songs. Therefore, the process of converting them into a stage performance can be quite rewarding and exciting. In addition, the use of the narrative tales as a form of dramatic expression can help develop children in a variety of ways.

If used effectively, therefore, the dramatised narrative tales can help in the development of children and youths in the same way that games and plays engaged in by African children help in their development. As Mtonga says, the plays and games serve four areas of need, which he lists as, emotional support, intellectual stimulation or capacitation, physical support, and responsibility training. (Chilala, 2002/3, p. 23).

REFERENCES

Chilala, C. F. K. (2002/2003). Where adults fear to tread: Children's theatre in Africa. In W. Schneider (Ed.), *ASSITEJ Yearbook 2002/3* (pp. 22–25). Frankfurt: ASSITEJ International.

Ford, B. (Ed.). (1983). *The new pelican guide to English literature - The present* (Vol. 8). Middlesex: Penguin Books.

Goldberg, M. (1974). *Children's theatre: A philosophy and a method.* Englewood Cliffs, NJ: Prentice-Hall, Inc.

Mwansa, D. (1999). *Zambian theatre: From traditional art forms to movements for cultural expression.* Lusaka: House of Art Foundation.

Schipper, M. (1982). *Theatre and society in Africa.* Johannesburg: Ravan Press.

Cheela F K Chilala *is a Special Research Fellow and lecturer at the University of Zambia in Lusaka, Zambia. He is also President of ASSITEJ Zambia.*

SECTION V: DIFFERENT POPULATIONS AND THEIR NEEDS

ANDY KEMPE

27. DRAMA AND THE EDUCATION OF YOUNG PEOPLE WITH SPECIAL NEEDS

Keywords: special educational needs, learning difficulties, aesthetic learning, drama-therapy

The use of drama in the curriculum for children with special needs is sometimes automatically equated with dramatherapy. Such an assumption may arise from the mistaken belief that if a child has some kind of learning disability, the only type of drama of any value for them must be designed to help them with their particular individual need. Dramatherapy is a developing approach to the treatment and education of specific groups based on the work of J. L. Moreno. While some children with special needs might benefit from the approach, it should not be assumed that any child needs dramatherapy any more than they need physio or electro-convulsion therapy (Kempe, 1996, pp. 10–11). Indeed, as Irwin (1979) has argued, to make such an assumption is contrary to the belief that any well structured and carefully monitored work in drama can be 'therapeutic' by merit of the fact that it can give the individual a greater sense of competence in the activity being focused upon resulting in heightened self worth. Given that drama is a social art form (as opposed to something that can productively be engaged with in a solitary way), active engagement in dramatic activity can facilitate positive social outcomes such as a sense of belonging to a group. While the generation of such feelings may be seen as beneficial to all (Gallagher, 2007), they may have particular importance for children who, because of their particular needs, may be excluded from a number of social situations that others take for granted.

A major problem encountered in any discussion concerning special needs is that of terminology. This is apparent in the paragraph you have just read! By categorising young people under the catch-all heading of 'special needs' we are in danger of implying that a) they are in some way similar, whereas, in truth, the specificity of their needs may make them a wildly disparate group of individuals, and b) that their needs are grounded in some deficit on the part of the individual, rather than resting in the educational system (Raban & Postlethwaite, 1988, p. 2). In England, a child is deemed to have special educational needs (SEN) if, after rigorous assessment, it is agreed that they need something different from or additional to what is provided for other children of the same age in order to make progress in their learning. Most usually, this occurs as a result of one, or a complex combination of any of the following:
– Cognitive and learning difficulties
– Emotional, behavioural and social difficulties
– Communication and interaction difficulties
– Sensory and/or physical difficulties

S. Schonmann (ed.), Key Concepts in Theatre/Drama Education, 165–169.

It is worth noting here however that 'special educational needs' (SEN) and special needs are not interchangeable terms. Special needs may be shared by children in a similar socio/cultural or linguistic context. A recently relocated child for whom English is an additional language but whose physical and mental capabilities are in no way impaired would be considered to have a special need. Special needs are thus distinct from the individual experiences of learning difficulties that constitute a special educational need (children who are especially gifted and talented may also be considered to have special educational needs on account of the fact that normal mainstream educational may not, in itself, be satisfactory for them).

The amount of research which explores the use of drama and SEN is limited (Jindal-Snape & Vettraino, 2007, pp. 107–117) and this can make it difficult for teachers wishing to develop their practice in this field. In the case of students with autism, for example, Sherratt & Peter (2002, p. 17) note that 'Play and drama are rarely used with children with autism in any purposeful way.' With this particular group of children, there is often an underlying deficit in imagination and the desire for rigidity or patterns of behaviour; the unpredictability of the drama medium can prove difficult for them to accommodate and be challenging for teachers lacking in confidence. This can, in turn, lead to teachers' prejudice against using this medium for addressing the specific needs of this group. (Billington, 2006, p. 2). On the other hand, if the flexibility of the medium is embraced, it can lead to the creation of a teaching situation that has little scope for failure for students and therefore represents a 'safe environment' in which to practice important social skills (Attwood, 2006). In every aspect of drama education, it is an established paradox that the safest lesson is often the one in which the teacher takes the most risks no matter what group is being taught.

While considerable debate has taken place in recent years about the relationship between drama as a medium for achieving specific learning objectives, and the teaching of drama as an art form in its own right, it is worth considering how any of us come to learn anything in the first place. Ward (1989) has argued for an emphasis to be placed on the arts in education of young people with special needs on the grounds that arts activities for their own sake have a general therapeutic value. He bases his plea for such entitlement on the proposition espoused by educationalists such as Louis Arnaud Reid (1986) and Jerome Bruner (1962) that there is such a thing as 'aesthetic knowing', that is, a knowledge other than that which concerns objective facts but is based in sensate experience. Such knowledge is of a personal and fluid nature, offering new insights and structures for understanding and assessing one's place in the world. Ward pinpoints five key areas of aesthetic knowing . Each may be related to the art form of drama with the result that the potential of drama in the education of young people with special needs becomes persuasively alluring:

1. Sensation

In the first instance we come to know the world through our senses. For example, if somebody sticks a finger into your back you will most likely feel the pressure. 'Most likely' because some special needs of children arise as a result of an inability to sense aspects of the world because of the impairment of one or more of their primary senses (sight, hearing, touch, taste, smell). Drama is polysemic, that is to say that meaning is conveyed through a multiplicity of sign systems in the art form (Aston & Savona, 1991). While in mainstream theatre this most often involves communicating through the visual and aural, both children's theatre companies such as Theatre Centre and contemporary companies such as Stan's Cafe have explored the possibilities of focusing on the kinaesthic (sense of movement), gustatory (sense of taste) and olfactory (sense of smell) in the creation and performance of drama.

2. Perception

Perception is the registration of what has been experienced sensually. It involves fitting the sensation into a scheme or pattern and is thus a cognitive process. For example, if you feel a pressure being applied to your back you may assume that it is a stick, a gun or a finger or something else depending on what other information you are receiving and cognitively processing in the situation. Here again though, not all children derive the same patterns either because of a sensory deficiency or a neurological failure to recognise and place a sensory experience. Drama however is, by its very nature, resistant to fixed interpretation: because there are many ways of representing the same thing in drama, it must be accepted that any representation is open to differing interpretations. In the education of young people with special needs this may be seen as a liberating factor for the pupil in that the task of making sense and moving on becomes more the responsibility of the teacher.

3. Representation

This is a particularly strong feature of aesthetic knowing which has clear links to the drama medium in that it involves the use of the body to somehow represent a sensory experience, for example, physically demonstrating your reaction to something being stuck in your back after the event. Observing pre-verbal babies may provide insights into how humans learn through representation. For example, while opening and closing a box in front of an infant one might observe either their hand or mouth mimicking the action of the box (an early manifestation of working in role perhaps!) Some children are extraordinarily gifted in some modes of representation though they may have a special need deriving from some other specific disability. Because drama is an art form that may employ the visual, verbal, kinaesthetic it offers choices of exploration and expression.

4. Synthesis

Children with unimpaired senses relate to things through multi-sensory activity. For example, on being stuck in the back most people would employ their hearing to ascertain what it is behind them; they may turn and use their eyes to see what it is. Some people do not anticipate the world in such a way however. Artists such as David Hockney, and Wassily Kandinsky, novelist Vladimir Nabakov and composer Franz Liszt were all, for example, synaesthetics and so experienced a primary sensory stimulation in a secondary form (for example, experiencing sound as the sensation of colour). When dealing with children with special needs it is useful to deliberately employ one sense in order to support and complement an- other; fortunately, the art form of drama readily lends itself to this.

5. Structuring

Humans seem to have a phenomenal desire to wish to 'close' or complete an experience. Gestalt psychology offers us an understanding of this and can be used to deliberately tease out a response. For example, do we treat being stuck in the back as a joke, an affront, an accident? By pigeon-holing it in some way we can recall it in future incidents. We cannot assume though that all pupils with special needs will structure experiences in a predictable way; it may be that what makes them 'special' is that they structure experience in a way that seems strange to most other people. Cecily O'Neill (2006) is one of a number of contemporary practitioners and comment- ators of drama education who has recognised the need for both structure and spontaneity in drama education. One might of course wonder how dull the world would be and how bereft of any art if all human beings did structure experience in exactly the same way. This is not to say that, in drama, anything goes. Far from it; if a dramatic enterprise, be it a role play, improvisation or formally presented play, fails to communicate anything to anyone then it is hard to see how it can be classified as drama at all. It is here that Vygotsky's theories (1933) regarding the necessity of adult intervention in a child's learning help us recognise the need for the teacher to be actively involved in the creation and development of the drama in order not only to help them make sense of their own experience but communicate that to others.

For David Ward, arts education for young people with special needs serves exactly the same purpose as arts education for anyone. In all cases, the task for the teacher is to pinpoint which of the five key areas operates well and use this capability to support the development of other areas. In discussing her practice of using drama with people who are physically disabled in different ways, Sue Jennings (1973, p. 4) noted that the work did not 'differ in content or technique from other types of drama, although great care must be taken in selecting and applying drama techniques.' The emphasis in practical drama work with all young people should concern recognising and developing existing capabilities in such a way as to foster new skills, knowledge and insights rather than confronting inability and lack of knowledge. Aesthetic activity proves that we are alive by awakening our senses and forcing us to make our own sense of what they seem to be telling us. Conversely, that which is anaesthetic deprives us of our consciousness and ability to act. No doubt we have all had anaesthetic experiences in the theatre: let those of us who teach drama to young people with special needs try to avoid subjecting them to the same.

REFERENCES

Aston, E., & Savona, G. (1991). *Theatre as sign-system: A semiotics of text and performance*. London: Routledge.
Attwood, T. (2006). *The complete guide to Asperger's syndrome*. London: Jessica Kingsley.

Billington, T. (2006). Working with autistic children and young people: Sense, experience and the challenges for services, policies and practices. *Disability & Society, 21*(1).

Bruner, J. (1962). *On knowing: Essays for the left hand.* Cambridge, MA: Harvard University Press.

Gallagher, K. (2007*). The theatre of urban: Youth and schooling in dangerous Times.* Toronto: University of Toronto Press.

Jennings, S. (1973). *Remedial Drama.* London: Pitman.

Jindal-Snape, D., & Vettraino, E. (2007). Drama techniques for the enhancement of social-emotional development in people with special needs: Review of research. *International Journal of Special Education, 22*(1), 107–117.

Kempe, A. (1996). *Drama education and special needs.* Cheltenham: Stanley Thornes Publishers.

Irwin, E. (1979). Drama therapy with the handicapped. In A. Shaw & C. G. Stevens (Eds*.), Drama/theatre and the handicapped.* Washington, DC: American Theatre Association Publication.

O'Neill, C. (2006). *Structure and spontaneity: The process drama of Cecily O'Neill.* Stoke on Trent: Trentham Books.

Raban, B., & Postlethwaite, K. (1988). *Classroom responses to learning difficulties.* London: Macmillan.

Reid, L. A. (1986). *Ways of understanding and education.* London: Heinemann.

Sherratt, D., & Peter, M. (2002). *Developing play and Drama in children with autistic spectrum disorders.* London: David Fulton.

Vygotsky, L. S. (1933/1976). Play and its role in the mental development of the child. In J. Bruner, et al. (Eds.), *Play: Its role in development and evolution.* London: Penguin.

Ward, D. (1989). The arts and special needs. In M. Ross (Ed.), *The claims of feeling.* Oxford: Pegamon Press.

***Andy Kempe** is Head of Initial Teacher Training at the University of Reading where he is also Senior Lecturer in Drama Education.*

ANDY KEMPE

28. WHAT DRAMATIC LITERATURE TEACHES ABOUT DISABILITY

Keywords: disability, dramatic literature, special needs

Disabled people have always been represented in dramatic literature. However, the appearance of disabled characters prior to the mid 20th century may be considered primarily in terms of their dramatic functionality and symbolic value rather than representing any explorations of disability itself. Tiresias, for example, is an embodiment of the proverb that 'there are none so blind as those who will not see', while Richard III's deformity and both Lear's and Hamlet's 'madness' are manifestations of 'something being rotten in the state' as a result of the 'natural order', or 'great chain of being' having been disturbed.

This chapter explores what young people might learn about disability through the dramatic literature they may encounter in the school curriculum or theatre which is available to young audiences. Any such discussion is likely to be controversial not least because the language associated with disability is highly contested. For example, in the world of education the term 'special needs' is used as an umbrella (some might say euphemism) for physical disability, cognitive impairment and mental illness. It can also be used to refer to people of such intelligence or giftedness that they fall outside of what is perceived as the 'normal range', yet 'normality' is itself a problematic term, though a feature of many successful dramas lies in the way notions of normality are challenged or inverted. Indeed, the arts world tends to embraces the term 'disability' in order to establish an aesthetic which can directly counter ablist agendas that either ignore its existence or simply doesn't know how to engage with it for fear of seeming patronising, ignorant or offensive. The question is, to what extent does dramatic literature provide young people with insights into the lives of people who are disabled and society's response to them?

The invisibility of disability in pre-twentieth century dramatic literature is hardly surprising given the way those who were disabled have been treated in the past and continue to be treated in many places. In England, for example, it was not until 1893 that school boards were instructed to provide education for children who were blind or deaf (Barnard, 1947, p. 223). Six years later the Education (Defective and Epileptic Children) Act directed that children 'not being imbecile and not being merely dull and backward' should be provided for in special classes (Tansley & Gulliford, 1960, p. 3). In the USA a 'free and appropriate education for all handicapped children' wasn't mandated until 1975: before then, some 4,000,000 children with disabilities did not receive the necessary support and another 1,000,000 received no schooling whatsoever (Connor & Ferri, 200, p. 63). The inclusion of children with special educational needs into mainstream schools continues to be a contentious

S. Schonmann (ed.), Key Concepts in Theatre/Drama Education, 171–175.

issue (Ainscow & Booth, 1998; Hodkinson & Vickerman, 2009) with the result that what many young people learn about disability from dramatic representations may go unmoderated by any first-hand experience.

Perhaps the most commonly studied piece of literature in which the protagonist has an identifiable disability is Of Mice and Men. Steinbeck wrote the story in such a way that it could be read as either a novel or a play. It was first performed on stage in 1937, the same year that it was published as a novel. It is the story of Lennie, a gentle giant with the mind of an innocent child, and his friend George who attempts to protect him from a cruel and unsympathetic world. A common reading of the narrative would be a liberal humanist one in which George's final act of killing Lennie is seen as a compassionate and selfless 'act of kindness'. However, it could equally be argued that the characterisation of Lennie as a victim imparts a negative view of those with learning difficulties in that, ultimately, he becomes a burden that is simply too great for George to bear. Such a reading is cognate with the argument expressed by Snyder and Mitchel (2001) that disability has persistently been used to bolster ablist discourses and ideological frameworks. But the play may be considered in other ways. For example, it may be seen as a metaphor for American society in that Lennie and George live in a land built on the principle that dreams can come true. However, like Willy Loman in Miller's Death of a Salesman, it is clear that not all dreams do come true and that the 'best laid plans o' mice and men gang aft agley.' The fact that the play/novel was banned by some state and school libraries for promoting euthanasia and holding an anti-capitalist stance supports the notion that the world of Lennie and George may indeed be a metonymic representation of American society.

Of Mice and Men is a useful touchstone in that its depiction of a disability may be interpreted in different ways, each of which may be employed in discussions of other plays depicting characters with some form of impairment. In the first instance, it is worthy of consideration because the story is so commonly studied in schools (albeit most usually in the form of a novel rather than a play) even though it was not written specifically for a young audience. Other plays that have appeared on examination syllabuses in England would include The Glass Menagerie in which Laura is depicted as both emotionally and physically 'crippled'; Peter Nichols' tragi-comic exploration of the challenges faced by parents trying to look after their pro-foundly and multipli-disabled daughter in A Day in the Death of Joe Egg; Peter Shaffer's dramatisation of an apparently true (though actually unverified) story of an emotionally disturbed teenager in Equus; and Brian Clark's dramatic moral debate on euthanasia for those left paralysed after an accident, Whose Life is it Anyway? In the context of curriculum study, students are likely to be required to focus on the text as a piece of literature and discuss narrative, structure and character development. Alternatively, they may be required to consider what is involved in moving from page to stage, how to play the characters and how to achieve dramatic impact. What the plays may be saying about disability and responses to it tend to remain largely undiscussed in such a context. Is this, in itself, a manifestation of an ablest agenda that cares only to view disability through the lens of objectified study? Or is it a result of teachers simply not knowing quite how to open up the issues for discussion?

Another groundbreaking play that offers insights into a specific disabling condition and the challenges faced by those with the condition and those around them is William Gibson's 1957 play The Miracle Worker. Based on Helen Keller's own writings, the play imparts the didactic message that children with disabilities should be treated like any others in terms of having high expectations held of them. The play upholds the belief that, given discipline and structure, they can learn, become independent and behave in a socially acceptable way. In contrast, Arne Skouen's 1984 play Ballerina tends to sentimentalise the problems that occur when social norms are rejected and a disabling condition is indulged. The central character of the play is an autistic teenage girl, Malin, whose mother has snatched her from an institution and built a communication system for her based on balletic movement. When the mother's circumstances change she is forced to ask for help only to find that no-one feels able to share the esoteric world she and her daughter have created.

Ballerina has certain similarities to A Day in the Death of Joe Egg in that Malin's condition is both the cause of tension between her parents and a lens through which the inadequacies of adult relationships may be examined. In fact, the reflection of adults' foibles and failures in children's disabilities appears to be quite a common feature with disability serving as a trope for adults' emotional or moral instability. Joe's mother Sheila, for example, blames herself for her daughter's condition because she was promiscuous. In Spoonface Steinberg, the father is blamed for his daughter's condition because she fell off a chair and banged her head while her parents were arguing about his infidelity, while in Dennis Potter's Brimstone and Treacle, Pattie's vegetative state is the result of her being knocked down by a truck while running away after catching her father in flagrante delicto. Another Potter play commonly studied in English schools is Blue Remembered Hills in which the slow-witted Donald Duck is noted to have a mother of loose morals. While all of these plays offer sympathetic portrayals of disabled characters, what may be learnt from them is that disability is a punitive manifestation of some fundamental code of normality being broken; in a sort of human embodiment of pathetic fallacy the protagonist is effectively de-humanised by being reduced to a dramatic device.

The use of disability as a metaphor for dysfunctionality is not, of course, limited to inter-personal relationships. Stoppard's Every Good Boy Deserves Favour uses mental illness to comment on the lunacy of a totalitarian regime while McDonagh's The Pillowman questions the morality of both extreme parental and state control and freedom of expression when a character with learning difficulties murders three children after reading his brother's grotesque, yet in one case autobiographical, 'fairy tales'. Here again, the end result of such representations is that contemporary young audiences experience disability as standing for something else in much the same way as Greek or Shakespearean audiences may have done rather than being encouraged to reflect on disabilities in their own right.

There are, however some plays where the purpose is to explore a particular disabling condition. Even here though, the most commonly perceived argument is that society in general is ill equipped to deal with aberrations from the norm.

For example, it may be argued that Equus is more about the psychiatrist's frustration with his own ability to make a positive difference:

I'll heal the rash on his body. I'll erase the welts cut into his mind by flying manes. When that's done, I'll set him on a nice mini-scooter and send him puttering off into the Normal world where animals are treated properly: made extinct, or put into servitude, or tethered all their lives in dim light (Shaffer, 1983, p. 92).

In some cases humanitarian frustration is replaced by a furious indictment of society's response to the disabled though this may be expressed more forcibly in the author's introductory notes that in the playscript itself. Examples of this would include Nabil Shaban's play about the Nazi's treatment of the disabled, The First to Go, and Haresh Sharma's Off Centre, which became a milestone when it was admitted to the curriculum in Singapore notwithstanding the Ministry of Health withdrawing funding for its development because its depiction of mental illness was considered too extreme.

A number of plays originating in the late 20th century explore mental illness (Wald, 2007) and some of these have proved popular with young audiences perhaps because the protagonists are themselves young people. Find Me, Gum and Goo, Adult Child Dead Child and 4.48 Psychosis have all proved to be popular vehicles through which young performers may demonstrate their acting talents. The question is, are these plays studied because of the insight they give into mental illness, or because the anger that gives them their dramatic power serves as a vehicle for the teenage angst of those performing them? There are nonetheless a small number of plays written especially for young audiences that offer good opportunities for young performers as well as attempting to provide thoughtful and sensitive explorations of disability as experienced by young characters. Stronger Than Superman, for example, a play originating from the Berlin based Grips Theatre, is a humorous portrait of a 10 year old boy with spina bifida while Strugglers, a play about a class in a school for children with special educational needs, won both the Sunday Times Playwriting Award and National Student Drama Festival in England in 1988.

In conclusion, it may be regarded as something of a paradox that while drama educationalists have consistently and persuasively argued the efficacy of the medium as a means of challenging negative attitudes and highlighting social issues, dramatic literature offers relatively few possibilities for developing young people's understanding of people with special needs. This is not to say, however, that drama teachers and theatre companies working with young people are not addressing the issues through practical workshops or by devising and writing their own plays, some of which, in my view, fully deserve to be published and made available to a wider audience.

REFERENCES

Ainscow, M., & Booth, T. (Eds.). (1998). *From them to us: International study of inclusion in education.* London: Routledge.
Barnard, H. C. (1947). *A history of English education from 1760.* London: University of London Press.

Connor, J., & Ferri, B. (2007). The conflict within: Resistance to inclusion and other paradoxes in special education. *Disability and Society, 22*(1).

Hodkinson, A., & Vickerman, P. (2009). *Key issues in special educational needs and inclusion.* London: Sage Publications.

Shaffer, P. (1983). *Equus.* Harlow: Longman Group.

Snyder, S., & Mitchell, D. (2001). *Narrative prothesis: Disabilities and the dependence of discourse.* Michigan, MI: University of Michigan Press.

Tansley, A. E., & Gulliford, R. (1960). *The education of slow learning children.* London: Routledge & Kegan Paul.

Wald, C. *(2007). Hysteria, Trauma and Melancholia: Performative Maladies in Contemporary Anglophone Drama. Basingstoke: Palgrave Macmillan.*

PLAYS CITED IN CHRONOLOGICAL ORDER OF PRODUCTION

1937	Of Mice and Men	John Steinbeck
1944	The Glass Menagerie	Tennessee Williams
1949	Death of a Salesman	Arthur Miller
1957	The Miracle Worker	William Gibson
1967	A Day in the Death of Joe Egg	Peter Nichols
1972	Whose Life is it Anyway	Brian Clark
1973	Equus	Peter Shaffer
1977	Brimstone and Treacle	Dennis Potter
1977	Every Good Boy Deserves Favour	Tom Stoppard
1977	Find Me	Olwen Wymark
1979	Blue Remembered Hills	Dennis Potter
1980	Gum and Goo	Howard Brenton
1980	Stronger Than Superman	Roy Kift
1984	Ballerina	Arne Skouen
1987	Adult Child Dead Child	Clare Dowie
1987	Effie's Burning	Valerie Windsor
1988	Strugglers	Richard Cameron
1993	Flowers for Algernon	Bert Coules
1993	Off Centre	Haresh Sharma
1996	The First to Go	Nabil Shaban
1997	Spoonface Steinberg	Lee Hall
2000	4.48 Psychosis	Sarah Kane
2003	The Pillowman	Martin McDonagh

Andy Kempe is Head of Initial Teacher Training at the University of Reading where he is also Senior Lecturer in Drama Education.

PARASURAM RAMAMOORTHI AND ANDREW NELSON

29. DRAMA EDUCATION FOR INDIVIDUALS ON THE AUTISM SPECTRUM

Keywords: autism, drama, masks, communication, social skills

The drama-in-education community is facing a new and exciting challenge: providing meaningful drama and arts experiences for individuals on the autism spectrum. Autism Spectrum Disorder (ASD) is a neurological disorder that often profoundly affects a person's communication, socialization, and play skills. One recent U.S. study concluded that approximately 1 in 150 people are on the autism spectrum (Centers for Disease Control and Prevention, 2007), and interventions range from behavior-based therapies to sensory integration techniques. More recently, drama and art education approaches have gained greater attention and the arts are being applied in a wide variety of ways and settings to help individuals with autism. Also, many adults and young people with ASD are finding their unique voice through the arts.

The authors propose a Drama Education model that simultaneously helps individuals develop artistic talents and careers while using specific art techniques to address social skill development, communication, empathy, and other issues common to ASD. This chapter will focus on the use of drama to achieve these two goals.

Drama is an effective medium for introducing new skills to individuals with autism. *The Diagnostic and Statistical Manual of Mental Disorders-IV-TR* (American Psychiatric Association, 2000) lists communication, socialization, and restricted play repertoires as the main criteria for an autism diagnosis while further describing issues related to emotion expression and recognition, empathy, and group dynamics. When one asks the question "what is required of a successful theatre artist" the list generated looks remarkably similar to the DSM criteria. Acting behavior is a learned process that can be systematically taught (Bloch, Orthous, & Santibañez-H, 1987) and autism-theatre professionals have recognized the connection between autism deficits and what drama can offer.

Masks have been used in child development for many decades. Pollaczek (1954) suggested that masks help children explore new roles, deal with negative images in new ways, and increase engagement, citing the example of one child who leaped up and down with excitement when wearing a mask. Masks are being used with people on the spectrum to improve eye contact and thereby help social interaction skills (Ramamoorthi, 2008). Masks also help to develop attention and focus since the mask-wearing actor with ASD can only look through the holes meant for the eyes, minimizing peripheral distractions. Masks can increase confidence by allowing timid actors on the spectrum to temporarily hide themselves from public gaze and

S. Schonmann (ed.), Key Concepts in Theatre/Drama Education, 177–181.

scrutiny. One young man with autism shielded his face with his arm without stopping for two days during a drama workshop, but when he and others were given masks his arms dropped and he danced with his peers. He then brought a mask home with him and wore it to his special school where he greeted his school master for the first time with confidence the following week. Masks are fun and colorful and can be used to encourage the creative play often absent or delayed in individuals with ASD. Parental involvement is also a key component of mask work and meaningful parent-child connections can happen during mask work. One mother in a mask workshop heard her son comment on her face and hair features for the first time in his life as he painted a mask on her face.

Richard Schechner (1977) calls acting "restored behavior." The authors use another term "rehearsed response" to describe the process of drawing from our experience and memory when we are on stage. Our emotional memory is a reservoir or archive from which we draw images and behavior patterns when we play a role. Young people with ASD often have a strong visual memory but may lack the ability to plan and prepare for novel settings or events. They may have problems attending birthday parties or weddings, going to a restaurant for dinner, or being in a public space. Rehearsed response or role play techniques can be used to help prepare for social situations like first dates, greeting a stranger of the same sex and the opposite sex, boarding an aircraft, ordering in a restaurant, coping with stress, and a wide variety of other skills and scenarios. Visual supports such as pictures of places, items, or people are shown to an individual and a rehearsal is arranged before the actual event. The whole scene is pre-arranged and perfectly played as in a theatre rehearsal. Props from the anticipated environment can be used to create an authentic rehearsal as well. This process allows the person with ASD to practice social behavior and interactions just as the actor rehearses his or her part. Also, rehearsed response games provide fun opportunities to play roles or watch others playing their roles, and placing one's self in an imaginary situation is important for developing empathy. In our work we have seen how role playing can increase flexibility. One actor in a recent integrated theatre production was asked to play additional parts as one of his fellow actors fell sick just before the show was to open. This particular actor rose to the challenge, played multiple parts in the drama, demonstrated calm and focused behavior throughout the process, and ended up being a terrific model for some of the younger actors. During another "Arts for Autism" festival in Madurai, India 15 children and their families from all areas of India gathered to explore and express through the arts. As part of the retreat organizers had arranged for a trip to a large, crowded, and ancient temple in the heart of the city. The group decided to role play going to the temple two times before actually going on the outing. Children and their parents practiced and discussed a variety of key points related to the temple visit. As a result of this "rehearsed response" and other preparations the children on the spectrum had zero upsets and were calm and content during the two hour visit to the temple.

Nearly 40% of people on the autism spectrum are non-verbal (CDCP, 2007). They may not have any functional communication but produce some simple sounds. Oftentimes there are situations on stage when an actor grunts, screams, and yells but does not speak and actors intersperse their text with sounds for emphasis. Based on this experience a model for communication has been created and is being used by some families to develop a customized language called *Soundscape* (Ramamoorthi, 2008). Research in this direction might lead to the creation of a language like Braille or sign language. People with ASD have difficulty communicating what they want and what they feel. Parents are often at a loss when trying to understand their wants and needs. Peers do not understand and often this social confusion results in abusive behavior. To overcome this issue the *Soundscape* method is being tried with non-verbal children. The philosophy of language learning starts with the acquisition of sounds. Human beings can communicate their basic needs through sounds and in fact we do often resort to sounds rather than a language for communication. This needs to be systematized and children and adults on the spectrum, after speech therapy has failed, may be encouraged to use sounds for communication. Each family can create a dictionary of sounds, using basic vowels, to communicate their needs. For instance "aa" could mean communicating a need to go to the toilet. Soundscape experiments are being followed by some families in India with the goal of multiple families sharing sounds with one another to increase communicative partners and social opportunities.

Actors commonly use focal points when performing to suggest a particular place, mood, or the presence of another person or object. Often these focal points are placed somewhere in the house area of the theatre and an actor practices locating and accessing these focal anchors in rehearsal and performance. An actor can shift his or her eyes and attention to multiple points in the theatre space and can assign different emotional and physical qualities to these points (ex. Hamlet picturing his uncle's face, etc). Scientists have studied the mechanical processes of the eye, including saccadic eye movements (Fischer & Breitmeyer, 1987) and focusing systems (LaBerge, et al, 1997) in order to better understand how we shift between focal points in our environment. These studies tell us a great deal about peripheral focus, how the human eye moves between engaged and disengaged states, and the time delays involved in such transference. Recently, this work has been applied to individuals with autism spectrum disorders (Van der Geest, et al., 2001; Townsend, Harris, & Courchesne, 1996) revealing slower shifts of focal attention between points when compared to typically developing subjects. Focal point techniques are being used by the authors with actors on the autism spectrum to develop four main communicative skills: eye contact, joint attention, emotion recognition, and emotion expression. First, a flash light is used to help actors with autism quickly locate focal points in a given space and shift between multiple spots, with the goal of quickly fading the flash light once focal points are committed to muscle memory. Next, an emotion is assigned to each focal point either using emotion images (happy, sad, angry faces, etc.) fixed to the wall or using muscle memory only. Actors then shift between the various emotion focal points and either mimic/express the emotion or respond to what they see with their own emotion or physicality. Again, a flashlight may be needed at first to help actors with autism make clear shifts between focal anchors. Focal point training is a fun, efficient way to teach simple eye contact and joint attention shifting as well as the more complex emotion work associated with acting.

Drama troupes and performing arts-based activities for individuals with ASD are growing in popularity around the world (Schneider, 2007; Nelson, 2008). Autism theatre groups with a performance element help take drama beyond a mere skill-building technique to an event that ties performers with autism to their community. Audiences connect with their neighbors and peers on the spectrum and the arts become the forum for dialogue, play, and understanding. For instance, in July 2009 a drama camp was formed at the Autism Society of America Conference in Illinois. An integrated mix of individuals on the spectrum and their typical peers spent 2 rigorous days in acting classes and used a combination of improvisation and scripting to create a musical based on an Aesop Fable. This integrated experience brought actors together from every corner of the U.S. and a true community was created. One actor on the spectrum sent a retrospective letter to us saying "My experience was awesome, because if I hadn't done it at all, even without the King's Robe, lion mask, or manufactured crown, I would have been bored... I had a great experience with the play! I also liked the jokes at the end of the play...Thank you so much for this opportunity. I really needed it." Drama groups for actors with ASD do utilize specific techniques to support new skills however the goals of the group more closely resemble those of any other typical theatre club or company. Through these performances the authors have met several artists who, with proper coaching and social supports, could have viable careers as actors, stand-up comedians, scene painters, or stage managers.

Drama techniques are being used creatively to help individuals with autism develop new skills and perspectives. The over-arching goal, however, is to develop the "artist within" and not merely a set of skills or behaviors. Hopefully, teachers, parents, and caregivers will continue to use drama and the arts to help individuals with autism express themselves and thrive in the world. Individualized arts education that capitalizes on strengths can radically change the lives of people with ASD. Artists who are nurtured by their education system can discover their authentic voice and perhaps one day have a viable career in the arts.

REFERENCES

American Psychiatric Association. (2000). *Diagnostic and statistical manual of mental disorders-IV-TR*. Washington, DC.

Bloch, S., Orthous, P., Santibañez-H, G. (1987). Effector patterns of basic emotions: A psychophysiological method for training actors. *Journal of Social and Biological Structures, 10*(1), 1–19.

CDCP - Centers for Disease Control and Prevention. (2007). *Autism information center*. Retrieved July 30, 2009, from http://www.cdc.gov/ncbddd/autism/index.htm

Fischer, B., & Breitmeyer, B. (1987). Mechanism of visual attention revealed by Saccadic eye movements. *Neuropsychologia, 25*(1), 73–83.

LaBerge, D., Carlson, R. L., Williams, J., & Bunney, B. G. (1997). Shifting attention in visual space: Tests of moving-spotlight models versus an activity-distribution model. *Journal of Experimental Psychology: Human Perception and Performance, 23*(5), 1380–1392.

Nelson, A. (2008). *Social skills for individuals with asperger syndrome: A proven method using theatre and the arts*. Hyderabad, India: Prachee Publications.

Pollaczek, P. P. (1954). Use of masks as an adjunct to role-playing. *Mental Hygiene, 38*, 299–304.

Ramamoorthi, P. (2008). *ARTRAN: Conversation with Co-Founder Dr. Parasuram Ramamoorthi.* Official Podcast of the Applied Theatre Research and Autism Network. Retrieved from www.autismtheatre.org

Schechner, R. (1977). *Performance theory.* London: Routledge.

Schneider, C. B. (2007). *Acting antics: A theatrical approach to teaching social understanding to kids and teens with Asperger syndrome.* London: Jessica Kingsley Publishers.

Townsend, J., Harris, N. S., & Courchesne, E. (1996). Visual attention abnormalities in autism: Delayed orienting to location. *Journal of the International Neuropsychological Society, 2*(6), 541–550.

Van der Geest, J. N., Kemner, C., Camfferman, G., et al. (2001). Eye movements, visual attention, and autism: A saccadic reaction time study using the gap and overlap paradigm. *Biological Psychiatry, 50*(8), 614–619.

Parasuram Ramamoorthi, *PhD, formerly Professor of Theatre Arts Madurai kamaraj University. Chairman, VELVI. Playwright and director. Specializes in drama for mental health and for autism.*

Andrew Nelson, *M.Ed, International Association of Theatre for Autism and West Virginia Autism Training Center at Marshall University. Author of Foundation Role Plays for Autism.*

BURCU YAMAN NTELIOGLOU

30. DRAMA AND ENGLISH LANGUAGE LEARNERS

Keywords: drama education, English Language Learning, language skills, Second/
Foreign/Additional Language Education

Researchers in drama education have investigated the cognitive, emotional, social and
aesthetic potentials of drama. Even though important literacy and drama connections
have been explored by drama educators (e.g. Booth & Neelands, 1998), they have
rarely looked at the strong connections between drama pedagogies and second/
foreign/ additional language learning.

The terms ELL (English Language Learner), ESL (English as a Second Language),
EFL (English as a Foreign Language), EAL (English as an Additional Language)
and LEP (Limited English Proficient) are used interchangeably in the literature. I will
be using the more up-to-date term ELL whenever it is appropriate. The term ELL
refers to students whose first language is not English and who are learning the
language in the context of an English speaking environment. ESL (English as a
Second Language) is contrasted with EFL (English as a Foreign Language), which
refers to English language learners who are learning the language in the context of
a non-English speaking environment. The term ESL has been seen as problematic
because for some students English is not their second, but maybe third or fourth
language; that is why the term English as an Additional Language (EAL) is offered
by some educators.

Cognitive psychology has had a strong presence in the field of Second Language
Acquisition (SLA), but Firth and Wagner (1997) have called for its reconcept-
ualization – one that resists the mainstream view of SLA as solely a cognitive and
individual process and suggests a socio-cultural approach to language learning.
Because of its social nature, teaching through drama has the potential to provide
this kind of socio-cultural orientation to language learning with a focus on purposeful
interaction (Wilhem & Edmiston, 1998). Drama provides ELLs with opportunities
to express themselves in English for a "meaningful" purpose (Krashen, 1982),
going beyond vocabulary and grammar drills (Dodson, 2002). Drama pioneer
Dorothy Heathcote suggested that the main purpose of drama is to educate students
"to look beyond the surface action, to the personal and cultural values, to sustain
them" (Heathcote & Bolton, 1998, p. 160). Therefore, the application of drama is
valuable not only for the enhancement of language skills but also for helping ELLs
to understand how culture(s) operate(s).

The use of drama activities has long been advocated by teachers and researchers
in the field of foreign and second language education. More recent publications such
as Kao and O'Neill's *Words into Worlds* (1998), Robbie, Ruggirello and Warren's

S. Schonmann (ed.), Key Concepts in Theatre/Drama Education, 183–188.

Using Drama to Bring Language to Life (2001) and Burke and O'Sullivan's *Stage by Stage* (2002) provide information about how dramatic techniques can be practically applied in language classrooms.

Most of the research on drama and EAL has been theoretical and there is little classroom research in this field. The majority of the existing classroom research concentrates on the benefits of drama for speaking skills. Miccoli's (2003) research with EFL University students in Brazil showed that taking risks in drama activities led to improvements in students' oral skills. McCafferty (2000) discussed the significant benefits of drama for language learners for describing and interpreting gestures and non-verbal communication in the target language, skills that will help them comprehend the language and express themselves in it. Only a few classroom research studies focus on drama and second language reading and writing skills. Hertzberg (2004), working in a school in Australia, found that drama helps children think better about their ideas; it engages them in the learning process and at the same time enhances the language and literacy development of the EAL students in particular. Liu (2000) used Readers Theatre (RT) activities in an American university EAL writing class. Students read aloud from the source text, discussed the passages, and created their own conclusions to the story in written dialogue. Then the students were encouraged to act out the imaginative ending of the story by reading their dialogues aloud with feeling and dramatic facial expressions. Liu stated that drama is an interesting and interactive way of getting students to think, reflect, and write.

This examination of the impact of drama on segregated language skills, as described in the studies above, is important. However, because drama has great potential to naturally integrate all language skills, it is also important to research the integration of all language skills (reading, writing, speaking, listening, viewing and representing) through drama. This kind of integrated-skills approach, as opposed to a purely segregated approach, exposes English language learners to authentic language in its multiple forms and challenges learners to interact naturally in the language (Peregoy & Boyle, 2001).

My 2007 study focused on the use of drama to integrate and support all language skills (the listening, reading, speaking and writing skills) of language learners, and to investigate the role of drama in negotiating language, culture and identity within a multicultural Canadian context. The participants in this study were first-year university students in an ESL/Humanities course. They had been admitted to the university as matriculated students, but still needed the kind of continued language support that this course was designed to provide. The course was content-based, and included a substantial body of social science and humanities materials for students to learn. When students completed the course they earned nine academic credits toward their undergraduate degree, and therefore the content of the course was given major importance. In collaboration with the classroom instructor, who was completely new to drama, I implemented drama education strategies designed to cover the necessary course content and create a context for reflecting the ELLs' own lived experiences. Students negotiated between fictional and actual experiences, past and present, and made use of in-role and out-of-role reflection throughout.

This study showed that the drama tasks did provide opportunities for the integration of different language skills while focusing on the content of this humanities course (i.e. Immigration, Canadian Identity and Multiculturalism). For example, in one of the units, students read the Canadian Charter of Rights and Freedoms and the Canadian Multiculturalism Act and then each group focused on one specific right (e.g. fundamental freedoms; mobility rights; democratic rights; language rights). Using the "mantel of the expert" and "teacher in-role" drama strategies, the groups learned about the significance of the specific right, provided examples and presented to the class in-role as experts. At the end of this unit, they individually wrote a letter in-role to be submitted to a hypothetical government committee examining whether to keep the Canadian Charter of Rights and Freedoms and the Multiculturalism Act. Other examples of the integration of language skills through drama included listening to a radio play, discussion, and writing an in-role journal entry.

During the one-on-one interviews, many students mentioned that although they did a lot of reading, writing assignments and listening to lectures in their classes at university, they did not really have a chance to interact or share their thoughts with others. They reported that the learning that took place through drama activities was deeper and better retained because of the interactive (rather than passive) listening that these activities required, and because they could communicate with others, discuss difficult vocabulary and their ideas with each other and negotiate their different opinions.

> The role-playing is enjoying. It is not easy, it's challenging. It [the information to be presented] is complicated and you have to show a lot of things in one moment... and it is most challenging because you must give input in the group and participate. It's not like in normal class where you just sit there and listening and stop listening because no one knows whether you are listening. So in drama activities you have to participate, it's challenging... People have to communicate, discuss and think what way we can present the information, thoughts, emotions better. I have to... think about how can I use body and facial expression. I have to think how can I best give the message. (Student interview, Ru-bing interview II, November 2005)

Many students like Simba (see below) said that they did not like, in fact they feared, writing in English in general but that they enjoyed both the individual and group writing in-role exercises in the drama activities. This experience of researching and writing in-role proved different and motivating because students explored this topic using their different language skills through drama activities and they included their own experiences in the drama. Simba said that because he was in-role as the expert, he could write about what he knew well without having to state that he was, himself, a victim. This distancing through role introduces the notion of safety in the fictional world of drama.

> Simba: I wanted to report that's why I wanted to write as the expert. I did not want to be the one in the place of the victim... As a victim, I thought that people always seem to complain about everything so I, so... I had

to take on a different voice to express my feelings and the feelings of others. So, that's why I wrote as the expert.

Burcu: I know you told me before that you don't like writing, how did you like writing this letter?

Simba: I liked writing because I wanted to say something. That's why. Although I didn't have that passion to write, I wasn't very comfortable in the beginning to write either, but the topic... our conversations in group convinced me to write... I had to compare what may happen here which is not happening now in some other countries. For example those rights are not taking place in other places... I wrote about what happened in Sudan, countries like Lebanon... Because it has happened to my place, my people. My relatives have been killed. So in that role I wrote. For example, the governments decide to use power to impose religious view. So... but if those people are allowed to have their own freedom to worship, there will be no problems. So that's why I chose Sudan, that's why there was war in my country... that's why I wanted to write as expert.

The course instructor also commented on the letter in-role activity (the students handed in this assignment for grading) and highlighted the incorporation of personal experience in the activity:

I think that the writing a letter in-role assignment was more motivating for them than the kind of work I would have normally given them... I might have said "Write an essay making the case for keeping the Charter" – which is not that different from what you do, but they were doing it in-role when they were doing it with you – they were sort of personalizing it. I think that made it easier for them... (Instructor, Interview II, February 2006).

Di Pietro (1982) stated that when students are able to include some parts of themselves in the activities, they are more likely to benefit from the language learning process. Since drama activities are learner-centred, and learners are asked to bring personal experiences to the tasks, these tasks create personal involvement and motivation (Kao & O'Neill, 1998; Liu, 2000; Miccoli, 2003; Hertzberg, 2004).

The findings of this study suggest that introducing drama in a university content-based humanities/language classroom can engage ELLs in significant ways and create room to integrate as well as support all language skills, while providing the kind of support that is recommended by second language researchers: opportunities for collaborative learning, multiple representations, and practices that build on prior knowledge and that are culturally responsive (Yaman Ntelioglou, 2007). The field of drama and language education is an exciting and growing field; however rigorous and long-term classroom research is still needed. It is important to continue empirical research in this field with different age groups (elementary, secondary, high-school and university students); different classroom settings (whether it is an ESL, EFL or content-based classroom setting with high numbers of English language learners); different language proficiency levels; and with teachers who have little, some or extensive drama background. Since studies in this field are mostly action research studies focusing on the researcher's own classroom practice, it is also critical to conduct research using other qualitative and quantitative methodological approaches. I would like to end with a quote from a student, Daniel, who describes what many other students in this classroom have mentioned during my informal conversations and interviews with them. For these students it was important that drama activities incorporated embodiment and interaction, instead of solely focusing on isolated language instruction or the passive learning that they experience most of the time at university. These students felt that because of this interactive, active and embodied nature of learning drama they improved not only their understanding but also their retention of the information.

In university, people here rarely interact, always read book that's it... If you learn with drama, it opens the students' eyes to new things. The experience stays with them. This experience will probably stay with the class, stay with me even after I finish university. Basically we take notes at university. There are no courses like this where we can learn doing drama. Drama doesn't really involve taking notes. It is the experience of doing things in drama rather than taking notes and this is what helps the learning. (Student interview, Daniel, November 2005).

REFERENCES

Booth, D., & Neelands, J. (Eds.). (1998). *Writing in-role.* Hamilton: Caliburn.

Burke, A. F., & O'Sullivan, J. C. (2002). *Stage by stage: A handbook for using drama in the second language classroom.* Portsmouth, NH: Heinemann.

Di Pietro, R. J. (1982). *The concept of personal involvement in foreign language study.* ERIC Clearinghouse. (ERIC Document Reproduction Service No: ED 227684).

Dodson, S. (2002). The educational potential of drama for ESL. In G. Brauer (Ed.), *Body and language: Intercultural learning through drama* (pp. 161–179). Westport, CT: Ablex.

Firth, A., & Wagner, J. (1997). On discourse, communication and (Some) fundamental concepts in SLA research. *Modern Language Journal, 81,* 286–300.

Heathcote, D., & Bolton, G. (1998). Teaching culture through drama. In M. Byram & M. Fleming (Eds.), *Language learning in intercultural perspective: Approaches through drama and ethnography* (pp. 158–178). New York: Cambridge University Press.

Hertzberg, M. (2004). Unpacking the drama process as intellectually rigorous - "The teacher gives you the bones of it and we have to act the muscles". *NJ (Drama Australia Journal), 28*(2), 41–55.

Kao, S., & O'Neill, C. (1998). *Words into worlds - Learning a second language through process drama.* London: Ablex.

Krashen, S. D. (1982). *Principles and practice in second language acquisition.* Oxford: Pergamon Press.

Liu, J. (2000). The power of readers theatre: From reading to writing. *ELT Journal, 54*(4), 354–361.

McCafferty, S. G. (2000). Gesture and creating zones of proximal development for second language learning. *Modern Language Journal, 86*(2), 192–203.

Miccoli, L. (2003). English through drama for oral skills development. *ELT Journal, 57*(2), 122–129.

Peregoy, S. F., & Boyle, O. F. (2001). *Reading, writing, & learning in ESL: A resource book for K-12 teachers* (3rd ed.). New York: Longman.

Robbie, S., Ruggirello, T., & Warren, B. (2001). *Using drama to bring language to life: Ideas, games and activities for teachers of languages and language arts*. North York, ON: Captus Press Inc.

Wilhelm, J., & Edmiston, B. (1998). *Imagining to learn: Inquiry, ethics and integration through drama*. Portsmouth, NH: Heinemann.

Yaman Ntelioglou, M. B. (2007). *Crossing borders: Drama in the second language classroom*. Saarbrücken, Germany: VDM Verlag.

Burcu Yaman Ntelioglou *is a doctoral candidate in the Department of Curriculum, Teaching and Learning at the Ontario Institute for Studies in Education, University of Toronto.*

SECTION VI: SHAKESPEARE AND BRECHT

ALISTAIR MARTIN-SMITH

31. LOOKING FOR SHAKESPEARE

Transformation through Double Framing in the Adolescent Journey

Keywords: Shakespeare, youth theatre, transformation, identity, framing

Shakespeare is appropriated by educators and others to serve their own purposes (Allen, 1991, p. 42–43), whether they be to teach the heritage of English literature, to perpetuate the examinations system, the Shakespeare industry and its Bardolatry, or, in this case, to promote adolescent response. The perspective from which Looking for Shakespeare begins is that of an inquiry into the layers of personal meaning in the play: Shakespeare's "open text" challenges participants to reassess and transform their perceptions and their worldview (Allen, 1991, p. 45). A four-week intensive theatre workshop for adolescents which began at New York University in 1999, the program was conceived for inner-city adolescents who may not have had any theatre background to get to know and to perform a Shakespeare play. We adopted an integrated arts approach, employing improvisation, role play, visual art, creative writing, movement and music to explore and illuminate the text.

What is often missing for participants in traditional drama education is learning to hold several different worlds in the mind simultaneously, in order to reflect on the personal meaning that is generated as the metaphors are explored. With this in mind, Looking for Shakespeare attempts to build a bridge between the historical and cultural world of Shakespeare, and the contemporary world of the participants. Underpinned by Jan Kott's (1965) seminal text, *Shakespeare our Contemporary*, we worked together to find meanings in the text that resonated with the participants' lives. We encouraged them to make a connection between the play's themes and their own lives, so that young people would discover Shakespeare and experience transformations of self-image in the process. The adolescents built a bridge to Shakespeare by creating contemporary characters, which then played Shakespeare as a play within a play; each young person would play a role within a role (Martin-Smith, 2000). The development of the project can be traced back to 1999 when we explored scenes from *Hamlet*, *Macbeth* and *Much Ado* as a troupe of players. The second summer it was *Twelfth Night* and *A Midsummer Night's Dream*, performed at a young person's rave. The third summer, our focus was on *As You Like It*, set in the fictional Arden Correctional Facility for Exceptional Juveniles, where the worlds of juvenile detention and the banished Rosalind and Duke Senior co-existed. The participants were in role as inmates who performed the play as part of their prison therapy. The fourth summer, we performed *Cymbeline* as a way to settle a turf war between two Lower Manhattan gangs, The Royals and The Army of Darkness. Over these four years in New York, the artistic team continued to weave elements

S. Schonmann (ed.), Key Concepts in Theatre/Drama Education, 191–195.

of contemporary life and Shakespeare together in a way that resonated with the young people and our local community.

In 2004, we brought Looking for Shakespeare to Goldsmiths University of London. We set *Romeo and Juliet* in the midst of 1960's East End gang culture. The worlds of the Mods and Rockers from the film *Quadrophenia* (1979) and the world of the Montagues and Capulets were juxtaposed, and provided a forum for discussions of different types of parental authority (Martin-Smith & Hayton, 2006). The second year, we performed *A Midsummer Night's Dream* in a futuristic Athens, with the mechanicals as secret police modelled after the Keystone Cops. The play was set in the authoritarian world of Theseus, King of Athens, co-existing with the fairy world of Oberon and Titania. Inspired by Marian Warner's (2000) essay "Rough Magic and Sweet Lullaby," our outdoor production explored the dark world of Titania's fairies, who emerged onto the stage through the windows of the ivy-covered walls of Goldsmiths College only to be threatened by Puck, played by four actors simultaneously.

The third year we performed Shakespeare's journey play *Pericles: Prince of Tyre*, set at a fictional Thames River Festival, while telling the participants' own immigration stories. Pericles' journey is a story of sorrow, suffering and joy: the loss of his kingdom, as well as the loss of his wife Thaisa and daughter Marina. To understand Pericles' journey, the adolescents were challenged to take a longer perspective of life than they possessed. Yet they resonate with Pericles' suffering because they too have suffered on their long journeys to London, with or without their families. Shakespeare's play helped them to focus time, both speeding it up and slowing it down, so they could connect their stories with Pericles' story. The Looking for Shakespeare production of *Pericles* employed Shakespeare's original text, co-written with 17th Century Southwark brothel owner George Wilkins, to echo issues of child slavery in our contemporary world. Actively experiencing these multiple perspectives helped the young people to transform their self-images through personal narrative to include virtual times and cultures. Transformations in their self-images, their contemporary characters and their Shakespeare characters were revealed in their "Me Projects", life-size self-portraits in pastel and coloured marker on brown paper (Martin-Smith, 2010).

The most important benefit to young people in engaging them in the performance of Shakespeare's plays is that the engagement is not primarily about the plays themselves. Rather, performances of Shakespeare's plays, which hold a "mirror up to nature", engage young people in a reflection on their own lives. *Hamlet*, for example, is not only a play about the killing of a king: the killing of a king is a metaphor for Hamlet's self-destruction because of a secret he cannot reveal. Looking at *Hamlet* in this way encourages young people to make personal meaning through the performance of the play. Antonin Artaud's *Theatre and its Double* helps us to understand the power of the play within the play as a framing device for the life journey:

> ... if theatre doubles life, life doubles true theatre... This title will comply with all the doubles of the theatre which I thought I'd found for so many years: metaphysics, plague, cruelty... the pool of energies which constitute Myths,

which man no longer embodies, is embodied by the theatre (Artaud, quoted in Schumacher, 1989).

Dorothy Heathcote (Heathcote & Bolton, 1996) created a double framing strategy called "mantle of the expert". In order to help young people understand the culture of King Arthur's 6th Century England, Heathcote framed participants as 20th Century beekeepers at an international conference, in which they had to explain bee-keeping techniques for a television audience. Looking for Shakespeare used double framing to help young people make the connection between theatre and their lives. Shakespeare's play within the play in *Hamlet*, the *Murder of Gonzago*, is a double framing strategy. Our double framing strategy in Looking for Shakespeare is an extended play within the play in which participants play double roles as a Shakespeare character and as a contemporary character. Cecily O'Neill calls this role doubling "role playing within the role" (O'Neill, 1995, pp. 82–85).

The power of this framing strategy is that it creates an aesthetic distance that enables reflection in safety for adolescents. As Hamlet can observe Claudius' guilt without accusing the King of his father's murder, so a young participant in Looking for Shakespeare can reflect on her or his personal journey of immigration to London, while reflecting on how Pericles responds to the trials of his fictional journey to becoming King of Pentapolis. This extended play within the play engages the abilities of the young participant to focus in both the short aesthetic distance to reflect on their personal journey and to focus on the longer aesthetic distance of Pericles' journey. The resulting cognitive/emotional/physical gymnastics strengthened the young person's ability to apply this mode of metacognition to past and immediate situations requiring distancing and reflection, rather than violence, to solve problems. The use of double framing in Shakespeare has been observed by Cynthia Malone in *Hamlet* to be transformational (Malone 1991, p. 59).

In an article about the transformational processes in Looking for Shakespeare (Martin-Smith & Schonmann, 2005), we point out that questioning was at the core of our theatre outreach process:

> The young people, the graduate students, and the staff conducting the project were constantly asking questions about the procedures, the goals, the content and the form, as well as the social and ethical aspects of the project. As the questioning process became an integral part of the research procedure, it was given a formal slot in the timetable, usually when doing *check-out* at the end of the day: *What are we doing? Why are we doing it? How are we doing?* Such questions allowed us to reflect on the process at different points of time in the project.

Another important aspect of this experience was that the group consisted, with some exceptions, of young people who, when they began the workshop, were strangers to one another. During the four weeks they bonded in varying degrees to produce an artistic ensemble. We consciously facilitated their getting to know each other and becoming more trusting of their peers.

One way of seeking independence from the parents is to rely more on peers as attachment figures. These strong relationships form because adolescents share the same mind set at that age - they are trying to break away from their parents, so it is easy to rely on each other. This transfer of reliance from parents to peers is an important process in the adolescent's life because it is usually a struggle at first, but it encourages their adult attachment styles to develop fully (Lee, 2003).

From the perspective of attachment theory, Looking for Shakespeare can be viewed as an extension of the bonding of the family and of the classroom. Educational drama and theatre lacks longitudinal studies which could investigate the benefits and limitations to the field of attachment perspectives. Of the young people who voluntarily returned year after year, all spoke highly of the experience, crediting it with their decision to pursue a college or theatre career. The cultural capital generated by Looking for Shakespeare has been discussed at length in relation to our production of *A Midsummer Night's Dream* (Martin-Smith, Hayton, & Ishiura, 2007).

Due to the importance of peer pressure in adolescence, a young person's meaning-making process is interdependent on his or her peers. In Looking for Shakespeare, the young participants were given daily opportunities to reflect on the meaning of both their Shakespeare character's journey and their personal journeys, drawing annotated self-portraits and sharing them with the ensemble. Personal meaning that was generated during the rehearsal process was regularly shared, so not all participants needed to play each character to benefit from that character's perspective. Each participant's personal journey story was intertwined with their character's story like strands in a rope, resulting in transformative personal meaning. The young people created not just personal meaning, but also new selves. They constantly moved back and forth between their characters and themselves in a reflexive way. Once this dynamic is set up in the rehearsal process, transformation of the self-image begins. In his analysis of Shakespeare's characters, *Role Playing in Shakespeare*, Thomas Van Laan suggests that negotiating and transforming social relationships is identity-building (1977, p. 25).

Providing opportunities to reflect "out of time" (as in the play within the play), slows down real time for the purpose of learning. We were asking the young people to learn not just about Shakespeare's play, but also to build a bridge between Shakespeare's play and their own lives. Building the bridge takes time and energy, but once built it makes possible the flow between the two worlds. The paradox is that by investing time, time is saved. Another essential paradox is that by taking considered risks in the dramatic world, you can sometimes avoid taking dangerous risks in the real world. This does not mean that taking risks in the fictional world is without danger, yet being able to anticipate and weigh the risk is a definite advantage. Traditional education may have succeeded in rendering the social world so sterile that young people seek unacceptable risks through gangs, violence, drugs and binge drinking.

From the "natural education in self-governing communities" that Caldwell Cook established through drama with his pupils at the Perse School in Cambridge at the turn of the century (Cook, 1917), to the adolescent-centred community in Looking for Shakespeare, over the past hundred years we have deepened our understanding of how young people can actively engage with Shakespeare. A playful attitude is essential for alleviating the fear of making mistakes that often prevents them from creating their own personal meaning from his plays (Salomone & Davis, 1997; Gibson 1993). Following the lead provided by Dorothy Heathcote in her "mantle of the expert", Looking for Shakespeare demonstrated that double framing enables and empowers young people to reflect on the connections between the characters and events in Shakespeare's plays and their own lives. Attachment theory may help us to understand why it is essential for young people to share their personal experiences and meaning-making in a supportive environment, but more research applying this theory within the context of drama education is necessary. The resulting process and culminating performance is transformational on many levels, resulting in identity-building and the creation of cultural capital. Looking for Shakespeare has demonstrated that it empowers young people from inner-city backgrounds to achieve personal transformations and to set achievable career goals.

REFERENCES

Allen, B. (1991). A school perspective. In L. Aers & N. Wheale (Eds.), *Shakespeare in the changing curriculum* (pp. 40–57). London: Routledge.

Cook, H. C. (1917). *The play way*. London: Heinemann.

Gibson, R. (1993). Teaching Shakespeare in schools. In S. Brindley (Ed.), *Teaching English* (pp. 140–148). London: Taylor & Francis Ltd.

Heathcote, D., & Bolton, G. (1996). *Drama for learning: Dorothy Heathcote's mantle of the expert approach to education.* Oxford: Greenwood Press.

Kott, J. (1965). *Shakespeare our contemporary.* London: W.W. Norton and Co.

Lee, E. J. (2003). *The attachment system throughout the life course: Review and criticisms of attachment theory.* Retrieved July 7, 2009, from http://www.personalityresearch.org/papers/lee.html

Malone, C. N. (1991). Framing in Hamlet. *College Literature, 18*(1), 50–63.

Martin-Smith, A. (2000). Looking for Shakespeare: Role-playing within the Role. *Drama Research, 1,* 93–107.

Martin-Smith, A. (2010). The journey of looking for Shakespeare's *Pericles*: Inspiring identity transformation in young people's theatre. In J. Coventon (Ed.), *Drama to inspire.* London: Trentham Books.

Martin-Smith, A., & Hayton, A. (2006). Romeo and Juliet: A timely morality play for young mods and rockers. *Youth Theatre Journal, 20*(23), 110–123.

Martin-Smith, A., Hayton, A., & Ishiura, M. (2007, March–June). Emancipating Shakespeare: Cultural transmission or cultural transformation? *Caribbean Quarterly.* Retrieved June 1, 2010, from http://findarticles.com/p/articles/mi_7495/is_200703/ai_n32229367/

Martin-Smith, A., & Schonmann, S. (2005). Looking for Shakespeare: Anatomy of a youth theatre project. *IDEA Journal/ Applied Theatre Researcher, 6,* Article No. 7. Retrieved from http://www.griffith.edu.au/arts-languages-criminology/centre-public-culture-ideas

O'Neill, C. (1995). *Drama worlds: A framework for process drama.* Portsmouth, NH: Heinemann.

Salomone, R. E., & Davis, J. E. (Eds.). (1997). *Teaching Shakespeare into the twenty-first century.* Athens, OH: Ohio University Press.

Schumacher, C. (Ed.). (1989). *Artaud on theatre* (pp. 87–88). London: Methuen.

Van Laan, T. (1977). *Role playing in Shakespeare.* Toronto: University of Toronto Press.

Warner, M. (2000). Rough Magic and Sweet Lullaby. In J. Uglow (Ed.), *Signs & wonders: Essays on literature and culture.* New York: Vintage.

Alistair Martin-Smith *has taught theatre/drama education at the University of Windsor in Canada, New York University in the US, and Goldsmiths University of London in the UK.*

ERIKA HUGHES

32. BRECHT'S LEHRSTÜCKE AND DRAMA EDUCATION

Keywords: Brecht, Lehrstücke, He Who Says Yes/He Who Says No, student-actor, große Pädagogik

The term *Lehrstücke*, or learning-plays, describes a series of experimental works written in the 1920s and early 1930s by Bertolt Brecht and a number of collaborators, including Kurt Weill, Hanns Eisler and Elisabeth Hauptmann. The intention behind writing and performing these experimental plays was not necessarily to culminate in a finished, final product to be replicated exactly during each performance. Rather, the ideal *Lehrstück* performance is also something of a rehearsal, or, as Frederic Jameson (1998) describes it, "one continuous master class" (p. 62–63). Jameson suggests that the process of acting in a *Lehrstück* is the end result: "the decision to act out this particular gesture; or not to act it out, or to act out its opposite—now proves to be the annulment of difference on another, and perhaps even more basic, one: namely, that between actors and public" (p. 65). As performer and audience are synthesized, this opens up a new realm of possibilities for action and choice within the framework of the play.

In experimenting with the fundamental dynamics of the stage through the *Lehrstück*, Brecht dissolves the difference between player and spectator, and instead advocates a *"große Pädagogik"* which "only recognizes actors who are simultaneously students" (Brecht, 2003, p. 88). Whereas difference is eradicated in terms of actor/spectator, it is highlighted in the potentials open to the characters within the world of the drama. In focusing not on one final product, but rather on the process of artistic development as in a rehearsal, the *Lehrstück* aims to bring about a kind of self-realization in those taking part. Brecht suggested that "[t]hese experiments were theatrical performances meant not so much for the spectator as for those who were engaged in the performance. It was, so to speak, art for the producer, not art for the consumer" (Brecht, 1964, p. 80). As this essay explains through an examination of the process and development of the 1930–31 *Lehrstücke* for young audiences, *Der Jasager* (He Who Says Yes or, He Said Yes) and *Der Neinsager* (He Who Says No or, He Said No), audience members were empowered as they became engaged in the process of production. As such, Brecht's *Lehrstück*-theory can be useful to both practitioners of theatre for young audiences and its scholarly community.

While children factor into Brecht's ideas on pedagogy and theatre, the *Lehrstücke* are not traditionally thought of as children's theatre; only *Der Jasager* and *Der Neinsager* were written for young people. Much of Brecht's *Lehrstück*-theory deals with adult participants, both as performers and audience members, yet these ideas

S. Schonmann (ed.), Key Concepts in Theatre/Drama Education, 197–201.

can and should be applied to new works for young audiences. In his essay "Theory of Pedagogies," Brecht writes that "young people should be educated by play-acting," a pedagogical method that turns actors "into people who are simultaneously active and contemplative," creating student-actors who are equal parts learner and performer (Brecht, 2003, p. 89). This distinction does not imply that a performance will take place in the traditional sense, but rather privileges education and process over a final product:

> By virtue of the fact that young people, when performing, carry out actions which they themselves scrutinize, they are educated for the state. These performances must be invented and executed in such a way that the state benefits. What decides the value if a sentence, or a gesture or an action, is thus not beauty, but whether the state benefits if the performers speak that sentence, carry out that gesture and proceed to take that action (p. 89).

Brecht abandons a traditional system of value judgment for the theatre, and instead shifts the focus toward theatre's usefulness for society and the state, encouraging a pragmatic pedagogy through rehearsal-performance of the *Lehrstück*. Roswitha Mueller (1994) notes that, "the historical basis for the *Lehrstücke* is a society in transition to socialism. Within this context, the central concern is to find ways of learning that are adequate for the new state" (p. 82). Brecht's texts do not reiterate a larger goal of teaching a specific idea; rather, they teach how to think, or, as Mueller paraphrases Reiner Steinweg, "the *Lehre* is to be understood not as 'recipes for political action,' but as the teaching of dialectics as a method of thinking" (Mueller, 1994, p. 85).

Brecht's major accomplishment with the *Lehrstücke* is not rooted in specific ideology (particularly Marxism) transmitted through plots, but rather as Jameson notes, his "doctrine is simply the method itself" (Jameson, 1998, p. 99). An examination of Brecht's *Lehrstücke* reveals many examples the student-actor can follow in the space of the performance-rehearsal or master class. The characters within *Lehrstücke* are asked to make and execute critical life-changing decisions. The dialogue is often comprised of explanations for why characters made the decisions they did; for example, in *Die Maßnahme* (The Measures Taken), a group of communist agitators from Russia illustrate and explain why they killed their comrade. The *Lehrstück* structure encourages the performer to both enact and examine his or her character's actions. In *Der Jasager* the young protagonist decides, in the first version of the play, to let himself be killed, but in *Der Neinsager* he rejects this idea, and describes his reasons for doing so.

Der Jasager and *Der Neinsager* are based on the 15th century Japanese Noh play *Taniko*; Brecht's adaptations were written between 1930 and 1931. The original version of *Der Jasager* was composed as an opera for students for which Kurt Weill composed the score. The play was rewritten twice: Brecht created *Der Neinsager* as a response to the earlier play, and then later rewrote *Der Jasager*. Neither *Der Neinsager* nor the rewrite of *Der Jasager* were set to music. Brecht wanted the two versions of *Der Jasager* to be performed together with *Der Neinsager*, as a trilogy. However, the opera *Der Jasager* and *Der Neinsager* only appeared together once during Brecht's lifetime, in a 1951 Living Theatre production in New York (Willett, 1997, p. 342). The rewrite of *Der Jasager* was not part of the production.

Despite the fact that *Der Jasager* and *Der Neinsager* were written for and influenced by children, it is clear that the lens through which scholars view these plays is not one specific to children's theater. Important strides have been made in examining these plays as 'teaching pieces,' but when essays mention the children's response to and interaction with the original text of *Der Jasager*, it is usually as a means through which to attack the plays in a product-oriented manner for being inconsistent or flawed. Yet from a process-oriented perspective it becomes clear that the trio of plays exists, along with their course of revisions, as an example of children's theater that served to empower students.

In the first version of Brecht's *Der Jasager*, a young Boy wants to accompany his Teacher and Three Students on a dangerous journey across the mountains to obtain medicine for his ill mother. While traveling, the Boy becomes tired and ill, which prompts the Teacher and Three Students to discuss the local Custom: "all those who fail the climb should be thrown into the valley" (Brecht, 1997, p. 52). The Custom also stipulates that the Boy himself should be asked, but that he should then consent to death. The second version of *Der Jasager* employs several significant changes to the plot. The Custom is done away with—in this version the climbing party decides to leave the Boy behind, as the mountain is too difficult to cross while carrying the boy. The group of travelers is also seeking medicine for the town, and its survival depends on their success. The Boy initially consents to being left behind, but then asks the climbing party to instead hurl him into the valley, as he is "frightened to die alone" (ibid, p. 56). This time, it is the Boy who demands that the Three Students must consent to hurling him down, reversing the power dynamic. Both versions of *Der Jasager* end with a Chorus describing the death of the Boy.

In *Der Neinsager*, which opens with the same text as the first version of *Der Jasager*, the final scene begins with the Teacher informing the Boy of the Custom, that he should be hurled into the valley, and that he should consent to such action. Yet the scene plays out very differently, as the Boy *"pauses for thought,"* then replies, "No, I do not consent" (ibid, p. 58). The Teacher and Students do not know what to make of the Boy's decision, but the Boy explains his reasons, advocating the abandonment of the old Custom in favor of "a new Custom, which we should bring in at once, the Custom of thinking things out anew in every new situation" (ibid, p. 59). The climbing party, faced with such a reasonable rejection of their ancient ways, returns back to the town. The play ends with the Chorus commenting on the new Custom and the group's solidarity in the name of reason.

The changes in the play can largely be attributed to the suggestions made by a group of students who were at the premiere of the first version of *Der Jasager*. According to John Willett (1997), Brecht was not present, but among those who attended was a music teacher from a progressive Berlin school. "[S]ince Brecht himself appeared open to suggestions," the teacher "brought a group of students round to the writer's flat to talk their problems over" (Willett, 1997, p. 341). The comments were collected by the teacher and given to Brecht, who employed a number of them in the two subsequent versions of this play—first, the composition of *Der Neinsager* as a companion piece, and later the revision of *Der Jasager*. The alternatives that were not evident to the Boy stood out to the students who commented on this play, and their abilities to interact with this text, through Brecht as a conduit, empowered them to challenge the educational ideological apparatus as it appeared onstage.

Reiner Steinweg began exploring Brecht's *Lehrstück*-theory in the 1970s; it has since been employed by directors such as Heiner Müller and Andrzej Wirth. Its influence can also be seen in the development of Augusto Boal's Theatre of the Oppressed. The use of *Lehrstück*-theory in drama for children can be seen in the British play *On Trial* by Brian Way (1973). The play is told mostly through flashback, recounting the story of an adult guide, David Abbott, whose decisions while on an expedition saved hundreds of lives at the expense of several of his men. Much as in *Jasager/Neinsager*, the deaths are not played out onstage but the decision-making process is reenacted. The play begins and ends with the jury out, and the audience is without a verdict. The play closes with David turning to the audience and saying: "You, the jury, must decide. You, the jury" (p. 28).

The Berlin GRIPS Theater's *Voll auf der Rolle* presents the process of the *Lehrstück* at work in a play-within-a-play that features contemporary Berlin students staging a historical drama about anti-Nazi resistance and the persecution of Jews during the Third Reich. The students gravitate to roles somewhat similar to their own in real life: a young Turkish boy, the son of a foreign worker who faces deportation, agrees to play a Jewish boy in hiding, while his classmate, a right-winger, wants to play a member of the Hitler Youth. As Gerhard Fischer (1988) notes, this play "demonstrates in an exemplary manner some of the central issues of Brecht's *Lehrstück*-theory while at the same time making a thoroughly original and theatrically innovative statement" (p. 372). In *Voll auf der Rolle*, only through the synthesis of stage role and social role do students come to understand the relevance of history.

Young audiences can be engaged in critical thinking processes and empowered through the interaction between spectator and actor in plays that are influenced by Brecht's *Lehrstück*-theory. The *Lehrstücke* not only address the potential for theatre to educate young people, but also work reciprocally. They allow young audiences to respond to what has been presented onstage by suggesting different alternatives for the characters, thereby diminishing the delineation between actor and spectator, and in the case of *Der Jasager* and *Der Neinsager*, the delineation between teacher and child.

REFERENCES

Brecht, B. (1964). The German Drama: Pre-Hitler. In J. Willett (Ed. & Trans.). *Brecht on theatre: The development of an aesthetic* (pp. 77–81). New York: Hill and Wang.

Brecht, B. (1997). He Said Yes/He Said No. In J. Willett & R. Manheim (Eds.), *Bertolt Brecht, collected plays* (Vol. 3, pp. 45–59, 333–342). London: Methuen.

Brecht, B. (2003). Theory of pedagogies: The major and the minor pedagogy, theory of pedagogies. In T. Kuhn & S. Giles (Eds.), *Brecht on art and politics* (pp. 87–92). London: Methuen.

Fischer, G. (1988). The Lehrstück experience on a contemporary stage: On Brecht and the GRIPS-Theater's Voll auf der Rolle. *Modern Drama, 31*(3), 371–379.

Jameson, F. (1998). *Brecht and method*. London: Verso.
Mueller, R. (1994). Learning for a new society: The Lehrstück. In P. Thompson & G. Sacks (Eds.), *Cambridge companion to Brecht* (pp. 79–85). Cambridge: Cambridge UP.
Way, B. (1973). *On trial*. Edmonton, Alberta: Young Audience Scripts.
Willett, J. (Ed. & Trans.). (1997). *Collected plays* (Vol. 3). London: Methuen.

Erika Hughes, PhD, will be a fellow at the United States Holocaust Memorial Museum in 2010–2011. In 2011–2012, she will be a research fellow at the Freie Universität Berlin.

MARÍA INÉS FALCONI

33. CLASSICS AND YOUNGSTERS

Keywords: classic theatre, classic literature, young people, adolescents, young performing

Just to mention "classics and youngsters" in the same breath apparently supposes
falling into a contradiction. "Classics" addresses history, past, permanence, excellence,
whereas "youngsters" refers to updated, present and transitory. Is it possible to join
these two extremes in an interesting and creative action? This is the question we
will try to answer here.

Often when we talk about a classical text (literature or theatre) with young people
(ages 13–18 or even older) our discourse immediately awakens in many of them
a reaction of rejection. Shakespeare, Cervantes, Lope de Vega, the Greek Theatre
and even the more contemporary Federico García Lorca are often synonymous
with feelings of obligation and boredom. These texts are usually topics of obliged
reading in Literature lessons at school and are frequently presented as rigid textual
structures, to be analyzed, to be memorized, but never to be enjoyed. To read classic
texts, with their "ancient" language, incomprehensible words (unfamiliar only because
such words are out of use), complex grammar, or even poetry, is hard work for
young people. We need to help our students find meaning in what they are reading.
We need to seek ways to interest them in their reading not simply leave them alone
in front of a text they cannot understand.

What does engagement with any text (classic or not) require in order to raise our
interest? First, it is essential that we can understand it. Then, we need to be able to
identify ourselves with the story, the characters, the themes or the situations. As a
third point, a text needs to have a strong and interesting dramatic structure that make
us curious to know the ending.

For a classical text to fulfil these three conditions it is necessary that an adult
mediate between the text and the youngster, whether that youngster is an actor, a
reader or a member of the audience. If we succeed in our role of "guides",
youngsters will be more willing to take on a challenging text, rather than abandon
it in frustration.

Comprehension: first is first. It is difficult to get close to those things that we do
not understand. Classical texts need "translation", not from one language into another
one, but from one shape into another one. As educators we need to be aware that
youngsters nowadays are absorbed in a variety of fast informatics communications.
Not only have users significantly reduced the number of words they use to communicate with each other, but also the letters that they use to write their communications.
In addition, often, to our surprise, we find ourselves having to explain the meaning

S. Schonmann (ed.), Key Concepts in Theatre/Drama Education, 203–206.

of words within a text; words that seem obvious to us, but which youngsters say they have never heard of in their whole life. Or perhaps, they have heard these words spoken by others, but they ignored them or have never used them, so, as they say, the words "do not exist".

Something similar happens with metaphors, sayings, proverbs and so on. Youngsters read them and even repeat them as a sequence of words but without any meaning-making. Such literary devices, historical references and sayings "have to be learned". Often, in my experience, students will not put any effort into understand the meaning embodied within these phrases or sayings. Perhaps, after you have spent months of listening to youngsters repeating such phrases, if you ask them about the meaning, they will answer that, "they have no idea", they are just repeating the words.

As text mediators, we have to try (and better at the beginning of our working with the text rather than months later) to help students learn how to read difficult texts, to recognize literacy devices and references, to think, to find out. I advise that, as educators, we are the ones who will have to surface in the text the paragraphs, phrases or words that our students do not understand. They are not going to identify these by themselves, or perhaps more truthfully, they will not pay any attention to that which they do not know. To enlighten those parts of the text that need explanation or analysis, we should, then, read the text not from our experienced point of view, but in the way we might imagine that the youngsters would read it: with surprise, mis-comprehension, and in doing so, we will discover that those points that are very clear for us, are perhaps, not so clear for our students. When we help youngsters puzzle out, for example, a metaphor, their reaction is often characteristic and surprising: they will say "Ahhh" with their mouths wide-open, and then they will smile, and then, they will become aware and say "Sure!" full of satisfaction. And meaning comes to light and the text opens up to them.

But sometimes, the process of understanding a text is not only related to meanings but also to different ways of talking in one time period compared to another. As educators, we need to find the parallelism between the classical text we are reading and our current way of talking and the words we use nowadays (or the words our students use). So, for example, Shakespeare's text: "Part, fools; put up your swords; you know not what you do" is perhaps more comprehensible if it is translated into present-day language: "Go away, assholes! Don't you see the mess you are doing?" Please understand that I am not suggesting that we should not use the original text, on the contrary. I am just stating that in order to be able to use the original text properly, we need to understand it, and to be able to understand it, it is useful to translate it into our everyday life language, the one that we know very well.

About identification, it is clear to us, as adults, that the classics address universal and timeless topics, existential human conflicts through time. It may not be so clear for young people, even when day after day they may experience similar situations. For example, perhaps some students will not understand why it is impossible for Romeo to fall in love with Juliet. What does it mean, to entertain such a ridiculous situation between two enemy families? But, what happens if some parents' prohibitions prevent youngsters from socializing with certain groups of people? Even nowadays, what happens in situations involving lovers of different religions or ethnic groups? Is the story so "old"?

"Doña Rosita, the single" spends years waiting for her cousin to come and marry her, but he never comes. Nobody would be able to cope with such endless despair of waiting in the XXI Century, that's for sure, but, how many hours might a young girl spend in front of her computer or with her mobile phone waiting for a call from the boy she likes while rejecting everybody else? When working with the classics, it is useful to use contemporary examples when interpreting the text with your students. Once more, it is by holding an adult's hand that youngsters are able to puzzle out the relevance or validity of the conflicts contained within classic texts and in this way, recognize and understand similar situations with their own real life.

The third item, dramatic structure, is only a consequence of the two previous ones. Once you can understand the language and the situations, once you have recognized the conflicts and the characters, you will be easily captured and moved by the plot, and in most circumstances, like a great movie, you will hang in suspense up to the end.

After reading the text, we face the challenge of staging the play. We could say that difficulties will repeat themselves in the same way but now come through the action, embodied within the performance. Each teacher, director or playwright will adapt and stage a play according to his or her own creativity and experience. There are no formulas (and nor should there be either), but I think there is a premise that should be taken into account: youngsters, when they play the classics need to have fun, even when they are performing a tragedy. And the audience (generally youngsters) has to have fun too. Humour is the master key. To find out that, to allow it and to share it, that is critical to success.

When working with youngsters, I never come to them with a finished adaptation, with actors already selected for each character and the stage design decided. I come to them with guidelines just ideas to begin to work with, ideas that perhaps will be used or which perhaps will be modified during the process. I allow youngsters to improvise different situations, to play different characters. I allow them to interject their own personal mood or interpretations, to suggest crazy and impossible ideas: that's to say, to become owners of the project. Then it's time to fix the play, the speech, the characters and the aesthetic. Everything is about bringing together the play's genius and the group's creativity. This is the coordinator's duty. I would like to point out that this way of staging a play is not the result of a "group's creation" that comes about just by chance. The play and the staging are transformed not only by the group's creative contribution, but also on the basis of a written text and rigorous staging. On the other hand, and related to the text, I think it is necessary to use the original text, mixed with an up-dated one, simpler if necessary, shorter too and so on; but incorporating the author's words and poetry, his or her images, his or her particular way of telling has to be present, in the actor's voices and in the audience's ears.

Finally, I will briefly touch upon production. It is important that the group be involved in the whole project. This is not only about hopping onstage and performing, but also, about being responsible for other duties involved in producing the play, according to each individual's abilities. Perhaps, there is a musician in the group who could compose the music, play or record it. Perhaps you could find someone who is clever in the visual arts, who could participate in costumes or stage design; or someone who likes mathematics who could take care of the production; or others who could write a press release and implement an advertising plan. All groups are different and it is a coordinator's duty to find out who has which abilities suitable and to encourage youngsters to develop them. Where possible, youngsters should have the support and advice of a professional in the field, as they fulfil their production responsibilities and performances so that their experience will be one of learning. I don't know how many youngsters discover their vocation during this process but I can ensure you that by creating the opportunity for children to engage and be successful in the arts we contribute to the health and wellbeing of the arts and that of the children.

This process, so briefly described, has as its aim not only the training but also the intention of bringing youngsters closer to classical literature. Trying to have them become friends, to open doors to new knowledge and discoveries for young actors and young audiences. After performing or seeing a well-treated classical play, one that takes their interests into account, which engages them with pleasure and not with obligation, youngsters will more readily reach for the original text with interest, without fear or prejudices. They will start to read if only to see what they have heard or said on stage is also written in the original text. They will be surprised when they find the paragraphs they have already heard; they will take a critical glance at the text to discover what was changed or omitted; and, perhaps, they will take on the risk of reading new authors and new texts.

Classics will go on living and youngsters will live better, awakened to the possibilities that the classics through the arts offer.

María Inés Falconi, *Playwright and Writer, Theatre Director, Drama and Play-writing Teacher. Vice- president of ASSITEJ International, Secretary of ATINA Universidad Popular de Belgrano Boards of Directors.*

SECTION VII: CREATIVITY AND TECHNOLOGY

SHARON BAILIN

34. CREATIVITY AND DRAMA EDUCATION

Keywords: creativity, drama education, originality, imagination, critical judgment

The claim is often made that drama is a creative enterprise and that participation in drama can foster creativity. Determining whether and in what way this may be the case poses challenges, however, as the term creativity is ambiguous in several ways. For one thing, it can be applied to a number of different referents. We speak of creative persons, as in "Tom Stoppard is a creative playwright," creative processes, as in "Tom Stoppard thinks creatively," and creative products, as in "Arcadia is a creative play." In addition, there is a particular ambiguity when the term creativity is applied to the arts. The arts are, by their nature, creative in the sense that they involve activities of actual creation - of paintings, music, dances, dramas, and art-works of various sorts. Thus, by engaging in the arts, one is being creative almost by definition. That cannot, however, be all that is meant by the arts being creative since it is commonly thought that some art processes and products are more creative than others and that certain ways of teaching the arts in general and drama in particular are more likely to foster creativity. We usually mean more by creativity than simply engaging in creative activities, since we distinguish among the products of these activities in terms of their creativity. Not all creations are equally creative.

This observation highlights one of the problems which has plagued the concept of creativity in education in general and in arts education in particular. Arts education has been strongly influenced by a form of Romantic naturalism (Hornbrook, 1998) which views the person in his or her natural state as essentially good and views culture as potentially damaging to this natural goodness (Hornbrook, 1988). Education, then, becomes a liberation and development of what is within rather than an acquisition and assimilation of what is without. Although the popularity of this perspective has waxed and waned in recent years, it has had a strong hold on drama education in the past, and this hold is still evident in some contexts today. Manifestations of this view include an emphasis on process over product, an emphasis on originality viewed as novelty, and the downplaying of skills of the discipline and knowledge of dramatic tradition, all in the name of facilitating the emergence of the natural creativity within the individual (Bailin, 1998).

The majority of theorists working on the notion of creativity agree that at its core creativity must include some element of novelty or originality. They also agree, however, that novelty is not enough. What is required as well is an element of value in the products produced. This implies that there is some sort of outcome, product or achievement which can be deemed creative, thus rendering the process emphasis problematic. An additional implication is that works which are seen as having value, even highly innovative works, must be connected to and viewed within the context of the artistic traditions out of which they arise. Thus creative production necessarily involves the skills, knowledge and judgment which arise from an in-depth understanding of these traditions and the criteria which are embodied within them. The appropriate attitude toward these traditions is one of flexibility and openness, however, involving a willingness to take seriously what they have to offer but also to go beyond them should the need and occasion arise (Bailin, 1988/1992).

A fundamental problem with the Romantic view of creativity is that it assumes that creativity implies total freedom and fails to realize that it is possible to be creative within constraints. Indeed, all artistic creation takes place within constraints of some sort, and the majority of artists are not radical innovators of form but rather work within the limits of technique inherent in a particular style. Yet there is certainly scope for creativity within these limits. Creativity in drama is not confined to spontaneous improvisation but is possible in all aspects of dramatic work.

We can see, for example, the many ways in which directing a play is an arena for creative achievement. Because a script is usually pre-determined and fixed, there are constraints upon the creating from the outset (Eco, 1992). Nonetheless, there is considerable leeway in how the script is brought to life on stage, and this provides possibilities for originality and freshness. Although a script is the blueprint for a theatrical production, within the confines of what is actually presented in the script, there is vast scope for interpretation (Miller, 1986; Brook, 1996). The interpretation of the characters, both overall and at any particular moment, and the decision as to the meaning of the play, as well as the means to achieve these, rest ultimately on the judgment of the director. A particular production may, then, differ radically in interpretation from past productions of the same play, and if the innovative treatment creates new insights into the play, then the production would be considered very creative. But even in productions in which the way in which a play is treated is not a radical departure from conventional approaches, there will still be a specific interpretation guiding what transpires which may be, in some respects, unique. There may be a particular portrayal, a particular interaction, a particular moment which conveys a fresh perception. If the script is animated in a manner which enhances its dramatic values and brings fresh insights to the play, then such productions will also be considered creative.

We can see, also, how the interplay between invention and critical judgment is evident in this facet of dramatic work. In developing a new interpretation of a play, the director requires considerable judgment at every step of the interpretive process, from seeing that a particular play presents interesting interpretive possibilities, to judging the aptness of possible interpretations, to predicting the likely effect on an audience, to judging the feasibility of execution, to deciding on the particular form in which the interpretation will be manifested, to developing the interpretation in production. Thus, for example, Ian McKellan's innovative film interpretation of Richard III, with its setting in a fictional post-war fascist England, had to have arisen from his thorough understanding of the play's text and themes and incisive judgment regarding the evocative power with which those themes could be presented for contemporary audiences using such a setting.

The creative element in a work is often associated with imagination, but we can see from these examples that imagination and skill are closely interconnected. There is imagination manifested in the execution of skill and skill involved in the development of an imaginative vision. We view the imaginative element in directing as reflected in the interpretation which is embodied in the production, and this interpretation is very much a product of the director's skill. The director must bring out the dramatic values inherent in the script, and doing so is largely a matter of solving the problems which the script presents. What emerges in the actual production as the director's imaginative vision is not, then, an arbitrary flight of fantasy, but is a carefully worked through whole based on work with the script and the actors, knowledge of dramatic principles, and dramatic problem-solving abilities (Bailin, 2001).

As another example, the act of playwriting, even when it does not involve the creation of a new genre, is an arena for creativity. Writing a play involves the creation of a script which portrays images of human experience and visions of human possibility crafted in such a way that they can be brought to life through production. And some plays may do this in a creative manner, revealing new insights, uniquely touching our sensibilities, or crystallizing ideas or feelings in novel ways. We might be tempted to view the creation of such insights and vision as embodying the creative dimension of playwriting and relegate the skills of the playwright to a mechanical process. Yet this vision is expressed in the dialogue of the characters – in the choice in words, and in what is said and not said; in the stage movement indicated and envisaged; in the setting suggested; in the dramatic structure created. It would be somewhat misleading, then, to say that the imaginative vision is expressed by means of the playwright's skilled use of language and dramatic techniques. Rather, the former is developed through the latter. The vision is a dramatic vision, and the imagination of the playwright is a dramatic imagination.

There is considerable scope for creativity for actors working with scripts. Acting for an audience can be more than a kind of purely technical signaling (Bolton, 1992). Indeed, a distinction if often drawn between acting purely technically and acting in an imaginative manner. The former refers to acting which is superficial and relies on a repertoire of conventional gestures and responses, acting which lacks depth, genuine feeling, and real insight into the character portrayed. Imaginative acting, on the other hand, involves the creation of a unique and believable character and involves depth of feeling and real understanding. It is often pointed out that an actor may be technically proficient in terms of skills of presentation and performance but yet lack these other elements. Yet surely it is also the case that the actor's skill goes beyond movement on stage, control of the voice and body, projection and similar abilities. The ability to understand a character and to create a believable presence on stage is a part of the actor's skill as well. Such a characterization comes not purely from a pre-existing abstract vision, but rather from the actor working with the script, director, and other actors and developing the characterization through technical abilities and acting skills. Once this is recognized, we can see here again that imagination and skill are closely intertwined.

A similar interplay of between imaginative invention and knowledge of the form is evident in dramatic innovation in which some of the rules of the form are violated. It is an understanding of the rules and conventions, of the reasons for them, and of what is at issue in complying with them which enables an artist to know when to violate these rules. Thus a novice director may inadvertently block an actor with her back to the audience thus losing her lines upstage. But an experienced director who is well aware of the rules of stage movement, who understands the reasons for the general injunction against turning one's back to an audience may choose to defy this rule at a certain point in order to achieve a particularly startling effect of focus. Similarly, skills and knowledge in no way inhibit radical innovation in the sense of going beyond established frameworks. Many great artists have done precisely this, and the majority have not been artistic innocents, unsullied by the skills of a prevailing style, but have been masters of these skills. It is, in fact, this mastery which puts the artist in a position to know when the techniques will no longer suffice to express a new insight or point of view, to know when the possibilities of the present form are exhausted. New ground is broken through critical judgment, but this judgment is itself based upon a repertoire of acquired and assimilated skills and knowledge (Bailin, 1988/1992).

Ultimately, creativity has to do with actual creating and with quality production, and such production takes place within cultural forms and traditions. Thus, in order to be creative, students require the resources which will enable them to engage knowledgeably and skillfully with these traditions. In the case of drama, this means acquiring the skills and knowledge of dramatic art as well as an understanding of the multiple and diverse dramatic traditions past and present which are the embodiment of creative achievement. Such traditions have within them tensions and contradictions as well as the mechanisms for criticism which make evolution possible. Thus critical judgment is central to creativity. Fostering creativity is not a matter of withholding critical judgment, but rather of developing it (Bailin, 1998).[1]

NOTES

[1] Many of the arguments in this paper are drawn from Bailin 1988/1992 and Bailin 1998.

REFERENCES

Bailin, S. (1998). Creativity in context. In D. Hornbrook (Ed.), *On the subject of drama* (pp. 36–50). London: Routledge.

Bailin, S. (1988/1992). *Achieving extraordinary ends: An essay on creativity*. Dordrecth: Kluwer, Norwood, NJ: Ablex.

Bailin, S. (2001). In the space between the words: Play production as an interpretive enterprise. *Journal of Aesthetic Education. 35*(2), 67–75.

Bolton, G. (1992). *New perspectives on classroom drama*. Hemel Hempstead: Simon & Shuster Education.

Brook, P. (1996). Epilogue: Six hemispheres in search of... In M. M. Delgado & P. Heritage (Eds.), *In contact with the gods? Directors talk theatre*. Manchester: Manchester University Press.

Eco, U. (1992). *Interpretation and overinterpretation*. Cambridge: Cambridge University Press.

Hornbrook, D. (1988). *Education and dramatic art*. London: Routledge.

Hornbrook, D. (1998). Drama and education. In D. Hornbrook (Ed.), *On the subject of drama*. London: Routledge.
Miller, J. (1986). *Subsequent performances*. New York: Viking.

Sharon Bailin *is Professor Emeritus in the Faculty of Education, Simon Fraser University, Vancouver Canada. Her main areas of research are creativity, critical thinking, and arts and drama education.*

LAURA A. MCCAMMON, AUD BERGGRAF SÆBØ
AND LARRY O'FARRELL

35. "CREATIVITY REALLY COMES BY WHAT'S INSIDE OF YOU"

Drama/Theatre Teaching and Learning and Creative Achievement

Keywords: creativity, creativity and play, effective teaching

> "...*creativity really comes by what's inside of you. Teachers should show you how to create certain stuff, but from a base, you have to go on your own.*" (O'Farrell, 2009, p. 6)

A secondary student in a Canadian performing arts school articulates one of the interesting dichotomies when it comes to promoting creative achievement in young people: For the individual student, it is likely that creativity is perceived as a form of self-expression, something that happens within themselves or in their group. While, for the teacher, promoting creative achievement depends on the structuring of the class and assignments and observing student growth as s/he masters an art form. This comment from an elementary teacher in Jamaica illustrates, "In teaching creativity, teachers need to provide opportunities where students are allowed to give their own idea and present what they are feeling which also will help to develop critical thinking skills" (Sæbø, McCammon, O'Farrell, & Heap, 2008, p. 51).

Both perspectives are critical to promote creative achievement. According to pioneering creativity educator, Doris Shallcross (1981), creative activities should be structured to remove the barriers occurring both within the individual and outside the individual. The challenge, then, for drama/theatre educators is to provide the structure and environment for their students to perceive their own successes. This paper will look briefly at the literature on teaching for creative achievement and how it applies to drama/theatre education.

WHAT IS CREATIVITY?

Historically creativity has proven to be a difficult concept to define. There is general agreement, however, that creativity results in something new, useful and, hopefully, ethical. According to Fisher (2004), there are three levels of originality:

- Individual: being original in relation to one's previous thoughts, words or deeds; e.g. "I have not thought or done this before."

S. Schonmann (ed.), Key Concepts in Theatre/Drama Education, 215–220.

- Social: being original in relation to one's social group, community or organization; e.g. "We have not thought or done this before."
- Universal: being original in terms of all previous known human experience; e.g. "No one has thought or done this before." (p. 9)

There is agreement in the literature that creativity is a distinctly human trait and that all humans have creative capacity. Craft (2005) places creative potential on a continuum from everyday acts of creativity, which she calls "little c", to highly creative innovations or "Big C". According to Shallcross (1981), "Creative abilities exist in varying degrees among us, as do other kinds of intelligence. It's a matter of getting those abilities to surface and making them work for us" (p. 2).

There are four general contexts for creativity: creative persons, creative processes, creative products or ideas, and creative environments. These four are not independent of each other and frequently overlap. There are a number of elements frequently associated with creativity including: imagination/flexibility of the mind, divergence and convergence, risk-taking, problem solving, critical thinking, playfulness, new insights or ideas, rebelliousness and challenges to the status quo, ethical commitments, liminality, achieving a "flow" state.

Teachers who have clear understanding of what creativity is and how it can apply to teaching and learning will be better able to promote creative achievement in their students.

TEACHING FOR CREATIVE ACHIEVEMENT

Following the rationale that creative capacity exists in all of us, there is, therefore, general agreement among educators that creativity can be taught (e.g., Craft, 2005; Fisher, 2004; NACCCE, 1999; Shallcross, 1981). Doris Shallcross, one of the first to offer a method for teaching creativity, tended to see creativity as a problem solving method. Her approach was to develop multiple forms of divergent thinking through brainstorming and then convergent thinking to pull all the ideas together to develop a solution or plan. While in many ways, drama/theatre pedagogy has moved beyond Shallcross's method, some of her original tenets set up basic understandings for how drama/theatre classrooms can develop creative capacity more effectively.

Nurture the Social Context

Shallcross (1981) notes that there are two important barriers to teaching creativity: those coming from within the student (psychological) and those coming from outside the student (sociological). She begins with the sociological barriers since these are the conditions most in the immediate control of the teacher.

Sociological barriers. Several factors are at play here. First, are the social group roles and issues of adolescent identity that students bring with them into the classroom (Cahill, 2009). Examples include the influence of peer pressure on both boys and girls, the conflict between male identity and drama participation, and "academically successful students" reluctance to risk participation outside their control.

The social environment strongly affects creative behavior because, first and foremost, creative expression involves personal risk. Shallcross (1981) advocates building a strong sense of emotional safety through constant demonstration and reinforcement, good classroom structure, and a clear set of expectations. Her method builds mental flexibility and comfort through small first steps, built in successes, building associative powers and fluency through brainstorming. Most drama/theatre educators spend time carefully establishing their classroom community and setting up expectations for respectful and playful interaction. Peer feedback which benefits both the giver and the receiver is often used effectively in all aspects of drama/theatre teaching and learning.

Psychological barriers. Within each student are unique psychological barriers which impede creative interactions. Shallcross (1981) cites rigidity and inflexibility, fear of ridicule and failure, reliance on authority, habits of mind or routines that prevent divergent thinking as forms of psychological barriers. In schools two adverse conditions are especially dangerous to motivational states: anxiety and boredom. According to Csikszentmihalyi, Rathunde and Whalen (1993), even talented teens did not want to be doing what they were doing in schools most of the time. Arts students, however, tend to find that their learning is not only challenging but also fun (McCammon, 2009). Research suggests that drama that includes improvised activities strongly motivates the students to be creative in the learning process (Sæbø, 2009). Because students perceive drama activities to be different, they are more engaged in their learning especially when they can use fantasy and creativity as they learn (Sæbø, 2005).

Participation in drama/theatre activities gives young people and their teacher the opportunity to confront and manage both the psychological and the sociological barriers. When young people, for example, have the opportunity to explore other roles and perspectives they can broaden their view of the world, learn empathy for others, and develop a stronger sense of themselves. This can happen both in process based drama activities and in the more structured performance-based theatre. In play production, for example, young people take on roles in the play (playing a character) but also outside the play (director, designer, dramaturg).

Using Play to Generate a Safe and Receptive Space for Creativity

The creative drama movement in the early years of the 20th century grew out of the understandings of children's pretend play (McCaslin, 2006). The study of play and its relationship to development of young people continues to provide useful insights for a discussion on creativity. Brown (2009) defines play as "an absorbing, apparently purposeless activity that provides enjoyment and a suspension of self- consciousness and sense of time. It is also self-motivating and makes you want to do it again" (p. 60). According to Brown, humans need to play to continue to develop brain functioning as play stimulates multiple centers of perception and cognition across the whole brain. There is, moreover, a strong link between play and memory; because the play state promotes both heightened attention and emotional rewards, students are more motivated to remember what they learned.

Through play and fantasy, young people not only develop cognitive skills, but also their imaginations which, in Brown's (2009) view, are key to not only creativity but more fundamentally to emotional resilience and creativity. "Imagining the inner life of others and comparing it to ones own - is one of the keys to developing empathy, understanding, and trust of others, as well as personal coping skills" (p. 87).

The impulse to create art, according to Brown (2009) is a direct result of the play impulse; furthermore, art promotes community. "It is literally a communion" (p. 62). When arts are created in schools, a sense of "belonging" is generated which can put young people "in sync with those around [them]. It is a way to tap into common emotions and thoughts and share them with others" (p. 63).

Brown (2009) identifies various types of play critical for human development. It is important to note that each can be found in a drama/theatre classroom:

– Body and Movement Play - through movement play, individuals learn to think in motion and learn about self-movement. Brown advocates getting up and moving around to stimulate play and creative thinking in adults.
– Object Play - there is pleasure and play in the manipulation of objects - putting together a puzzle, kicking a ball. The hand and brain work together to solve problems.
– Imaginative Play - children's pretend play which translates into the adult tendency to "make up storylines in our heads". Imaginative play is the key to emotional resilience.
– Social Play - social play takes three forms - friendship and belonging, rough-and-tumble play, and celebratory and ritual play.
– Storytelling and Narrative Play - the mind structures events most effectively in narrative form; story becomes a way of "learning about the world, oneself, and one's place in it."
– Transformative-Integrative and Creative Play - "when we engage in fantasy play at any age, we bend the reality of our ordinary lives, and in the process germinate new ideas and ways of being." (pp. 80–94).

Promoting play in the classroom in the form of improvisation, theatre games, process drama is one of the major ways that drama/theatre teachers develop creative capacity. Expanding their world through improv, for example, opens them up to divergent thinking, accepting offers, challenging themselves (Johnstone, 1981). Through play both teacher and student can live in those liminal spaces between fantasy and reality. Through the protection of role and dramatic playing, young people can challenge the status quo, transgress and rebel, take on new social roles, expand their imagination and flexibility of mind.

While play can stimulate what Shallcross (1981) saw as divergent thinking, young people also need the process of convergence - coming together in the creative act. Activities like writing in role, developing original monologues, and learning a scripted role all enable the student to pull together diverse thoughts into a coherent whole.

It is also important to note that most drama/theatre activities promote both individual creative acts and collective moments.

Use Effective Teaching Strategies

There is little doubt that effective, creative drama/theatre teachers are more capable of enhancing creative capacity in their students. Several characteristics of effective teaching for creative achievement emerge from the literature. Effective teachers:
- Have knowledge of their field and to continue to learn and practice their own art form (Craft, 2005; Csikszentmihalyi, Rathunde, & Whalen, 1993; O'Farrell, 2009).
- Focus on learner empowerment and passing control to the learner, through imaginative approaches, giving learners choices, setting interesting tasks, encouraging and valuing learner contributions, and making learning more interesting (Craft, 2005; Fryer, 1996).
- Build confidence by starting with simple tasks, building in successes, standing-back and letting students come up with their own solutions (Fryer, 1996; Shallcross, 1981).
- Provide structure and clear expectations while still allowing room for experimentation (O'Farrell, 2009; Sæbø, 2009; Shallcross, 1981).
- Are enthusiastic, confident, and willing to take risks themselves (Fryer, 1996).

Drama/theatre has enormous potential to uncover and enhance the creativity capacities of young people as individuals and as members of a social group. Effective teachers, both those who specialize in the drama/theatre and those who use drama/theatre as a way to learn other subjects, are the key to removing those barriers.

"Creative teaching demands a sure, secure, and brave teacher and then creative teaching creates secure and brave students" (Norwegian elementary teacher) (Sæbø, McCammon, O'Farrell, & Heap, 2008, p. 54)

REFERENCES

Brown, S. (2009). *Play: How it shapes the brain, Opens the imagination, and invigorates the soul.* New York: Avery/Penguin Books.
Cahill, H. (2009, July 14–19). *Re-thinking the fiction/reality boundary: Investigating the use of drama in HIV prevention projects in Vietnam.* Paper presented at the 6th International Drama in Education Research Institute, Sydney, Australia.
Craft, A. (2005). *Creativity in schools: Tensions and dilemmas.* London: Routledge.
Csikszentmihalyi, M., Rathunde, K., & Whalen, S. (1993). *Talented teenagers: The roots of success and failure.* New York: Cambridge University Press.
Fisher, R. (2004). What is creativity? In R. Fisher & M. Williams (Eds.), *Unlocking creativity: Teaching across the curriculum* (pp. 6–20). London: David Fulton Publishers Ltd.
Fryer, M. (1996). *Creative teaching and learning.* London: Paul Chapman.
Johnstone, K. (1981). *Impro: Improvisation and the theatre.* New York: Routledge/Theatre Arts Books.
McCammon, L. A. (2009, August 8–12). *"It becomes a second family": The role of community in theatre participation.* Paper presented at the joint conference of the American Alliance for Theatre & Education and the Association for Theatre in Higher Education, New York.
McCaslin, N. (2006). *Creative drama in the classroom* (8th ed.). New York: Longman.

National Advisory Committee on Creative and Cultural Education (NACCCE). (1999). *All our futures: Creativity, culture and education.* London: DFEE.

O'Farrell, L. (2009). *Creativity in arts education: A case study in an arts magnet school.* Unpublished paper.

Sæbø, A. B. (2005). *Drama og Elevaktiv Lærning/Drama and student active learning.* Trondheim: NTNU.

Sæbø, A. B. (2009). *Didaktiske Utfordringer ved Drama som Læringsform I Skolen/Pedagogical challenges when drama is integrated as a learning form in education.* Stavanger: UiS.

Sæbø, A. B., McCammon, L. A., O'Farrell, L., & Heap, B. (2008). *Connecting with their inner being: An international survey of drama/theatre teacher's perceptions of creative teaching and teaching for creative achievement.* Technical Report.

Shallcross, D. J. (1981). *Teaching creative behavior: How to teach creativity to children of all ages.* Englewood Cliffs, NJ: Prentice Hall.

Laura A. McCammon *is Associate Professor, teaches Theatre Education at the University of Arizona in Tucson and has presented papers and published internationally on drama/theatre teaching and learning.*

Aud Berggraf Sæbø*, PhD, is a teacher educator and researcher in drama/theatre at the University of Stavanger, Norway. She has published textbooks, research reports and articles.*

Larry O'Farrell *is Professor and UNESCO Chair in Arts and Learning, Queen's University, Canada. He is also Chair, Canadian Network for Arts and Learning.*

NANCY SMITHNER

36. CREATIVE PLAY

The Importance of Incorporating Play, Liminality and
Ritual in Teaching K-12

Keywords: play, drama, creativity, teaching, imagination

Most educators would readily agree that creative play is a necessary prerequisite to learning, mental health and developmental growth. As an educator of pre-service teachers, as well as a director and performer, I view the natural intersection between play and creativity as an inspirational yet complex phenomenon. In play, meaning is imparted to action, as all play means something in the moment. As educator and artist Nellie McCaslin articulates: "A creative act does not happen once, it is an ongoing process, which with encouragement and guidance becomes a way of life" (2006, p. 25). Play is a means to an end, an aesthetic tool, and a rehearsal for life. Play teaches adaptability and resilience, and in the rapidly changing technological pace of the 21st century, creativity, which arises from play, is an essential survival skill encompassing the ability to be alert in the moment, have either conscious or unconscious insights, and to continually learn and imagine something new.

Creative play is a visceral and embodied process incorporating ritual, flow and liminality, which I believe should be woven into the fabric of learning in all grades and subject areas, as a basis for cultural, pedagogical and sociological enlightenment. When children play, they operate at their highest possible level, in the "zone of proximal development" (Vygotsky, 1978). The human species is innately adaptable, and children creatively and playfully exercise this human capacity through their own imaginative coping.

Creative play has been incorporated into many early childhood and elementary school curricula, (Hendy & Toon, 2001; Catron & Allen, 2008), including creative play-based lessons that recognize the importance of the development of creative individuals and the interrelatedness of developmental areas. In arts education, creative play can encompass as well as enliven all of the art forms (Cornett, 2003). It is manifested through role play, process drama, visual art projects using various mediums such as paint or sculpture, song, musical games, collaborative or improvisational dance, to name just a few. In drama, lessons, units and curriculum maps have been created for integration of the art form into the curriculum from K-12 by Neelands, O'Neil, Heathcote, Bolton, McCaslin, Taylor, Fleming and many others.

Indeed, the use of creative drama, in particular, is widely considered to enhance the ability to think critically, improve communication skills, increase knowledge of

S. Schonmann (ed.), Key Concepts in Theatre/Drama Education, 221–225.

self and develop understanding and appreciation of the cultural backgrounds and values of others (McCaslin, 2006, p. 6). It is this cultural awareness that lucidly draws my attention, in the ongoing contemporary re-definition of play, thus it is important to acknowledge the postmodern view that we do not exist in a cultural vacuum, and are influenced by multifaceted interactions, divergent viewpoints, and diverse cultural norms.

In the 21st century, theorists have come to recognize play as a culturally structured activity that varies widely across cultures not only in its content, but in the types of social interactions experienced, the way gendered play is interpreted, as well as the resources which are available, including material objects, space and time, and in quantity and quality (Goncu & Gaskins, 2007). In Euroamerica, play is a highly supported activity, and is believed to encourage cognitive, social and emotional development. In this view, "play is the child's work." However this interpretation of play is not always either acceptable or possible in other cultures, where it must be curtailed or is encouraged less frequently. Therefore, it is important to remember that there is not a universal blueprint for play or childhood experience. Cultures have different levels of investment in play, and it is not always a privileged and unique activity in children's lives (ibid, 2007). Educators working in diverse environments need to acknowledge these various levels of interpretation, expectation and understanding.

Additionally, the changes in contemporary play culture must be framed in terms of exposure to commerciality and all forms of technology, especially the dominance of television and video games. Much play is brief and fragmented (Kalliala, 2006, p. 134). Creative play needs time and space, and imaginative and make believe play is not always encouraged in the home or in day care centers. Furthermore it is unrealistic to believe that the ideal circumstances for play are created in the context of formal schooling.

Intersections of Play and Creativity

Play has historically been a difficult topic to define and study, as it is not a monolithic notion with a single definition, but rather a perplexing set of related behaviors or actions that do not combine easily into a single phenomenon (Goncu & Gaskin, 2007). Before attempting to define play himself, Victor Turner claimed that play was indefinable: "it does not fit in anywhere particular, it is a transient and is recalcitrant to localization, to placement, to fixation – a joker in the the neuro-anthropological act" (1982, p. 4). However, definitions are necessary for discourse, and as Richard Schechner points out, the ambiguous and multi- dimensional nature of creativity aligns well with that of the flowing concept of play (1995). Play is "fluid rather than fixed, vivid rather than formalist and reticular rather than patently mappable" (Clark as cited in Gonco & Gaskin, 2007, p. 290). Play is voluntary, detached from ordinary life, unpredictable, imaginative yet serious - it must be played according to the rules. It involves preoccupation, concentration, cannot be easily left, nor can it easily admit intrusions, and reaches its own saturation point. It is essentially satisfying, even when there is tension or anxiety.

How then is it possible to reign in play for use in a planned curriculum? How can creative play be engendered? Is play eroding? One might further ask: What is creativity? Can anyone be creative? Can you teach someone to have curiosity? Creativity can mean using ordinary resources of the mind and body in unusual and extraordinary ways, and in order to generate original ideas that have value, creative thinking strategies must be cultivated. Sir Ken Robinson, in a televised talk for TED (Theatre, Education and Design) in 2006, asserted that creativity is as important as literacy and should be treated with the same status. In formal assessment of children, and in the stigmatization of "mistakes", we are "educating kids out of their creative capacities." According to Rollo May, creativity is the act of repatterning the known world into meaningful new configurations (as cited in McCaslin 2006, p. 25). As teachers, we must find opportunities to approach information in new and different ways versus presenting only facts and single answer formats.

To engender creativity and play, first we must value these notions as educators, and have belief in and enthusiasm for the ability to be creative. A major part of the school day needs to be spent engaging students in creative problem solving; the arts provide the most fertile ground for growing this indispensable high-order thinking. Creativity involves different kinds of thinking strategies: metaphoric, divergent, convergent, combining opposites, finding contradictions. A person does not create in a vacuum, but rather is involved in other's ideas and foundations of others, and thus experiences repetition, notices patterns, makes realizations and moves forward. The opportunity to frame ideas in different ways can be put into action, using the playful concepts of brainstorming, word association, and collaborative thinking through active creative engagement. Additionally, acknowledging the notion that students learn and express themselves through multiple intelligences can expand the possibilities for engaging them in a creatively motivated pedagogy. The ability to be engaged actively through physicality, aurality, and visuality changes the entire atmosphere of learning.

Unfortunately, teaching often takes place in an educational environment in which there is an obsession with efficiency, objectives, standards and targets, where movement is discouraged, and spatial use of the classroom is never varied. Creative play, however, works against the notion of constant assessment and evaluation, judgement, competition, emphasis on the product, following explicit directions, lack of time to ponder, asking questions, taking things too seriously, and staying within the lines. The use of questioning where the first idea is not immediately seized upon, the invitation for discussion, and the notion to "agree to disagree" allow the student to move beyond just following directions into an open-ended terrain. Furthermore, creative play involves the body, promotes physical development and corporeal articulation and listening.

Liminality and Ritual

The diverse roles play has in children's experience can have important developmental consequences in terms of affect, cognition, interpersonal relations and language. Developmental theorists seek to identify the stages through which children pass as part of their natural development, in order to promote learning. These stages could be defined as liminal states, or rites of passage, which are characterized by ambiguity, openness, and indeterminacy. One's sense of identity dissolves to some extent, bringing about disorientation. Turner suggests that in these transitional states, normal limits to thought, self-understanding, and behavior are relaxed, leading to situations which ultimately reveal new perspectives (1982). A liminal state is often one of vulnerability, involving struggle, as an individual faces change, or prepares to cross a threshold. Passing through these transitions, whether they be personal or academic, although difficult for an individual can be facilitated by the use of play or ritual, thus bringing order to chaos, overcoming obstacles, discovering patterns, and engaging in risk taking, involving an education for the whole being.

Players who are truly immersed in play experience "flow" (Csikszentmihalyi, 1990). Flow is the pleasurable experience of becoming so absorbed in an activity that the sense of the passage of time is suspended, and an activity becomes effortless and unselfconscious. As flow is inherent in play, there exists a heightened concentration and focus, and thus, a sense of personal control over the situation or activity, which is intrinsically rewarding. This effortlessness of action has been called being in the "play world," "the zone," or "the groove." Playing is inherently exciting and precarious, "the interplay of the subjective interpretation, and that which is objectively perceived (actual, or shared reality)" (Winnicott, 1986, p. 52). Students who explore their own liminal states through play and improvisation may create their own rituals, stories and forms of expression.

Classroom teachers in all subject disciplines should be flexible, responsive, attuned to the play culture around them. In structured settings, play cannot be dictated to the child, but rather adults need to foster situations enabling flexible, self directed and imaginative forms of expression. As creativity is more present in the searching than in the finding, a playful sense of being should be embraced in the teaching of research methods. Children should take pleasure in the energetic repetition of math and the intriguing experimentation of the science lab. Ritual should enter into the study of language, literature, and history. The focus should be on process, not always on product.

Conclusion

Children are imaginative by nature, but imagination requires nurture and encouragement at all ages. There is a great need for arts based inquiry in this area; a methodical examination of creative play in the classroom would surely reveal the inherent benefits for communication, socialization, emotional and aesthetic expression, empathy and group dynamics. Therefore, why shouldn't creative play be at the center of the curriculum? As Huizinga states: "Now in myth and ritual the great instinctive forces of civilized life have their origin: law and order, commerce and profit, craft and art, poetry, wisdom and science...all are rooted in the primeval soil of play" (1955, p. 5). Play engenders flexibility and patience, enabling us to rearrange intellectual and artistic capacities in unforeseen ways.

While play is often viewed as the opposite of work, musician Stephen Nachmanovitch believes that creative work is play, "the creative mind plays with the objects it loves" (1990). In the arts this is especially apparent. Students should be encouraged to take joy in the practicing of an art form, for without skill there is no art. According to Richard Courtney play is the principle instrument of growth. Without play there can be no normal adult cognitive life; without play, no healthful development of affective life; without play, no full development of the power of will (1974). Further investigation of the use and benefits of symbolic play, fantasy play and role play in the upper grades is in order.

As educators and trainers of pre-service teachers, we must break through the dualistic world of form versus content, structure versus experience, and logic versus meaning, thus embracing multiple perspectives. Any attempt to tame or direct imagination, on the part of a teacher, parent, or helpmate, could be the stifling of an imaginative and creative developmental process. Education should tap into the relationship between play and exploration, between multiplicity and openness, as students learn how to navigate and contribute to the new creative and cultural developments of the future.

REFERENCES

Catron, C. E., & Allen, J. (2008). *Early childhood curriculum: A creative play model.* Saddle River, NJ: Pearson/Merrill Prentice Hall.

Cornett, C. (2003). *Creating meaning through literature and the arts.* New Jersey, NJ: Merrill Prentice Hall.

Courtney, R. (1974). *Play, drama & thought.* New York: Drama Book Specialists.

Csikszentmihalyi, M. (1990). *Flow: The psychology of optimal experience.* New York: Harper & Row.

Goncu, A., & Gaskins, S. (2007). *Play and development.* New York: Taylor and Francis.

Hendy, L., & Toon, L. (2001). *Supporting drama and imaginative play in the early years.* Philadelphia, PA: Open University Press.

Huizinga, J. (1955). *Homo Ludens.* Boston: Beacon.

Kallialla, M. (2006). *Play culture in a changing world.* Berkshire, England: Open University Press.

McCaslin, N. (2006). *Creative drama in the classroom and beyond.* New York: Longman.

Nachmanovitch, S. (1990). *Free play.* New York: Jeremy M. Tarcher/Perigree Books.

Schechner, R. (1995). *The future of ritual.* London & New York: Routledge.

Turner, V. (1982). *From ritual to theatre: The human seriousness of play.* New York: Performing Arts Journal Press.

Vygotsky, L. (1978). *Mind in society.* Cambridge, MA: Harvard University Press.

Winnicott, D. W. (1986). *Playing and reality.* New York: Routledge.

Nancy Smithner, PhD, performer and director, teaches performance skills, play theory and pedagogy at New York University's Program in Educational Theatre.

AMY PETERSEN JENSEN

37. THEATRE EDUCATION AND NEW MEDIA/DIGITAL TECHNOLOGIES

Keywords: digital technology, transmedia storytelling, convergence, digital literacy

THEATRE AND DIGITAL TECHNOLOGIES

Digital technologies are pervasive in the contemporary world. Mobile devices, social networking sites, and other online and portable technologies are prominent aspects of every day social interactions and engagements for most people. These new technologies allow individuals to regularly access information, receive and produce content, and connect with others at will.

Digital technologies are important in the theatre world because many conceptions of the present-day theatre space have been shaped by these technologies. Since the advent of modernism, theatre practitioners have employed forms of communicative technologies in theatre productions to explore and expand on notions of time, space and spectacle. Scholars argue that the advent of film in the late 1900s and the subsequent incarnations of that technology allow for a "uniquely pliable and poetic [theatre] space" (Dixon, 2007, p. 14–15) that could not exist previously in the fixed perspective of the theatre spectator. Like earlier media technologies, digital technologies influence the non-linear presentation of theatrical materials, the fragmentation of time and space, and invite contemporary spectators to re-consider what live performance means (Auslander, 1999).

The use of digital technologies is also gaining prominence in Theatre for Young Audiences (TYA) productions. For example, global for-profit edutainment companies such as Nickelodeon re-purpose popular television programs like Dora the Explorer or Blues Clues in live arenas capitalizing on theatrical conventions to expand their popular, global brands into local communities; and professional TYA companies including Melbourne's Arena Theatre Company (Play Dirty, 2002) and the Minneapolis Children's Theatre (Fashion 47, 2007) are producing works that engage audiences in technological experiences, or situate characters in online or digital environments, in an effort to explore themes and issues created by those technologies.

Each of these examples demonstrates a common twenty-first century interest in circulating texts - theatre, media, and other commercial content - across a variety of media platforms and systems of representation. Media scholar Henry Jenkins labels this cross population of media forms as an indication that we currently reside in a convergence culture. Jenkins asserts that within this new cultural mind set producers and viewers are exposed to "a whole range of new technologies [which]

S. Schonmann (ed.), Key Concepts in Theatre/Drama Education, 227–232.

enable consumers to archive, annotate, appropriate, and re-circulate media content and in the process, these technologies have altered the ways that consumers interact with core institutions of government, education, and commerce" (2006a, p. 8). The advent of this convergence culture has allowed for a significant shift in cultural structures that can allow young people more participatory experiences in culture, politics, and social settings.

Young people are active participants in convergence culture and have been introduced to the technology tools and concepts that shape convergence in their out-of-school environments. They regularly engage with their online and offline worlds with digital tools that allow them to experiment with identity formation, engage in new forms of relationship building, and test the boundaries of time and space in their personal interactions. Because new media tools are constantly present in young people's social and cultural worlds, educational leaders and policy makers have encouraged school systems and teachers to embrace digital technologies as a means of reaching and teaching today's students (Partnership for 21st Century Schools, 2004).

NEW MEDIA AND NEW LITERACIES IN THE EDUCATIONAL THEATRE SPACE

Reacting both to globalism and the complexity of the new digital tools required to facilitate effective teaching and learning in these environments, education leaders call on schools and teachers to engage in new multiliteracies. Specifically, they encourage teachers to embrace the "multimodality of contemporary communications environments, particularly digitally mediated environments [that overlay] linguistic, visual, audio, gestural, and spatial modes of meaning" (Kalantzis, 2005, p. x).

In the fine and performing arts, educators are beginning to embrace digital technologies. These educators are seeking avenues of connection between new media and their art forms to enhance their classrooms. The International Handbook of Research in Arts Education devotes a large section of their two-volume work to the exploration of digital technology and its interface with the pedagogy of each unique art form. Authors in this volume argue that "ultimately, it is arts educators who have a large role to play in helping children deal with the challenges of the digital world, [and that] education in digital literacy should be a central component of contemporary arts curricula." They go on to say that "developing the curriculum and identifying new styles of teaching and learning in arts education that take account of young people's everyday uses of new media represents the key research challenge" (Snyder & Bulfin, 2007, p. 1307).

Drama education researchers similarly argue that while drama teachers must remain committed to teaching the live art form, "technology often can and does enrich and extend the imagination of students." Recognizing the tension that drama/theatre teachers might feel between the real and the mediatized they continue, "If we allow the mediatised and the live to become a dichotomy we are in danger of losing our young students/audiences as they seek relevant performance forms in the mediatised world they have been born into." (Carroll, Anderson, & Cameron, 2006, p. xvi).

I have argued elsewhere that because technologies have a profound effect on our society, and often outpace our ability to properly assess or understand their implications, young people must become critical and active agents in their interactions with the new media forms. Arts education, specifically theater education, is uniquely positioned to substantially contribute to interactions between teachers and students as they acknowledge and explore the new forms of literacy that are essential to navigating contemporary culture. Because of this, arts educators must effectively engage with their students' multimodal concerns through interactions that value new multimodal literacies. (Jensen, 2008).

So what are these multimodal literacies and how do they intersect with educational drama conventions and processes? Henry Jenkins (2006b) argues that: "Participatory culture shifts the focus of literacy from one of individual expression to community involvement" (p. 4). This shift requires a new set of skills that aid students in thinking about how they might become actively involved in community building. For Jenkins these new skills include:

- Play – the capacity to experiment with one's surroundings as a form of problem-solving.
- Performance – the ability to adopt alternative identities for the purpose of improvisation and discovery.
- Simulation – the ability to interpret and construct dynamic models of real-world processes.
- Appropriation – the ability to meaningfully sample and remix media content.
- Multitasking – the ability to scan one's environment and shift focus as needed to salient details.
- Distributed Cognition – the ability to interact meaningfully with tools that expand mental capacities.
- Collective Intelligence – the ability to pool knowledge and compare notes with others toward a common goal.
- Judgment – the ability to evaluate the reliability and credibility of different information sources.
- Transmedia Navigation – the ability to follow the flow of stories and information across multiple modalities.
- Networking – the ability to search for, synthesize, and disseminate information.
- Negotiation – the ability to travel across diverse communities, discerning and respecting multiple perspectives, and grasping and following alternative norms. (2006b, p. 4).

These new media literacies, as described by Jenkins, dovetail with many of the goals of process drama and applied theatre. Both can effectively engage students in the development of social skills that are expanded through collaboration and networking. Each is built on a foundation of meaning making. Additionally, they encourage students to learn research skills, technical skills, and develop an aptitude for analysis and reflection. In combination they provide a space for educators to connect with students who are increasingly interested in the role that technology plays in their everyday lives.

DIGITAL TECHNOLOGIES AND DRAMATIC PLAY

Two examples illustrate how Jenkins guidelines of participatory interactions with new media can be effectively utilized in drama settings.

The first, an out-of-school example, demonstrates how the principles of play, performance, collective intelligence, and negotiation might work in a setting that combines drama and media. In 2000, Arizona State University's Department of Theatre initiated a community based theatre and performance residency program in the United States called Place: Vision and Voice. The program combined drama and new media tools to engage young creators in conversations about their community.[1]

Stephanie Etheridge-Woodson, the project initiator, designed the program to aid young people as they worked to "process and negotiate adult-arbitrated landscapes to create and re-create their own identities" (2004, para. 1). Working collaboratively, the young people and adult facilitators from the university devised and edited multimedia digital stories that incorporated music, graphics, and video elements. These digital stories were then combined with traditional process drama activities devised by the young people which including creative movement, creative writing and scripted presentation. The young people brought the productions back into their unique communities. The performances, which explored notions of authority and regulation as they played out in their lives, were then used as conduits for conversations amongst themselves and the adults in their communities. According to Woodson, the project aided students in understanding and creating a space for democratic dialogue, taught young people how to effectively elicit response on critical issues affecting their lives, and opened up communities for open conversations (2004).

In the second example drama educators John Carroll and David Cameron demonstrate how the new media concepts of simulation, appropriation, and transmedia navigation can be used in classrooms. Carroll and Cameron created an in-school project in which student participants engaged in new media to extend and expand a drama story that they were developing together in their classroom. Using facilitator-generated online social networking and mobile media devices, the students examined issues of mistaken identity through the technologies as an exploration of themes from Shakespeare's Twelfth Night. Carroll and Cameron developed and facilitated drama activities in which students discovered dramatic story lines and addressed themes that they would encounter in the dramatic text through multiple media platforms including email, digital still images, weblogs, digital videos and mobile devices (2009, p. 296). The co-creators integrated these digital technologies with recognized process drama conventions, such as dramatic pre-text and role-based improvisation to create "digital pretexts."[2] These environments that combined drama and media engaged students in story creation and understanding. Carroll, Cameron, and their students explored and performed dramatic texts by intermingling the conventions inherent within both theatre and media to achieve their story goals. The educators reported that students, who acted as co-creators of the technology-infused drama, explored a variety of social and cultural issues important to the participants, and were especially invested in conversations about identity and power in spaces affected by digital technology (p. 309).

DIGITAL LITERACY IN DRAMA/THEATRE EDUCATION CLASSROOMS

Constructs and representations of characters, settings, and situations that are identifiable to an audience have been at the very heart of theatre from ancient times. While the positive and negative effects of digital technologies and mediatization on theatre will continue to be debated, it is clear that these technologies and the societal conventions that are created by them are an increasingly present part of our world. However, what must be recognized is that digital interactions and conventions make our world fundamentally different. Drama/theatre education practitioners have an impetus to engage in digital environments because these technologies and tools have a direct impact on conceptions of time and place, and those new conceptions bring new possibilities for creative constructs and representations that new/young audiences, can identify with. Great portions of their world are digitized, many of their most intimate communications are mediated; they project their presence daily into a global community that in reality can only be comprehended through the same tools and technologies that create this new world. Digital stories are the stories young audiences want to hear, and they are the stories that young artists want to tell - they are the stories of their world, their societies, their communities, and their lives.

NOTES

[1] According to Woodson, Place: Vision and Voice operated two residencies: one at the Ira H. Hayes Memorial Applied Learning Center on the Gila River Indian Community (GRIC), and the second, a program for children in long-term foster care with Child Protective Services (CPS) in Metropolitan Phoenix.

[2] Carroll and Cameron are borrowing the concept of pre-text from Cecily O' Neill who describes it as a launching strategy of non-scripted collaborative dramatic enactment that begins without any text. Improvisations and process drama lead to understandings that allow a future text to be more fully explored. The pre-text, then is a "latent" text (in Drama Worlds, 1995 p. 19). For Carroll and Cameron the digital materials they provide become "framing" texts that help participants to "define the nature and extent" of the dramatic world in which they are engaged (299).

REFERENCES

Auslander, P. (1999). *Liveness: Performance in a mediatized culture*. London: Routledge.
Carroll, J., & Cameron, D. (2009). Drama, digital pre-text and social media. *Research in Drama Education, 14*(2), 295–312.
Carroll, J., Anderson, M., & Cameron, D. (2006). *Real players: Drama, technology, and education*. London: Trentham.
Dixon, S. (2007). *Digital performance: A history of new media in theatre, dance, performance art, and installation*. Cambridge, MA: MIT Press.
Etheridge-Woodson, S. (2004). *The place vision and voice program: Power, authenticity, and ethics*. Retrieved from http://www.communityarts.net/readingroom/archivefiles/2004/05/place_vision_an.php
Jenkins, H. (2006a). *Convergence culture: Where old and new media collide*. New York: NYU Press.
Jenkins, H. (2006b). *Confronting the challenges of participatory culture: Media education for the 21st century*. New York: MacArthur Foundation.
Jensen, A. P. (2008). Multimodal literacy and theatre education. *Arts Education Policy Review, 109*(5), 19–28.

Kalantzis, M., & Cope, B. (2005). *Learning by design*. Illinois, IL: Common Ground.
Partnership for 21st century skills. (2004). *Skills framework*. Retrieved from http://www.21stcentury skills.org/index.php?option=com_content&task=view&id=254&Itemid=120
Snyder, I., & Bulfin, B. (2007). Digital literacy: What it means for arts education. In L. Bresler (Ed.), *The handbook of research in arts education* (pp. 1297–1310). Netherlands: Springer.

Amy Petersen Jensen is an Associate Professor in the Theatre and Media Arts Department at Brigham Young University where she studies youth, theatre, and media culture.

SECTION VIII: MODES OF THEATRE, EXPRESSIONS AND PERFORMANCE

ANTHONY JACKSON

38. PARTICIPATORY FORMS OF EDUCATIONAL THEATRE

Keywords: audience participation, applied theatre, theatre in education, forum theatre

Audience participation of some kind has been at the heart of much theatre for young people, just as it has been for other theatrical forms that claim an educational or 'interventionist' role. Arguably, all theatre is participatory to a degree. Even the audience sitting in formal rows in a traditional auditorium are not passive: their engagement in the drama is an active process of de-coding, responding, and constructing meaning from the variety of stimuli presented. The focus here, however, is with theatrical activity that transgresses the traditional boundary-lines between stage and auditorium and aims to generate an engagement from the audience that is 'overt and direct, and will often be physical, active and sometimes verbal in form' (Jackson 2007, p. 136). While audience participation has a rich history throughout the twentieth century (from 1930s agit-prop to Brecht's lehrstücke to children's theatre), it is the search for theatrical ways of communicating information, and for generating active learning, that has produced some of the most innovative and challenging forms.

What, then, are the forms that participatory theatre tends to take? And what are the purposes and implications – artistic and educational – of engaging audiences actively in a theatre event? And the risks? The specific references in this essay will be to the practices known as theatre in education (TIE) and forum theatre, fields of theatre practice in which audience participation is pivotal, and which have education as one of their primary goals. By TIE is meant the use of theatre designed specifically and explicitly for presentation in schools and other educational settings, in which the subject matter relates directly to topics and themes relevant to the curriculum and/or the social needs of specific age groups, and the dramatic form is created to serve the educational goals and connect with the likely interests of that age group. At its best, such theatre will go well beyond the mere delivery and illustration of a message and will engage its audience at many levels: emotional as well as intellectual, making full use of what live theatre can achieve. Its portability and its reliance on minimal set and lighting are not (in the best practice) an excuse for the second rate – closeness to its audience often requires acting, and indeed an ability to communicate, listen and generate discussion, of a very high order. Forum theatre is one of the main participatory theatre techniques developed by Augusto Boal as part of his repertoire of practices and strategies collectively known as 'theatre of the oppressed' (Boal, 1979) – and widely used in theatre for development, theatre in prisons and museum theatre as well as TIE and classroom drama.

S. Schonmann (ed.), Key Concepts in Theatre/Drama Education, 235–240.

ANTHONY JACKSON

The Main Participatory Forms in Educational Theatre

In 1976, John O'Toole categorised the main formats of participation evident in
TIE, identifying three basic kinds: peripheral, extrinsic and integral. It was, and
continues to be, a useful rule of thumb, but, given the growth and spread of TIE
and related practices over the past four decades, some updating and revision are
inevitably needed. The following is a modest attempt in that direction:

1. *Peripheral participation*. This refers to theatre events, especially those for
   younger children, in which the role of the audience is simply to contribute when
   prompted to the dramatic mood or the excitement of particular narrative moments.
   Children may, for example, be asked to help create suitable sound effects or
   movements or vocally to warn characters of impending danger (loud choruses of
   'He's behind you' being one all-too-obvious example). It may sometimes involve
   audience members joining the cast on stage, but as 'extras' rather than as
   'characters', obeying instructions and amplifying the number of 'townspeople'
   needed on stage, for example. Their participation may add to the texture and
   enhance the sense of excitement or atmosphere but in no way influences the
   progress of the narrative or its outcomes. Well handled, it will add to the
   enjoyment of the performance but the participation is decorative rather than
   essential.
2. *Extrinsic participation*. This refers to the kind of educational theatre programme
   generally favoured for work with teenagers and young adults. Usually the
   audience do not take on a role – they respond and contribute as themselves. The
   participation takes place outside the framework of the dramatic narrative, and
   participants do not influence the course of that narrative, but the workshop
   elements allow for a deeper understanding of the issues raised, and of the
   alternative outcomes that might have been possible if the characters had acted
   differently. The many variations include:
   - A short play followed (or sometimes punctuated) by workshop techniques such
     as 'hot-seating' the characters, that is, pupils interrogating (and challenging)
     one or more characters from the drama.
   - An introductory, exploratory workshop (using, for example, Image Theatre,
     Simulation or varieties of role-play exercises) followed by a play that explores
     the issues in a more focussed way, concluding with an out-of-role discussion.
3. *Forum theatre*. The enactment of a drama centring on the problems faced by
   a protagonist, identified as the 'oppressed', leading to crisis; the audience are
   invited to help resolve the crisis by identifying and revisiting the key moments
   of the narrative, and themselves stepping into the shoes of the protagonist to try
   out alternative ways of acting and changing the situation. It closely resembles
   the extrinsic formats described above but with a very specific set of goals and
   working methods, facilitated by a neutral so-called 'joker', and distinctive in its
   encouragement of the audience (or 'spect-actors') to influence the outcomes of
   the drama.
4. *Integral participation*. Here the participation is sustained throughout the course
   of the drama, and is usually thought to be more appropriate for younger pupils

(up to about 10–11 years old), generally readier to 'willingly suspend disbelief' for sustained periods of time. Participants' involvement (which will include dialogue with characters, perhaps voting on a course of action to be taken, etc.) often has a bearing on the progress of the narrative. The variations include:

- The actors remain in role throughout (apart, usually, from a brief out-of-role introduction); the children remain as themselves or 'lightly enrolled' for functional purposes – drawn into the story as, for example, reporters.
- The actors and children are in role from beginning to end, the children taking on identifiable and significant roles in the story – factory workers whose livelihoods are threatened by impending redundancy, for example, or villagers whose village is threatened by plans to flood their valley to create a reservoir. In these scenarios, pupils are often required to research the social background in advance in order to deepen their grasp of the issues.
- The actors are again in role; the children take on roles but at pivotal moments in the narrative come out of role to reflect, as themselves, on the issues and decisions to be taken. One of the actor-teachers may act as 'facilitator' throughout, whose job is to intervene at critical moments in the narrative to ask questions about what the children have seen, their own interpretations and questions arising from the action. Alternatively, the actors themselves may stop (or 'freeze-frame') the action and come out of role to discuss the action with children. There are substantial overlaps with extrinsic participation, but here the out-of-role interventions may, and often do, affect the narrative outcomes.[1]

There are many permutations of the above, including performances in which audience roles may be implied and introduced momentarily, for example for just one scene. It must be stressed finally that these categories are not prescriptive, nor do they claim to cover all possible kinds of participation.[2]

Why Participation?

There are many reasons why participation has been embraced as an important ingredient in educational theatre. The shift away from the traditional 'one-way traffic' models of education, rooted in positivist notions of epistemology, has been accompanied by the increased development of participatory models of education, constructivist theories of learning and a belief in the importance of 'experiential learning (Kolb, 1985); likewise, aesthetic theories and the growth of interest in reception studies, that emphasise the readers' and audiences' roles in making meaning (Jackson, 2007), have all helped to create a more receptive climate for participatory theatre. Audience participation in young people's theatre is therefore based on a number of assumptions, namely that young people learn best through doing; that they should be encouraged to take a degree of responsibility for, and ownership of, their own learning; that the degree of engagement, effort and two- way dialogue required in dramatic participation and role-play are beneficial in embedding learning, developing ownership and empowering the learner (Freire, 1996); finally, that participation in drama can be in part a way of rehearsing for 'real life' and of preparing us for active participation in society at large. The latter notion explicitly drives forum theatre and other Boalian techniques, and constitutes a proactive attempt to create theatre that works directly to promote social change. The extent to which theatre can and does contribute directly and immediately to changes in society is of course highly debatable, and examples are difficult to locate. There is more robust evidence for the impact of participatory drama at the level of the individual (Allen, Allen, & Dalrymple, 1999; Etherton & Prentki, 2006; Jackson & Kidd, 2008). Irrespective of impact, however, audience participation has drawn critical fire from many quarters.

Participation – Problems and Pitfalls

From different perspectives, and across both pedagogic and non-pedagogic contexts, many critics (Allen, 1979; Cole, 1975; Harris, 1985; Langer, 1953; Levy, 1987) argue the need for a clear boundary between actors and audience so that the special qualities inherent in the act of theatre – the 'sacredness' of the acting (Cole); or aesthetic distance, that is, the clear separation of the stage-world from the audience's world, allowing the author's narrative to unfold unimpeded (Harris, 1985; Levy, 1987) – are not compromised by actively participating spectators. But this assumes a rigid and necessary demarcation between actor and audience and fails to allow for the more fluid and dynamic practices becoming increasingly common by the end of the 20th century (Schechner, 1977; Jackson, 2007). Audience participation and aesthetic distance do not have to be mutually exclusive: audiences can be actively engaged in ways that retain a degree of aesthetic distance, even if the nature of that 'distance' may appear to be of a markedly different kind from that found in conventional theatre practice (Jackson, 2007). In any event, it is agreed by most commentators that when participation takes place, it changes theatre utterly. In Schechner's words, audience participation 'expands the field of what a performance is' and is 'incompatible with the idea of a self- contained, autonomous, beginning-middle-and-end artwork' (1994, p. 40). Participatory theatre then highlights a characteristic of much contemporary live theatre – it problematises the conventional divide between actor and audience.

Pedagogically, too, there are challenges and risks. Activity per se does not necessarily equate to purposeful participation, just as experience per se does not guarantee anything will be learnt from it (Dewey, 1938). Learning by doing is the mantra that is called into play to justify participatory drama because it gets children actively engaged and therefore more likely to recall and 'own' the learning they undertake. But, just as Dewey notes that experience on its own is not necessarily educational, so participation for its own sake is not necessarily going to produce learning. Not only can poorly structured and mishandled participation lead to confusion or distraction, but it can sometimes do more damage than good. In broader, applied theatre contexts, too, participation has come under intense critical scrutiny (Etherton & Prentki, 2006). Cooke and Kothari, for example, asked in 2001 whether, in development programmes in the third world, including some theatre for development programmes, participation had become 'the new tyranny'. In various applied theatre practices, participatory workshops designed to 'empower', inviting community groups to set the agenda, can, in reality, often prove to be counter-productive and actually cement existing power relations within a group or community and consequently disempower the already-disempowered. By the same token, participatory theatre that apparently enacts a philosophy of equality and dialogue can, sometimes, if unintentionally, do precisely the opposite: give space and status to those in the class, or the audience, already confident enough to voice their own opinions at the expense of those cast as the 'quiet' or the 'backward' ones. At its best, such theatre will transcend the entrenched classroom behaviour patterns and surprise teachers as much as the pupils themselves in its generation of genuine, open debate and the opportunities for some of the least forward or least motivated to find their voice. At worst, the participatory moments will be token and reinforce pre-existing prejudices and behavioural norms. Schechner, from the standpoint of a performance practitioner, puts the matter even more pungently, arguing that 'participation is legitimate only if it influences the tone and possibly the outcome of the performance; only if it changes the rhythms of the performance. Without this potential for change participation is just one more ornamental, illusionistic device: a treachery perpetrated on the audience while disguised as being on behalf of the audience.' (1994, p. 77)

The contentiousness of the debates reminds us that audience participation, of whatever kind and for whatever purpose, intervenes directly in the personal response of spectators and invites – sometimes requires – a personal commitment in return. Genuine, willing participation cannot be taken for granted. We need to recognise the risks involved in work that disguises itself as participation but serves rather different agendas in reality – that casts its audience as mere extras and coerces individuals into collective action that serves only the 'grand design' or at worst the ego of the facilitator. Before it is employed in any educational theatre context, therefore, the pedagogic and aesthetic implications require the most careful consideration. The need for critical thinking and widening of awareness of best practice has become paramount.

NOTES

[1] See also 'teacher-in-role' and 'mantle of the expert' approaches in classroom drama (Bolton & Heathcote, 1996).
[2] See also Invisible Theatre and Legislative Theatre (Boal, 1979, 1998), and first and third person interpretation at historic sites (Roth, 1998).

REFERENCES

Allen, G., Allen, I., & Dalrymple, L. (1999). Ideology, practice and evaluation: Developing the effectiveness of theatre in education. *Research in Drama Education, 4*(1), 21–36.

Allen, J. (1979). *Drama in schools.* London: Heinemann.

Boal, A. (1979). *Theatre of the oppressed.* London: Pluto Press.

Boal, A. (1998). *Legislative theatre: Using performance to make politics.* London: Routledge.

Bolton, G., & Heathcote, D. (1996). *Drama for learning: Dorothy Heathcote's mantle of the expert approach to education.* Westport, CT: Greenwood Press.

Cole, D. (1975). *The theatrical event.* Middletown, CT: Wesleyan University press.

Cooke, B., & Kothari, U. (Eds.). (2001). *Participation - the New Tyranny?* London: Zed Books.

Dewey, J. (1938). *Experience and education.* New York: Macmillan.

Etherton, M., & Prentki, T. (2006). Drama for change? Prove it! Impact assessment in applied theatre. *Research in Drama Education, 11*(2), 139–155.

Freire, P. (1996). *Pedagogy of the oppressed.* Harmondsworth: Penguin Books.

Harris, A. (1985). Plees make more. In N. McCaslin (Ed.), *Children and Drama* (3rd ed., pp. 117–127). Lanham, MD: Rowman & Littlefield.

Jackson, A. (2007). *Theatre, education and the making of meanings.* Manchester: Manchester University Press.

Jackson, A., & Kidd, J. (2008). *Performance, learning & heritage: Research report.* Retrieved from www.plh. manchester.ac.uk (last accessed 03/01/10).

Kolb, D. (1985). *Experiential learning.* Englewood Cliffs, NJ: Prentice-Hall.

Langer, S. (1953). *Feeling and form: A theory of art.* London: Routledge & Kegan Paul.

Levy, J. (1987). *A theatre of the imagination.* Charlottesville, VA: New Plays Inc.

O'Toole, J. (1976). *Theatre in education: New objectives for theatre: New techniques in education.* London: Hodder & Stoughton.

Roth, S. (1998). *Past into present.* Chapel Hill, NC: University of North Carolina Press.

Schechner, R. (1977). *Essays on performance theory.* New York: Drama Books Specialists.

Schechner, R. (1994). *Environmental theater.* New York: Applause Books.

***Anthony Jackson** is Emeritus Professor of Educational Theatre at The Centre of Applied Theatre Research, The University of Manchester, UK.*

HELEN NICHOLSON

39. APPLIED DRAMA/THEATRE/PERFORMANCE

Keywords: disciplinary field, critical practice, professionalization, idealism, artistic
practices

I first heard the term 'applied theatre' sometime in the mid1990s from a colleague
who had heard it used at an academic conference. At the time I didn't ask which
conference he had attended, although of course now I wish that I could locate the
history of this keyword more precisely. There is, however, a general vagueness that
accompanies all accounts of the derivation of the term, suggesting that it is not a
phrase that was coined by a particular individual to describe a very precise set of
practices or concept, but that the term that emerged haphazardly and spread like
a rhizome to fill a gap in the lexicon. Locating the ways in which this keyword
is used, therefore, is not a search for the authentic roots or the essential meaning
of applied drama, theatre and performance, but in recognising its pliability and
porousness. Inevitably there are ways of thinking about this field that I find more
persuasive than others, but my entry marks an attempt to reflect some of the
different ways in which the term has been understood rather than to insist on a
particular derivation or single meaning. As the theatre historian Joseph Roach
points out, 'improvised narratives of authenticity and priority may congeal into
full-blown myths of legitimacy and origin' (1996, p. 3).

Although the terms applied drama/theatre and performance are differently inflected,
it is widely understood to refer to theatre practices that are applied to educational,
institutional and community contexts. This work is usually led by professional
theatre-makers and is intended to be socially or personally beneficial to participants.
It is often, but not always, funded by charities or the public sector who have
particular interests in promoting the well-being of a particular community group, or
in encouraging public engagement in specific issues. Judith Ackroyd (2000) was
one of the first to point out that applied theatre (as it is widely known) is not a
particular set of dramatic practices or performance methodologies, but an 'umbrella
term' used to describe many different forms of educational and community-based
theatre – including theatre-in-education, reminiscence theatre, theatre for development, theatre in hospitals - all with their own specialist agendas.

The appearance of a collective noun, and the speed with which it spread, suggests a
willingness to question whether there are family resemblances between the different
movements and ways of working, and an interest in investigating their shared
concerns and common principles. It is interesting that my colleague first heard the
term in an academic setting; unlike many other nomenclatures within the wider
field of community arts, applied theatre was a term that emerged in universities
rather than developed by practitioners. Undergraduate and postgraduate programmes

S. Schonmann (ed.), Key Concepts in Theatre/Drama Education, 241–245.
© *2011 Sense Publishers. All rights reserved.*

called 'applied theatre', 'applied drama' or 'applied performance' were introduced at different UK universities towards the end of the century, a new on-line academic journal was established in Australia in 2000, and newly formed research centres secured funding around the turn of the century. Publishers were not slow to spot this trend, and three books with similar titles were published between 2003 and 2005 to support the growing academic market (Taylor, 2003; Thompson, 2003; Nicholson, 2005). A materialist analysis of this intellectual history would note that the rapid spread of this term within universities was partly indebted to the pragmatics of academic funding and the economics of the job market; it is easier to recruit students for degree courses that have a broad remit rather than for those that focus on one specialised aspect of the field (such as TIE or theatre in prisons, for example). The proliferation of careers for theatre practitioners in community and educational settings meant that there was a demand for courses that interrogated questions of pedagogy and the principles of theatre-making in different communities and institutional settings. Furthermore, arts academics across the world have been increasingly pressured to attract research funding, and research centres which offer the capacity to work in multi-agency and inter-disciplinary teams promise to strengthen funding applications. More idealistically, the context in which the term emerged suggests that the millennium ushered in a new scholarly interest in theorising forms of drama that take place in a range of community and educational settings, and that the university training of community-based theatre practitioners meant that their work was becoming increasingly professionalized.

It is not just the place in which the term emerged that is important, the timing is also significant, not least because it sheds light on how the common principles that underlie different forms of theatre-making in community and educational contexts were re-conceptualised in the twenty-first century. There is a long tradition of community arts and educational theatre which had its roots in the political Left, and to which contemporary practice is indebted. During the twentieth-century, however, theatre activists often articulated their political intentions in revolutionary terms; theatre was instrument through which capitalism might be overthrown (Nicholson, 2005; Govan et al, 2007; Jackson, 2007; Prentki and Preston, 2009). Although social change remains an important tenet in applied theatre, without the old certainties of mid-twentieth century Marxism there was a need to re-evaluate the principles that informed socially engaged theatre. The 1990s brought in, as Baz Kershaw identified, a 'new world disorder' in which political theorists analysed systems of power in a globalising world, and cultural critics were pressed to re-imagine the social meaning of democracy following the fragmentation of the political Left after the collapse of Communism (Kershaw, 1999, p. 6–7). It was within this political climate that the term applied theatre took hold, begging questions about how the democratic principles that had been associated with all forms of community and educational theatre might be re-envisioned for the new millennium.

I have always understood that the term applied drama/theatre/performance does not announce a specific set of dramatic methodologies nor a particular political pedagogy, but indicates a discursive practice and defines a scholarly field in which drama that aspires to be publicly and socially beneficial might be theorised and its ideological values debated (Nicholson, 2005 p. 14–16). Vocabularies that had been taken for granted by community and educational theatre-makers in the political landscape of the twentieth-century became ripe for reassessment in this emergent scholarship; words such as 'empowerment' and 'transformation' that followed the legacy of Romanticism in suggesting that the arts are inherently redemptive were opened for critical scrutiny (Butler, 1981). Without a foundational belief that active, community participation in the arts necessarily benefits society, intellectual interest became focused on ideas that had been accepted by community-based practitioners. With the grand political narratives of the twentieth-century displaced, James Thompson memorably described this process of reflection and analysis as 'bewildering' to those on the political Left who struggled to understand how to maintain a commitment to radical, democratic principles (Thompson, 2003). This struggle was further compounded by the recognition that theatre practices that had been developed with political 'empowerment' in mind, particularly those articulated by the influential Marxist theatre director Augusto Boal, had been applied to corporate settings with the objective of empowering the kind of workforce required to further global capitalism (Nicholson, 2005 p. 46–51). This not only raises complex questions about the political use of participatory theatre forms, it also asserts the need for open-handed and informed debate about the relationship between politics, theatre form and critical practice. Informed discussion about how the discourse relates to democracy and the politics of identity (Neelands, 2007) and to the intercultural politics of theatre form (Chinyowa, 2009) have enriched the terms of the debate.

Scholarship is not, of course, remote from practice but intimately connected to it. This is particularly the case for students who follow university courses in applied theatre where they are often invited to test out theories against practice. Students taking university courses in applied theatre might also reasonably expect to prepare for inter-agency theatre practice by reading and debating theories of community, citizenship, creativity, representation and other significant key concepts. Course descriptions reveal that students are also likely to consider the politics and pragmatics of funding, learn ways to work productively in multi-agency settings and raise questions about how to work ethically and sensitivity with community groups as a cultural outsider. Academically, this learning is likely to reflect the inter-disciplinarity of the field, with readings garnered from areas as diverse as anthropology, cultural geography and philosophy as well as education, theatre and performance studies. This process aims to encourage students to developing a 'praxis' or, in other words, an informed and theorised understanding of their own values and principles as practitioners and scholars.[1]

Although there may be widespread agreement that theatre-making should be based on egalitarian and democratic principles, definitions of practice have tended to focus either on the particular sites in which they took place (hospitals, schools, prisons and so on) or referred to the particular communities or social groupings with which they engaged, such as children, the elderly or refugees (Thompson, 2009, p. 5). Precisely which forms, styles and genres of theatre might be productively applied to these different settings or social groups is less clearly articulated. For some (and I would include myself here) this lack of precision is a virtue; any attempt to define which forms of theatre-making or workshop practices 'count' as applied theatre risks limiting creativity and producing work that artistically impoverished. If applied theatre is built on inclusive principles, theatre practitioners who are interested in applying their craft as devisors, playwrights, directors, puppeteers, storytellers, shamans or even stand-up comedians will be welcomed into different settings and communities. Of course, good practitioners complement their knowledge of theatre-making metho- dologies with an awareness of what it means to work in particular contexts, and enrich their practice by understanding how to use appropriate participatory pedagogies. Seen in this light, collaborative work with community participants may develop into a myriad of artistic forms, including site-specific performance, installations, autobiographical performance, scripted plays and multi-media performance.

There is another way of looking at this debate that reflects the changing uses of this keyword. As graduates from applied theatre courses have moved into the creative industries, a new ambiguity has arisen around the terminology used to describe their professional role and artistic practices. I have recently heard some theatre-makers referred to as 'applied theatre practitioners' who are proficient in something called 'applied theatre' and use 'applied theatre techniques'. Some work with people called 'clients', a term borrowed from dramatherapy and the social services. I have also heard some North American practitioners draw distinctions between the genres of 'applied theatre', 'applied drama' and 'applied performance', although written documentation of these definitions has so far eluded me. Delineating applied theatre as a form of practice in this way - or delimiting it, depending on your point of view - rather regarding it as an intellectual field in Bourdieu's terms (Bourdieu, 1977), represents a significant shift in thinking. There may be advantages for newly professionalized practitioners to define their labour and to claim specialist forms of knowledge, but there is also a risks that its practices becomes either too tight and restrictive to foster creativity, or that its definitions are too loose and open-ended to serve any useful purpose (see Thompson, 2009, p. 3).

As a relatively recent keyword, there is more work to be done on how applied drama/theatre/performance is conceptualised and understood in different contexts. If the term is to be useful to practitioners and scholars who are passionate about the effects, affects and efficacy of their work, its meanings will change and evolve. There is a need for further research into what constitutes the professional knowledge of theatre-makers who apply their skills to community settings and social groupings, and how their work might be theorised and extended rather than becoming fixed by restrictive boundaries. It is in this context that informed debate is to be welcomed; this entry is intended not only to offer a reading of some of the debates have shaped the discourse but also to keep the field alive by stimulating new discussions and help shape alternative ways of thinking.

NOTES

[1] See, for example, advertised descriptions of courses in applied theatre at Central School of Speech and Drama, University of London www.cssd.ac.uk; The University of Manchester, www.manchester. ac.uk; and Royal Holloway, University of London www.rhul.ac.uk/drama, all accessed 14.8.09

REFERENCES

Ackroyd, J. (2000). Applied theatre: Problems and possibilities. *Applied Theatre Journal, 1.* Retrieved from http://www.gu.edu.au/centre/atr/

Bourdieu, P. (1977*). Outline of a theory of practice.* Cambridge: Cambridge University Press.

Butler, M. (1981). *Romantics, rebels and revolutionaries.* Oxford: Oxford University Press.

Chinyowa, K. C. (2009). Emerging paradigms for applied drama and theatre practice in African contexts. *RiDE: The Journal of Applied Theatre and Performance, 14*(3), 329–346.

Govan, E., Nicholson, H., & Normington, K. (2007). *Making a performance: Devising histories and contemporary practices.* London: Routledge.

Kershaw, B. (1999). *The radical in performance: Between Brecht and Baudrillard.* London: Routledge.

Neelands, J. (2007). Taming the political: The struggle over recognition in the politics of applied theatre. *Research in Drama Education, 12*(3), 305–317.

Nicholson, H. (2005). *Applied drama: The gift of theatre Basingstoke.* Basingstoke, UK: Palgrave Macmillan.

Prentki, T., & Preston, S. (Eds.). (2009). *The applied theatre reader.* London: Routledge.

Roach, J. (1996). *Cities of the dead: Circum-atlantic performance.* New York: Columbia University Press.

Taylor, P. (2003). *Applied theatre: Creating transformative encounters in the community.* Portsmouth, NH: Heinemann.

Thompson, J. (2003). *Applied theatre: Bewilderment and beyond.* Oxford: Peter Lang.

Thompson, J. (2009). *Performance affects: Applied theatre and the end of effect.* Basingstoke, UK: Palgrave MacMillan.

Helen Nicholson *is professor of drama and theatre at Royal Holloway, University of London where she specialises in contemporary performance, applied drama and theatre education.*

EVA ÖSTERLIND

40. FORUM PLAY

A Swedish Mixture for Consciousness and Change

Keywords: forum play, forum theatre, values clarification, socio-analytical role-play, theatre of the oppressed

Resistance to change is a common problem in society as well as on the individual level. Normally it takes more effort to alter something than to let it remain 'as usual'. Sometimes we want to change ourselves but are not able to, or we can refuse to change even when the circumstances call for it. French sociologist Pierre Bourdieu (1990) used the concept of *habitus* to explain social reproduction and why change is so hard to achieve. Habitus is very resistant to change – it is not only internalized in the mind by traditions and lifestyles, but is also inscribed in the body, in how we move and carry ourselves. "Seemingly, everyday experiences, internalised psychological patterns, life conditions and social structures all contribute to maintain the status quo" (Österlind, 2008a, p. 72).

Educational Drama, however, has shown itself to be useful in order to promote change. Cecily O'Neill (1996), states that "Drama has the power to enlarge our frames of reference and to emancipate us from rigid ways of thinking and perceiving" (p. 145), and according to Jonothan Neelands (2004) it seems to be the rule rather than the exception that drama work generates personal and social transformation. This might be due to the fact that drama involves intellectual, emotional and physical aspects in a process of social inter-action, and thereby provides an excellent opportunity for participants to try out new ways of thinking, feeling and acting.

This entry's purpose is to present Forum Play, a drama method for liberation and social justice, to a wider audience and exemplify how drama and other concepts merge and develop in relation to each other. The building blocks of Forum Play have in common a focus on the relation between individual and society, aiming for increased consciousness, empowerment and change. Forum Play is the result of a mixture of three concepts, namely Socio-analytical role-play, Values Clarification and Forum Theatre. Before going into the characteristics of Forum Play these three concepts are briefly described, beginning with the least known.

INGREDIENTS

Socio-analytical role-play, developed by Björn and Helena Magnér, originates from drama work with teenagers in the suburbs of Gothenburg during the late sixties. The idea of Socio-analytical role-play is that the participants "...based on their personal experiences develop knowledge about the connections between individual and society, create visions of a more joyful and human society and formulate strategies for actions of change" (Magnér, 1980, p. 1, EÖ translation). Magnér describes how the method evolved from unspecific drama work like fantasy improvisations to thematic role-playing, based on the participants' personal experiences and framed by a set of discussions, aiming at increased consciousness. Socio-analytical role-play was used in many different settings in Sweden during the seventies and eighties, but was later almost forgotten. The method is fairly structured, which probably was one reason for its popularity, but at the same time it was experienced as rigid and criticized for being too intellectual.

The first step in socio-analytical role-play is a 'pre-discussion' of a chosen theme, which should be of genuine interest to the participants. The purpose is to establish a difference between first-hand knowledge and other kinds of information, through questions such as 'How do you know that?', 'How can you be so sure?', and noticing what is taken for granted. The second step is a role-play on the theme, prepared by the leader, and a 'post-discussion' immediately after the play to explore the situation and the characters from several perspectives. In the third phase the 'final discussion' turns to questions related to here and now. The participants compare their opinions from the pre-discussion and insights from the role-play and post-discussion: 'Are there any general opinions that differ from what you found in the role-play?', 'Do they fulfill any function in society?' The last part focuses on how the participants until now have acted in situations related to the theme, and how they might want to change their actions in the future.

Values Clarification was presented as an alternative way of transferring values from adults to young people in western society (Raths, Harmin & Simon, 1966). It was introduced in Sweden by John Steinberg to encourage students to develop their own ethical values instead of copying someone else's or relying on un-reflected routine. It is a structured way to 'teach valuing instead of values' by analyzing one's values, attitudes and actions, becoming aware of their origin and consequences, and investigating alternatives. Participants get a chance to consider, express and motivate their choices, listen to and respect other points of view, and to reflect. The aim is to realize the possibility of making conscious choices to be proud of and tell others about, choices that will guide one's future actions. In other words Values Clarification is a method to consider the gap between words and deeds, establish what Steinberg calls 'active values' and start to walk your talk.

Forum Theatre was developed by Augusto Boal as one of the techniques in Theatre of the Oppressed (Boal, 1974), which I assume is well-known to the reader. Essentially, Forum Theatre is a rehearsed play about some kind of oppression, ending in a clash. The purpose is to stop the oppression and create a better solution. The audience is invited by a Joker to get on stage and take the role of the oppressed in order to confront the oppression, overcome the obstacles and explore different ways of solving the problem. Exchanging the oppressor is not permitted since that would be 'magic' and not useful as preparation for future action. Forum Theatre evolved when Boal's theatre company was playing for peasants and workers in Brazil. The performance showed a conflict ending in a crisis, and the audience was invited to suggest possible solutions on how to deal with the oppression. Their suggestions were performed by the actors. On one occasion, a spectator was not satisfied with the actor's performance of the solution, and finally was invited on stage. At that moment a significant change took place, as from then on nobody – audience, volunteer or actors – knew what would happen next. This characteristic of audience participation gives a significant presence, an authentic flavor to Forum Theatre. Forum Theatre has proven to be a powerful tool, used around the world (cf. Österlind, 2008b), and several adaptations have been made (e.g. DRACON, 2005; Saldaña, 2005). One such adaptation is Forum Play.

PROCEDURE

The ingredients of Forum Play have their roots in leisure time activities for youth, formal education of students, and theatre performances for adults. Forum Play, developed by Katrin Byréus (1990, 2006), has been applied extensively in varying contexts with children, young people and adults. Byréus initially used the Socio-analytical method and experienced that the role-playing was often lively and intense, but that the participants' involvement decreased in the discussions afterwards. It was hard for them to sit down and reduce something that had involved the whole person to an intellectual matter. Many times those who were watching wanted to take action and try to solve the problem by creating alternative endings. However, Byréus followed the procedure of Socio-analysis until she finally allowed the participants to do as they wished. One day a boy spontaneously stood up: 'I know what I would do', he said. When he had acted out his solution everybody was touched – and Byréus changed her way of working.

The participants now created their own role-plays based on personal experiences, and showed them to the rest of the group who were invited to step in and try out alternative solutions. Byréus describes this way of working as quite unstructured, until she came in touch with Boal and Theatre of the Oppressed (TO). Since 1979 she has been working with the tools of TO, meeting thousands of children, teenagers and adults. She describes Forum Play as a fusion of Forum Theatre and improvised play combined with values clarification. Byréus says she has kept the idea from Socio-analytical role-play of working on a theme, but frames the play with activities like games and value exercises related to the theme, rather than just discussions. "A Forum play depicts problems and dilemmas in easily identifiable everyday situations. The play ends in unresolved conflict in order to stimulate the audience into actively intervening with the purpose of resolving the simulated conflict" (www.byreus.com).

The introduction consists of warming-up exercises, like physical activities and games (cf. Boal, 1992), in order to achieve a certain level of energy and establish an atmosphere where participants feel safe to express themselves. This introduction is followed by exercises exploring participants' values and attitudes related to the chosen theme. In smaller groups the participants then create a forum-play, an improvised role-play, on the theme. The play should contain an escalating problem and some kind of injustice or oppression, and end when the dilemma has been fully displayed and the conflict is at its peak. Each play is performed to the other groups

EVA ÖSTERLIND

who are then asked by the leader/Joker "– Do we want to see this happen again? What can we do to make a change?" Several solutions are tried out, based on exchange of the person exposed to injustice and sometimes also the witness(es), and short discussions are held between and after the interventions. To ensure that all the participants have a chance to express themselves it is possible to conclude with value exercises.

REMARKS

Comparing the three ingredients of Forum Play, we see that Socio-analytical roleplay and Values Clarification focus more on increasing consciousness and freeing oneself from restricting attitudes, while Forum Theatre focuses on changes in behavior and action. Two are more 'analytical', looking at impact, agency and the interplay between individual and society, while one is more 'executive', heading for problem solving. Forum Play combines elements from all three, working with a relevant theme, looking at personal values and acting out solutions. It is crucial that the theme under investigation is chosen by the participants. In my view, imposing sensitive issues on people is a form of oppression.

Forum Play, in my experience, can be used as a 'social laboratory' where we can try new ways of behaving, and rehearse for situations in our everyday life. Working with Forum Play is appealing since no formal stage, no manuscript and no equipment are needed, but of course the leader needs education and preparation. The leader has to establish an open atmosphere that is supportive and non- competitive. Forum Play can be used almost anywhere, as long as there is a trained leader and a group ready to explore a theme of interest to them. Sometimes, though, working through Forum Play can be problematic. Working on a theme like bullying can be risky in groups where this is a current problem, especially if the leader is not well informed about the situation. Another challenge is if the leader and the participants disagree on who is the oppressed that should be exchanged. Forum Play, as any method, can be misused. If, as in this case, the method is powerful, it has to be thoughtfully and respectfully applied.

What all these concepts have in common is that reflection and action are intertwined, taking the participants' personal experiences as the point of departure. Personal experience is very important but participants are encouraged to step out of strictly private experience and reframe it in a social and societal perspective. The idea is to enhance commitment by creating distance to that which is usually taken for granted, and in doing so opening for new perspectives and new ways to think and act. Arne Engelstad (2004) says about Forum Theatre that, "[The] synthesis of passionate involvement (as in the 'Aristotelian' dramaturgy) and critical rationality (as in Brecht's theatre) gives the audience of the Theatre of the Oppressed the passion and desire to *transgress*..." (p. 203), which I believe can also be said about Forum Play. As habitus is resistant to change and 'old habits die hard', the need to cultivate reflective and creative thinking and action is infinite. Hopefully this example of how drama concepts evolve, merge and are adapted can serve as inspiration for future work towards increased consciousness and change.

250

REFERENCES

Boal, A. (1974/2000). *Theatre of the oppressed*. London: Pluto Press.

Boal, A. (1992/2007). *Games for actors and non-actors*. London: Routledge.

Bourdieu, P. (1990). *The logic of practice*. Cambridge, UK: Polity Press.

Byréus, K. (1990/2001). *Du har huvudrollen i ditt liv. Om forumspel som pedagogisk metod för frigörelse och förändring* [You play the main part in your life. Forumplay as an educational method for emancipation and change]. Stockholm: Liber.

Byréus, K. (2006). *Bella - Rubble and roses 2: For girl groups*. Stockholm: KSAN.

DRACON International. (2005). *Bridging the fields of drama and conflict management. Empowering students to handle conflicts through school-based programmes*. Malmö: Malmö University.

Engelstad, A. (2004). *Poetikk og politikk. Augusto Boal og De undertryktes teater*. [Poetics and Politics. Augusto Boal and the Theatre of the Oppressed]. Diss., English summary. Åbo: Åbo Akademi University press.

Magnér, B. (1980). *Hur vet du det? Socioanalys i praktiken*. [How can you know for sure? Socio-analysis in practice]. Göteborg: Esselte studium.

Neelands, J. (2004). Miracles are happening: Beyond the rhetoric of transformation in the western traditions of drama education. *Research in Drama Education, 9*(1), 48–56.

O'Neill, C. (1996). Into the Labyrinth: Theory and research in drama. In P. Taylor (Ed.), *Researching drama and arts education: Paradigms and possibilities* (pp. 135–146). London: Routledge Falmer.

Österlind, E. (2008a). Acting out of habits - Can theatre of the oppressed promote change? Boal's theatre methods in relation to Bourdieu's concept of habitus. *Research in Drama Education, 13*(1), 71–82.

Österlind, E. (2008b). Forum theatre - a way to promote active citizenship. *TmačaART Magazine, 10*(39), 44–51.

Raths, L. E., Harmin, M., &, Simon, S. B. (1966/1978). *Values and teaching: Working with values in the classroom*. Columbus, OH: Merrill Publishing.

Saldaña, J. (2005). Theatre of the oppressed with children: A field experiment. *Youth Theatre Journal, 19*, 117–133. www.byreus.com/english.php (downloaded 2009-08-14)

Eva Österlind, PhD, Associate Professor and drama pedagogue, works with postgraduate students at the department of Education in Arts and Professions, Stockholm University, Sweden.

LARRY O'FARRELL

41. FORMAL EXPRESSION IN DRAMA/
THEATRE EDUCATION

Keywords: form, drama, theatre, text, performance

The varied terminology used when specialist teachers discuss drama/theatre education gives an indication that teaching the elements of formal expression in drama/theatre education is by no means a consistent or even an uncontested practice. While some specialists in the field refer to their work as 'theatre' education, others use variations on the term 'drama' to identify their work - creative drama, process drama, developmental drama, drama as a learning medium, or simply drama. When the term 'theatre' is used, it may be implied that formal expression will be an element in the curriculum because the production of a play before an audience involves a wide range of decisions about expressive elements in acting style, set and costume design, etc. Some of the approaches identified by the term 'drama', particularly the American tradition derived from Winifred Ward's creative dramatics, also recommend that teachers lead their students toward a stage production, implicitly including consideration of the elements of formal expression. However, other drama educators have clearly rejected the option of a public performance of student work and, to some extent, the implied attention to theatre form. Some of these practitioners address aspects of formal expression within the context of classroom drama while refraining, in whole or in part, from teaching the aesthetics or techniques of theatrical production. Before it is possible to consider ways in which the formal elements of theatre may be included in a drama/theatre education program, it is necessary to acknowledge the dichotomy that has emerged between those educators espousing the art form widely known as theatre and those who either reject it outright or limit its application.

Although the debate has extended beyond the English-speaking world, its origins can be traced to the work of practitioners working and writing in the United Kingdom. As early as the beginning of the twentieth century, innovative British educators like Harriet Finlay-Johnson (1911) and H. Caldwell Cook (1917) reported using elements of drama/theatre to enhance the teaching of other subjects. The instrumental use of drama/theatre in education was revived, mid century by Brian Way and Dorothy Heathcote. Although their methods and philosophies varied substantially, both Way and Heathcote published statements intended to differentiate the 'drama' that they used to engage children from conventional theatre practice.

Describing his approach as 'development through drama' Way (1967), advocated 'learning by doing'. His goal was not to teach theatre as an art form but, rather, to use improvised drama to help young people to achieve personal development. Heathcote's use of drama was also instrumental, aimed at a blend of emotional response and cognitive engagement in support of standard disciplines in the school

S. Schonmann (ed.), Key Concepts in Theatre/Drama Education, 253–257.

curriculum such as history and literacy. She aimed to expand the students' awareness of the issue or theme inherent in the drama through unscripted role-playing. Heathcote acknowledged using theatre understanding in her teaching but largely rejected theatrical production as a component of her work. She wrote, "Drama has become accepted but many headmasters still think of it as watered down theatricals, not because they are stupid, but because they themselves have only seen theatricals or done theatricals in their own time in school." (Heathcote, 1984, p. 31) The legacy of these influential practitioners is more fully described elsewhere in this book. Important for the current discussion is their unequivocal differentiation of 'drama' from 'theatre' and the weight they attached to the instrumental outcomes of drama in preference to a study of the art form per se.

By the 1990s, the method advocated by Heathcote had gained ascendency in the British discourse about drama/theatre education. At that time, however, an impassioned rejection of her approach was initiated by fellow British educators who argued that an educational drama program that denied students an opportunity to perform their work in public and to study theatre as an important cultural form was inadequate and misguided. David Hornbrook spoke out against what he described as "all the worst aspects of school drama's progressivist legacy." (Hornbrook, 1992, p. 16). He advocated that the drama curriculum include the 'dramatic product' (featuring performance for an audience) and a wide range of dramatic literature representing various forms and conventions. Peter Abbs (1992) blamed Heathcote's approach for causing the neglect of "drama as a distinctive arts discipline (with its many genres, texts, techniques, modes of performance and reception and its many commanding, imaginative, and expressive achievements from Greek Tragedy onwards)." (Abbs, 1992, p. 3) Hornbrook articulated three elements in the discipline of drama - making, performing and responding - to which Abbs added a fourth - evaluating. These elements appear in various combinations in the current drama/ theatre curricula of a number of countries, often with complementary consideration given to theatre history and theories of theatre and performance.[1]

Having acknowledged an important debate that continues to the present day, it is beyond the scope of this article to resolve it. However, Gavin Bolton (2007) offered one possible accommodation when he wrote, "In my own practice at Durham University I tried to bring theatre form to a combination of Heathcote/Way approaches, arguing that dramatic play and theatre should be seen as a continuum." (p. 53) Because, the concept of a continuum is widely articulated by drama/theatre educators, the remainder of this article will be predicated on the assumption that an extensive (multi-year) educational program in drama/theatre will include both dramatic play and formal expression through the art of theatre. For the sake of clarity, the term 'theatre' will be used in reference to the art form as a whole and 'drama' will refer to dramatic play when used as a pedagogic tool.

The lists offered by Hornbrook and Abbs suggest a range of expressive components of theatre art. They include forms, conventions, genres, texts, techniques, modes of performance and reception. Heathcote, too, offers an analysis of how expression is understood in her approach to drama. The six elements that she identifies are darkness and light, stillness and movement, silence and sound. (Heathcote, 1984,

p. 32) Heathcote explains that these elements, in various combinations and gradations, constitute humanity's living environment. She considers these elements to be deeper than what she calls "stage effects". Her objective for the participants is to immerse them in the dramatic experience rather than teaching them how to convey this experience to others. She says, "[Teachers] have to learn how to employ this magic, to make the experience a real one at the moment of its happening, so that those who actually make it, learn the magic of it and get the experience themselves, not give it to the onlookers." (Heathcote, 1984, p. 32).

The distinction between the emphasis on performance and reception proposed by Hornbrook and Abbs and the emphasis on the participant's own experience proposed by Heathcote may be accommodated by Bolton's continuum concept. Within this hypothesis, when the focus of practical work is on dramatic play and process oriented drama at one end of the continuum, the participants will experience dramatic expression through engagement in a select number of expressive components without necessarily learning how to use these components to affect an audience. When the focus is on theatre art, at the other end of the continuum, the participants will encounter a wider range of expressive elements with a view to learning how to employ them to engage and move an audience.

Both positions have been affected by an Aristotelian tradition. For centuries, following a renewal of interest in Classical thought during the Renaissance, European dramatic theories were dominated by Aristole's analysis of Greek tragedy. According to this analysis, tragedy in Fifth Century BC Athens consisted of six elements: plot, characters, thought, diction, melody and spectacle. Although the six elements were regarded as interdependent, foremost among them was plot, with character in second place.

Tragedy is essentially an imitation not of persons but of action and life, of happiness and misery. All human happiness or misery takes the form of action; the end for which we live is a certain kind of activity, not a quality. Character gives us our qualities, but it is in our actions – what we do – that we are happy or the reverse. In a play accordingly they do not act in order to portray the Characters; they include the Characters for the sake of the action. (Aristotle, trans. 1920, p. 37)

Because Aristotle relegated the performance elements of melody and spectacle to an accessory function, his analysis gave rise to a tradition in which the art form was conceptualized as performed text. From an Aristotelian perspective, it was the playwright who was responsible for the three most important expressive elements - plot, character and diction (which refers to how a character's thought is expressed in words and not to the way an actor pronounces those words). As a result, the text produced by the playwright came to be synonymous with the work as a whole. Indeed, Aristotle argued that the tragic effect could be achieved without a public performance or actors. One remarkable result of this view has been the publication of numerous works of dramatic literature that were never intended for performance at all. Included among these are the closet dramas of such Romantic poets as Browning and Shelly.

By contrast, theatrical experiments in the twentieth century introduced a conception of the art form as essentially one of performance. Seminal to this discussion is the revolutionary manifesto, The Theatre and Its Double published by Antonin Artaud in Paris in 1938. Artaud (trans. 1958), rejected the tradition of theatre as performed text.

> For the Occidental theater the Word is everything, and there is no possibility of expression without it; the theater is a branch of literature, a kind of sonorous species of language, and even if we admit a difference between the text spoken on the stage and the text read by the eyes, if we restrict theater to what happens between the cues, we have still not managed to separate it from the idea of a performed text. (Artaud, trans. 1958, p. 68)

In place of this restrictive tradition, Artaud proposed a theatre of cruelty in which a play would be "composed directly on the stage, realized on the stage." (Artaud, trans. 1958, p. 41) Drawing on Eastern forms of theatre, he rejected performed text, seeking expression through the pure theatrical language of the mise en scène which he defined as "the visual and plastic materialization of speech" and "the language of everything that can be said and signified upon a stage independently of speech, everything that finds its expression in space, or that can be affected or disintegrated by it." (Artaud, trans. 1958, p. 69)

Three decades after the publication of Theatre and Its Double, Artaud's ideas resonated in the work of such notable theatre innovators as Peter Brook and Charles Marowitz in the United Kingdom (Brook, 1968), Jerzy Grotowski in Poland (Grotowski, 1968), and Richard Schechner in the United States (Schechner, 1988). Schechner argued, for example, that traditional methods and vocabularies for analysing theatre were inadequate. He proposed the use of a diversity of non-literary tools for this task including "mathematical and transactional game analysis, model building, comparisons between theatre and related performance activities. (Schechner, 1988, p. 27) Around the same time, a greater interest emerged in applying a study of semiotics theatre and drama. Because this science is concerned with how meanings are generated and conveyed, a semiotic study of a theatrical production will take into consideration not only the literary elements of the play script but also such performance and production elements as "movement, settings, music and the rest." (Elam, 2002, p. 190)

Returning to the original question of how the formal elements of theatre may be included in a drama/theatre education program, it is necessary to consider where, on Bolton's proposed continuum from drama to theatre, a specific lesson or project is being devised. In a lesson that makes use of dramatic play, a special focus may be given to the six elements identified by Heathcote. In a theatre project, a wider range of elements is likely come into play. Another factor to be considered is whether the approach to theatre being taken in a specific unit of study is derived from the text based Aristotelian tradition or from the performance centred innovations of the twentieth century. If the project involves the interpretation of a play script, attention may need to be paid to the Aristotelian elements of theatre as performed text. Indeed, a program that features the study of dramatic scripts is, by implication, influenced by the Aristotelian tradition. At the same time, however, it seems unlikely that any theatrical project, whether text based or performance centred, will proceed without consideration of a wider range of visual and auditory elements associated with the broad poetic field that Schechner has identified as performance.

The contribution of this chapter has been limited to a discussion of how the expressive elements of theatre may be situated within conflicting (or at least dichotomous) approaches to drama/theatre education and in the context of both text-based and performance-centred analyses of theatre art. Apart from the lists developed by theorists cited above, a systematic delineation of the many elements that might be included in an extended program of theatre studies is beyond the scope of the chapter. However, Artaud's comprehensive vision of "everything that can be said and signified upon a stage" gives an intimation of the depth and diversity of the considerable potential for formal expression in educational drama and theatre.

NOTES

[1] For example, a Canadian curriculum guideline (Ontario, 1999) is built around three "Strands" – "Creating", which includes devising and performing drama/theatre pieces; "Theory", which includes a study of plays and theatre history; and "Analysis", which includes reflection on one's own creative work and that of others.

REFERENCES

Abbs, P. (1992). *Abbs replies to Bolton. Drama, 1*(1), 2–6.
Aristotle. (trans. 1920*). On the art of poetry* (I. Bywater, Trans.). Oxford: Clarendon Press.
Artaud, A. (trans. 1958). *The theatre and its double* (M. C. Richards, Trans.). New York: Grove Press.
Bolton, G. (2007). A history of drama education: A search for substance. In L. Bresler (Ed.), *International handbook of research in arts education* (pp. 45–62). New York: Springer.
Brook, P. (1968). *The empty space*. London: MacGibbbon & Kee.
Cook, H. C. (1917). *The play way*. New York: Fredrick Stokes.
Elam, K. (2002). *The semiotics of theatre and drama*. London: Routledge.
Finlay-Johnson, H. (1911). *The dramatic method of teaching*. London: Blackie.
Grotowski, J. (1968). *Towards a poor theatre*. New York: Simon & Shuster.
Heathcote, D. (1984). *Collected writings on education and drama* (L. Johnson & C. O'Neill, Eds.). London: Hutchinson.
Hornbrook, D. (1992). Can we do ours, miss?: Towards a dramatic curriculum. *The Drama/Theatre Teacher, 4*(2), 16–20.
Ontario. (1999). *The Ontario curriculum, grades 9 and 10: The arts*. Queen's Printer for Ontario.
Schechner, R. (1988*). Performance theory* (Rev. ed.). New York: Routledge.
Way, B. (1967). *Development through drama*. London: Longman.

Larry O'Farrell is Professor and UNESCO Chair in Arts and Learning, Queen's University, Canada. He is also Chair, Canadian Network for Arts and Learning.

KARI MJAALAND HEGGSTAD

42. FRAME AND FRAMING

Keywords: performance distinction, primary frameworks, role, keying, situation

Through a study of TIE practice, *framing* became a central concept, which in turn provided a closer reading of primary texts in the field.[1] Drama concepts that seem simple and clear within the English language might easily become strange and unclear seen from a different language perspective. The reader will hesitate at concepts and formulations that are not easily transformed into ones own mother tongue and thereby search for nuances and backgrounds for the concept to better ones understanding. Framing is one of these concepts that seem to be somewhat too simple and concrete and at the same time diffuse and unclear.

Etymologically the roots are found in Old English language *framian* (to profit, be helpful, make progress) from *fram* (vigorous, bold) and originally *fremman* (help forward, promote further, do, perform, accomplish). Roots are also found in Old Norse *fremja* (to further, execute) (Online Etymology Dictionary, read: 04.17.07). The meaning of the concept has been changing and with parallel meanings through the centuries. In modern language the concept seems to have a static nuance. In this article I will study primary texts – looking for new perspectives, searching for flexible nuances and versatile understandings.

When Dorothy Heathcote introduced framing in drama she was inspired by the social anthropologist Erving Goffman's (1922–1982) theories. In some of her speeches and articles between 1978 and 1980 she refers to Goffman's *Frame Analysis* (first published in 1974).[2] O'Toole, however, says that the drama educational use of *framing* can be tracked back to play theories for instance Bateson's *play-frame*, where a number of signals tells that the activity is *play* (O'Toole, 1992, p. 109). Goffman himself refers to Bateson: "[...] it is in Bateson's paper that the term "frame" was proposed in roughly the sense in which I want to employ it" (Goffman, 1986, p. 7).

Goffman uses the term *frame* when he studies the social role-play that goes on when people meet and communicate with each other. Bennet M. Berger quotes Goffman in his foreword to *Frame Analysis* "[...] that his strengths as an observer lay in his attention less to the interaction itself than to the implicit rules that, by "defining the situation" shaped the meanings generated within it" (Goffman, 1986, xiii). When framing is used in ordinary social interactions, it becomes necessary, according to Goffman, to use theatre concepts to describe that part of the communication that deals with giving off expressions (Goffman, 1959, p. 4). Goffman uses a spectrum of theatre terms like role (and role-distance), performance, scene, audience, stage–arrangement, set, dramatisation, dramaturgy and dramaturgical skills and strategies. He also talks about teams playing against each other, primary framing, key and keying, fabrication strategies, face-to-face behaviour (often referred to as face-work), and backstage-front stage etc.[3]

Goffman presents five distinctions of performances (Goffman, 1986, p. 125–127). He starts with the most 'pure' performance distinction; *dramatic scripting*. This is theatre performance and other staged performances with a watching audience (if no audience no performance). A sub category here is what he calls "ad hoc performances". The arena is now in the domestic circle, and the performer (story-teller, musician, reciter etc.) performs for others. Goffman calls this the "optional beguilement" of other guests. The performer in this more informal setting provides the tools and props needed.

The next performance distinction is *contests and matches* where the contest itself is more important to the participants than the entertainment of the viewers (this include the whole continuum from matches with a few viewers to large champion-ships). A "less pure" performance distinction is *personal ceremonies* like weddings and funerals, where the watchers function as witnesses and guests. Goffman says: "[…] ceremonials tend to provide a ritual ratification of something that is itself defined as part of the serious world" (op.cit. p. 126).

The next performance distinction is *lectures and talks*, which is, according to Goffman, a very mixed class as to purity; briefing sessions, demonstrations, political analysis by stand up comedians – and "gifted" speakers that has the capacity to conceal for the listeners that the form is more at stake than the content. The last performance distinction is the most "impure"; *work performances*, for instance at constructions sites or rehearsals. Here there is no concern for the dramatic elements of the labour. The audience simply watch people doing their work.

In an article from 1980, "From the particular to the universal", Heathcote interprets Goffman's distinctions of performances.[4] She divides the five distinctions into six levels of purity, but for some reason she turns the continuum a bit around, by for instance moving "optional beguilement" to the less pure part of the continuum – and "work performance" in the opposite direction. She also partly changes the content of some performance distinctions. The interpretation is interesting, since she creates an order, where Goffman seems to be more vague and "flexible".

When Goffman elaborates on his *primary frameworks* and *keying* he uses headings that except for the last one are closely connected to the five distinctions of performances (op.cit. p. 47–77): 1. *Make-believe* (playfulness; fantasy or day-dream and dramatic scriptings); 2. *Contests*; 3. *Ceremonies*; 4. *Technical redoings* ("practicing"; demonstrations; replays of recordings; group psychotherapy and other role-play; and "experiments"); 5. *Regroundings*; Goffman finds the last category the "most troublesome". Here the performer's motives for the actions can be both "within the normal range of participation", and with motives that "leave the performer outside the ordinary domain of activity" (op.cit. p. 74). The performance will not be a simply read performance, because the performer is acting for other reasons – for instance when late King Olav of Norway performed as a bus passenger under the petrol crises in 1973; or when a young person is assisting (with little or no pay as a trainee) a professional in order to learn through practice; or when a lumberjack's work is done as recreation. Goffman says there is a participant-observation in regroundings, at least when they are done with prior self-disclosure (op.cit. p. 75).

Goffman's performance distinctions and his categorisation of some of the basic keys employed in our society is part of his examinations in his frame analysis. He is, as earlier mentioned, reading social encounters as different frames where different kinds of "performances" take place. The application of Goffman's theories to a drama in education context implies frames prepared by the leader/teacher and constructed and transformed by the participants. Different choices of performance distinctions can, the way I see it, provide some new perspectives and challenges in the drama field.

Going back to Heathcote, we find an interesting perspective on framing in her figure "Pieces of Cake" in "Material for significance" (Heathcote, 1984, p. 135).[5] (see figure 1)

Here Heathcote makes use of Goffman's five distinctions (with only one change of position) – and ends up with eight distinctions all together by dividing Goffman's

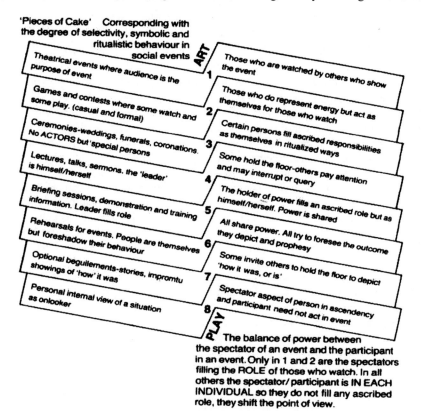

Figure 1. Heathcote's "Pieces of Cake".

work performance into *briefing sessions* and *rehearsals* – and at the end adding a separate audience perspective; a *personal internal view of situations as onlooker*. She connects each performance distinction to a description of performer/audience activity – going from "art" to "play".

The balance of power between spectator and participant is indicated. Heathcote claims that it is only in a *theatrical event* and in *games and contests* that the "spectators [are] filling the ROLE of those who watch" (ibid). One could here add the "optional beguilement" category (*ad hoc performances*). Some of Heathcote's descriptions of the performance distinctions differ from Goffman's, which also entails a slight change of content. This is probably done to better fit in with a drama in education thinking. However an elucidation on her transformation and adoption of Goffman's distinctions (with reference) would have given a theoretically better transport to her own perspective and development of frame and framing.

In her article from 1982 "Signs and (Portents?)", Heathcote presents frame and framing in drama and TIE.[6] She explains 'frame' in a footnote:

> In any social encounter, there are two aspects present. One is the action necessary for the event to progress forward towards conclusion. The other is the perspective from which people are coming to enter the event. This is frame, and frame is the main agent in providing (a) tension and (b) meaning for the participants. (Heathcote, 1982, p. 21)

An interpretation of this explanation of *frame* is that *frame* is not only a situation with some acting participants. It is also a *situation* and interpretations of a situation by the participants involved and by possible viewers. Any participant will enter any situation with a certain luggage and motives, trying to make sense of the social encounter. But any situation will also implicate some rules. The participant (either in role or not) will interpret from a special point of view. Thus meaning is constructed through the interpretations – and the following actions. What happens in the situation between the participants therefore has a potential of tension. Imbedded in tension and suspense is, the way I see it, both temporality and shifts of power. Temporality provides the next inexperienced moment, a potentiality moment where the unknown will take place and where shifts of power can happen according to the understanding of the situation and of the meaning making that is going on.

Will a Heathcotian explanation differ from a Goffmanian understanding? Probably not, but Goffman rarely gives clear and exact explanation himself. With Goffman there is always more explanations, more details, more to return to. His infinite regress can easily lead the reader off focus. He is also a creator of new verbal constructions and using terms in new and sometimes unexpected ways – quite similar to Heathcote's writing.

In 1980 Heathcote presents a concretisation of *frame distances* through a diagram called "General role-function in relation to frame distance" where nine frames behind each other is presented.[7] Heathcote's visualisation is well known with the artist transforming the event in the one end and the participation *in* the event in the other. The diagram is made for a certain context, but used *out of context* the continuum of frames can to some extent be troublesome. It is probably questionable if this frame model is applicable for other contexts. I find both the main conceptualisation of frame rigid and the selection of frame perspectives somewhat restrictive. Another problem is the "hierarchic" order that arise when *numbering* categories.

Relevant questions are: Can we at all talk about different *types* of distances for different role types? Can distance be divided into different levels (parallel to classes of "purity" in the distinction of performance)? A situation can be viewed from different perspectives through roles inside the fiction or from outside the fiction. There will always exist a distance in the perception of the situation.

In conclusion a suggestion is to combine Goffman's theories and perspectives on performance frames together with Heathcote's educational perspective into a broader framing concept.[8] This way each step of a DIE or TIE session from beginning to end provides frames of different kinds that can be scrutinised from versatile perspectives. Heathcote argues for the significance of exciting the pupils through a special *relationship* to the action:

> I take it as a general rule for myself that people have most power to become involved at a caring and urgently involved level if they are placed in a quite specific relationship with the action, because this brings with it inevitably the responsibility, and, more particularly, the viewpoint which gets them into an effective involvement (Heathcote, 1982, p. 27).

The educational and aesthetic aims challenge the drama teacher's planning and construction of frames and framings.

NOTES

[1] The TIE research was part of a lager Project Arts Didactics (2004–2008) at Bergen University College conducted by professor Aslaug Nyrnes. See more in Heggstad, 2007, 2008 and 2010.

[2] I have found three different articles from this period where Heathcote refers to Goffman. Two of them are referred to here. The third one is "Drama as context for talking and writing" (Heathcote, 1984).

[3] These "Goffmanian" terms will not be commented further in this article, but for instance *key and keying* seem to be important ways of signing in Heathcote's work, according to Sandra Heston's thesis from 1994 *The Dorothy Heathcote Archive.*

[4] The article is based on Heathcote's speech at the conference *Theatre – Education: An Exploration in the Riverside Studio in London, UK, 1978* (Heathcote, 1980, p. 7–15).

[5] This text was first published in 1980 in the booklet *The Treatment of Dr. Lister: a language functions approach to drama in education,* edited by John Caroll, Michell College of Advanced Education, Bathurst, Australia (Heathcote, 1984). In the article Heathcote refers to Goffman twice (p. 131 and p. 132). Later (p. 135) she transforms his distinction in an illustration.

[6] The first publication of the article was in SCYPT Journal, no. 9, 1982. In 1984 a slightly changed version was published in Johnson and O'Neill, 1984. The last version of this article that I have seen is in the booklet *People in Movement* from 2000 (Cooper et al.). Heathcote's article is very often referred to in drama literature, for instance in Neelands (1984), O'Neill (1995), Bolton (1998) and Ackroyd (2004) and belongs (in my opinion) to the canon of drama and theatre in education.

[7] Stig A Eriksson presents this diagram together with three later adaptations of it in his thesis *Distancing at Close Range* (Eriksson, 2009, p. 141–150).

[8] See examples in Heggstad (2008, 2010).

KARI MJAALAND HEGGSTAD

REFERENCES

Ackroyd, J. (2004). Role reconsidered: *A re-evaluation of the relationship between teacher-in-role and acting*. Stoke on Trent, UK: Trentham Books.
Bolton, G. (1998). *Acting in classroom drama: A critical analysis*. Birmingham, UK: Trentham Books.
Cooper, C., Gillham, G., & Yeoman, I. (Eds.). (2000). *People in movement*. A handbook of Materials on Theatre-in-education Methodology to accompany the course led by SCYPT at the ICTIE Conference in Amman, Jordan. Rhondda: SCYPT Publication.
Eriksson, S. A. (2009). *Distancing at close range: Investigating the significance of distancing in drama education*. PhD dissertation. Vasa, Finland: Aabo Academy.
Goffman, E. (1959). *The presentation of self in everyday life*. New York: Anchor Books.
Goffman, E. (1986). *Frame analysis: An essay on the organization of experience*. Boston: Northeastern University Press. [first edition 1974].
Heathcote, D. (1980). From the particular to the universal. In K. Robinson (Ed.), *Exploring theatre & education* (pp. 7–51). London: Heinemann.
Heathcote, D. (1982). Signs (and Portents?). *SCYPT Journal, 9*.
Heathcote, D. (1984). Signs and portents. In L. Johnson & C. O'Neill (Eds.), *Dorothy heathcote: Collected writings on education and drama* (pp. 160–169). London: Hutchinson.
Heggstad, K. M. (2007). "TIU i retorisk perspektiv - et analyseeksempel". ["TIE in rhetoric perspective - an example of analysis"] In B. Rasmussen (Ed.), *Drama Boreale*. Trondheim: Tapir - Gnist.
Heggstad, K. M. (2008). Prosperos nyve og den sokratiske orden. En undersøkelse av en TIU-praksis via begrepet'framing'. [Prospero's frown and the Socratic order. An investigation of a TIE practice via the concept 'framing'] In A. Nyrnes & N. Lehmann (Eds.), *Ut frå det konkrete*. Olso: Universitetsforlaget.
Heggstad, K. M. (2010). TIE - In winds and calm: An attempt at reframing 'framing'. In A.-L. Østern, M. Björkgren, & B. Snickars-von Wright (Eds.), *Drama in three movements. A Ulyssean encounter*. Report no. 29/2010; Vaasa: Faculty of Education, Åbo Akademi University.
Neelands, J. (1984). *Making sense of drama*. London: Heinemann.
O'Neill, C. (1995). *Drama worlds: A framework for process drama*. Portsmouth, NH: Heinemann.
O'Toole, J. (1992). *The process of drama: Negotiating art and meaning*. London: Routledge. Online Etymology Dictionary: http://www.etymonline.com/index.php?search=frame&searchmode=none (Read: 04.17.07)

Kari Mjaaland Heggstad is Associate Professor in drama at Bergen University College, Norway. Research interest: TIE and drama in education. Participating in DICE, an EU research project.

ROBERT COLBY

43. DRAMA AND SOCIAL HISTORY

Keywords: applied drama, applied theatre, theatre-in-education, social history, labor history, social justice

Small acts, when multiplied by millions of people, can transform the world.
Howard Zinn (*The Optimism of Uncertainty*, 2004)

Since the mid 1990s one of the initiatives of the theatre education program at Emerson College has been the teaching of United States social and labor history through drama, along with the development of related curriculum units and devised performance pieces intended primarily for young people in school settings. Several of these drama/theatre-in-education hybrids were created in collaboration with Bethany Nelson, Jonathan Neelands, James Robinson, Rachel Dickinson, and other drama educators, theatre artists and classroom teachers and have been shared at U.S. and international conferences and workshops. Representative topics have ranged from 19th and 20th century labor disputes (the Ten Hour Movement, the Bread and Roses Strike, the Ludlow Massacre) to the plight of migrant workers during the Great Depression and a re-examination of the trial and execution of Sacco and Vanzetti in light of the 21st century so-called "war on terror." Placed in the context of contemporary applied drama and theatre research and theory by such scholars as Tim Prentki and Sheila Preston (2009), Helen Nicholson (2005), and Philip Taylor (2003), these examples of praxis illustrate some of the evolving methodologies employed in the field and expand and clarify the rationale for addressing social and labor history through drama in schools.

Social history emerged as an interdisciplinary specialty in the 1960s and 70s, primarily as a response to what many felt was the elitism of established practices of political and economic history. Its initial concerns were with disenfranchised groups and their interactions, rather than with affairs of state, and though the field has broadened and overlaps with sociology and ethnology, its focus remains on "history from below" and how everyday people, rather than their leaders, shape the events of history. The textbook *Who Built America? Working People and the Nation's History* (American Social History Project, 2008) provides an example of how this field has been embraced by American education, though most would credit progressive historian Howard Zinn (1980) for catapulting the study of social history into the mainstream with the publication of his *A People's History of the United States* and the 2009 documentary film, *The People Speak* (Damon et al., 2009).

Just as Zinn has been central to the development of social and progressive history in the U.S., it is not possible to describe the evolution of applied drama and

S. Schonmann (ed.), *Key Concepts in Theatre/Drama Education*, 265–269.

theatre without reference to 20th century progressive political theatre movements, Bertolt Brecht's theories of epic theatre, and especially the work of Augusto Boal, whose shadow can be felt across much of what is practiced under the various labels of community theatre, theatre for social change, theatre for development, and theatre-in-education. And as the theories and methodologies of process drama, drama education and its related forms are also gradually being subsumed under the wider umbrella of applied theatre, it is worth noting the long history of connections among social history, progressive education and the principles and practices of drama for, as, and in education. Boal was significantly influenced by Paolo Freire's theories of critical pedagogy, and similarly the philosophical origins of the contemporary practice of drama in schools lie with progressive educators stretching back even before the 20th century. Jonathan Levy has pointed out that some of the earliest drama and theatre practices with young people in the U.S. date from Charles Stearns' use of "dramatic dialogues" at the Liberal School in Lincoln, MA beginning in 1792. In *The Wooden Boy: The Folly of Local Prejudice*, Stearns dramatizes the schoolyard clash of "cits" and "clowns" (city vs. country dwellers) with insights and motivations that would be familiar to 20th century social historians and progressive educators (Levy, 1992, pp. 87–90). By the 1960s and 70s when social history was emerging as a distinct discipline, examples of drama being used to teach history were already abundant. John Hipkin's *The Massacre of Peterloo* (1968) describes a school-wide, interdisciplinary experiment involving the participation of hundreds of students in a production about this episode in labor history. In the early 1970s Oliver Fiala noted the Brechtian elements in Dorothy Heathcote's pioneering drama work, practice that significantly influenced historian John Fines' book with Raymond Verrier, *The Drama of History: An Experiment in Co-operative Teaching* (1974).

As a series of political changes swept across Europe and the U.S. in the 1980s, they were accompanied by challenges to our understandings of culture, representation, identity, and citizenship that emerged from research. The possibility that progressive drama practices could lead to transformations of individual understandings about the nature and structure of political and economic systems and thereby to a re-imagining of those systems toward the goal of increased social justice were challenged and interrogated by theorists, researchers and practitioners, including and sometimes especially those from the Left (Nicholson, 2005, pp. 10–13). Meanwhile, the fragmentation of the Left in Europe after the fall of the Soviet Union, as well as the rise of the Right in the U.S., made many educators in the U.S. cautious in advocating for the role of drama in teaching social history or even of addressing the more contentious episodes in labor history in schools at all. In time, a neo-liberal response to this rightward drift contributed, as Chantal Mouffe has noted, to the refusal by some liberal theorists "to acknowledge the antagonistic dimension of politics and the role of affects in the construction of political identities because they believe that it would endanger the realization of consensus, which they see as the aim of democracy. What they do not realize is that, far from jeopardizing democracy, agonistic confrontation is the *very* [italics in the original] condition of its existence" (Mouffe, 2009, p. 77).

The present-day tension between Mouffe's agonistic approach to a revitalized democracy and what has been variously described as a rational, non- confrontational, dialogic "Third Way" is best understood in the context of social and labor history, which is rife with examples where a series of agonistic confrontations over time actually helps contribute to a climate that allows for dialogue and a resolution of conflict. Yet, any act of civil disobedience or "speaking truth to power" carries enormous risks to and requires extraordinary courage of those who participate, as Depression-era pea pickers who allowed themselves to be photographed by Dorothea Lange or 19th century factory workers signing petitions for shorter workdays were well aware. However, to paraphrase Zinn, such small acts, multiplied, were transformative. What helps individuals understand the nature of power, how democracy flourishes rather than wilts in the heat of vigorous debate, and how to develop an individual capacity and courage to stand up to injustice even against an instinct for self-preservation have been among the overarching questions addressed by many in the disciplines of applied theatre.

Threads Through Time, a site-specific T.I.E. piece examining the struggle for a ten-hour workday by the Lowell, Massachusetts "Cotton Mill Girls" in the 1840s ran for several years and provides some examples of how these goals can be addressed. The performance was developed in collaboration with the Tsongas Industrial History Center at the Boott Cotton Mills Museum in the Lowell National Historical Park and was part of a daylong program for students from ages 10 to 14 exploring the early industrial history of the city. As Nicholson, Prentki and Preston have pointed out, tensions in such collaborations can be expected as the challenges of one community entering into a relationship with another and the ethics of such border crossings and interventions are complex and demand careful attention and ongoing dialogue.

The young people participating in the program arrived in role and frequently in costume as historical figures of the 1840s that they had previously researched. To enter the mill, they had to cross a narrow wooden bridge over a canal, the symbolism of which was exploited in the drama activities that followed, which were focused on a representation of that bridge and the connections and conflicts between the worlds inside and outside the mill that the structure called to mind. When the students entered the playing space, the actor teachers engaged them in role, and the era of the 1840s was evoked with a series of projections and labor songs. Shortly thereafter, the students confronted and explored the relative power and status of their roles as mill workers, owners and managers, and other townspeople of Lowell by enacting how they might pass one another on that crowded narrow bridge.

With the news that an immigrant mill girl had died from injuries she sustained as the result of long hours and a "stretch out," Sarah Bagley, a former mill worker now a union activist, called the mill workers together at the foot of the bridge and urged them to sign a petition calling for a ten-hour workday. Management responded by threatening to fire and blacklist anyone signing the petition, and as owners, overseers and boardinghouse keepers slowly crossed the bridge toward the gathering of mill workers, intending to make good on their threat, the action was halted several times to allow students the opportunity to speak or in some way try to alter what seemed about to happen. Mill workers, management and townspeople all had to make decisions about where they stood, with real risks attendant on those choices. If enough mill workers stood together and were joined by some of the townspeople, the managers were turned back; otherwise, management tore up the petition. The program concluded with the facilitator informing the students over the strains of the labor song "Step by Step" that when the Massachusetts legislature received such petitions they chose not to intervene until thirty years later. In one memorable performance, the balance of power in the final confrontation lay in the hands of a group of African American girls playing mill workers. After conferring amongst themselves, they chose to step back and return to work declaring, "We're not going to help them [the other workers] – this is not our fight." The implications of their words and actions resonated through the space and launched several rich discussions amongst the students and actor teachers alike.

A number of the core features of this approach to teaching social history through drama are evident in this example. In terms of content, these features include the necessity of directly addressing the nature of power and its imbalances, identifying the confrontational nature of most historical social movements, and embracing the complexity and multiplicity of perspectives that are informed by questions of culture, as well as by political, sociological and economic pressures. These principles are evident in the explicit language about power and status used in several of the activities, and the framing of the final event around the students' understanding of the social and economic issues in play.

With regard to form, praxis has revealed that a variety of structures that are both embodied and informed by Gardner's concept of multiple intelligences are central to the initial and continued engagement of students, attention to the aesthetics of theatre is essential, and an emphasis on the role of affect and emotions, even passionate ones, in both the learning and drama activities is critical. These features are present here in the opening structures, the bridge crossing exercise, and the staging of the final confrontation. In terms of both form and content, the problems faced in the worlds of both the drama and students' lives must be authentic and the resonances between them clear and explicit, the possible solutions explored in the drama should involve real choices, and the outcome of the work and the students' understandings about it cannot be pre-determined. Many of these precepts are central to the work of other applied theatre artists as well, particularly those who have worked in theatre-in-education since the late 1960s.

With each new project, the challenges of "making a difference" as Nicholson puts it, loom ever more acutely, particularly with regard to the issues of identity, culture and community that contemporary researchers such as Nelson have illuminated (2009). In the end, Nicholson describes this challenge well as "an attempt to straddle an irresolvable tension – between the overarching ideal of a radical, just and inclusive democracy for all and a respect for local circumstances, the social contexts of the participants and cultural differences" (p. 13). As for why the struggle matters, Zinn reminds us in a 2004 essay, "...human history is a history not only of cruelty but also of compassion, sacrifice, courage, kindness... If we remember those times and places – and there are so many – where people have behaved magnificently, this gives us the energy to act, and at least the possibility of sending this spinning top of a world in a different direction."

REFERENCES

American Social History Project. (2008). *Who built America? Working people and the nation's history* (3rd ed., Vols. 1–2). New York: Bedford / St. Martin's.

Damon, M., Brolin, J., Moore, C., Arnove, A., & Zinn, H. (Executive Producers), Moore, C., Arnove, A., & Zinn, H. (Co-Directors). (2009). *The people speak* [Motion Picture]. United States: The History Channel.

Fiala, O. (n.d.). *Brechtian elements in Dorothy heathcote's approach in preparing teachers to use drama: With implications for teacher training.* The Dorothy Heathcote Archive, AC095. Manchester, UK: Manchester Metropolitan University.

Fines, J., & Verrier, R. (1974). *The drama of history: An experiment in co-operative teaching.* London, UK: New University Education.

Hipkin, J. (1968). *The massacre of Peterloo.* London, UK: Heinemann.

Levy, J. (1992). *The gymnasium of the imagination: A collection of children's plays in English, 1780–1860.* New York: Greenwood.

Mouffe, C. (2009). On the political. In T. Prentki & S. Preston (Eds.), *The applied theatre reader* (pp. 77–79). London, UK: Routledge.

Nelson, B. (2009). Beyond belonging: The relationship between community and power for urban students of color. *Drama Research: International Journal of Drama in Education,* 1, 60–74.

Nicholson, H. (2005). *Applied drama: The gift of theatre.* New York: Palgrave.

Prentki, T., & Preston, S. (Eds.). (2009). *The applied theatre reader.* London, UK: Routledge.

Taylor, P. (2003). *Applied theatre: Creating transformative encounters in the community.* Portsmouth, NH: Heinemann.

Zinn, H. (2004). *The optimism of uncertainty.* Retrieved from http://www.thenation.com/doc/20040920/zinn

Zinn, H. (1980). *A people's history of the United States: 1492-Present.* New York: Harper Collins.

Robert Colby, *Associate Professor of Performing Arts, Emerson College, Boston. Graduate Program Director. Widely recognized for his contributions to the fields of theatre education and theatre for young audiences.*

MOSES GOLDBERG

44. THE THEATRE PRODUCT IN RELATION TO TEACHING DRAMATIC PROCESS

Keywords: arts experiences, field trips, audience benefits

Over thirty years ago - practically in the dawn of arts education in the United States - *Coming to our Senses: the Significance of the Arts for American Education* was published. This report, funded by the Rockefeller Arts, Education, and Americans Panel (1977), makes many assertions about the value of the arts in accomplishing the overall mission of the educational system. It was one of the first documents to spell out a three-pronged approach to arts education, and it advocated making all three components essential and interdependent if the results are to be demonstrable and effective. The three ingredients in their recommendations for an effective arts program are *arts instruction, arts processes incorporated into the classroom*, and *arts experiences*. In Chapter Three of my recent volume, *TYA: Essays on the Theatre for Young Audiences* (2006), I have described these three areas as a three-legged stool, providing a solid foundation in the arts, maximizing the positive influences on the child's total education, and significantly improving the chances of that individual child reaching his or her fullest potential as a human being and contributor to society.

Arts instruction involves learning the core components of the art form. In theatre that would mean a basic vocabulary - plot, character, theme, conflict, etc.; and identifying them in works of art the student makes or sees. It would include an opportunity for arts production, perhaps including the performance of a rehearsed or improvised play before an audience. It would also include arts appreciation. *Arts instruction* gives each child the opportunity to express themselves as a developing artist and to recognize and appreciate the artistic expression of others.

Arts processes as a part of the regular classroom asks the classroom teacher to understand and utilize the mental processes integral to the arts as part of his or her classroom management and instruction. Artists often embrace non-logical connectivity, mental abilities other than cognition (Multiple Intelligences), kinesthetic or sensory exploration, and open-ended (even ambiguous) solutions to problems. Collaboration and revision are common in drama activities, but rare in the teaching of facts. **Facts** are less important to the artist than **truths**. Another goal of the classroom use of arts processes should be to make every teacher more flexible, and better at reaching the students in the classroom – each with their individual learning styles.

Arts experiences are the actual exposure of the child to the artistic product – a great painting in a museum or the excellent performance of an age-appropriate play. Typically, in the theatre area, this means a field trip to a nearby arts agency,

S. Schonmann (ed.), Key Concepts in Theatre/Drama Education, 271–274.

perhaps to see a play specifically produced for the students, or at least a school-time matinee of a production from the regular season deemed appropriate for the student population. Alternatively, a troupe of actors may be brought into the school for an assembly program featuring a performance, although some of the benefits listed below belong exclusively to the field trip experience. The goal should be to present the students with a production of high quality, teaching them that the theatre is meaningful as well as enjoyable. The argument ought to be that our children deserve to know and experience great moments of artistry. While empty slapstick and pratfalls may entertain them for the moment, the opportunity to inspire them is stolen away by condescending or poorly executed productions.

A significant amount of research exists to demonstrate the benefits of *arts instruction*, and even some focusing on the effectiveness of *arts processes* in the classroom. As a sampling, the Americans for the Arts (see ref.) maintains a website listing recent and ongoing research projects in educational settings for all major art forms. Recently, this site reported studies ranging from the benefits of creative drama on early reading skills to the use of drama in socializing special needs youth. But evidence of the effectiveness of *arts experiences* - the actual attendance at a play, for example – is almost all anecdotal! Asking adult theatre practitioners or audience members how they first got involved in theatre almost always evokes a vivid description of a childhood experience – perhaps being taken to the theatre by a parent or grandparent, or acting in a children's company or drama class. Although an examination of a theatre's subscriber list would probably reveal that American theatre goers tend toward being wealthier and better educated than the general population, still there are few studies which have shown scientifically that people who attend the theatre are actually different in some functional way from people who don't, and the lack of such evidence is critical because funding decisions within a school system are often based on demonstrable outcomes. In today's educational environment, **accountability** is a (maybe **the**) driving force, and principals and teachers are often reluctant to spend school time on activities that may not translate into higher test scores. Here is a clearly articulated issue – widely assumed to be valid; but which cries out for statistical evidence by way of scholarly research.

Clearly, there are recognizable benefits of arts experiences, and most educators can cite them, even though they cannot prove that they exist. At a recent focus group session with a dozen classroom teachers from Maryland, with teaching assignments ranging from elementary to high school, I posed the question, "What are the benefits to the child involved in arts education from attending a performance of a well-produced production of an age-appropriate play." (Goldberg, 2009). The ensuing lively discussion produced many responses, which seemed to fall into seven distinct groups. Their suggestions paralleled and expanded upon benefits I have previously described (Goldberg, 2006, p. 29).

- Modeling – Seeing a performance by well-trained actors gives them a behavioral model for their own classroom arts activities. Student athletes demonstrate hero-worship toward professional sports figures. Should not aspiring artists have access to similar role models?

- Legitimacy – The finished product validates the processes that they are learning and gives them a recognizable goal to strive toward. It is always easier to teach a concept – for example, "characterization," if you can discuss actual examples. How did that actor let you know that Huck was ashamed of his feelings of friendship toward Jim?
- Variety – Since their own dramatic activities are limited by the pressure of multiple curriculum goals within the school setting, it is important to see many different types of plays in order to learn that a range of styles and genres exists. The contemporary theatre scene includes an eclectic range of theatrical forms. How can we become comfortable with forms other than television realism, etc.?
- Communality – Watching a production alongside other students, perhaps from different backgrounds, reinforces the values of a pluralistic community, and allows them to experience, in a non-judgmental way, how others may respond differently to the same event. For example, teachers and parents often laugh at different things than children do. What does this teach us about the adults in our lives, or about ourselves?
- Gift from adult society – Attending a production in an out-of-school venue demonstrates that one's community values the arts, sometimes creates arts events especially for the child population, and perhaps has gone so far as to establish a dedicated theatre building for the purpose of presenting these experiences to their valued future citizens. How often do children see direct evidence that their community cares about them and is willing to provide them with special resources for their stimulation and entertainment?
- Application – Seeing the play, and discussing it in a structured way with the teacher, or informally with their peers, allows them to apply the arts instruction and arts processes they have learned to a new experience. Arts appreciation must be practiced to be fully learned. How often do the students evaluate their television or film experiences with the guidance of an adult?
- Fun – Ideally, they will have a sense of attending a special event, enjoyable in many ways – not the least of which is simply leaving the school environment for a pleasurable exploration of a community resource. What else during the school day is offered as an activity intended to give pleasure to the students?

It would, no doubt, be difficult to design research studies which demonstrated statistically the existence of these various benefits, or others. The pervasiveness of film and television experiences would make it difficult to separate out any effect from exposure to a live theatre experience. One research study that creates a method of quantifying the child's response to a play was developed by Patricia D. Goldberg (1983), and it has been used as a training tool for students at Arizona State University, but – to my knowledge – no large scale or longitudinal studies have actually been published. That would certainly be a worthy issue for the field to explore, and one which might make it easier for dedicated teachers and administrators to carve out precious school time to make arts events a regular part of the school year.

One important caveat: the arts experience must be age-appropriate, challenging and rewarding, neither so far beneath his or her interest that it becomes condescending, nor so far above that it becomes confusing. In Chapter Nine of *TYA: Essays on the Theatre for Young Audiences* I have expanded my consideration of this issue, frequently overlooked by theatre practitioners who seem to regard childhood as monolithic, erroneously assuming that "one size fits all."

High quality *arts experiences* complement and significantly expand upon the *arts instruction* and *arts processes* that take place in the school, and should be part of a comprehensive program to bring young learners to the world of theatre art.

REFERENCES

Americans for the Arts Website: http://www.americansforthearts.org/public_awareness/artsed_facts/002.asp

Arts, Education, and Americans Panel. (1977). *Coming to our senses: The significance of the arts for American education.* New York: McGraw-Hill.

Goldberg, M. (2006). *TYA: Essays on the theatre for young audiences.* Louisville, KY: Anchorage Press Plays.

Goldberg, M. (2009, July 20). *Focus group discussion on arts in education.* Unpublished. Westminster, MD: McDaniel College.

Goldberg, P. D. (1983). Development of a category system for the analysis of the response of the young theatre audience. *Children's Theatre Review, 32*(2), 27–32.

Moses Goldberg has recently retired after twenty-five years as Producing Director of Stage One: The Louisville Children's Theatre. He now works as a freelance director, teacher, and playwright.

SECTION IX: THEATRE FOR YOUNG AUDIENCE

MANON VAN DE WATER

45. FRAMING CHILDREN'S THEATRE

Historiography, Material Context, and Cultural Perception

Keywords: theatre, children, youth, culture, context, historiography

Historiography, or the writing of history, has gained significant ground in theatre scholarship over the past few decades, but its impact on children's theatre, or Theatre for Young Audiences (TYA) as it is now commonly referred to, has been generally ignored. Nonetheless, the way in which historians constructed a narrative based on the critical examination of their selection of facts, colored by their own ideological position and identity location, has greatly impacted theatre for young audiences. The field of TYA, that is professional theatre *for* young people *by* adults, is fraught with myths and axioms perpetuated through history in various cultural and socio-logical contexts. From Mark Twain in the United States (US) to Alexandra Gozenpud in Soviet Russia writers have claimed "firsts," "most significants," and "influentials," constructing an image of the field that was at the very least incomplete, periodizing and situating it in a liminal and limiting frame of what Roger Bedard (2003) coined as "theatre-but-not-theatre" (p. 98).

In the first decade of the 20th century Mark Twain proclaimed that "[it] is my conviction that children's theatre is one of the very, very great inventions of the 20th century" (Ward, 1939, p. 33; 1950, pp. 33–4). U.S. theatre for young audiences historian Nellie McCaslin (1997) posits Alice Minnie Herts's Children's Educational Theatre, founded in 1903, as "[a]cknowledged by all authorities to be the first significant theatre for children" (1971, pp. 3, 5–6; 1997, p. 3). Alexandra Gozenpud (1954–61), one of the leading historians of theatre for young audiences in the former Soviet Union, makes a claim for Soviet Russia: "In the very first months after the victory of the Great October Socialist Revolution, the first theatres for children in the history of world theatre were organized in the Soviet nation," (p. 421).

These select examples suggest two widely perpetuated historiographical assumptions: first, that theatre for children and youth is a twentieth century pheno-menon; and second, that among theatre audiences we can from now on distinguish a special population, namely children and youth. Both of these assumptions have wide implications. Regardless of the culture, TYA as an identifiable field only came into existence with the recognition of a special audience, which needed a different kind of theatre than what was offered to adults. These differences had not to do with quality but were framed into the presumed needs of children: spiritual, moral, educational. A close examination of how the history of TYA is constructed in two very different countries: the U.S. and (Soviet) Russia, offers some remarkable parallels from a historiographical perspective.[1]

S. Schonmann (ed.), Key Concepts in Theatre/Drama Education, 277–281.

Soviet Russia may perhaps rightfully claim that they created the first state supported professional theatre for young audiences. Evidence suggest that they were not only the most prolific and largest in size, but also that they served as a model to be emulated throughout the world, including the US (Ward, 1950, pp. 19–20; Swortzell, 1986, pp. 8–10). However, the way this theatre was *posited* as a model to emulate was deliberately constructed and highly ideological. From its inception the theatres for young audiences became increasingly appropriated and commodified by the regime as instruments of perpetuating the official ideology of Marxism-Leninism through repertories and production practices. Choices of plays and theatrical and educational practices were tightly supervised by both the Ministry of Education and of Culture and Enlightenment. The theatres for young audiences generally played to full houses, as they were part of the school curriculum's mandatory "aesthetic education." Teachers were obliged to offer monthly field trips to, among other places, the theatre. This framing of Soviet children's theatre as an educational tool to which each child was mandatory exposed, clearly affected both the *generation* of this theatre by the artists involved (playwrights, directors, actors, designers), who were coerced to espouse messages in line with the official ideology through unambiguous signs and signifiers, and the *perception* of this theatre by its target audience, who became preconditioned to interpret these messages in the spirit of Marxism-Leninism. The same holds true for the historians who wrote about this theatre, most notably Alexandra Gozenpud, Lenora Shpet (1971), and the founder of Soviet theatre for children, Nataliia Sats (1960; 1972). All wrote under the official doctrine of Marxism-Leninism, which rejected any ideological critique; scholars were expected to glorify the contributions of the revolution, Marxism, the Soviet state, and its leaders. Quotes from Lenin were required, and contributions from the state to the overall benefit of the subject in question were to be highlighted. Regressions or failures had to be downplayed or ignored.

For the theatres for young audiences, or *tiuz* (teatr iunogo zritelia), the political changes of the mid-1980s raised profound questions about their mission and educational function under the new political, cultural, social, and economic material circumstances. Although it was not reflected in official documents, theatre for young audiences was in an abominable state: the repertory was stilted as there was a great lack of new plays, especially for adolescents; the quality of the productions was often poor; the average age of the actors in 1987 was 43; and, the auditoriums were full only thanks to the mandatory field trips of mostly reluctant students. The positive image of the pre-*Perestroika tiuz* was sustained by the *tiuzes*' status as official government institutions, which were in the former Soviet Union beyond criticism, and perpetuated in historical documents.

The revelation of the formerly hidden problems of the theatres for young audiences with *Glasnost* caused a change, a *Perestroika*, in material circumstances and organizational structures, and in repertory and production practices. From an official government institution with an explicit ideological function, theatre for young audiences changed into an art form for young people now allowed to convey through its repertory and theatrical practices a pluralism of ideologies. This led to the question whether the theatres for young audiences would be able to (and were willing to) adapt themselves to the rapid ideological shifts without losing their identity as theatres specifically for young audiences. By 1987 the leading Soviet theatre journal *Teatr* in its *teatr i deti* or "theatre and children" section acknowledged the dilemma and published a feature discussion centered around the opening article of V. Dmitrievskii (1987): "*Tiuz* Today: To Be or Not to Be?"

In the US, meanwhile, the founding of professional theatre for young audiences was less clearly cut, more spread out over time, and on a smaller scale. The afore-mentioned quotes by Mark Twain and Nellie McCaslin, picture children's theatre more as art education than art for its own sake, and indeed the Children's Educational Theatre was a settlement house, a place where much of the theatrical activities for children at the turn of the 20th century started. The Junior League, founded by Mary Harriman also greatly influenced the conception of children's theatre as amateur and educational as junior league productions for children sprouted up in the country for decades to come. In 1915 Constance D'Arcy Mackay published *How to Produce Children's Plays*, one of the first widely disseminated sources on children's theatre. Germinating a conception of children's theatre that defined the field until well after the middle of this century - and in various aspects beyond that time period - Mackay weaves the history of children's theatre into a narrative of "appropriateness," closely tied to educational values - both in form and content. Mackay by and large ignored professional/commercial theatre for children - particularly Broadway spectacles, vaudeville, and the popular Buffalo Bill shows - all specifically advertised for child audiences (see Salazar, 1989). She provided writers in the field with a source of evidence on theatrical activities at the turn of the century that was limited and contextualized by the dominant ideologies of her times. The significance of this becomes evident when comparing Mackay's conception of the field with that of later influential children's theatre practitioners and historians, such as Winifred Ward, who is considered to be the mother of formal theatre for and informal drama with young people, and Nellie McCaslin, the U.S. historian of the field. Ward's theories about children's theatre appear little more than reiterations of Mackay's. Through her writing, the perception of children's theatre as "appropriate," "educational," and "moralistic," and above all "amateur" was strongly reinforced. Nellie McCaslin published *Theatre for Children in the United States: A History* in 1971, followed by two more editions in 1987 and 1997, all based on her 1957 dissertation. She reiterates, among other things, that children's theatre has remained, in general, outside and independent of the adult professional theatre. Although Winifred Ward and Nellie McCaslin wrote decades after Mackay, their framing of the children's theatre field as conceived in their writings is virtually identical to that described by Mackay: namely, that children's theatre is an amateur activity directed primarily to educational and social ends. To this day, many professional theatres for young audiences could not survive if they could not rely on school audiences - this reliance, in most cases, means that they have to conform to school ideologies and notions of appropriateness if they want to keep these audiences and forge any kind of partnership with educational institutions.

Hayden White in *The Content of the Form* (1989) writes:

Myth and the ideologies based on them presuppose the adequacy of stories to the representation of the reality whose meaning they purport to reveal. When belief in this adequacy begins to wane, the entire cultural edifice of a society enters into crisis, because not only is a specific system of beliefs undermined but the very condition of possibility of social significant belief is eroded (p. x).

Although theatre for children and youth in Soviet Russia and the US operated under very different material circumstances, which affected the generation and perception of this theatre in both countries, one could make some careful comparisons of the ways the respective histories have been constructed in narratives that have led to a predominantly limiting perception of what this type of theatre could or should be. The most obvious one, perhaps, is that in both histories an ontological relationship between children, education, and appropriate entertainment is assumed. In Soviet Russia this presumed relationship was commodified by the regime, and officially legitimated the *tuizes* right of existence. White's quote directly speaks to the crisis in Soviet Russian children's theatre when its official function of providing aesthetic and ideological education in the spirit of Marxism-Leninism was contested by *Glasnost* and *Perestroika*. On the other hand, U.S. theatre for young audiences apparently has to maintain its belief in the adequacy of this ontological relationship in order to survive.

The recognition of a separate audience of children and youth in the early 20th century and the subsequent positioning of children's theatre in an educational and social context, framing it as a pedagogical tool that used aesthetic representation as a means rather than an end, constrained the generation and perception of this theatre in both countries. While the radical changes in material circumstances in Russia forced the *tiuzes* to reexamine their historical function, leading to significant structural and ideological changes that affect current repertory, practices, and perception of this theatre; U.S. Theatre for Young Audiences seems to have a much harder time to escape an image that is historically constructed and reinforced by the contemporary material circumstances under which it has to operate and survive. After a decade of uncertainty, during which some proclaimed the "death" of Soviet/Russian TYA, Russian TYA regrouped, abandoning first of all their education sections and the forced field trips. Perhaps the field, in the US at least, just needs a crisis to escape its written and unwritten past.

NOTES

[1] For detailed historiographical accounts of TYA in these countries see Manon van de Water "Constructed Narratives" (2000), *Moscow Theatres for Young People* (2006), and "Russian Drama and Theatre in Education" (2004). Due to the space limitations of this essay much supporting evidence, nuances, and examples had to be omitted, which makes the essay itself, ironically, a prime example of historiographical construction.

REFERENCES

Bedard, R. L. (2003). Negotiating marginalization: TYA and the schools. *Youth Theatre Journal, 17,* 90–101.
Dmitrievskii, V. (1987). Tiuz Segodnia: Byt' ili ne Byt'? *Teatr, 2,* 95–106.

Gozenpud, A. N. (1954–61). Teatry dlia Detei (Theatre for children). *Ocherki Istorii Russkogo Sovetskogo Dramaticheskogo Teatra* (Essays on the History of Russian Soviet Dramatic Theatre). (Vol. I, 421–443, 719–730; Vol. II, 355–401, 695–715.) Moscow: Akademii Nauk.

Mackay, C. D. (1915). *How to produce children's plays*. New York: Holt.

McCaslin, N. (1971). *Theatre for children in the United States: A history*. Norman, OK: Oklahoma UP.

McCaslin, N. (1987). *Historical guide to children's theatre in America*. New York: Greenwood.

McCaslin, N. (1997). *Theatre for children in the United States: A history* (Revised and updated ed.). Studio City: Players Press.

Salazar, L. G. (1989). Theatre for young audiences in New York City, 1900–1910: A heritage of jolly productions. In R. L. Bedard & C. J. Tolch (Eds.), *Spotlight on the child* (pp. 25–34). New York: Greenwood.

Sats, N. (1960). *Deti Prichodiat v Teatr*. Moskva: Iskusstvo.

Sats, N. (1972). *Novely Moei Zhizni*. Moskva: Iskusstvo.

Shpet, L. (1971). *Sovetskii Teatr dlia Detei* [Soviet Theatre for Children]. Moskva: Iskusstvo.

Swortzell, L. (Ed.). (1986). *Six plays for young people from the federal theatre project (1936–1939)*. New York: Greenwood.

Teatr i Deti [Theatre and Children]. (1987). *Teatr, 2*, 95–135.

van de Water, M. (2000). Constructed narratives: Situating theatre for young audiences in the United States. *Youth Theatre Journal, 14*, 101–113.

van de Water, M. (2004). Russian drama and theatre in education: Perestroika and Glasnost in Moscow theatres for children and youth. *Research in Drama Education, 9*(2), 145–160.

van de Water, M. (2006). Moscow theatres for young people: *A cultural history of ideological coercion and artistic innovation, 1917–2000*. New York: Palgrave.

Ward, W. (1939). *Theatre for children*. New York: Appleton.

Ward, W. (1950). *Theatre for children* (Rev. ed.). Anchorage: Children's Theatre Press.

White, H. (1989). *The content of the form: Narrative discourse and historical representation*. Baltimore: Johns Hopkins UP.

Manon van de Water *is a Professor of Theatre Research and Director of the Theatre for Young Audiences Program at the University of Wisconsin-Madison. Chair of ITYARN.*

ROGER L. BEDARD

46. THEATRE FOR YOUNG AUDIENCES AND CULTURAL IDENTITY

Keywords: theatre, children, culture, ideology, childhood

The activity of theatre performed by adults for young audiences (TYA), has, over the last forty years in particular, coalesced as a loosely unified field - a recognizable and coherent economic, artistic and social structure. While there is much diversity in TYA, the field coheres around at least one (obvious) trait: the production of theatre for children. The relative coherence or incoherence of the field varies in terms of the questions posed (Smelser, 1992, pp. 22–25), but all theatre for young audiences occupies a unique discursive and practical "space," born of the union of the complex and often seemingly disparate, culturally-inscribed worlds of "children" and "theatre." The complexities of this relationship become clearer in considering the degree to which TYA, as a field, both promulgates and is marked and contained by multiple ideological dimensions. While I am aware of the problems arising from considering TYA as a seemingly essentialized field, it is useful to explicate some of what Eisenstadt explains, as both the "order maintaining and order transforming dimensions" of the social structure (1992, p. 83).

I am concerned here with issues of identity construction and cultural hegemony, and how TYA gains the appearance of a specific substance through negotiations with other discourses and social entities external to and often dominant over TYA. Cultural hegemony is not the imposition of ideology, but, rather, as theorist and historian Bruce McConachie reminds us, "cultural hegemony works primarily through legitimation, the half conscious acceptance of the norms of behavior and the categories of knowledge generated by social institutions... viewed as 'natural' by the people whose actions they shape" (1989, pp. 3–4).

The TYA "Performative"

The theatre for young audiences (TYA) field gains its unique identity - that is, it is perceived as an entity separate from other entities - through the literal "performance" of TYA. We are what we do, or, more precisely, the identity of TYA comes from the perception of others of how we "perform" the field, because, without this performance TYA does not exist. It is important here to consider that this "performing" includes far more than what we put on our stages (the literal theatre event), as all aspects of theatre for young audiences comprise the semiotics of TYA. Critical theorist Judith Butler offers a useful theoretical corollary for this discussion in her theories of the construction of gender and other ritual social dramas. In her writings about identity construction she describes the necessity of "a performance that is *repeated*. This repetition is at once a reenactment and reexperiencing of a set of meanings already socially established; and it is the mundane and ritualized form of their legitimation" (Butler, 2007, p. 381). TYA carries a kind of virtual reality, what might be called (using Butler's terminology) "the appearance of substance... a constructed identity, a performative accomplishment" (p. 381). In considering the "performative accomplishment" of TYA, we are obviously concerned with both the written and performance texts that support theatre production about which much has been written. But these constitute only a *very small part* of the TYA "performative accomplishment," and focusing on these leaves unexamined much of the nature of this constructed identity. All aspects of TYA discourse and production figure into this performance of identity: from marketing, to union contracts; from play titles, to educational "support" materials; from audience "talk-backs,' to day time performances; from school buses delivering audiences, to the length of performances; from teacher previews to actors in the classroom. The sheer number of such signifiers that are ancillary to the theatre event itself underscore the complexity of the TYA semiotic system. While a detailed analysis of these semiotics is beyond the scope of this paper, it is important to note that this signifying system does not inscribe a blank slate, but, rather, it is given meaning through the "reexperiencing of a set of meanings already socially established." In the case of TYA it is a re-constitution of meanings related to the often more dominant concepts of *children* and of *theatre*, and TYA carries meaning through simultaneous understandings of the always already present signification of these concepts within which the TYA performative is firmly nested.

Members of any society carry within themselves a working definition of childhood, its nature, limitations, and duration. (Calvert, 1992, p. 67).

The cultural construction of children and childhood is perhaps the single most dominant discourse through which TYA must negotiate identity. TYA does not exist without children. Indeed, virtually all aspects of the TYA performative explicitly point to or signify the focus on children, and in doing so TYA both reifies commonly accepted ideas of children and childhood and reinforces the adult/child binary in the meaning making system. While it may seem an absurd redundancy to say TYA is for children, in order for this performative to rest comfortably within that defining focus (to *be* what it *is*) it must explicitly reflect the "order maintaining and order transforming dimensions" of this defining - and subordinate - meaning-making relationship with children. While some contemporary theatre artists struggle against what they see as artistic limitations in TYA, many of those limitations grow logically from societal expectations of what is perceived as appropriate for children. And while TYA companies are free to shape their performative (and their theatre performances) as they choose, if this conflicts with prevailing ideas of children and childhood, they will quickly be labeled as outliers (a "different kind" of TYA company) or they will be denied all recognition as a company for children.

As noted above, cultural theorist Karin Calvert argues that our culture operates with a "working definition" of children and childhood. While people "may not explicitly discuss this definition, write about it, or even consciously conceive of it as an issue, ...they act upon their assumptions in all their dealings with, fears for, and expectations of their children" (Calvert, 1992, p. 67). A historically dominant (and, by most accounts, the prevailing) ethos in the US is one of the "innocent" child who must be protected. According to noted child historian Philip Aries, this has "resulted in two kinds of attitude and behavior towards childhood: firstly, safe-guarding it against pollution by life and particularly by ...sexuality; ...and secondly, strengthening it by developing character and reason" (Jenkins, 1998, p. 16). U.S. TYA companies, in order to keep their cultural "place," are expected to avoid any content that interrogates the trope of childhood innocence (such as nudity, profanity, sexual themes) and to present positive, character-developing messages.

A recent headline in the *London Guardian* theatre and performing Arts blog exclaimed: "Children's Theater Must Grow Up." This headline (and the article accompanying it) was a response to a theatre critic from another London newspaper, who had declared that a TYA play at London's Unicorn Theatre "should be taken off the Unicorn stage at once" because the material presented was not "suitable" for children (Gardner, 2008). While this particular instance of censorship on the behalf of children may have a higher profile than most arguments about the "proper place" of TYA, anyone working within TYA has dealt with these issues of "containment" in situations both profound and ludicrous.

But, can *children's* theatre *grow up*? I suggest we cannot ignore the inherent contradiction in that statement about an art form whose very identity is inextricably bound in the identity politics of children and childhood.

The theatre *is* now, and *ever has been*, A SCHOOL OF FALSE SENTIMENT AND OF LICENTIOUS PRACTICE. (Miller, 1812)

In addition to negotiating identity in terms of concepts of children/childhood, TYA must also assume an "order maintaining" identity as a kind of theatre, which itself carries significant cultural and social resonances. Historians have clearly documented Western society's 2000 years of distrust, and sometimes disdain, for the theatre, particularly when it might be experienced by children. As a result, the relationship between theatre and children has been uneasy if not outright condemned. Over two thousand years ago Plato explicitly argued for the protection of morals of children as the primary reason for banning the poet/dramatist from his ideal state. Yet, notably, he also praised the skills of these mimetic artists (Plato, 1921, p. 377). While many religious leaders throughout history have condemned the theatre, as early as the 16th century Jesuit educators, acknowledging the power of theatre, skirted these prejudices by introducing "school drama" into their pedagogy (Levy & Floraine, 1996). In 1762, when the governor of Colonial New Hampshire refused a license to performers, the petition against the theatre noted plays "would be of very pernicious consequences... to morals of young people" (Bryan, 1993, p. 27). Yet, just a few years later, Charles Stearns, a respected Massachusetts minister and school headmaster, directly confronted the moral dilemma of theatre and children by situating a kind of theatre, dialogues, as a useful part of proper schooling consistent with the concept of the "innocent" child. In the introduction to this book, *Dramatic*

Dialogues for the Use of the Schools, Stearns asserts that when properly "managed," performances of *dramatic dialogues* can "be productive of a most innocent and rational amusement, and not only improve the outward carriage of the students; but implant the most useful morals in them, and in the minds of their friends, who attend their performances" (Stearns, 1798, p. 7).

A semiotically reconstituted (rehabilitated?) and safe theatre thus entered the early U.S. schools, signified in the discourse not as theatre (the "seminary of vice"), but as dramatic dialogues, "rational amusements" that projected a kind of theatre-but-not-theatre which, when properly "managed," was of use in the proper education of young people. It is important to note that in these early efforts to place drama in the schools, the re-signification came at the hands of educators, not theatre artists, who, at this point in time appeared to pay little heed to child audiences. These historical arguments of theatre as a kind of moral poison for young people verses drama as an important form of moral education, coupled with the historical divide between the artist and the educator, figure prominently in the contemporary discourse.

In the contemporary TYA performative, this activity is clearly presented as something other than "regular" theatre. Certainly the focus on the child suggests that difference, but virtually all aspects of the discourse surrounding TYA clearly reinforce the pedagogical and "innocent" nature of the work to be presented. With these descriptors and others like them, the TYA performative assumes its "proper place" within the social structure to, in effect, normalize the activity and accrue relative value within that structure. This is a dynamic, ongoing negotiation for TYA to engage in the process of what cultural theorist Michael Apple calls "winning consent to the prevailing order." It is through this process that TYA finds its place in a sort of "ideological umbrella under which different groups who usually might not agree with one another might stand" (Apple, 1996, p. 15).

Toward Agency

TYA has grown to be an identifiable subset in the world of culture designed for and directed to children. As such it is a site of significant power in reifying all that is "appropriate" for young people. Yet, within the TYA performative, some theatre artists struggle for an identity that is equally rooted in the sometimes "dangerous" world of art, which, by definition, questions, interrogates and offers new ways of understanding reality. As cultural theorist Henry Giroux argues: "Culture is the ground of both contestation and accommodation" which "produces the narratives, metaphors, and images for constructing and exercising a powerful pedagogical force over how people think of themselves and others" (Giroux, 2000, p. 133). Theatre for young audiences graphically illustrates this "contestation and accommodation" binary as its struggles to maintain a cultural identity that accommodates both concepts of theatre art and children/childhood. While not always pleasing the artists involved or even always satisfying parents and teachers who bring their children to the theatre, the TYA performative has secured a "place" in contemporary culture through reinforcing dominant childhood values and shielding young people from the "evils" historically associated with the theatre. This remains a delicate negotiation, and it is only through a thorough understanding of these identity politics that contemporary theatre artists working with young people can become agents in assuming a more dominant position in this cultural dance.

REFERENCES

Apple, M. (1996). *Cultural politics and education.* New York: Teachers College Press.
Butler, J. (2007). Subversive bodily acts. In S. During (Ed.), *The cultural studies reader* (3rd ed., pp. 371–382). New York: Routledge.
Bryan, G. B. (1993). *American theatrical regulation 1607–1900 conspectus and texts.* Metuchen, NJ: Scarecrow Press.
Calvert, K. (1992). *Children in the house: The material culture of early childhood, 1600–1900.* Boston: Northeastern University Press.
Eisenstadt, S. N. (1992). The order-maintaining and order-transforming dimensions of culture. In R. Munch & N. J. Smelser (Eds.), *Theory of culture* (pp. 64–98). Berkeley, CA: University of California Press.
Gardner, L. (2008). Children's theatre must grow up. *The blog theatre & performing arts.* Retrieved from http://blogs.guardian.co.uk/theatre/2007/10/childrens_theatre_must_grow_up.htm
Giroux, H. A. (2000). *Impure acts: Practical politics of cultural studies.* Florence, KY: Routledge.
Jenkins, H. (Ed.). (1998). *The children's cultural reader.* New York: NYU Press.
Levy, J., & Floraine, K. (1996). The use of the drama in the Jesuit schools, 1551–1773. *Youth Theatre Journal, 10,* 56–66.
McConachie, B. (1989). Using the concept of cultural hegemony to write theatre history. In T. Postlewaite & B. McConachie (Eds.), *Interpreting the theatrical past* (pp. 37–58). Iowa City, IA: University of Iowa Press.
Miller, S. (1812). *"A Sermon delivered January 19, 1812." Home page of the reformed Presbyterian church (Covenanted).* Retrieved from http://www.covenanter.org/SMiller/millertheatre.htm
Plato. (1921). *The Republic* (B. Jowett, Trans.). Oxford: Clarendon Press.
Smelser, N. J. (1992). Culture: Coherent or Incoherent. In R. Munch & N. J. Smelser (Eds.), *Theory of culture* (pp. 3–28). Berkeley, CA: University of California Press.
Stearns, C. A. M. (1798). *Introduction: Dramatic dialogues for the use of the schools.* Leominster, MA: John Prentiss & Co.

***Roger L. Bedard**, Evelyn Smith Family Professor of Theatre, directs the Theatre for Youth MFA and PhD Programs at Arizona State University.*

JEANNE KLEIN

47. CRITICISM AND APPRECIATION IN THEATRE FOR YOUNG AUDIENCES

Keywords: Theatre for Young Audiences, criticism, appreciation, children

Criticism refers to the public act of discerning, analyzing, interpreting, and judging theatre performances and dramatic literature. Its artistic purpose is to convey one person's aesthetic experience of a theatrical event and its observable "effects" on other spectators by justifying one's opinions with artistic criteria and evidence interpreted from performances. In contrast, Elliot Eisner refers to appreciation as the private act of appraising a performance's artistic qualities, but with no obligation to justify one's opinions about its emotional effects other than to articulate one's culture-specific criteria (1991, p. 85). As Wolfgang Schneider reminds us, Goethe (1819) noted "three types of [spectators]: one who appreciates without criticizing, another who criticizes without appreciation, and the intermediate one who appreciatively criticizes and critically appreciates; this latter one essentially reproduces a work of art again" (1995, p. 71).

When applied to Theatre for Young Audiences (TYA), artistic criticism and aesthetic appreciation are fraught with significant problems, largely because adults' observations of children's behaviors during performances in no way signify a production's artistic qualities. As Shifra Schonmann discovered during two inter-national festivals in Haifa, an enormous gap exists between the critical and appreciative opinions of adult and child critics (ages 6 to 13). When asked to judge and award prizes for the best performances, adults considered children's choice of the best play to be the worst play in these festivals (and vice versa) (2006, pp. 119–143).

This all-too-common gap occurs because children's cross-cultural criteria differ a great deal from adults' highly variable artistic criteria or Western standards of theatre practices. Across industrialized nations, 6 to 12 year olds from all socioeconomic classes use seven main criteria to evaluate dramatized stories in this prioritized order: 1) comprehensibility, 2) involving dramatic action, 3) humorous entertainment, 4) informative child characters, 5) realism, 6) innocuousness, or violence or romance, and lastly, 7) aesthetic qualities. These overlapping artistic values and aesthetic criteria have been corroborated by international TYA reception studies.

When asked to verbalize their aesthetic experiences after performances, children use these inductive criteria to explain the publically available images they remember seeing and hearing and the privately held meanings they interpreted. Their responses depend entirely on the specific questions they are asked to answer and whether they are asked to articulate their appreciations and/or criticisms of adult-created

JEANNE KLEIN

productions. More often than not, adults want to know whether children appreciated their artistic intentions to please them. So children often feel obligated to justify why they did or did not appreciate adults' worthy attempts to please them – but without criticizing artists' success and/or failure to communicate their intended meanings – perhaps because they do not want to hurt adults' feelings for all their hard work.

In contrast to aesthetic appreciation, public acts of artistic criticism ask spectators to judge a performance's artistic merits by answering Goethe's (1821/1921) three basic questions: 1) What is each artist trying to do? 2) How well has each artist done it? and 3) Was the performance worth doing? Children already know that adult artists are trying to please them, and they presume that any performance is worth doing because adults already created it and caretakers took them to see it. What they don't know is what each artist (actor, director, designer, playwright) is trying to accomplish; that is, his or her more specific artistic intentions. All they know for certain is what they perceived and comprehended from artists' performed actions.

In order to identify artists' intentions then, any spectator (regardless of age) first needs to speculate by inferring or guessing what each artist was trying to express and communicate, before they can judge how well each artist accomplished his or her intentions. After answering these two questions, they can then judge for themselves whether a performance was worth doing based on their cultural tastes. We must never forget then that it is artistic intentions, and not cultural tastes, that initiate, cause, and drive aesthetic experiences. Cultural tastes merely reflect the by-products or aesthetic effects of intended meanings as an end-result of the communication process.

Yet who is ultimately responsible for persuading whom that their critical assessments of TYA performances are justified and worthy of public consideration? Do adult critics need to persuade child spectators that their "expert" critiques are more viable and trustworthy than children's judgments? How might child critics persuade adults that their artistic criticisms are just as (if not more) viable and valid as adults' judgments?

To resolve this conundrum, my studies have asked child critics to infer and interpret what artists were trying to do when expressing various metaphors and main thematic ideas as conceptualized in respective performances. I then compare children's speculations against artists' known intentions in order to judge how well artists communicated their intended meanings to young spectators. This method of questioning and cross-cultural reception analysis places the public obligation and ethical responsibility of theatre criticism squarely on the shoulders of adult artists and critics who respectively produce and critique theatre for all audiences.

To appreciatively criticize and critically appreciate the artistic worthiness of TYA performances, responsible adult critics ideally need to know TYA artists' actual intentions–with an empathetic appreciation for and direct acknowledgment of their cross-cultural communication efforts. In most cases, when they don't actually know artists' specific objectives for certain, they need to speculate by analyzing each artist's implicit intentions very critically in direct relation to child spectators. For example, is the playwright respecting or mocking childhood? Do thematic

290

ideas emerge organically from dramatic actions, or are they simply announced in prescriptive dialogue? Are directors inducing and keeping young minds focused on comprehending metaphoric meanings, or are they diverting children's attentions elsewhere during staged moments? Are actors encouraging children to laugh with them, rather than at them, to satisfy whose sense of humor? Are designers using artistic effects to support a play's metaphors, or are they merely trying to awe youngsters by showing off their cleverness and technical wizardry?

Moreover, responsible adult critics need to not only appreciate but also prioritize whatever meanings children comprehend, and then criticize artists if they fail to communicate intended meanings and praise them when they succeed. However, unlike child critics who know what they comprehend, the pivotal problem adults face is that they seldom know or even bother to find out the specific meanings that child spectators actually comprehended after performances. So how can they possibly judge a performance's artistic worth if they haven't even compared and questioned their speculative meanings directly with child spectators?

When adult critics fail to appreciate children's comprehension efforts by excluding their articulated meanings from public critiques, they render children's ostensible presence invisible. When they dismiss young cultural tastes as "inferior" to their own by applying their own artistic standards rather than children's own criterial values, they exclude child spectators from practicing and participating in adults' theatre cultures. When they believe that TYA critiques are of dubious value to child spectators (e.g., children won't read published reviews), they feel no obligation to justify how they arrived at their criticisms to young audiences. Instead, they simply direct their reviews to parents and teachers by describing how artists pleased children's appreciative emotions and by not criticizing artists' dubious intentions. For these reasons (and more), critics of TYA (and too few academicians) have largely failed to produce an artistic body of theatre criticism worthy of young people (Klein & Schonmann, 2009).

Brief reviews of *A Year with Frog and Toad*, a vaudevillian musical adapted from Arnold Lobel's books and produced by the Children's Theatre Company in Minneapolis on Broadway in 2003, offer a case in point. Typical adjectives included "adorable, amiable, charming, cheerful, clever, delightful, gentle, heartwarming, imaginative, ingratiating, innocuous, lighthearted, lovable, straightforward, sweet, uncomplicated, upbeat, whimsical, witty," "quaint but not cutesy," and "simple without being simplistic." Despite these "rave" reviews and three Tony Award nominations (for Best Musical, Best Book of a Musical, and Best Original Score), the production failed to recoup its capital investment after fifteen previews and seventy-three performances. Nevertheless, this "little" musical went on to live a longer life with subsequent productions, and the Children's Theatre Company became the first TYA institution to win the Regional Theatre Award granted by the American Theatre Critics Association.

This example highlights several consequences of criticism. While stimulating a company, playwrights, and their play's future destiny, critical acclaim often functions apart from public opinions as dwindling audiences ultimately determine a production's fate. In general, published criticism seldom affects audience development or further innovations in artistry because critics, artists, and audiences tend to operate in completely separate spheres of institutional influence. In fact, this entry may become moot as critics themselves predict the "death" and failure of criticism to explain the cultural necessity of live theatre among non-lovers (Kalb, 2003; Gener, 2008). As audiences age and lose appreciation for the liveness of theatre, they drift online for more news-worthy cultural information than local theatre events, spurring artists and critics alike to search for alternative means of attracting and developing younger audiences worldwide. Given the widespread lack of public demand for theatre in current market economies, as evidenced by declining attendance figures, the myth of future theatre audiences can no longer be ignored by critical writers (National Endowment for the Arts, 2008; Delgado & Svich, 2002).

Despite re-conceptualizations of TYA as an artistic profession with its own "special" audience over the last three decades, repairing the sorry state of theatre criticism may not suffice, especially when critics are forced to defend the cultural worth of childhood itself–a daunting challenge. To alter overprotective parental assumptions regarding TYA's contested educational values, child spectators need to be championed as professional critics with the same civic rights of creative self-expression and communal responsibilities as any self-avowed critic. By making young critics' reviews visible and public–online where young people now congregate–young spectators may be fully recognized, not only as competent co-participants in adults' theatre cultures, but as artistic co-creators of their own aesthetic experiences.

Aside from offering their appreciations, child critics need to be invited specifically to share their imagined speculations regarding artists' intentions. Analyzing their critical reviews through the lenses of their culture-specific criteria would then allow TYA observers to resolve their own speculations concerning children's emotional behaviors during performances. By embracing children's interpretations and evaluations, artists could qualify their successes and failures and then pursue alternative strategies to optimize young aesthetic experiences in future performances. Rather than advocating their notoriously variable artistic standards or attempting to settle unresolvable arguments between "low" (child) and "high" (adult) class cultural tastes, TYA leaders could instead refocus their conversations on how best to satisfy their intended missions directly with young people.

In these ways, TYA could re-establish itself as a cultural necessity, truly driven by young communities, that moves beyond parental expectations for "innocuous" entertainment toward more purposeful artistry that crosses generational divides. By harnessing schools' access to the Internet (not to mention personal mobile devices), children, teachers, and parents could participate together in theatre criticism directly. For instance, by showcasing child actors in heroic child roles, child critics could conceivably counter parents' and teachers' attacks over "age-appropriate" content and stimulate some really fascinating blogs. These and many other yet-to-be-imagined strategies could, in effect, revolutionize theatre education itself from the outside in and thereby democratize educational institutions. If children and youth are to remain a "special" audience, then TYA leaders need to position them as such and re-conceptualize TYA as a more inclusive community of cross- generational participants.

REFERENCES

Delgado, M. M., & Svich, C. (Eds.). (2002). *Theatre in crisis? Performance manifestos for a new century*. New York: Manchester University Press.

Eisner, E. (1991). *The enlightened eye*. New York: Macmillan.

Gener, R. (2008). The future of criticism: Notes on heart and mind or, the promise of theatre criticism in the republic of broken dreams. *American Theatre, 25*(2), 38–41, 70–73.

Goethe, J. W. (1821/1921). On criticism (1821–24). In J. E. Spingarn (Arr.), *Goethe's literary essays: A selection in English* (pp. 140–142). New York: Frederick Ungar. (Original work published in 1821)

Kalb, J. (2003). The death (and life) of American theater criticism: Advice to the young critic. *Theater, 33*(1), 44–57.

Klein, J., & Schonmann, S. (2009). Theorizing aesthetic transactions from children's criterial values in theatre for young audiences. *Youth Theatre Journal, 23*(1), 60–74.

National Endowment for the Arts. (2008). *All America's a atage: Growth and challenges in nonprofit theatre*. Washington, DC: NEA Office of Research and Analysis.

Schneider, W. (1995). 'Rosy cheeks' and 'Shining eyes' as criteria in children's theater criticism. *The Lion and The Unicorn, 19*, 71–76.

Schonmann, S. (2006). *Theatre as a medium for children and young people: Images and observations*. Dordrecht, Netherlands: Springer.

Jeanne Klein is a theatre professor at the University of Kansas where she teaches theatre for young audiences, drama with children, and children and media.

EVELYN GOLDFINGER

48. THEATRE FOR BABIES

A New Kind of Theatre?

Keywords: theatre for babies, baby theatre, theatre for the very young

Theatre for the very young has garnered the interest of numerous artists, investigators and parents. Over the past few years, the words "theatre for babies" and "baby theatre" have echoed in new productions in different parts of the world and been discussed in theatre conferences.

When learning of this new kind of theatre, many artists, researchers and parents ask why it is so relevant to discuss or even make theatre for babies, given that one can entertain a baby with pretty much any action. Or why turn to theatre when one can capture a baby's or very young child's attention by an action as simple as revealing and then hiding an object? Interestingly enough, one could say that this argument echoes the same thinking or prejudice that many people have regarding theatre for children in general: "why do children need theatre? Why, when they can be entertained so easily?"

This writer understands theatre for babies as professional theatre led by adults performing for an audience of babies from months old to toddlers approximately one and a half to two years old accompanied by a parent or adult companion. Babies usually sit on their caregiver's lap or in a stroller, and watch a play - usually between 30 to 45 minutes long - designed especially for them.

Given theatre for babies' newly emergent and contemporary status, it seems too soon to write its historiography. But one can say with confidence that theatre for babies productions emerged in Europe during the 1990's in places such as Italy (La Baracca), Sweden (Unga Klara troupe), France (Acta-Agnès Desfosses) and the United Kingdom (Polka), among others[1]. Small Size, a European Network for the diffusion of performing arts aimed at early childhood (0–6) "aims to promote an awareness of the significance of performing arts for early childhood....."[2] At International theatre festivals for early childhood audiences one can find entries such as "Visions of future, visions of theater" (La Baracca, Bologna, Italy), "Rompiendo el cascarón" (Teatro Fernán Gómez, Madrid, Spain) and "Theater von Anfang an!" (Dresden, Germany). In Argentina, two-year olds have attended theatre for children productions for many decades.

Theatre for babies productions tend to follow the aesthetics and manners of local TYA. In Europe, for example, one can see abstract productions with non-linear plotlines, audience members are received onstage, and performers play with objects such as water, shoes or musical instruments. At times, audiences are invited to interact

S. Schonmann (ed.), Key Concepts in Theatre/Drama Education, 295–299.

with the performers, as they did in Norway's Teater Fot production "De røde skoene" (The Red Shoes)[3] and Swedish Unga Kara's "Baby Drama".

Another thing happens in Argentina, where two years old have been brought along to theatre for children for many decades. In "Chiches"[4] (Toys), one of the few local productions intended for babies, there is a simple storyline, conflict, defined characters, songs, no use of microphones and no interaction with the audience. This production pays special attention to the stage and audience area settings and to avoid over stimulation from loud music, blackouts and infantilizing the characters. During the production process the company worked on understanding the special audience they will face: babies in strollers or sitting at the adult's laps, adults "explaining" what is happening onstage to their babies, no verbal response, crying, etcetera. As the variety of theatre for babies productions illustrate, there is no single one way to design theatre for babies. One can also observe that the baby-caregivers audiences also respond differently in each part of the globe.

Production play processes are similar around the world: recalling the actors' personal experiences (as infants or with babies), watching baby videos, observing babies in relationship with their parents and/or conducting workshops with baby and caregiver audiences that are filmed and adults are asked for feedback.

Many theatre productions for babies include in the play development process perspectives and experiences from both artists and scholars from the psychology and pedagogical field. Suzanne Osten (director) and Ann-Sofie Bárány (writer and psychoanalyst) from Swedish troupe "Unga Klara"[5] respond to criticism that babies are too young to understand:

> "...part of the message is that we underestimate the intelligence of the new born. 'If you can speak to a three-month-old baby and get laughter from them, you must be able to write an interesting play for them,' said Osten."[6]

But a significant question persists among some theatre practitioners and theatre researchers: is theatre for babies theatre? French semiologist Patrice Pavis stresses that the word *theatre* comes from the Greek word *Theatron* that translates as balcony or vantage point. *Theatron* manifests a fundamental feature of this art, which is contemplation: it is the place where the audiences observe an action that is presented to them in another space[7] (Pavis, 1998, p. 425).

According to Argentinean scholar Jorge Dubatti,[8] there are three moments of internal structure that must be present in an event in order for it to be considered theatrical: the convivial[9] event; the poetic event (theatrical poíesis\theatrical poetics), that is, the artistic production, what happens onstage; and the expectatorial event (poetic and convivial expectancy), the role that the audience plays (Dubatti, 2007, pp. 35–36).

Theatre for babies corresponds with Dubatti's theory: there is a convivial event, a poetic event and an expectatorial event; a vantage of a certain (artistic) event. But Dubatti also states that there is an ontological leap between the convivial event (that is, real life) and the poetic event (the artistic parallel world that is being presented to the audience). Like the fictional pact in literature, in theatre, audiences know that they are facing something that it is not real. Through convention (Pavis, 1998,

p. 94), audience members put their credulity aside to accept this poetic world with its own laws, different from the real world. Semiologist Fernando De Toro states that theatre presents a situation where everything on stage is real, and at the same time, nothing is. This means that the material dimension of the representation is real: actors, objects, costumes, etcetera, but at the same time none of these are real in the sense in the sense that they are symbolizing something that is fiction (De Toro, 1992, p. 168).

When faced with the question "do you think of theatre for babies as theatre?" Argentinean actor, director and playwright Rafael Spregelburd reflects that theatre for babies can not be considered as theatre because the spectator doesn't know he is part of an illusion. Therefore it is an act of deceit, a deception[10].

But how do we understand that theatre is but an illusion? How do we learn to participate in this convention? One can observe that in theatre, children go back and forth from the everyday life to the poetic world. They may ask their parent a question, and then yell at the bad wolf, and then ask to go to the restroom in less than five minutes. Children learn to become theatre spectators -and theatrical conventions- by going to the theatre. They "acquire a competence that deepens and broadens their experience's perimeter" (Sormani, 2004, p. 29). They learn that what's happening before their eyes is an illusion each time they revisit the theatre. True, a child might have heard from a teacher, a parent or seen on TV how theatre works. But even when that child knows that theatre is an illusion, for a moment he or she may cry because of the bad wolf, forgetting that an actor is playing the wolf. Children believe they are in conviviality with the character. And one may ask isn't that what theatre is about? Buying into the illusion?

With theatre for babies this concept of theatre as an illusion becomes even more complicated. How can babies understand they are engaging in an illusion when they attend a theatre production, when they are just beginning to learn what everyday life is? And the question rises again: do we think of theatre for babies as theatre? What does representation stand in place of when babies have not yet incorporated the real world? Can babies understand that they are facing an (hopefully wonderful and well crafted) illusion and that the character talking or moving in front of them belongs to a poetic world? Moreover: is that understanding even relevant? Why?

One possible answer is that theatre can be not only as representation, but as an event: an "artistic practice that allows in an exchange between the actor and the spectator" (Pavis, 1998, p. 191). I would suggest that theatre for babies experiences can be related to a theatrical event: generally, as mentioned earlier, there are no defined characters, little to no text, no lineal plot, no fable. Most performers receive the audience while playing and showing objects such as masks, shoes, water. Sometimes, the stage is defined by a fine line on the floor, or is suggested by lighting. At times, toddlers are invited onstage or performers step into the audience space[11]. And some new questions arise: is theatre for babies an artistic installation?[12] Or is it perhaps some other kind of live entertainment? How do babies see theatre and what's the difference between that and any other kind of entertainment adults put in front of infants and toddlers? Can one think of theatre for babies as a more sophisticated kind of game?

These questions lead to further questions: can we evaluate theatre for babies with the same tools we appraise TYA? How can theatre for babies be evaluated when the younger members of the audience can not answer back? Is it enough to ask the opinion of their adult companions? Is it enough to watch babies watch a performance with full attention? How do we know that they are being entertained or fascinated and not over stimulated?

Australia Council Fellow Tony Mack (2009) has developed the following criteria:

1. Close observation of the children. Good work for the very young tends to engender an almost fierce concentration and focus, whole body engagement, occasional mimicking of actions and expressions, and elements of the play slip into subsequent creative play after the performance...
2. The quality of the total experience for the audience. Theatre is a communal activity... observing the body language of the caregiver and the way they interact with the child afterwards can also provide evidence of the impact of a work.
3. The normal criteria of theatre. Your normal aesthetic instincts still apply, even if the theatrical form responds to humans at a different stage of development than adult observers...[13]

When considering why many practitioners are creating theatre for babies at this time, one can contemplate a number of possible motivations. In a general context, babies nowadays are seen as a target of cultural consumption. There are many products designed for babies, such as clothes, DVDs, books and TV shows (even though parents and grandparents are the actual purchasers). Joël Brée affirms that "children constitute a new category of consumers particularly eager of new products" (1995, p. 18). Which contributes to a trend of early stimulation. According to Pavis, the everyday confrontation with mass communication media affects the way we perceive and think of reality. It impacts our habits of perception, including the way we make and see theatre (Pavis, 1998, p. 59). Even small children have become used to screens and the presence of special effects, loud sounds and high-speed rhythms. And babies are now being actively introduced to this multi-media techno-logical world. Another possible motivation is that babies are brought along to theatre productions for (older) children and artists are choosing to create something appropriate or intended for these younger siblings. Since a child learns how to become an audience member by going to the theatre, one could say that theatre for babies may be creating new generations of theatre goers from the cradle; as performers take a new step towards engaging young children and infants in early drama education. Last but not least, theatre for babies may be an emergent response to artists' need to explore further than what is already known. Most likely, theatre for babies arises from a combination of the many possible motives mentioned above.

One can evaluate the production, the content, the aesthetic and research further, but one should not question the act of creating theatre for babies because it is ultimately the artists' right (provided it does not hurt the babies in any way[14]).

It may be time for theatre theory to recognize and study the emergence of theatre for babies – whether theatrical installation or performance-, and the accompanying new practices required for its production. We need to take into account the arrival of a new kind of spectator, babies: a spectator who may not be able to distinguish everyday life from fiction or provide a talking feedback, but who is watching expectantly.

NOTES

[1] Some exploratory experiences started in the mid- 1980's, like shows created for children attending crèches in Italy. See Schneider, Wolfgang (ed.). Theatre for Early Years; researching in performing arts for children from birth to three. Frankfurt, Peter Lang GmbH: 2009.

[2] Online source, <http://www.smallsize.org/>.

[3] "De røde skoene" (The Red Shoes), directed by Lise Hovik.

[4] "Chiches" (Toys), by Maria Inés Falconi. Argentina.

[5] They've created "Baby Drama," an hour long interactive play for babies, about the creation of life.

[6] Online source, < http://livingwithpeanut.blogspot.com/2006_01_01_archive.html>.

[7] Frequently on stage.

[8] In other words, there is conviviality among the audience, the performers, and the technicians, andthere is conviviality among all three of these groups, at the same time.

[9] Dubatti derives the concept of conviviality from the literal meaning of the word in Spanish, the co-presence of people, based on con-vivio or "living with." The concept indicates an encounter in time and space where we let ourselves get affected by the presence of the other.

[10] As interviewed by the author of this entry at the Forum "Teatralidad", Tecnoescena 08: International Theatre, Art and Tecnology Festival, Centro Cultural Recoleta, Buenos Aires, Argentina. November 1st, 2008.

[11] This kind of theatre is specially presented in Europe, where abstract theatre for children is more commonly explored than in others part of the globe.

[12] Interestingly, Norway's Teater Fot theatre company referrers to its production "De Røde Skoene" (The Red Shoes) as an "Interactive installation for the very young; a performance". Online source, <http://www.teaterfot.no>.

[13] Mack, Tony, "Theatre from the very beginning", Lowdown Magazine, Australia's youth performing arts magazine, Adelaide, February 2009.

[14] This work focuses on the artistic point of view. We leave it to the psychologists and other trained professionals to analyze what is best for the babies.

REFERENCES

Brée, J. (1995). Los niños, el consumo y el marketing. Buenos Aires: Paidós.

De Toro, F. (1992). Semiótica del Teatro: Del Texto a la Puesta en Escena. Buenos Aires: Galerna.

Dubatti, J. (2007). Filosofía del Teatro 1: Convivio, Experiencia, Subjetividad. Buenos Aires: Atuel.

Mack, T. (2009, February). Theatre from the very beginning. Lowdown Magazine, Australia's youth performing arts magazine, Adelaide.

Pavis, P. (1998). Diccionario del Teatro. Dramaturgia, Estética, Semiología. Buenos Aires: Paidós.

Sormani, N. L. (2004). El Teatro para Niños; Del Texto al Escenario. Buenos Aires: Homo Sapiens.

Evelyn Goldfinger, researcher, performer, playwright, director devoted to TYA. Member of ITYARN. Board member of ATINA, Buenos Aires, Argentina.

ANNIE GIANNINI

49. QUEER REPRESENTATIONS IN TYA

Keywords: gay, lesbian, queer, TYA, representation

Gay and lesbian theatre proliferated in the nineteen nineties in the United States, yet theatre by and for young people remains largely unaffected by this phenomenon. In both theatre for young audiences (TYA) and high school theatre, plays including gay and lesbian characters or any mention of homosexuality are rare, reflecting the degree to which heteronormativity dominates the field. When homosexuality is represented in TYA it is often treated as a calamity, discreetly packaged in plays intended to teach lessons about tolerance. In the last decade, a small body of drama for young people has emerged that includes gay and lesbian characters characterized by a discourse of "troubled gay youth," which limits representation to those who are victimized because of their sexuality. This negative discourse perpetuates the notion that "being gay" puts youth at risk for a plethora of problems by indicating that lesbian, gay, or queer youth will likely become either victims of self-hatred or victims of social hatred. However, queer plays that move beyond these hetero-normative restrictions have developed in countries outside of the U.S. and are readily available for production.[1]

While some form of representation might be seen as an achievement in a context in which sexuality in general, and especially homosexuality, is taboo, the presence of gay and lesbian characters reinforces heteronormativity, which Warner and Berlant (1998) define as "the institutions, structures of understanding, and practical orientations that make heterosexuality seem not only coherent—that is, organized as a sexuality—but also privileged" (p. 548). Heteronormative thinking relies on monolithic notions of heterosexuality, fixed definitions of gender and sexual orientation, and the heterosexual/homosexual binary mode of representation. Plays that reinforce heteronormativity support the idea that homosexuality is never desirable, but that it is always already an affliction that leads to extreme punishment, psychically and/or physically.

Plays with gay and lesbian characters or anything hinting at homosexuality are often forbidden for young people to perform at school or attend in children's theatres. Jennifer Chapman (2005) provides the most significant study of these issues in her dissertation on heteronormativity in U.S. high school theatre. She discusses the de facto rule in high school theatre that "plays should not be overtly sexual or have non-heterosexual characters (unless for the purpose of a joke)" (p. 2). High school theatre students typically address homosexuality through performing plays such as The Children's Hour (Hellman, 1953), Tea and Sympathy (Anderson, 1953), and The Laramie Project (Kaufman et al, 2001), which focus on perils related to the homo-sexual label thereby eliding positive and depictions of gay, lesbian, or queer lives.

S. Schonmann (ed.), Key Concepts in Theatre/Drama Education, 301–305.

Educators who produce theatre with or for young people that include lesbian, gay, or queer relationships must work under the looming threat of censorship. In 1999, seventeen-year-old Samantha Gellar's play, "Life Versus the Paperback Novel," won a young playwrights festival put on by the Children's Theatre of Charlotte and Charlotte-Mecklenburg Schools; however, the festival refused to produce the play because it involved two lesbian characters who fall in love. The festival organizers argued that the play was inappropriate for young people, eventually staging it for an older audience. The controversy around the incident drew the attention of prominent artists in New York, including Holly Hughes, who organized a staged reading of the play with Lisa Kron and Mary Louise-Parker as part of a benefit for gay and lesbian youth organizations. Nevertheless, the taboo on homosexuality in theatre for young people has not shifted significantly since 1999. For example, in 2009, productions of "Rent: the School Edition" were censored in three different states partly due to its homosexual content.

While homosexual representations for high school audiences are subject to censorship, the issue remains most controversial with regard to young children. In 2002, parents in Novato County sued their school district in Northern California for allowing their elementary school aged children to watch a performance of Cootie Shots: Theatrical Inoculations Against Bigotry for Kids, Parents, and Teachers, which has been the most widely produced drama written for elementary school aged children that includes gay and lesbian characters. The lawsuit against the school district in Novato was eventually dropped. However, Cootie Shots led to controversy again in 2005, when a school district in Morris, Minnesota prevented its elementary school students from attending a performance by the University of Minnesota.

Despite the controversy, complex portrayals of gay and lesbian lives in Cootie Shots are scant. The play includes oblique representations of homosexuality, mainly involving children's gay relatives and anti-hate speech messages. Norma Bowles and Mark E. Rosenthal (2000) of Fringe Benefits, an educational theatre company in Los Angeles, compiled the collection of skits, poems, and songs, which consist of pieces devised by young people and adults, as well as donated works from well-known gay artists such as Luis Alfaro and Tony Kushner. The collection's purpose is to educate youth about tolerance of differences in general, such as age, race, gender, sexuality, and class. However, the collection oversimplifies differences in its allegories. For example, "The Parable of the Stimples" appropriates discourses regarding gay and lesbian rights to a story about discrimination against people who make "funny noises" (p. 106).

For adolescent audiences and performers, there is a larger body of plays from which to choose. The plays range from the "anti-gay bashing" genre, which focuses on issues relating to homophobia and the coming out or unwanted outing of a troubled gay character, to the "queer" genre, which challenges heteronormative conceptions of sexual identity by depicting the positive and generative aspects of queer lives. Anti-gay bashing is the predominant genre in which queer young people are represented in the U.S. The most frequently produced plays, all focusing on queer male characters, are The Wrestling Season (2000) by Laurie Brooks, The Other Side of the Closet (2000) by Edward Roy, and A Service for Jeremy Wong (2000) by Daniel S. Kehde. These three plays are most commonly produced for and presented to young people through touring to schools or inviting school audiences. However, the reductive construction of young people in the plays precludes complex portrayals of their sexuality and the discourses of troubled gay youth, coming out/outing, and homophobia work to reinscribe heteronormativity by minimizing homosexuality and instead emphasizing simplistic moral messages. In all three plays, the central gay or suspected gay characters encounter tremendous acts of violence such as beatings, suicide, or murder.

In contrast to the anti-gay bashing genre, queer plays for young audiences move beyond the mythos that all gay and lesbian youth are destined to lead troubled lives. Sullivan (2003) provides a definition of what it means "to queer": "to make strange, to frustrate, to counteract, to delegitimise, to camp up-heteronormative knowledges and institutions, and the subjectivities and socialities that are (in)formed by them and that (in)form them" (p. vi). A queer play for young audiences breaks away from the restrictions of the anti-gay bashing genre by including: 1) the articulation and representation of same-sex desire; 2) manifestations of homosexuality both inside and outside of sexual identity categories; 3) fun in homosexuality; 4) communities that embrace homosexuality; 5) the extension of queerness beyond able-bodied, white, middle-class males.

In the U.S., The Geography Club (2003) by Brent Hartinger is perhaps the most queer youth oriented play that has been produced, however scantly due to its subversive nature. The comic play focuses on a on a group of gay, bisexual, lesbian, and straight students who form an alliance. Russel, the main character, narrates his journey through various high school strata and the trials and tribulations of his romantic relationship with a popular jock, Kevin. The play moves away from the previous models by involving both gay and bisexual/lesbian relationships, and showing young people coping healthfully and collectively with the hostile aspects of their environment, thus presenting a world that allows for the possibility of finding enjoyment rather than misery in homosexuality. Further, The Geography Club avoids reductively constructing young people by portraying them across various sexual identities with a wide array of moral compasses and levels of agency. Russel serves as the queer lens through which the play unfolds. This lens is important because, as in all the plays discussed so far, The Geography Club presents a high school where students face pressure to have heterosexual sex and includes discourses of troubled gay youth, coming out/outing, and homophobia. However, rather than perpetuating stereotypes through such discourses, Hartinger uses Russel's queer perspective to poke fun at them. For example, Russel frequently jokes about the isolation brought on by his gayness. Not only does Hartinger use humor to combat the sad and lonely stigma of gay youth, he also focuses on Russel's resilience rather than victimhood. Further, unlike the other gay male protagonists, Russel has no qualms when it comes to sharing his same-sex desires with the audience.

Queer plays for young audiences in counties such as Canada, Britain, and Australia move beyond the anti-gay bashing genre by foregrounding queer social relationships and relatively tame expressions of same-sex desire both discussed and embodied. Yellow on Thursdays (2002) by Canadian playwright Sara Graefe is one of the few plays for youth that centers on a girl who comes to embrace a lesbian identity. Two of the main characters, Katie and Rebecca, are best friends, but their friendship begins to deteriorate after a summer vacation apart during which Rebecca loses her virginity to a man at camp, while Katie stays at home dreaming romantically of her French teacher, Madame Dufresne. The third character, Mike, is a recent transfer to the high school; the self-proclaimed "boy crazy" Rebecca immediately latches on to him. Katie struggles with her same-sex desires as Rebecca obsesses over heterosexual sex and her relationship with Mike. The play explores homophobia, hegemonic masculinity, and pressure to engage in heterosexual sex, but these elements do not entirely obscure homosexuality.

While The Geography Club and Yellow on Thursdays present a step forward from anti-gay bashing plays by providing more positive outcomes for gay and lesbian young people within hostile environments, they are both still constrained, though not overwhelmed, by discourses of troubled gay youth, coming out/outing, and homophobia. Further, both plays limit young people's lives to high school communities that are oddly disconnected from outside social, political, and economic circumstances.

Vin, a one-act play by Australian playwright Stephen House (2003), provides a less sanitized and more complex depiction of young people's concerns and sexualities. House does not limit his characters to a high school community in which gossip about who is gay and who is not governs young lives. Instead, he focuses on urban and domestic spheres, depicting young people coping with poverty, neglect, and drug use. In a sense, the play portrays a group of "troubled" youth; however, these young people are not ontologically troubled due to their queer identities; rather, they are responding to socioeconomic circumstances. Moreover, while queer sexuality is not necessarily portrayed as a cause for celebration, homophobia and coming out/outing discourses do not circumscribe the play. The play incorporates queer elements such as the articulation and representation of same-sex desire, manifestations of homosexuality outside of sexual identity categories, and the extension of queerness to lower-class males. However, the characters remain unconstrained by the search for finite sexual identity. Likewise, Citizenship (2005) by the British playwright Mark Ravenhill includes complex representations of queer youth negotiating specific social, political, and economic environments and has been successfully performed by and for British youth.

In a political landscape in which diverse representations of human sexuality have been censored in schools, it is increasingly important to create opportunities for youth to publicly engage with and think about such representations. Can school drama and TYA become sites for such engagement? Or will TYA and school theatres continue to assuage adult anxiety regarding young sexuality? Clearly, there are no easy answers to these questions. Nevertheless, theatre with and for young people is in desperate need of a "queering," that is, an understanding of its heteronormativity and a deliberate subversion of it.

NOTES

[1] Discussions of these ideas are in (van de Water & Giannini, 2008) and (Giannini, 2009). A version of this essay was initially published in Youth Theatre Journal 24.1.

REFERENCES

Anderson, R. (1953). *Tea and sympathy*. New York: Samuel French.

Bowles, N., & Rosenthal, M. E. (Eds.). (2000). *Cootie shots: Theatrical inoculations against bigotry for kids, parents and teachers*. New York: TCG.

Brooks, L. (2000). *The wrestling season*. Woodstock, IL: Dramatic.

Chapman, J. (2005). *The theatre kids: Heteronormativity and high school theatre* (Doctoral dissertation). Available from Proquest Dissertations and Theses database. (UMI No. ATT 3175579).

Giannini, A. (2009). Young, troubled, and queer: Gay and Lesbian representation in Edward Roy's *The other side of the closet* and *Sara Graefe's Yellow on Thursdays*. *Youth Theatre Journal, 23*(1), 48–59.

Graefe, S. (2002). *Yellow on Thursdays*. Toronto: Playwrights Guild.

Hartinger, B. (2003). *The geography club*. Unpublished play.

Hellman, L. (1953). *The children's hour*. New York: Dramatists.

House, S. (2003). *Vin* (a play). Tasmania: Australian Script Centre.

Kaufman, M., et al. (2001). *The Laramie project*. New York: Vintage.

Kehde, D. S. (2000). *A service for Jeremy Wong*. Tallahassee: Eldridge.

Ravenhill, M. (2005). *Citizenship. Shell connections 2005: New plays for young people*. London: Faber and Faber.

Roy, E. (2000). The other side of the closet. In Rave: *Young adult drama* (pp. 7–55). Winnipeg, MB: Blizzard.

Sullivan, N. (2003). *Preface. A critical introduction to Queer theory* (pp. v–vii). New York: New York UP.

van de Water, M., & Giannini, A. (2008). Gay and Lesbian theatre for young people or the representation of 'troubled youth.' In F. Fisher (Ed.), *We will be citizens: New essays on Gay and Lesbian theatre* (pp. 103–122). Jefferson, NC: McFarland.

Warner, M., & Berlant, L. (1998). Sex in public. *Critical Inquiry, 24*(2), 547–566.

Annie Giannini *is a PhD student at the University of Wisconsin-Madison, specializing in theatre for youth.*

LORENZO GARCIA

50. LATINO TYA

Portraying Practices of Loss and/in Assimilation

Keywords: theatre, adolescents, assimilation, culture, bereavement

Curiously, despite the increased participation in the arts and growing demographics of Latinos,[1] little to no attention within the various publics currently served by U.S.-TYA is given to the history of resistance and intervention of Latino playwrights who struggle to contribute to the U.S. literary whole. Moreover, the syncretic dynamic to struggle against a totalizing homogeneity projected by what theatre critic M. Teresa Marrero (2002) refers to as a "stereotypical 'Latinidad'" is still a priority for current and future generations of Latino playwrights and, in effect, provides the philosophical grounding for a critique of U.S. society through modes of representation that mine "the ambiguity of the gaps, of the poetic, of the theatrical."

Interestingly, there are a large number of Latino plays that make visible complex and emotionally compelling adolescent characters. Equally interesting is that "diversity" has been one of the buzzwords of the last quarter century, though much of what I will sketch here depicts the push to make the experiences of Latino youth in the US far less "diverse." I first turn to *Bocón* (*Big Mouth*) by Lisa Loomer (1995), which can be viewed as an exemplary textual instance that provides a unique perspective on the painful practices of living with loss in a world full of problems. By appropriating the traditional coming-of-age genre, Loomer not only speaks to the options, futures, and responsibilities of her young narrator, but also, as if building on Marrero's insights, comments on the dominant U.S. society, even calling into question some of its core values.

In *Bocón*, Miguel, a 12-year-old boy, embarks on a dangerous journey northward to the "City of Angels" to testify about unspeakable acts of murder, hostility, and labor exploitation that his family and community of landless farmers have endured at the hands of corrupt and menacing Soldiers. The dramatic irony is that Miguel travels in silence for he lost his voice after witnessing the disappearance of his own parents. His journey, thus, begins with the yearning to break through the silence and accompanying isolation. It is a border-crossing journey fraught with fear and urgent need, as well as one that takes him into a realm of fertile chaos. To testify on behalf of his parents and on behalf of others who have endured great suffering is to transcend the everyday dimensions and limits of his life. The act of testifying connects him deeply to others who have suffered, as well as to something larger and more enduring than even his family's and community's history, and this sense of deep connection provides him by the end of the play with an exquisite aliveness that makes his daily fears more bearable.

S. Schonmann (ed.), Key Concepts in Theatre/Drama Education, 307–311.

Loomer's focus on a transnational connection uniquely foregrounds the investigation of identity formation, the central psychosocial task of adolescence (Erikson, 1968), in the context of historical and political conditioning. Interestingly, the next task in Erikson's hypothesized normal course of psychosocial development involves undergoing a transformation that establishes the capacity for intimate commitment. Loomer herself suggests that *Bocón* offers a young audience the opportunity to witness "a boy ... undertaking a transformation they might undertake themselves" (Jennings, 2005). Her use of *transformation* raises intriguing questions: What exact set of ideas or relationships does the transformation of which Loomer speaks disturb? What accomplishments, destinies, or intimate commitments does the metaphor of transformation signify for adolescents such as Miguel, and hasn't participating in the unauthorized acts of crossing borders actually shifted Miguel into the category of the undocumented, a people without status, place, or rights?

As Alicia Camacho (2008) persuasively argues, the transnational points to "a condition of alterity to, or exclusion from, the nation," and seeks to "speak for a new order of citizenship and shared interest, an order that follows from the struggles of people who move." This new order is critical for both the host and sending nations, as Camacho notes, "collude in producing a class of denationalized [migrant] subjects whose personhood is discursively consigned to mere economic being as disposable labor or is legally reduced to the mere status of criminal trespasser." Taking action and gaining voice are acts of refusal, and what Miguel refuses are the abject positions of "disposable labor" and criminal trespasser" that state officials are so willing to violently and indifferently impose on him. Beginning to emerge as interpellation misfires is what Judith Butler (1997) refers to as "a radically conditioned form of agency." For Miguel and thousands of others like him who every year enter the US not only seeking protection from human rights abuses but also unaccompanied by parents or guardians, agency within the vast terrain of transnational space comes at the high cost of reckoning with displacement and loss.

When armed combat, genocide, dislocation, and transnational migration enter the life story, resurrecting loss and its remains comes to suggest not only strong dissatisfaction but also a determined opposition that marks the overall effort of sustaining identity and community as desperate acts risking harm and even death. Replacing Loomer's use of "transformation" with "bereavement," which refers to "the process of losing a close relationship" (Raphael, 1984), raises important concerns related to the processes of regulation and integration - which are the same processes coming into play in the conceptualization of adolescence. And if it is bereavement through a violent death, as is the case for Miguel whose parents have "disappeared," might this not raise another set of questions about how to relate to the dead, and then how to inhabit and negotiate loss? Drawing on Jane Ribbens McCarthy's (2006) questions, the dilemma is clearly about how adolescents like Miguel are to deal with the grief that may accompany bereavement: "are they meant to 'let go' or not?" or "are they meant to control their emotions or express their grief, and in what contexts?" The questions serve as reminders that adolescents such as Miguel may have aspirations other than the pulls and tugs of socioeconomic upward mobility, raging hormones, peer relationships, or unbridled consumption perpetually circulated as confident characteristics of adolescent culture in the US (see Lesko, 2001).

By definition, Miguel at the point of arrival in the US is an exile as the concept describes persons who have fled war or other violence in their home country. However, while he may seek asylum in the US in order to escape life-threatening circumstances and while he may be terrified as he endures interrogation from the immigration "Judge," he is no way inclined to sever ties with his past. Undoubtedly, the loss Miguel carries will always be there, but it will never be just a loss. Rather, within the frame of exilic existence, the holding on to loss can be best viewed as providing a turn from mere endurance to recovery, which in the context of exile must include, according to Edward Said (2000), the harnessing of energy "to reassemble an identity out of refractions and discontinuities."

While the process of imaginative investment supplies energy and propels action, it also raises questions of value and, by extension, of the partiality or bias of valuing processes such as assimilation in which some ways of being are favored over others. Anthropologist Renato Rosaldo (1993) conceptualizes assimilation through its conflictual process of "cultural stripping away" that is put in the service of creating an image of the ideal citizen, making loss the very sign of the ideal national subject. In Rosaldo's view, assimilation requires a surrendering of a "meaningful past - autobiography, history, heritage, language, and all the rest of the so-called cultural baggage." On the other hand, the visibility of the "undocumented" serves to justify an increased militarization of the border -particularly the US-Mexico border - the same national border Miguel crosses in his journey northward, and the same border U.S. officials and civilians alike detain and abuse the undocumented with little regard for international human-rights conventions (see Camacho, 2008). National existence is reduced to a dialectic tension between a dominant center and a peripheral tradition - a biculturalism or psychic splitting that weaves between absorption and rejection but all the while is constrained by strict adherence to what Rosaldo calls "a peculiar ratio" in which "the more power one has, the less culture one enjoys, and the more culture one has, the less power one wields."

Extending Rosaldo's argument, one might also hypothesize, as Anne Cheng (2000) does, that the divided or bicultural subject plays out a lesson one might easily draw from psychoanalysis: that assimilation is "a form of internalization [or identification] so intense as to be almost a bodily incorporation of another." What is expected in the process of assimilation is the seamless identification with the socially prescriptive models of selfhood the dominant culture provides and imagines as perfection (e.g., "citizen"). A preoccupation with perfection establishes the conditions within which to carry out what Cheng refers to as the productive activities of "comparison" and "approximation," but as an organizing principle, it is often problematic. Living in a state of duality, as Cheng notes, amounts to "constantly seeking and staging the question of origin," as well as "anticipating and repeating a failed or painful experience of social entry and contact." However, the important point to consider, as David Eng and Shinhee Han (2003) emphasize, is the way in which assimilation demands that what is lost cannot ever be reinstated or recuperated into the psychic life of the individual. Precisely because the social injunction to measure up actually

LORENZO GARCIA

denies the social status of that lost object or ideal, Eng and Han claim it may actually
forestall the capacity to invest in new objects or ideals. This is particularly evident
in instances where sacrifice is viewed as an act of betrayal as in being American
comes at the sacrifice of being Puerto Rican. In these instances, assimilation cannot
guard against the trauma and loss the bicultural subject seeks to avoid. Measuring
up comes with uncomfortable understandings of disenfranchisement and dislocation,
and the nostalgic summoning of the lost ideal - Sigmund Freud's (1917/1955)
"shadow of the object" - serves to thwart the allure of assimilationist closure.

In the essay "The Location of Culture," Homi Bhabha (1994) proposes disrupting
assimilationist closure, what he refers to as an "ethnocentric" idea, with dissident
voices. The central point in Bhabha's argument is that the displaced, such as the
migrant and refugee, must invent their own "history" that "refigures" the past as
an "in-between space that innovates and interrupts the performance of the present."
On the basis of this hypothesis, holding on to lost presences can be read as a psychic
defense against oblivion - a productive intervention using a relatedness to a distant
past to address a making of an impending future. The impulse to disrupt power
and authority through the political project of rewriting national reality from the
experience of sociopolitical and cultural displacement points to the very desire to
recuperate submerged histories. Such recuperation can impart new facts in order to
problematize what Cheng calls "a scripting history" that is as dangerous as it is
unresponsive to difference and memory, denying the intricate relationships and
histories that bind various regions of the Americas.

One of the ways through which recuperation can occur, according to Bhabha, is
in literature, which I interpret broadly as "story." Taking my cue from Bhabha, but
also from Victor Turner (1982), I begin to understand the imperative of Loomer's
recurring use of "tell my story" as a form of social protest - in other words, a
responsible action to redress a social breach. The expectation is that the story
Miguel eventually tells will not be neutral. Rather, his story will be gripping and
instructive - aiming a bright light at the predicaments of the oppressed in ways very
similar to Augusto Boal's (1979) revolutionary hero who invites listeners/witnesses
through identification to see his situation in urgent need of corrective action. In the
recasting of story as redressive action lies the possibility that the loss can be
productively resurrected and, equally important, can gain expressive voice.

NOTES

[1] The term "Latino" is deployed as a pan-ethnic term that refers to the large population of individuals
residing in the US descending from Spanish-speaking groups, while calling attention to multiple
intersections within narratives of identity. Its use is an effort to rehearse a decolonialized practice
that acknowledges the use of the term as "the performance of a political stance [that] maneuvers
between, within, and against the nations of Mexico and the United States, the cultures of Spain and
Mesoamerica" (see Davalos, 2001).

REFERENCES

Bhabha, H. K. (1994). *The location of culture*. New York: Routledge.
Boal, A. (1979). *Theatre of the oppressed*. London: Pluto Press.

Butler, J. (1997). *The psychic life of power: Theories in subjection.* Palo Alto, CA: Stanford University Press.

Camacho, A. S. (2008). *Migrant imaginaries: Latino cultural politics in the U.S.-Mexico Borderlands.* New York: New York University Press.

Cheng, A. A. (2000). *The melancholy of race.* New York: Oxford University Press.

Davalos, K. M. (2001). Performing politics: Introduction. In C. A. Noriega, E. R. Avila, K. M. Davalos, C. Sandoval, & R. Perez-Torres (Eds.), *The Chicano studies reader: An anthology of Aztlan, 1970–2000* (pp. 243–252). Los Angeles: UCLA Chicano Studies Research Center.

Eng, D. L., & Shinhee, H. (2003). A dialogue on racial melancholia. In D. L. Eng & D. Kazanjian (Eds.), *Loss: The politics of mourning* (pp. 342–371). Berkeley, CA: University of California Press.

Erikson, E. H. (1968). *Identity, youth, and crisis.* New York: Norton.

Freud, S. (1917/1955). Mourning and melancholia. In J. Strachey (Ed.), The *standard edition of the complete psychological works of sigmund freud* (Vol. 14, pp. 237–258). London: Hogarth Press.

Jennings, C. (Ed.). (2005). *Theatre for young audiences: Twenty great plays for children.* New York: St. Martin's Press.

Lesko, N. (2001). *Act your age! A cultural construction of adolescence.* New York: Routledge Falmer.

Loomer, L. (1995). Bocón: A central American tale. In J. Rosenberg (Ed.), *Aplauso! Hispanic children's theater* (pp. 34–71). Houston, TX: Arte Público Press.

Marrero, M. T. (2002). From El Teatro Campesino to the Gay 1990s: Transformations and fragments in the evolution in Chicano/a Latina/o theater and performance art. In L. A. Ramos-García (Ed.), *The state of Latino theater in the United States: Hybridity, transculturation, and identity* (pp. 39–66). New York: Routledge.

Raphael, B. (1984). *The anatomy of bereavement: A handbook for the caring professionals.* London: Unwin Hyman.

Ribbens McCarthy, J. (2006). *Young people's experience of loss and bereavement: Towards an interdisciplinary approach.* New York: Open University Press.

Rosaldo, R. (1993). *Culture and truth: The remaking of social analysis.* Boston: Beacon Press.

Said, E. W. (2000). *Reflections on exile and other essays.* Cambridge, MA: Harvard University Press.

Turner, V. (1982). *From ritual to theatre: The human seriousness of play.* New York: PAJ Publications.

Lorenzo Garcia *is a Professor at the University of North Texas, USA, teaches and directs in the Department of Dance and Theatre, currently serving as department chair.*

PERSEPHONE SEXTOU

51. THEATRE FOR CHILDREN IN HOSPITALS

Keywords: theatre, children, health, well being

Theatre for children in hospitals is categorised under the umbrella of Applied Drama but it needs to be a flexible term because it includes a multitude of practices and practitioners, involving different circumstantial details concerning who is performing what in hospitals, how children are participating as audiences, what the effects of theatre are on hospitalized children's physiology and psychology and, how individual medical systems work. One of the things that make theatre for children in hospitals an exceptional experience for theatre professionals is that the journey goes beyond the stage into corridors, waiting areas, and along bedsides that are transformed into performance spaces for children without discrimination or charges. It can be liberating for actors who need to 'escape' from theatre venues, conventions and formalities, and who want to work in the community and, also for young audiences, families and hospital staff, who need to 'escape' from hospital routine, pain, stress and depression.

I appreciate the power of theatre to provide children with an improved quality of life and well-being in hospitals. However, I remain slightly uneasy when I consider the realities of health care being provided to children and families around the world. This is partly because the provision of health care raises political issues and questions that often seem to affect the work of professionals in arts programmes in hospitals. What quality of life is envisioned for children in hospitals? What activities are currently available to offer children joy and support while being patients? Whose values and interests does theatre in hospitals serve? Those of the patients, the theatre company, the health system, the funding agencies? In developed countries, some governments cannot cope with the total volume of cases in children's hospitals; health professions are sometimes under-represented and theatre in hospitals seems absolutely unfeasible. In developing countries or countries in crisis the picture is even more worrying. In Iraq, for example, there is no proper medical supply, no diagnostic accuracy and treatment for children, nor effective chemotherapy or access to antibiotics and no blood quality control that results in serious infections.[1] In Sri Lanka, injured children are victims brought down from the war zone and 'guarded by members of the same armed forces who were responsible, in some cases, for their injuries.'[2] Realities of this kind can easily make anyone who cares about children feel angry; how can one draw smiles to children's faces in a battle-field of sick and injured children? But then, it is common sense that the governments have their responsibilities, do they not? As theatre professionals, we have the opportunity to enter into these difficult places, and offer a helping hand to children in need in the best way we can.

S. Schonmann (ed.), Key Concepts in Theatre/Drama Education, 313–318.

Pluralism of Practice

The quality of treatment and care for sick children through the arts offer a range of examples of practice all over the world that demonstrate the breadth of this growing field. The field includes both professional and non-professional theatre performances often incorporating elements of drama, storytelling, poetry, live music and dance. Practitioners vary from actors who visit hospitals as individuals to theatre companies and, occasionally amateur drama troupes. Audiences come from a variety of age groups, socio-economic and education backgrounds. These initiatives range from mini shows of one actor presented at each child's bedside to portable performances of two to four actors based on fables, fairy tales, folk stories and devised classics. Clown visits, puppetry shows, drama workshops and productions on stories told by children attending hospital schools are also joining this category.

The pluralism of theatre practice in hospitals could not be possibly covered within the short space of this entry as increasing numbers of partnerships between hospitals and professional theatre companies are developing worldwide. Here are only a few representative examples. In the United Kingdom (UK), nine children from the Dialysis Unit of the Evelina Hospital school in Guy's & St. Thomas' Hospital and children from two primary schools in London have contributed to creating site-specific theatre that was produced by professional cast of the Unicorn Children's Theatre in London in 2009.[3] Soccorso, a professional Hospital Clown Theatre company in Italy with origins from Russia presents 'Strange Games.[4] The National Theatre of Northern Greece started touring performances into Thessalonica public pediatric and pediatric-oncology hospitals under the umbrella of its educational programmes in 2007.[5] In the US, Elephant Ensemble Theater tour plays in New York City hospitals[6] and Echo Theatre Company lead drama workshops and interactive performances in St. Louis.[7] Liu Brothers Hospital Clowns perform at the Beijing Women and Children's Hospital in China.[8] In Lithuania, Kaunas Puppet Theatre company runs a charity programme called 'Smiles on the Hospital Ward' and tour in hospitals and sanatoria in Kaunas.[9] In Russia, there has been a recent plan for an outreach programme for children in hospitals and orphanages in Moscow including clown visits and theatre activities.[10]

Motivations and Aims

Those of us who work in theatre for children in hospitals tend to be alert to our motives for engaging in the practice and research of this field. I am aware that I came to realize my need to make theatre for hospitalized children through personal experience. I recall myself as a parent in a children's hospital, in the midst of children lying on beds in pain, bored and unhappy with other children and parents in miserable moods. Dull colours on the walls, cold light, tired staff, strong blends of antiseptics and chicken soup made a rather unpleasant image. That image actually caused me to reflect on my joyful moments in the theatre, on happy children's faces, on colourful costume and settings, on cheerful music, and on fascinating shows that these children would probably not watch for a long time. I wanted to change that image, bring life and joy to that place, change the semiotics of the space, draw smiles to children's faces, and give hope to parents by watching their children being happy. So, I introduced theatre for children in hospitals to the National Theatre of Northern Greece (2007–2009) and turned my research towards the examination of theatre's contribution to children's health and wellbeing in NHS organizations (2010) in England.

The excitement of that time and my current research in health is informed by the belief that theatre might gradually change the way people interact with each other and with the community. (Nicholson, 2005; Prentki & Preston, 2009; Sextou, 2005, 2007; Somers, 1996). There is a humanistic motivation, assumption, and hope in this belief. As in making theatre for and with a community, theatre practitioners in hospitals are continually on the search of specific children's groups with common health experiences and medical treatment to either address their work or to engage them in creative, devising processes. The focus is, however, not on educating community audiences, as participatory theatre performances in hospitals are not used to explore or resolve social and political issues towards change. The focus is rather inspirational in a sense that it values children's life experiences; it aims to contribute to health and social care through theatre representations, dramatizations, staged or improvised readings, stories and creative narratives.

Benefits

Research evidence shows that significant benefits can result from a productive and creative relationship between theatre companies and hospitals. Healing and therapy is not considered as a direct target or result for theatre shows in hospitals. However, 'make-believed' representations of reality have healing affects on sick children in cases where theatre practitioners and drama therapists join their strengths with medicine professionals and researchers. It has been found that clownery in hospitals, for instance, may contribute to the child emotional health and well being by offering happiness and playfulness and by helping her to cope with her stay in hospitals. Participatory experiences between clowns and sick children are examples of opening up diagnosis and therapy to non-traumatic care provision. (De Lima *et al.*, 2009, p. 178) This finding matches with evidence that children cope with stress more efficiently, they become calm, relaxed and powerful when they remain active. (Kostenius & Öhrling, 2009; Aldiss *et al*, 2009) It has also been found that live performances promote nursing personal development, contribute to patient management, raise the quality of healthcare provision and improve working conditions for the medical and nursing staff. (Staricoff, 2006) In terms of Arts strategy and excellence in care, art projects in hospitals are described as 'high-kudos powerful marketing links' based on evidence which shows that patients exposed to art, theatre and music experience reduced stress and blood pressure, have shorter post-operative stays and improved mental health.[11] Within this context, it is not surprising that hospital and medical staff offer sick children theatre experiences in hospital settings in Canada.[12]

Regarding research methodologies where theatre and drama are used as data-collection methods for examining aspects of hospital care for children, attention is appropriately focused on ethics. (Sinclair in Aldiss et al, 2009; Powell & Smith, 2009) From my perspective, when entering children and families' 'pain area', it is useful to remember that sick children need no pity and emotional overflows. Theatre in Health raises ethical issues that need to be dealt carefully. In the UK, for instance, researchers need formal consents from children, parents and guardians as well as an ethical approval from the National Health System (NHS) and hospitals' Research Committees (REC). That is to perform in wards and use data from interviews and observations with children, especially in cases where actors use children's autobiographical stories to devise representations of them in hospitals. They need to do so respectfully with regards to the children's rights for privacy and care, and to their parents' decisions. Stories and experiences from illnesses and hospitalisation of individual children need to be treated and represented as the experience of composite fictional characters, within the safety of the dramatic context to avoid the repetition of traumatic situations and painful feelings.

Funding and Governmental Purposes

The cost and the provision of medical care and the government's proper use of resources for both health and the arts are some of the factors that might influence theatre practice in hospitals. In the UK, professional initiatives, creative partnerships between researchers, theatre companies and hospitals are commissioned by the support of a range of funding schemes such as the National Health System Foundation Trusts, the Mcmillan Cancer Support, the Department of Health's NIHR Biomedical Research Centre, the Wellcome Trust and City Councils. Some professional companies get support from a variety of organizations, which evidences that there is a growing appreciation of theatre for sick children and an interest to invest in Art & Health. Cahoots NI (Northern Ireland) are a good example of this practice.[13] In other countries, funding comes through the Ministries of Education and of Culture, donations from individuals and patrons (Piwacket Theatre for Children, US[14]) and other funding bodies and charities. Funding enables theatre companies to offer their work without charge and in some occasions; they receive official awards and recognitions of appreciation by the Arts Council and Foundations for the Arts for their contribution to the community.

Artistic Challenge and Limitations

Making theatre for children in hospitals is a great artistic challenge. That is first to turn white-painted, dull spaces into a performance space with the minimum of set, props and costumes. Then, to transform bored children who are in pain into lively and cheerful spectators hooked in a theatre. To make this possible requires acting of high professional standards, and the creation of a dramatic context where supernatural things may occur, where hope for cure and happiness can light the way out of trouble.

However, there is a question here of how children respond to theatre shows and how actors achieve high artistic quality with 'unhealthy' (sick) audiences in such peculiar circumstances. From my observations of plays for kids in Thessalonica hospitals, it becomes apparent that children's responses are mainly influenced by the type of clinic and medical incidents, the performance space and the nature of the audience. The type of clinic relates to the seriousness of the illness, the possibilities of death, the therapy (short-term or long-term) and the side effects of the medical treatment on a child's physiological and psychological well-being. The use of space is an issue in most hospitals and performing is often interrupted by passing visitors and hospital staff. I have seen actors easily lose their concentration and babble their words but I have also seen others deftly cope and respond naturally to interruptions as part of the play. The nature of audiences regards the age groups of participating children as an audience can be considerably mixed from two year olds up to adolescents. It is challenging to address a performance to a wide range of spectators overcoming age boundaries but, mixed audiences go hand in hand with various perceptions of the messages of the play, preferences for fantasy and realism, natural or supernatural heroes, limits of concentration and levels of engagement and satisfaction. This is where hospital professionals such as art and ward managers, nurses, doctors, special teachers and social workers can contribute by the way they 'treat' art/theatre programmes. They can help prepare the children to watch the performance, develop an interest in the plot and, encourage them to participate vocally and verbally.

A Realistic Epilogue

Theatre in the health sector is a growing strand thanks to a number of professionals who have the determination to contribute to their communities in creative and efficient ways. As this determination appears to have many benefits for patients and staff, further research on both non-clinical and clinical implications is recommended in order to determine specific results of the value and effect of theatre performances on particular diseases. Benefits for community agencies and facilitators also need to be further explored towards forming strong and durable community partnerships with theatre and health professionals. It is my hope that professional actors, theatre companies, researchers and funding bodies will implement similar partnerships in communities in crisis as those in developed countries. These will be the foundation of the future for combatting brutality, violence and cruelty, and introducing hope, friendliness and peacefulness in a world of hostility, torture, injustice and madness for children in hospitals worldwide.

NOTES

[1] Personal Communication with Professor Dr Salma Al-Hadad, Director of the Paediatric Oncology Clinic in Baghdad Hospital. Birmingham, 14th July 2009.

[2] Gethin Chamberlain (2009) 'Sri Lanka: child victims of the battle to end a bloody civil war' The Guardian, 25 May, p. 17. Also available at: http://www.guardian.co.uk/world/2009/may/24/srilanka-children-civilian-casualties (Accessed: 04 January 2010).

[3] The Prince of Wales (Available at: http://www.princeofwales.gov.uk/newsandgallery/news/the_duchess_visits_the_unicorn_theatre_in_southwark_london_74454649.html (Accessed: 4 January 2010).

4 Available at: http://www.etoth.com/downloads/biosoccorso.doc (Accessed: 04 January 2010).
5 National Theatre of Northern Greece, *Educational programmes for periods 2007–08 and 2008–09*, http://www.ntng.gr (Accessed: 04 January 2010).
6 *Thumbelina: The Story of a Brave Little Girl* (2008) Available at: http://www.tyascripts.com/Thumbelina.htm (Accessed: 04 January 2010).
7 *Outreach: Imagination Over Limitations*. Available at: http://www.echotheatrecompany.org/imagination.html (Accessed: 04 January 2010).
8 *Clowns bring laughter to children's wards*. Available at: http://www.magichospital.org/wards.htm, (Accessed: 19 May 2009).
9 Available at: http://teatras.mch.mii.lt/Teatras/Kaunas_puppet_theatre.en.htm (Accessed: 04 January 2010).
10 *Big Break, Moscow International Festival of Theatre for Children*. Available at: http://www.rtlb.ru/page.php?id=327 (Accessed: 04 January 2010).
11 *The Importance of Art in the New Hospitals* (not dated) Available at: http://www.equal-works.com/resources/contentfiles/5613.pdf (Accessed: 04 January 2010).
12 *The Hospital for Sick children in Toronto*. Available at: http://www.sickkids.ca (Accessed: 18 May 2009).
13 A Cahoots NI productions and Hall of Fun are supported by the Arts Council of Northern Ireland, Arts and Bussiness New Partners, Mi Wadi, Belfast City Council, Celebrate Belfast 2006, The Heritage Lotttery Fund, The National Lottery and Belfast Institute of Further and Higher Education. Available at: http://www.artscouncil-ni.org/news/2006/new08022006.htm (Accessed 18 May 2009).
14 *Outreach* Available at: http://www.piwacket.com/outreach.html (Accessed: 18 May 2009).

REFERENCES

Aldiss, S., et al. (2009). What is important to young children who have cancer while in hospital? *Children & Society, 23*(2), 85–98.
Kostenius, C., & Öhrling, K. (2009). Being relaxed and powerful: Children's lived experiences of coping with stress. *Children & Society, 23*(3), 203–213.
De Lima, R. A. G., et al. (2009). The art of clown theatre in care for hospitalized children. *Rev Esc Enferm USP, 43*(1), 178–185. Retrieved July 6, 2009, from http://www.ee.usp.br/reeusp/
Nicholson, H. (2005). *Applied drama*. London: Palgrave Macmillan.
Powell, M. A., & Smith, A. B. (2009). Children's participation rights in research. *Childhood, 16*(1), 124–142.
Prentki, T., & Preston, S. (Ed.). (2009). *The applied theatre reader*. London: Routledge.
Sextou, P. (2005). *Theatre-in-education programmes in schools*. Athens: Metaixmio.
Sextou, P. (2007). *Applied theatre in primary, secondary and elementary education*. Athens: Kastaniotis.
Somers, J. (1996). *Drama and theatre in education*. London: Captus University Publications.
Staricoff, L. R. (2006). Arts in health: The value of evaluation. *The Journal of the Royal Society for the Promotion of Health, 126*(3), 116–120.

***Persephone Sextou**, PhD, is a Senior Lecturer in Drama at Newman University College Birmingham. She is currently conducting research in Birmingham Children's Hospital-NHS.*

SECTION X: WAYS OF RESEARCH AND METHODOLOGY

LIORA BRESLER

52. ARTS-BASED RESEARCH AND DRAMA EDUCATION

Keywords: arts-based research, drama based research, qualitative research, arts education, embodied inquiry, performance

The concept of arts-based research (ABR) as a methodology was generated in the early 90s, grew and expanded rapidly, spawning distinct genres, approaches, and communities. This entry examines various approaches and genres under the umbrella of ABR, discusses the concept of embodied inquiry, and its realization through performance and the contributions made by drama-based researchers (DBR), and concludes with reflections on challenges to ABR.

Arts-based inquiry is based on the notion that the processes and the products of arts can contribute to research. The complex, characteristically antagonistic relationships between the constructs of "arts" and "research" and what counts as knowledge go back at least two and a half millennia. The dichotomous view of the senses and perception versus knowledge/truth, a legacy of Plato, was maintained and developed by some of the most important philosophers of the Western world, including Descartes and Kant. According to this dichotomy, arts-based research is an oxymoron.

The postmodern crossing of traditional disciplinary boundaries of the late 20th century has eroded this dichotomy. An early pioneer in the deconstruction of dichotomies is John Dewey, who argued that art and science share the same features with respect to the process of inquiry (1934). Using the metaphor of the *enlightened eye* (1991), Elliot Eisner was pivotal in drawing attention to the central role of the senses in inquiry and the knowledge embodied in artworks. In his conceptualization of research as connoisseurship and educational criticism, Eisner expanded what is considered legitimate forms of representations of research to include the visual, and the poetic as expressive forms that facilitate empathic participation in the situations studied and, in the process, raising consciousness of important social and cultural phenomena.

Eisner's *intellectual entrepreneurship* and his leadership role as president of the *American Educational Research Association* (AERA), enabled him to create structures and spaces for arts-based research. These include a Special Interest Group of ABR, featuring presentations, performances and exhibits of research through dance, drama, literature/poetry, and the visual arts, and a Winter Institute on Arts-Based Approaches to Educational Research taught bi-annually by himself and Tom Barone. Scholarly journals, new (e.g., *Qualitative Inquiry, The International Journal for Education and the Arts*) and established (e.g., *Educational Researcher, Studies in Art Education*) embraced ABR. Handbooks and books (e.g., Knowles and Cole's

S. Schonmann (ed.), Key Concepts in Theatre/Drama Education. 321–326.

Handbook of the arts in qualitative inquiry, McNiff's *Arts based Research*, Cahnmann and Siegesmund's *Arts-based research in education*), were dedicated to ABR.

Initially ABR focused on the literary arts, and the possibilities of transporting word-based art criticism into the field of education (Barone, 2006). Soon, researchers turned to address non-linguistic forms of representation (e.g. Bresler, 2005). Some shifted from ABR as qualitative research toward research-based art. Graeme Sullivan (2005) conceptualized ABR as the imaginative, critical, and intellectual work undertaken by artists as a form of research, taking place in community spaces, Internet studios, museums and galleries. Coming from the field of arts therapy, Shaun McNiff defines arts-based research as a method of inquiry which uses the elements of the creative arts therapy experience, including the making of art by the research, as ways of understanding the significance of what we do within the arts therapy practice (McNiff, 1998, p. 13).

Rita Irwin and her colleagues expanded ABR to address the seamless connections among art-making, research, and teaching (Irwin and de Cosson, 2004). Their concept of a/r/tography is a form of practice-based research, referring to the arts as a way of re-searching the world to enhance understanding, recognizing the educational potential of teaching and learning as acts of inquiry.

ABR consists of diverse "genres", including narrative inquiry, poetry, music, performance, dance, and the visual arts (Knowles and Cole, 2008; Leavy, 2009). Situated on the continuum from the most literary (narrative), to the one least verbal and most embodied (music and dance), drama is at the center, combining text with the non-linguistic embodied images, and sound.

DRAMA-BASED, EMBODIED RESEARCH AND PERFORMANCES

The connections between drama and research reflect a diversity of approaches. Drama-based research (DBR) can also be conceptualized as a way of knowing, highlighting embodied inquiry and communication. Grounded in perceptual awareness, research can turn to the body as a key medium of inquiry. The body and the senses have been used in the conduct of anthropological fieldwork (e.g., Csordas, 1999; Sklar, 2001, Stoller, 1989). Qualitative research can attend to how the body forms and informs the processes of data collecting – interviewing, observing, interpreting, and analyzing.

A second approach reflects drama-based research as a generative vocabulary for the conceptualization and understanding of human behavior (Pelias, 2008), including (i) drawing on qualities such as form and rhythm (Bresler, 2005); (ii) working from inside the body; and (iii) the presentation of self and models of social drama (in Pelias, 2008).

In my own work, I suggest that aesthetics is at the heart of both artistic experience and qualitative research, and that artistic processes, in particular, the space surrounding artistic and aesthetic experiences, can illuminate significant aspects of qualitative research, including data collection, data analysis, and writing. Examining the ways in which the arts provide rich and powerful models for perception, conceptualization, and engagement for both makers and viewers, I highlight their potential to cultivate habits of mind that are directly relevant to the processes and products of qualitative research. I focus on the research goal of empathic understanding which is based on an I-Thou connection within an aesthetic, cognitive/affective space. These dialogical relationships are intensified by the reality or expectation to communicate to an audience, creating a tri-pronged relationship. These connections, always embodied, support improvisation and creativity in data collection and identification of issues (Bresler, 2005).

A fourth approach regards DBR as a form of communication. Informed by Turner (1986) and Schechner (1993), who believed that cultural practices can be represented through embodied presentation, performance ethnography places cultural understanding on the stage (Pelias, 2008). Data collected through traditional qualitative methods such as observations and interviews can be conveyed in performance texts. Positioning audiences to respond in ways that are integral to the reciprocal participation required of arts experience has led to artist/researcher performance inquiries in the works of Norman Denzin, Donald Blumenfeld-Jones, and James Sanders, among others. Norman Denzin (1997), a key figure in advocating performances as part of research, argues: "The performance text is the single, most powerful way for ethnography to recover yet interrogate the meanings of lived experience." Performance-based methods can bring research findings to life, adding dimensionality, and exposing that which is otherwise impossible to authentically (re)present (Leavy, 2009). In social science research, performance can serve various research purposes, including consciousness-raising, empowerment, emancipation, political agendas, discovery, exploration, and education (Leavy, 2009).

CONTRIBUTIONS OF DRAMA EDUCATORS TO DBR

Focusing on the communication of research findings, one common type of performance is Readers Theater, a dramatic presentation of a written work in a script form, reading the text with expressive voices and gestures (Donmoyer and Donmoyer, 1995). Beyond communication, Shifra Schonmann (2001) identifies principles from several theatrical genres, including Playback Theater and Forum Theater, using them not only for presenting data but also for discussion and analysis for both researchers and informants to gain new perspective on the research processes and its findings.

Johnny Saldana addressed the conceptualization of research, as well as its processes and its communication, suggesting that there is a similarity between the aims of qualitative research and playwrights, in the sense that both aim to "create a unique, engaging, and insightful text about the human condition" (1999, p. 60). Theater practitioners share with qualitative researchers the skills of enhanced sensory awareness and observation skills, enabling an attuned sensitivity to fieldwork; the ability to analyze characters and dramatic texts, which transfers to analyzing interview transcripts and field-notes for participant actions and relationships; the ability to think conceptually, symbolically, and metaphorically – all essential for qualitative data analysis; and a proficiency in storytelling (Saldana, 1999).

DBR can be used for pedagogical processes. George Belliveau (2006), for example, presented key findings in the form of a drama. He aimed to capture the learning that emerged during the collective writing and rehearsing of a group of pre-service teachers who developed a play about anti-bullying as part of their teaching practicum. Belliveau uses drama as a method of inquiry, as well as a means of documenting the learning. The work of Kathleen Gallagher combines an arts-based approach with research-based drama, drawing on drama as a process, in what she refers to as experiment in theatre as methodology.

CHALLENGES: MEANINGS, AND CRITERIA

Barone and Eisner's (1997) criteria for Arts-based research are often referred to. They include: 1. The creation of a virtual reality. 2. The presence of ambiguity. 3. The use of expressive language. 4. The use of contextualized and vernacular language. 5. The promotion of empathy. 6. Personal signature of the researcher/writer. 7. The presence of aesthetic form.

Coming from arts therapy, Shaun McNiff (1998/2009) is less concerned with fitting standard definitions of research, and more about an "innate personal test of truthfulness" (p. 12) to determine whether or not the study corresponds to his sense of practice. His questions emphasize a personal reflection: Does the study appear real? Does it touch and illuminate qualities experienced in creative arts therapy? Will the study be of use to others and to the researchers? Will the process of inquiry help people in any way? Does the study resonate with the researcher's experience of creative arts therapy?

Meaning, argues Donal O'Donoghue (2009), resides not only in the work itself, in the relationship between content and form, in the time and place of performance and encounter, and in the nature of the encounter, but also in specific narratives surrounding the work that gives it particular meaning. O'Donoghue urges us to reflect on the place of the encounter and its impact on the nature of the encounter as an opportunity for interpretation. Indeed, the examination of the social conditions of the production is itself an act of interpretation. The question for arts-based-researchers, he suggests, is no longer, "can they go where artists go", but how much further must they go to make their work accessible to the academic community to which they belong, committing to ongoing development of theoretical coherence and epistemological innovation. Without a meaningful commitment to interpretation, O'Donoghue suggests, arts-researchers as academics fall short of that which is expected of them.

While some of the criteria for ABR are the same of qualitative research, (e.g., enhance perception, empathy, and understanding), criteria for the artwork and its quality are often missing. Jane Piirto (2002) questions whether there is a difference between "accomplished" art and art used for social purposes, and personal expression in the social studies, a distinction that I find is reminiscent of Langer's distinction between art and self-expression. In an era that cries out for interdisciplinarity, asks Piirto, is it necessary to have studied or performed the art in order to attempt to do it, display or perform it? Quoting Maxine Greene on the distinction between "art-like" and art, Piirto suggests that there is place for alternative expression. However, not all expression is art. Arts-based research, Piirto argues, should be evaluated by the peer-reviewers of the art-worlds.[1]

Criteria for the research aspect of ABR as research are similarly missing. Philosopher of science Denis Phillips' (in Pariser, 2008) criticizes Eisner's claim that "intelligent judgment" is used by both painters and social scientists alike, arguing that Eisner fudges the huge difference in the way these two professions function. Citing Dewey, Phillips notes that while art and literature are certainly examples of inquiry, in no way are they research in the sense of a methodical examination of a well-framed problem – and the hope of demonstrating the truth or falsity of a claim. Writing from the field of art education, David Pariser, (2008) skeptical about mixing the two worlds of arts and research, regards ABR as a "Trojan horse".

In my own thinking, I find the following criteria for the ARB work to be important: (1) enhances perception, (2) enhances understanding, cognitive and affective, (3) is conceptual, issue-orientated, (4) seeks good form, (5) inscribes substantiation by connecting description to explicit interpretation and conceptualization, (6) discusses subjectivity issues, the role and situated perspective of the researcher.

ABR is in its adolescence. We need ongoing, critical reflection on goals, criteria, and limitations, and, equally important, compelling examples of ABR and DBR to understand possibilities and contributions to knowledge and understanding. Within the area of research education, we want to reflect on the kinds of skills and sensitivities that need to be cultivated in the training of ABR researchers (Bresler, 2009), including the kinds of arts expertise essential in order to apply artists' sensibility to the research project.

I am indebted to Shifra Schonmann, Jeanne Klein, Joan Russell, and Aud BerggrafSæbø for their reading of this entry and their insightful comments.

NOTES

[1] A related issue concerns the spaces in which research and art operate. When considering research-based art, should works by artists that are based on extensive research and interviews with people, be considered research? For example, is Anna Deavere Smith's known for her "documentary theatre" style, featuring Smith as the performer of multiple and diverse characters, a researcher? Is Doug Wright's winner of multiple awards play "I am my own wife", based on extensive research of the main character, considered research?

REFERENCES

Barone, T. (2006). Arts-based educational research then, now, and later. *Studies in Art Education, 48*(1), 4–8.

Barone, T., & Eisner, E. W. (1997). Arts-based educational research. In R. M. Jaeger (Ed.), *Complementary methods for research in education* (2nd ed., pp. 73–98). Washington: AERA.

Belliveau, G. (2006, July 27). Engaging in drama: Using arts-based research to explore a social justice project in teacher education. *International Journal of Education & the Arts, 7*(5). Retrieved June 20, 2009, from http://www.ijea.org/v7n5/

Bresler, L. (2005). What musicianship can teach educational research. *Music Education Research, 7*(2), 169–183.

Bresler, L. (2009). Research education shaped by musical sensibilities. *British Journal of Music Education*, *26*(1), 7–25.

Cahnmann-Taylor, M., & Siegesmund, R. (2008). *Arts-based research in education: Foundations for practice*. London: Routeledge.

Csordas, T. J. (1999). Embodiment and cultural phenomenology. In G. Weiss & H. F. Haber (Eds.), *Perspectives on embodiment: The intersections of nature and culture* (pp. 143–162). New York: Routledge.

Denzin, N. (1997). *Interpretive ethnography: Ethnographic practices for the 21st century*. Thousand Oaks, CA: Sage.

Dewey, J. (1934). *Art as experience*. New York: Perigee Books.

Donmoyer, R., & Donmoyer, J. Y. (1995). Data as drama: Reflections on the use of readers' theater as a mode of qualitative data display. *Qualitative Inquiry*, *1*, 402–428.

Eisner, E. (1991). *The enlightened eye: Qualitative inquiry and the enhancement of educational practice*. New York: Macmillan.

Irwin, R., & de Cosson, A. (Eds.). (2004). *A/r/tography: Rendering self through arts based living inquiry*. Vancouver, BC: Pacific Educational Press.

Knowles, J. G., & Cole, A. (2008). *Handbook of the arts in qualitative inquiry: Perspectives, methodologies, examples, and issues*. Thousand Oaks, CA: Sage.

Leavy, P. (2009). *Method meets art: Arts-based research practice*. New York: The Guildford Press.

McNiff, S. (1998). *Art-based research*. Philadelphia: Jessica Kingsley Publishers.

O'Donoghue, D. (2009). Are we asking the wrong questions in arts-based research? *Studies in Art Education*, *50*(3), 352–368.

Pariser, D. (2008, November). *Arts based research: Shibboleths and Trojan horses an evaluation of a hybrid research approach. What Hath Eisner wrought?* Paper presented at the annual Canadian Society for Education through Art, Montreal, Canada.

Pelias, R. J. (2008). Performative inquiry: Embodiment and its challenges. In J. G. Knowles & A. Cole (Eds.), *Handbook of the arts in qualitative inquiry: Perspectives, methodologies, examples, and issues* (pp. 185–194). Thousand Oaks, CA: Sage.

Piirto, J. (2002). The question of quality and qualification writing: Writing inferior poems as qualitative research. *International Journal of Qualitative studies in education*, *15*(4), 431–445.

Saldana, J. (1999). Playwriting with data: Ethnographic performance texts. *Youth Theater Journal*, *14*, 60–71.

Schonmann, S. (2001). Beyond readers theatre: A perspective on research in aesthetic inquiry. *Arts & Learning Research Journal*, *17*(1), 132–154.

Sklar, D. (2001). *Dancing with the virgin: Body and faith in the Fiesta of Tortuga, New Mexico*. Berkeley, CA: University of California Press.

Stoller, P. (1989). *The taste of ethnographic things: The senses in anthropology*. Philadelphia, PA: University of Philadelphia Press.

Sullivan, G. (2005). *Art practice as research: Inquiry in the visual arts*. Thousand Oaks, CA: Sage.

Turner, V. (1986). *The anthropology of performance*. New York: Performing Arts Journal Publications.

Schechner, R. (1993). *The future of ritual: Writing on culture and performance*. New York: Routeledge.

Liora Bresler *is a Professor at the University of Illinois, Champaign, USA. Her research and teaching focus on Arts and Aesthetic Education, Qualitative Research Methodology, and Educational/Artistic/ /Intellectual Entrepreneurship.*

KATHLEEN GALLAGHER

53. THEATRE AS METHODOLOGY OR, WHAT EXPERIMENTATION AFFORDS US

Keywords: qualitative methodology, improvisation, space, youth, pedagogy

What would constitute a theatre methodology in social science research? Since the completion of my last study in drama classrooms in Toronto and New York schools, I have given much thought to the process of research and its relationship to the processes of improvised drama. In our collaborative qualitative research with young people in schools, we took methodological liberties. In my dictionary, a 'liberty' is defined in eleven different ways; my favourite is: "The ability to move without being limited by something such as tight clothing or lack of space". In other words, we dispensed with our tight clothing, that is, a finely-tuned research question about the pedagogies of drama and their relationship to questions of community and social cohesion in heterogeneous schools, and entered into fictional worlds with youth, so that we could better understand what mattered to them and how their imaginations were engaged in being and creating in the place called school. School, as we had conceived it though, was a too- small and insignificant space. 'Space', as Sherene Razack (1998) has argued, "determines who belongs to the nation state and who does not" (p. 367). If space is the ultimate arbiter, as Razack suggests, it was time to use our space, to transform it, as theatre does, to examine it more closely. Like good drama practitioners, we shed the research garb at strategic moments, and instead let the engagement in the improvised moment lead us. In what follows, I will attempt to take hold of what engaging in theatre-methodologically- affords the qualitative researcher.

Since this initial experiment in qualitative research, I have been thinking a great deal about 'drama methods' in the research moment and what, pedagogically, gets mobilized in order to discover knowledge differently and, in many cases, to discover different knowledge. Something pedagogical and methodological all at once? Something aesthetically attuned and politically engaged? I am thinking about these methods as more than simply interesting improvisational 'tools'. How might we understand applied drama methods as theoretically robust?

In our case, we used theatre to reframe the research context, which means positioning the researcher as 'do-er' or improviser, rather than 'observer'. And as a 'do-er'- in life and in art- you run the risk or gain the benefit of being in an area of not knowing how it is you know something. In this way, non-interpretation of a context, biding one's time, becomes as important as interpretation. The creative process of building a context together with research participants, as with art, takes considerable time and demands something we called 'open readings'. In an age of

S. Schonmann (ed.), Key Concepts in Theatre/Drama Education, 327–331.

measured outcomes and time-bound curriculum events in schools, however, or of re-emergent scientism in the social sciences, or of market-driven cultural production, these choices are not always easily made by teachers or researchers or artists.

Led by art, researchers, teacher, and students moved differently: We created an experiment in research that changed the terms of engagement, the levels of communication, and the modes of cultural production with a group of high school students. Convinced that working in improvised drama made available certain modes of communication, conduct, and embodiment, we were drawn to this research approach for the quality of talk and interaction that we thought it would solicit and for the kind of new insight into young people's worlds we might uncover together with them. We aimed to create a dialogue with them, and they with each other, in which, just as in life, the point was to communicate, a project at once larger and more immediate than an overtly pedagogic one or a narrowly-defined research-driven one. It is the quality of interaction in the improvised moment of creation between actors - a sociology of aesthetics- as I have come to understand it, which fosters a form of communication, and by extension, self-representation, not typical of the regimented social roles allocated to high school students.

This is theatre as methodology, theatre as a mode of devising a meta-world; to collaboratively and artistically frame a 'real' research problem or context in order to peer inside it. Engaging youth in research- theatrically- provides a robust environment for questioning, as the work deals in metaphor, or recreates 'real life' situations in which collaborators are able to more freely experiment with alternate strategies and perspectives in testing the validity of their own theories and insights about the world. Below, a glimpse at the experiment that led us to these conclusions:

In discussions and interviews with students, we were beginning to see emerge a theme from our data which I termed "Identity-Representation-Surveillance":

> First of all, I wouldn't have a jail. All I would ask the students [if I were the principal] is how they would like to see the school run. (Carter, grade twelve Redmount School)

> I think the locked bathrooms, the I.D. swipes and the sweep rules are totally unfair. (Damien, grade eleven Redmount School)

> It feels like we're a bunch of robots. (Adeline, grade twelve Middleview Tech).

Philip, a research assistant, and I devised an extended improvisation activity that we hoped would allow students to imaginatively enter into a created world that would ask them to both improvise and reflect upon their understandings of, and responses to this prevalent theme. Henry (2000) persuasively argues that:

> [t]he structures of qualitative research and of dramas take innovative forms in which means and ends, thought and action, intertwine in an unpremeditated, improvisational fashion. Both involve ways of knowing which people use in their everyday lives: existential knowledge. (p. 51).

In short, on this particular day, in the second year of the study, we decided to move the research inside the art frame. Shifting into role as two uncaring bureaucrats conducting an employee review, we moved inside the questions; we went from asking "how does it make you feel when?" and "what would you do if?" to the matter itself. In doing so, the students were faced with choices not just about how to react, but who they were enacting.

It occurred to me only in hindsight that this methodological shift was resonant with what Dorothy Smith (1999) sets up as an alternative to "established sociology". In this alternative, she does not treat experience as knowledge but as a place to begin inquiry where the aim of the inquiry is not to explain people's behaviour but to explain to people the social-or society- as it enters into and shapes their lives and activities (p. 96). Her alternative is built upon a social theory of knowledge, which "begins in a world of activity, the doings of actual people" (p. 98).

What we did with the students is artificial, to be sure. We created a "fictional" world/workplace of actual people in order to build theory together with youth, or as Foucault has suggested, to theorize in order to explain our experiences when we notice "...something cracked, dully jarring, or disfunctioning in things" (in Rajchman, 1985, p. 35–36). But is this theatre-making world any more "artificial" than a researcher's reconstruction of the "actual one" for the reader? *Theoria*, the form of knowledge that is called theory comes from the same root as does the word theatre (Lyman & Scott, 1975). New theories, I would suggest, become imaginable in the moment of dramatic improvisation, the moment when our latent, embodied and experiential knowledge is called on, when our "actions" become the fodder for the creative responses of others, and when the quality of our communication depends on our ability to take others in. What had been emerging in our conversations with youth, we aimed to re-present through the verisimilitude of the created world. What it afforded us was a shared point of reference, across a range of very diverse lived experiences, to examine precisely how the social, the political, the ideological, are entering and shaping our lives and activities.

"Interviewing," within a sustained improvisation, this analogous world, allows the researcher to consider carefully what "listening to youth" might mean. For youth, story and story-telling become an especially powerful means of communicating. If narrative knowledge is embodied in story-telling (Lyotard, 1984), the better question to ask, perhaps, is how, as researchers, do we enter into young people's fictions and re-tellings? We found one way to be through the remove of the fictional, the convention of creating an alternate world, that allowed us, ultimately, to co-construct knowledge with the youth.

There were about twenty-five students in the class on this day. The entire episode was recorded on video. We asked the group if they were prepared to go into role with us, to give us all another chance to work through some of the themes and issues we'd been discussing through the course of the research. They seemed quite keen to work with us in this different way. We reiterated that we would all be in role together, that Phil and I would be "employers", the bureaucrats, here for their six-month review. We also suggested that we would have time to "unpack" our fictional world together after the drama. Upon re-entering the room anew, we proceeded to call some "employees" up, while others were asked to wait in line. In role, I played the Processor, arbitrarily calling students up to be "fingerprinted" and verified in my laptop computer. I then sent them on to Phil, the Interviewer:

Interviewer (White, male, American-born): What department are you in?

Kayla (Black, female, Caribbean-born): [Straining to hear over the noise] Excuse me?

Interviewer: What department are you in?

Kayla: I don't know... I just started, nobody told me anything.

Interviewer: Hah! [To Processor, loudly.] She doesn't know what department she's in! [Laughs. The rest of class is momentarily quieted, then begins to react to Interviewer's display of contempt.]

Processor (White, female, Canadian-born): [To everyone waiting in line for interview.] We're assuming everyone knows what department they're in. [To individual employee.] Do you know what department you're in?

Interviewer: You don't know what department you're in. Where do you go everyday? [Pause.] This is a six-month review, you have been coming to work for six months and you don't know what department you're in?

Kayla: It's not my fault.

Interviewer: What do you mean it's not your fault?

Kayla: Because I am an employee, the employer is supposed to send me there.

Interviewer: Kayla Ford...now I have to look through the alphabetical list. [Pause, looking for her name on list.] Okay you're in Gardening, just for future reference, you're in Gardening. You know all those flowers and stuff? That's what you do.

[Looking over Manager's report.] Okay well this is fairly consistent...You are giving your manager Monique quite a bit of resistance. She says that you also, several times after work, have been seen loitering around the building.

Kayla: [Very serious, surprised.] Loitering around? That's funny. Every time I'm here I am working. [10 second pause]. If I am not shown respect, I will not give respect.

Interviewer: Okay, well that attitude is going to be problematic in a place like this. The customer comes first. If you expect the customers to hold your hand and bat their eyelashes at you...

(Gallagher, 2007)

Unsurprisingly, the heat of the moment swept us into ambiguous territory where our fabricated setting held real-world implications.

During the one hour of in-role work, students at the back of the room were engaging with each other while we fingerprinted and interviewed others at the front.

The whole experience had the feeling of uncertainty both in terms of the improvisation and for us as researchers. Throughout, it felt risky both dramatically and methodologically...

To the very last, our intent as Processor and Interviewer was to treat the employees with a disinterested discourtesy while forcing them to succumb to the privations of a badly-executed security and employment review. In doing so, we anticipated that we could shape events in such a way that it would be nearly impossible for the students to participate, at whatever level, without making sense of a) why they were here in the first place, b) their reaction to what was happening, and c) the implications (both personal and social) of going through such an experience. It was obvious to the students, I believed, that we were working in an analogous way and that we were asking them to think critically about the many complaints they had previously made to us in interviews and in general classroom discussions about the dehumanizing processes of schooling. In retrospect, our dramatic goals neatly corresponded with our goals as researchers inquiring into the knowledge students produce in drama classrooms in urban schools, an equivalence which, in our view, strengthened the argument for moving our research inside the art experience itself.

Our encounter with the fictional gave our subsequent interviews with students a quality and depth I imagine would be difficult to reproduce without having experienced, together, such a shared context; without having, however briefly, transformed our space. As bell hooks (1992) beautifully captures:

> Spaces can be real or imagined. Spaces can tell stories and unfold histories. Spaces can be interrupted, appropriated, and transformed through artistic and literary practices (p. 153).

REFERENCES

Gallagher, K. (2007). *The theatre of urban: Youth and schooling in dangerous times*. Toronto: University of Toronto Press.

Henry, M. (2000). Drama's ways of learning. *Research in Drama Education, 5*(1), 45–62.

Hooks, B. (1992). *Black looks: Race and representation*. Boston: Sound End Press.

Lyman, S. M., & Scott, M. B. (1975). *The drama of social reality*. New York: Oxford University Press.

Lyotard, J.-F. (1984). Phenomenology. Albany, NY: SUNY Press.

Rajchman, J. (1985*). Michel Foucault: The freedom of philosophy*. New York: Columbia University Press.

Razack, S. (1998). Race, space, and prostitution. *Canadian Journal of Women and the Law, 19*(2), 338–376.

Smith, D. E. (1999). *Writing the social: Critique, theory, and investigations*. Toronto, Buffalo & London: University of Toronto Press.

Kathleen Gallagher *is a Professor at the University of Toronto, holds a Canada Research Chair in Theatre, Youth, and Urban Schools, author of numerous books and articles.*

GEORGE BELLIVEAU AND GRAHAM W. LEA

54. RESEARCH-BASED THEATRE IN EDUCATION

Keywords: research-based theatre, education, ethnodrama, ethnotheatre, evaluation

The use of theatre in educational research has grown over the past three decades from a novel method for disseminating research results into an emerging methodology that has the potential to simultaneously gather, analyze, and disseminate data (Norris, 2000). This entry explores some of the literature on research-based theatre, looking at ways the work has been defined and some of the current debates and issues within the field. The authors then build upon Rossiter et al.'s suggestion of including a dramaturge into the development process as a way of navigating tensions in the field (Rossiter et al., 2008). Then, in an effort to further understand and validate this approach to research in education, the last section seeks systematic ways of evaluating research-based theatre.

DEFINING THE TERM

As the field of research-based theatre is emerging, its terminology is still varied and evolving. Ethnotheatre and ethnodrama are defined by Saldaña and Mienczakowski and Moore as modes of dissemination of data gathered and analysed using traditional qualitative research tools such as action research, narrative, interviews, and field notes (Mienczakowski & Moore, 2008; Saldaña, 2008). However, Norris (2000) argues that theatre can be more than a method of artistic dissemination of data suggesting that "the potential of drama [theatre] as research is fully realized, not when one translates data into a play, but when the dramatic activities shape the presentation in the same way as quantitative research uses numerical data through all stages" (p. 45). Similarly, Schonmann suggests Playback Theatre as a possible method of "simultaneously presenting data, analyzing and interpreting them, and delivering a clear meaning" (2001, p. 144). However, the use of theatre throughout the research process, as suggested by Norris and by Schonmann, is not explicit in current definitions of either ethnodrama or ethnotheatre.

In light of the literature in the field, ethnodrama and ethnotheatre appear to only serve part of the uses of theatre in the research process. The term research-based theatre seems more effective to describe the multiple ways of integrating theatre throughout the research process. Sinding, Gray, Grassau, Damianakis, and Hampson describe research-based theatre as "the use of dramatic form to capture research knowledge" (2006, p. 694). However, this understanding of research-based theatre focuses upon the capturing and dissemination of research data, not the analysis of research data using theatrical techniques as suggested by Norris. Mitchell, Jonas-Simpson, and Ivonoffski open the use of theatre throughout the research process

S. Schonmann (ed.), Key Concepts in Theatre/Drama Education, 333–338.

suggesting that research-based theatre is a way of "enhancing understanding of lived experience in different groups and communities" (2006, p. 198). This understanding of research-based theatre does not restrict the approach to "capturing" or disseminating research; instead, it permits the integration of theatre in any part of the research process, encompassing ethnodrama and ethnotheatre as well as research such as Norris's that uses theatre throughout.

INTEGRITY

While theatre is becoming increasingly used in educational research, Saldaña notes that "the legitimacy of ethnotheatre [and research-based theatre] as a credible genre of research reportage remains suspect to many scholars in the social sciences" (2008, p. 203). If the legitimacy of such research is in question, why then should research-based theatre continue to be explored as a mode of educational research? Denzin argues that "the performance text is the single, most powerful way for ethnography to recover meanings of lived experience" (1997, p. 95). When theatricalising data, researchers show, not tell the results of their research (Saldaña, 2008, p. 201) creating a three-dimensional presentation of their research data. This three-dimensional dramatic form "allows one to retain, at least somewhat, the human dimensions of the life experience qualitative research attempts to study [helping] to not lose research participants in the data or not transform them into dehumanized stereotypes" (Donmoyer & Donmoyer, 2008, p. 216).

Mienczakowski and Moore argue that theatricalizing data can extend the three-dimensional presentation of research to give "an empathetic power and dimension often lacking in standard qualitative research narratives" (2008, p. 451). This "empathetic power" offers insights between the research presentation and the audience in which "the overall performance becomes a shared context that the actor [supported by the researcher] and audience member intimately construct and relate to because of their own emotional link to the topic of the research/performance" (Mienczakowski & Moore, 2008, p. 452). Mienczakowski and Moore stress that when theatre is used as a research approach it is not "about a tradition of artistic endeavour but explanation and emotion evocation ... with one side critical and emancipator. . ., the other side evocative, self-expressing, and intentionally creative" (Mienczakowski & Moore, 2008, p. 452). Through this dual lens, research-based theatre can provide opportunities for a critical perspective through which to view research as well as openings for cathartic responses for audience members.

ART AND DATA

A balance should be maintained between the ethical responsibilities of the researcher to his or her data and the artistic responsibilities of the playwright to the art form. Saldaña describes the process of ethnodramatic playwriting as extracting the "juicy stuff" from ethnographic data (Saldaña, 2005, p. 16). The ethnodramatist "is not a storyteller, she's a story *re*teller. You don't compose what your participants tell you in interviews, but you can creatively and strategically edit the transcripts assuming you wish to maintain rather than 're-story' their narratives" (Saldaña,

2005, p. 20). On the other hand, Mienczakowski suggests that it is the "verbatim nature of the presentations themselves which lends meaningful authority, import, and significance to the resulting realizations" (2001, p. 468).

While the use of verbatim in ethnodrama may lend veracity to research-based theatre, being bound by the data may limit the aesthetic potential of a script. Jackson suggests that if we "lose sight of the aesthetic, the *capacity* of such theatre is diminished" (2005, p. 106). In *After the Crash: A Play About Brain Injury* Rossiter, Gray, et al. integrated dance to "capture physically and non-verbally some of the core *emotional* realities expressed in the focus groups, found often in the *tone* of the words spoken opposed to just the words themselves" (2008, p. 283). In the development of the dance, the playwrights noted a tension between the duty of the researchers to faithfully interpret their data, and presentations of the data that are deliberately left open to interpretation (Rossiter et al., 2008, p. 283). However, navigating the space between the aesthetic and the data is a difficult task and "in order to create a more artistically sound product there may be a danger of mis-representing the data" (Sinding, Gray, & Nisker, 2008, p. 465). Beare and Belliveau suggest that balancing art and research while "staying true to the essence of the data" may be "one of the biggest challenges of writing scripted data" (2008, p. 144).

DRAMATURGE

To help navigate the sometimes contentious divide between research and art, Rossiter, Gray, et al. suggest integrating a dramaturge - "a member of the production team who is concerned with the manner in which the ideas, themes and concepts are represented" - into the process of developing research-based theatre (2008, p. 279). The research-based theatre dramaturge should be fluent in the language and approaches of research and theatre in order to help the researchers and artists translate the "interdisciplinary and epistemological issues" (Rossiter et al., 2008, p. 279) introduced when transforming data to theatre. The research-based theatre dramaturge may help to balance the artistic and aesthetic with the research elements. By integrating a dramaturge into the development of research-based theatre, artists and researchers are better positioned to maintain artistic and research integrity, while exploring the meaning-making that may occur in such collaboration. However, the integration of the dramaturge must be done with care as an additional member in the research team adds another layer of analysis, possibly obscuring the data.

EVALUATION

To our knowledge there have, as of this writing, been no systematic studies evaluating the efficacy of research-based theatre in education. However, there is a body of evaluative research emerging from research-based theatre projects within the health sciences (Colantonio et al., 2008; Gray, Fitch, LaBrecque, & Greenberg, 2003; Kontos & Naglie, 2007; Mitchell et al., 2006; Rossiter, Kontos et al., 2008). This body of research has been surveyed by Rossiter, Kontos, et al. (2008) and can provide a framework for the evaluation of research-based theatre in education.

Rossiter, Kontos, et al. identify "three major methodologies [that] have been used [to evaluate research-based theatre] including unstructured forms of feedback, ... structured but open-ended questionnaires, and highly structured quantitative surveys" (2008, p. 139). Nisker, Martin, Bluhm, and Daar utilized unstructured feedback in the evaluation of their play *Sarah's Daughters*. After each of the twelve performances, the authors conducted and recorded discussions with the audience (2006). This discussion, along with "audience member comments forwarded to [the researcher] following the in-theatre discussion orally, or in electronic or paper mail" and demographic information of audience became the dataset upon which Nisker et al. evaluated the efficacy of *Sarah's Daughters* (2006, p. 230). However, Colantonio et al. note in their evaluation of *After the Crash: A Play about Brain Injury* that the use of post-show focus groups may not be "feasible as many audience members chose not to stay after the performance" (2008, p. 183). To address this, the evaluation of *After the Crash: A Play about Brain Injury* (Colantonio et al., 2008) and *I'm Still Here* (Mitchell et al., 2006) evaluated the efficacy of their research-based theatre productions through a post-show questionnaire structured by Likert-scale questions with spaces after each question for open-ended responses. While such structured yet open-ended surveys allowed audience members to participate quickly in the analysis without having to commit to a lengthy post-show discussion, the audience may not have had the opportunity to properly reflect upon the performance. If a production is aesthetically strong, audience members may be swayed by the artistry and rate the efficacy of the performance higher than they may given the opportunity to reflect a few days or weeks later.

Surveys conducted immediately post-performance such as those conducted for *After the Crash: A Play about Brain Injury* and *I'm Still Here* are unable to explore potential long-term impacts of theatre as a medium for research dissemination. Gray, Fitch, LaBrecque, and Greenberg addressed this limitation of post- performance surveys by studying the long-term impact of their production *No Big Deal?*, a play about men dealing with the effects of prostate cancer treatment (2003). The authors invited health researchers to participate in one pre and two post performance interviews, the first two weeks post-performance, and the other six months post-production. This design allowed the authors to examine the long-term perceptions and effects of research-based theatre; however, the participants were all health-care providers who had agreed to participate in the study, possibly skewing the responses (Gray et al., 2003, p. 227).

While the audience response has been favourable to both the productions and use of research-based theatre as a mode of disseminating research data Rossiter, Kontos, et al. identify three areas where research is lacking: the long-term effects of theatre as a tool for disseminating data, the "*aesthetic* quality of the productions," and "sustained quantitative inquiries" (2008, p. 139). Colantonio et al. suggest that "a randomized control trial that would expose an experimental group to the theatre production and a control group to the same ideas through a traditional form of knowledge... would facilitate a greater understanding of the effectiveness of this type of educational intervention" (2008, p. 184). Further, they suggest that a qualitative exploration of the "interdependence of the educational and aesthetic elements"

(Colantonio et al., 2008, p. 184) of research-based theatre should be undertaken to further the understanding of the efficacy of research-based theatre.

Clearly defined ways of systematically evaluating research-based theatre should benefit the integrity of current work in the field, and more importantly, help move this approach to research forward by offering robust ways of assessing all stages of the research: data collection, analysis, and dissemination. In many ways research-based theatre is still in its infancy as a research methodology, yet with growing numbers of scholars and artists engaged in the field and writing about their process and outcomes the field continues to emerge.

REFERENCES

Beare, D., & Belliveau, G. (2008). Dialoguing scripted data. In S. Springgay, R. L. Irwin, C. Leggo, & P. Gouzouasis (Eds.), Being with A/r/tography (pp. 141–149). Rotterdam: Sense Publishers.
Colantonio, A., Kontos, P. C., Gilbert, J. E., Rossiter, K., Gray, J., & Keightley, M. L. (2008). After the crash: Research-based theatre for knowledge transfer. Journal of Continuing Education in the Health Professions, 28(3), 180–185.
Denzin, N. K. (1997). Interpretive ethnography: Ethnographic practices for the 21st century. Thousand Oaks, CA: SAGE Publications.
Donmoyer, R., & Donmoyer, J. Y. (2008). Readers' theater as a data display strategy. In J. G. Knowles & A. L. Cole (Eds.), Handbook of the arts in qualitative research: Perspectives, methodologies, examples, and issues (pp. 209–224). Los Angeles: SAGE Publications.
Gray, R. E., Fitch, M. I., LaBrecque, M., & Greenberg, M. (2003). Reactions of health professionals to a research-based theatre production. Journal of Cancer Education, 18(4), 223–229.
Jackson, A. (2005). The dialogic and the aesthetic: Some reflections on theatre as a learning medium. Journal of Aesthetic Education, 39(4), 104–118.
Kontos, P. C., & Naglie, G. (2007). Expressions of personhood in Alzheimer's disease: An evaluation of research-based theatre as a pedagogical tool. Qualitative Health Research, 17(6), 799–811.
Mienczakowski, J. (2001). Ethnodrama: Performed research - Limitations and potential. In P. Atkinson, A. J. Coffey, S. Delamont, J. Lofland, & L. H. Lofland (Eds.), Handbook of ethnography (SAGE Publications ed., pp. 468–476) Thousand Oaks, CA.
Mienczakowski, J., & Moore, T. (2008). Performing data with notions of responsibility. In J. G. Knowles & A. L. Cole (Eds.), Handbook of the arts in qualitative research: Perspectives, methodologies, examples, and issues (pp. 451–458). Los Angeles: SAGE Publications.
Mitchell, G. J., Jonas-Simpson, C., & Ivonoffski, V. (2006). Research-based theatre: The making of I'm still here. Nursing Science Quarterly, 19(3), 198–206.
Nisker, J., Martin, D. K., Bluhm, R., & Daar, A. S. (2006). Theatre as a public engagement tool for health-policy development. Health Policy, 78(2–3), 258–271.
Norris, J. (2000). Drama as research: Realizing the potential of drama in education as a research methodology. Youth Theatre Journal, 14, 40–51.
Rossiter, K., Gray, J., Kontos, P. C., Keightley, M., Colantonio, A., & Gilbert, J. (2008). From page to stage: Dramaturgy and the art of interdisciplinary translation. Journal of Health Psychology, 13(2), 277–286.
Rossiter, K., Kontos, P. C., Colantonio, A., Gilbert, J., Gray, J., & Keightley, M. (2008). Staging data: Theatre as a tool for analysis and knowledge transfer in health research. Social Science & Medicine, 66(1), 130–146.
Saldaña, J. (Ed.). (2005). Ethnodrama: An anthology of reality theatre. Walnut Creek, CA: AltaMira Press.
Saldaña, J. (2008). Ethnodrama and ethnotheatre. In J. G. Knowles & A. L. Cole (Eds.), Handbook of the arts in qualitative research: Perspectives, methodologies, examples, and issues (pp. 195–207). Los Angeles: SAGE Publications.

Schonmann, S. (2001). Beyond readers theatre: A perspective on research in aesthetic inquiry. *Arts and Learning Research Journal, 17*(1), 132–154.

Sinding, C., Gray, R. E., Grassau, P., Damianakis, F., & Hampson, A. (2006). Audience responses to a research-based drama about life after breast cancer. *Psycho-Oncology, 15*(1), 694–700.

Sinding, C., Gray, R. E., & Nisker, J. (2008). Ethical issues and issues of ethics. In J. G. Knowles & A. L. Cole (Eds.), *Handbook of the arts in qualitative research: Perspectives, methodologies, examples and issues* (pp. 459–467). Los Angeles: SAGE Publications.

George Belliveau is Associate Professor at the University of British Columbia. His research interests include research-based theatre, drama and social justice, drama across the curriculum, and Canadian theatre.

Graham W. Lea is a PhD student at the University of British Columbia. His research interests include research-based theatre and integration of science and art in education.

LYNN FELS

55. A DEAD MAN'S SWEATER

Performative Inquiry Embodied and Recognized

Keywords: performative inquiry, research, learning, role drama, complexity

... one of these days, I'll be out fishing and I'll see my grandfather's boat returning to harbour. And he'll be bringing the fish back with him, millions of them jumping in the bow waves. And he'll yell, "Boy, hand over that there sweater of mine that you've been wearing. It's darn cold out here!"

I am in the heat of a performative moment, literally, sweating under the fisherman's white wool sweater, rain coveralls, life jacket, and sea cap, imagining the return of my dead grandfather and his crew all lost at sea years ago, off the coast of New-foundland. We are in the opening moments of our role drama on the Newfoundland cod fishery, the local processing plant has been shut down, the cod stock dissipated. In role as an aging fisherman, I regale my grandson about the days when "you could run across the backs of the cod to shore to fetch a forgotten lunch, the fish were so plentiful in those years."

I came to my doctoral studies with a desire to understand the learning that occurs during drama activities such as role drama (introduced to me by my thesis supervisor, Patrick Verriour), playbuilding, and other modes of improvisational creation. I was in search of a learning theory, a research methodology, and a way to share my learning through the arts with others. I was hopeful that I might through my work encourage teachers to engage in drama in education across the curriculum (Fels & Belliveau, 2008). What I did not anticipate was that I would conceptualize and articulate performative inquiry.

Initially I planned to explore how elementary science education might be impacted through drama and storytelling, and embarked upon a three-year research project with Dr. Karen Meyer in her science education course for pre-service teachers (Fels & Meyer, 1997). However, an over the fence conversation with my neighbour, Lee Stothers who was then embarking on her doctoral research in Asian theatre, turned my curiosity towards theorizing performance as an action-site of learning and inquiry (Fels & Stothers, 1996; Fels, 1998, 1999). "We know drama is learning," we agreed, "but how do we theorize it?" Lee sent me off to the library to research the term "performance" in an etymological dictionary (Barnhart, [Ed.], 1988).

Perusing the onion-thin pages, I learned that form refers to *form* or structure, and that *ance* means action (as in d/ance). The prefix, *per*, meaning "utterly, through-out and through," informs the adjacent word, in this case, *form*. If we draw upon Heidegger's understanding of knowledge as an active engagement simultaneously

S. Schonmann (ed.), Key Concepts in Theatre/Drama Education, 339–343.

LYNN FELS

embodying knowing, doing, being, and, as an earlier article I wrote proposes, "creating," we can then say that per/form/ance may be understood as "through form we come to action," recognizing that *action* means "knowing doing being creating" (Fels, 1995). Thus, through engaging with form we come to learning.

However, the prefix *per* is slippery, meaning also:

"to do away, away entirely or to [the] destruction" of form.

Thus, to my surprise, per/form/ance may be read as *"simultaneously* through form *and* through the destruction of form, we come to action, ie. knowing doing being creating. If we further understand that form embodies action, as art educator and theorist Elliot Eisner suggests, and that the shape and construction of a form, whether an object or structure or procedure as situated within an environment or given context reflects the actions, desires and prejudices of those who constructed either the form and/or the environment within which it exists (Christofferson, 2009), then our etymological reading of performance calls us to attention. Knowing that form is embodied action, simultaneously suspect, and accountable, and that we may through its interruption, reshaping and/or destruction come to new understanding, invites us to identify performance as a generative action-space of inquiry and learning.

While an etymological search may be dismissed as a playful jigsaw of meaning-making, what brought me to a standing ovation, much to the librarian's distress, was the complicity of the prefix *per*. With its doubled meaning, "through form and through the destruction of form," we suddenly find ourselves located in a space complexity theorists call "the edge of chaos," between structure and chaos where patterns of interrelations are continually created and recreated through an "endless dance of co-emergence" (Waldrop, 1992, p. 12). In new biology, the edge of chaos is recognized as a generative space of interaction which gives rise to emergent new life; within educational research, we might consider the edge of chaos as a fertile performative engagement of inquiry and reflection bringing forth new possible learning.

Complexity theory and enactivism which both inform performative inquiry draw our attention to what matters: to be mindfully aware of, or as Maxine Greene (1978) reminds us, in "wide-awakeness" to, the interplay of relationships, structures, practices, implications and complicities within embodied forms of action and inter-actions that in turn shape who we are and how we engage in our shared environments. "What we do," Varela says, "is what we know, and ours is but one of many possible worlds. It is not a mirroring of the world, but the laying down of a world..." (Varela, 1987, p. 62). As researchers, it is our task to be aware of how we are engaged and our own complicity and responsibilities as we seek meaning-making in relationship with others and our environment.

Far from merely existing relatively autonomously in the same location, individual and environment continually specify one another. Just as I am shaped by my location, so is my location shaped by my presence. (Davis, Kieran, & Sumara, 1996, p. 157)

Such a location calls to mind our Newfoundland role drama, where we are struggling as community members to come to terms with the processing plant's closure.

> A business tycoon comes to town with the promise of new prosperity, a new hotel on the plant's current location, employment for all. The student in role as the business tycoon is complicit in his promotion of his hotel as the community debates the benefits of tourism; he knows that the employment he offers are minimum wage jobs, that the bulk of the profits will end up in his back pocket and those of his investors. As one promise after another rolls off his tongue, I in role as the old fisherman become suspicious.

Engaging in performative inquiry through improvisational performances such as role drama invites participants and researcher to explore environments, issues, concerns, actions, in role through embodied play and reflection. On occasion (impossible to plan, always hoped for), participants may experience what Appelbaum (1995) calls a stop, a *moment of risk, a moment of opportunity*. Appelbaum's stop moments are those moments that interrupt, that evoke new questioning, that make visible our habits of engagement, our biases, issues we have overlooked or have never considered. It is through our questioning and reflection of these stop moments that new learning becomes possible. Such moments of recognition are those moments when we see a situation or issue from a new perspective, and while we may or may not embody this new learning within the role drama, it may influence us in future interactions. A stop is a moment that calls us to attention; a moment of recognition when we realize that there are other possible choices of action, other ways of being in engagement. And along with choices of action come ethical implications as participants listen for the absences of what has not yet been imagined.

> Tugging his drowned grandfather's sweater over his head, the fisherman thrusts it into the startled hands of the business tycoon. "We had dreams to save our community and you plan to steal it from us. Here. Take it! It's yours! I don't believe that my grandfather will sail home, the cod leaping in his bow waves, not anymore - take his dreams and mine with you back to the city." Nobody speaks. Nobody moves. The silence is deafening. And then the moment erupts into action.

A participant in role as a fisherman comes to my aid, throwing a comforting arm over my shoulder. As he writes later in his journal, my action of handing over my grandfather's sweater to the business tycoon nearly brought him to tears. In that moment, he reports, he realized that he had to respond, that it was his responsibility to come to my assistance. The handing of the sweater to the tycoon, was simultaneously a call to responsibility, a relinquishing of dreams. Recognition that our fishing community was in the process of being betrayed by the business tycoon became a pivotal moment in the role drama and in our inquiry into what may happen when a community loses its main source of economy and turns to others for assistance. This moment of recognition evoked questions as to our own responsibilities and complicity. *How could we give away responsibility for our community's survival to outsiders? What had we risked in disempowering ourselves? How might we now proceed?*

During our debriefing circle and subsequent journal writing - key components of performative inquiry - participants reflected on what had happened during the role play and the moments that had stopped us. While the angst of a dying outport in Newfoundland may be distant from our own experience, we can, if only for a moment of recognition, come to an embodied understanding of what matters and relate it to our own experience: the value of trust, responsibility and care for others and ourselves in relationship to our actions and our relationships within our own community. What matters in our performative engagement together becomes an embodied, symbolic, metaphorical, and ethical stopping point in our shared and individual journeys of inquiry.

What we experience and learn through performative inquiry may be considered within our own lives in relationship with others. Thus performative inquiry becomes a vehicle of investigation, learning, and reconsidering what is possible. Performative inquiry embraces performance - in creative action and interaction, critical thought and reflection - as an action-space of learning and exploration. Its tools of inquiry are our bodies, our minds, our imaginations, our experiences, our feelings, our memories, our stories, our biases, our judgments and prejudgments, our hopes and our desires, our curiosities and our questions - simply, our very *being, becoming.* The catalyst for inquiry may be a question, an event, a theme, an issue, a feeling, a line of poetry, a fragment of lived experience, a narrative quest, a human condition: any phenomenon which we wish to explore through performative engagement.

The performative researcher in concert with his or her participants is guided by questions embodied throughout the inquiry and upon reflection: *What if? What happens? What matters? So what? Who cares?* What is exciting about performative inquiry is that we enter a performative space of what is not yet known, and are challenged to experience our interplay together in ways that call what is absent or not yet recognized into presence. Cognition or learning is seen not as a mental operation separate from the body in action and interaction with others but as "*...an ongoing bringing forth of a world* through the process of living itself" (Maturana & Varela, 1992, p. 11, my italics).

> *it is in the meeting places between we become*
> *Here and Now, something happens. (Fels, 1999, p. 43)*

It is within these meeting places realized through performative inquiry that something happens - a moment of hesitation, a stop, a moment of recognition, that is our learning, our knowing, our being becoming. Writer Jana Milloy notes that a moment is "a child of duration" (2007, p. 157). Such moments may last a lifetime as we reimagine, reconsider, remember what matters, and explore how we may engage anew with each other in our shared environments of inquiry and learning. Through the lens and interplay of performative inquiry, unexpected moments of encounter call us to attention. And it is these communal and individual space-moments of recognition that performative inquiry seeks and maps, charting turbulent waters with navigational skills honed by the risk and possibility that is performance.

REFERENCES

Applebaum, D. (1995). *The stop*. Albany, NY: State University of New York Press.

Barnhart, R. D. (Ed.). (1988). *The Barnhart dictionary of etymology*. New York: H.W. Wilson.

Christofferson, R. (2009). *Dancing in the Belly: Performative inquiry in pregnancy*. Unpublished Master's thesis. Burnaby, BC: Simon Fraser University.

Davis, B., Kieren, T., & Sumara, D. (1996). Cognition, co-emergence, curriculum. *Journal of Curriculum Studies, 28*(2), 151–169.

Fels, L. (1995). Cross-country with Grumet: Erasing the line. *Educational Insights*. Retrieved from http://www.lane.educ.ubc.ca/insights/home.htm

Fels, L. (1998). In the wind clothes dance on a line. *Journal of Curriculum Theorizing, 14*(1), 27–36.

Fels, L. (1999). *In the wind clothes dance on a line: Performative inquiry - A (Re)Search methodology*. Unpublished doctoral dissertation. Vancouver, BC: University of British Columbia.

Fels, L., & Belliveau, G. (2008). *Exploring curriculum: Performative inquiry, role drama, and learning*. Vancouver, BC: Pacific Educational Press.

Fels, L., & Meyer, K. (1997). On the edge of chaos: Co-evolving world(s) of drama and science. *Journal of Teacher Education, 9*(1), 75–81.

Fels, L., & Stothers, L. (1996). Academic performance: Between theory and praxis. In J. O'Toole & K. Donelan (Eds.), *Drama, culture, and education* (pp. 255–261). Australia: IDEAS.

Greene, M. (1978). *Landscapes of learning*. New York: Teachers College Press.

Maturana, H., & Varela, F. (1992). *Tree of knowledge: The biological roots of human understanding* (Rev. ed.). Boston: Shambhala.

Milloy, J. (2007). *Persuasions of the wild: Writing the moment, a phenomenology*. Unpublished doctoral dissertation. Burnaby, BC: Simon Fraser University.

Varela, F. (1987). Laying down a path in walking. In W. I. Thompson (Ed.), *GAIA: A way of knowing - Political implications of the new biology* (pp. 48–64). Hudson, NY: Lindisfarne.

Waldrop, M. M. (1992). Complexity: *The emerging science at the edge of order and chaos*. New York: Simon & Schuster.

Lynn Fels is Assistant Professor at Simon Fraser University, Canada. She co-authored Exploring Curriculum: Performative Inquiry, Role Drama and Learning with George Belliveau.

STEFINEE PINNEGAR AND MARY LYNN HAMILTON

56. SELF-STUDY INQUIRY PRACTICES

Introduction to Self-study Inquiry Practices and Scholarly Activity

Keywords: action research, autoethnography, scholarship of teaching, narrative
inquiry, self-study of teacher education

The emergence of self-study inquiry practices requires a new conception of research
and scholarship for researchers in teacher education generally and theater education,
specifically. Lieberman (1992) introduced such a concept, "scholarly activity"
which captures the contradictory elements of self-study of inquiry practices by
marrying the idea of using systematic, critical, and empirical examination to develop
knowledge with an imperative to act to produce real rather than only theoretical
effects.

The work of theater education is fundamentally about scholarly activity since
teaching teachers to direct plays, to teach student actors and technicians, and
even to appreciate theater and all forms of dramatic media require both activity
in understanding and production, and scholarship in coming to understand the
context of a time and the tools needed to communicate ideas. Action Research
(including Collaborative Participatory Action Research), Auto-ethnography (Ellis,
2004), Narrative inquiry (Clandinin, 2006), Life History Approaches (Goodson &
Sikes, 2001), Scholarship of Teaching, Self-Study of Teacher Education Practices,
and Teacher and/or Reflective Practice Research (Cochran-Smith & Lytle, 2009)
are methodologies commonly employed for self-study of practice. They share
common and unique features which are outlined and articulated more completely in
Pinnegar and Hamilton's (2009) *Self-study of practice as a genre of qualitative
research: Theory, methodology, and practice.*

Common Features

Most self-study inquiry researchers regardless of methodology resonate with the
idea that as theater educators develop knowledge useful in understanding and guiding
teacher education, such knowledge and understanding should be evident in or based
on their practice, submitted to the crucible of public opinion through submission for
publication, and contribute and link to the research conversations in theater teacher
education specifically, and teaching and teacher education, generally. In research
conducted from a self-study of practice perspective, inquiry is seen as fundamentally
subjective and first person forms of expression appear in the manuscripts. Yet most
if not all of these methodologies can be characterized as empirical because the
inquirer constructs and collects observational data on which analysis is conducted

S. Schonmann (ed.), Key Concepts in Theatre/Drama Education, 345–350.

and what are traditionally called findings but in these inquires might be referred to as understandings, assertions for action, or wonderings emerge (e.g. & Pinnegar & Hamilton, 2009).

Another common feature is that the self is intimately involved and entangled in the inquiry. Theatre teacher educators might want to study how they teach pre-service teachers about how to engage their own students as actors, how to work with parents, or how to develop critical literacy skills. In such a study, the scholar would collect observational data that allowed them to examine the action they were taking in course organization, assignments, as well as one-on-one interaction. In this way the self-study conducted would be both self-initiated and self-focused (LaBoskey, 2004). Autoethnography researchers might construct careful auto-biographical field notes that would capture both their current experience working with pre-service teachers but might also develop recollections of their experiences from their own work as teachers or even their development as actors. Ellis (2004) argues we know the world through ourselves and our bodies and thus any research is essentially a study of self. Narrative inquirers (Clandinin, 2006) conducting studies might construct field notes that capture stories and narratives of their experiences both past and present as they lay their own experiences alongside those of their pre-service teachers attempting to become theatre educators. The stories of these experiences provide justification for their curiosity, investigation and interpretation in studying their practice.

The use of methodology rather than method here is a choice that reflects another common characteristic of these inquiry practices. Most people who engage in inquiry centered on their practice and through their perspective as the practitioner/teacher use standard methods such as interviewing, journaling, videotaping, surveying, observational field notes, or case study (to mention a few) in conducting their studies. They adhere to the specifications for these methods in their research design, data collection and analysis with the caveat that the self is part of the equation.

Tensions and Differences among Self-study Inquiry practices

Divergences in self-study of inquiry practices are evident in the title of this entry - self-study inquiry practices. First there is tension in the relationship between the self and the practice. For example, Autoethnography (Ellis, 2004) and Life History Approaches (Goodson & Sikes, 2001) are more oriented toward the self end of this dichotomous continuum. Through taking up a careful consideration of the self and the experiences of the self, inquirers develop understanding about experience and practice. Although study by study this varies, Scholarship of Teaching (Carnegie Foundation, http://www.carnegiefoundation.org/) and Action Research (McNiff & Whitehead, 2009) are on the other end of the continuum. From these perspectives inquiries explore, collect evidence from, and document practice and while the self is part of the practice being studied the target for inquiry is practice. McNiff and Whitehead (2009) insist such inquires must address the question - what would count as evidence of the practice? - and argue that the evidence must be presented in the voice of the others engaged in the practice.

The Scholarship of Teaching inquiries attempt to improve practice through increased understanding of students, content or teaching. Teacher Researcher/ Reflective Practice studies are mired in this tension since the researchers - public school teachers - must maintain relationships with all those involved - principals, parents, students or even district personnel. Self-study of teaching practices wholly embrace this tension asking that inquiries simultaneously consider the self and the other within the practice being studied (Pinnegar & Hamilton, 2009) and Narrative Inquirers studying their own practices exist uneasily within this same tension between studying self and practice (Clandinin, 2006).

Another point of divergence is represented in the tension in the pairing of inquiry and self. This tension is between basing the study's trustworthiness in ontology or epistemology. Some researchers orient themselves toward epistemology - turning true belief into knowledge. This orients the researcher toward debate about issues of validity within the norms of the scientific method. Others focus more on under-standing what is. They are more concerned with the accuracy of the account in uncovering the practice and the interrelationships of self and practice. Pinnegar & Hamilton as well as Clandinin provide discussion about this dichotomy and its relationship to methodologies. Action Research and Scholarship of Teaching Studies are more likely to focus on epistemology while Narrative Inquiry and Self-Study of Teacher Education practice are grounded in ontology. Teacher Researchers exist in tension between these two frames because their political positioning in practice requires attention to ontology but their position of power in the larger context of research requires intense attention to epistemology.

The final tension emerges from the pairing of inquiry and practice which concerns notions of objectivity and subjectivity in educational research. Within the positivist research tradition, objectivity is highly valued because it is essential for generaliz-ability - warranted findings from one setting can be legitimately transferred to another. Objective studies ensure that the perspectives, background experience, understanding or bias of the researcher does not enter into the study. Yet, self-study inquiry practices embrace the opinions, experience, understanding of the self as a valuable resource and a central feature in design, data collection, analysis, and representation.

This tension is present because the mere naming of a study as situated in personal experience (the self) marks it as subjective. Behind this tension is the concern that insights, wonderings, or findings from the study will be accepted as trustworthy, rigorous and useful for other researchers. As a result, self-study inquirers are concerned with convincing individual readers and the research community that their ideas have been vetted and are worthy of thoughtful consideration. Subjectivity may be less concerning for Autoethnographers than it is for Self-Study of Teacher Education Practice Researchers, Scholarship of Teaching Researchers, Action Researchers or other self-study inquirers who may attend more actively to tenets of objectivity in data collection and analysis. Autoethnographers and Life History researchers engage in studies knowing that the data they collect and their perspective on the question(s), situations, or topics they inquire about come from their personal subjective perspective. They realize from the beginning that their project will excavate their experience and opinion in relationship to an area of interest - a subjective stance. Teacher Researchers, more than any other group, are more often positioned as not quite as rigorous or scholarly as those doing more "traditional" research simply because of their location as teachers; thus, their desire to produce objective research may be greater and the research community as a whole may hold higher standards of objectivity for them.

FIVE CHARACTERISTICS

LaBoskey (2004) offers five characteristics for Self-Study of Teacher Education Practices inquiry: Self-initiated and focused, Improvement aimed, Interactive, Multiple primarily qualitative methods, Exemplar-based validation. They can be used to guide self-study of practice research.

Self-Initiated and Focused

The answer to the questions "who" is doing the research and "who" is being studied is the self. Professional practice embodies what practitioners know in, of, and about practice. Through cycles of critical reflection, the researcher uncovers and produces knowledge of practice. For Self-Study of Teacher Education Practices Researchers, this leads to reframing their practice.

Improvement Aimed

A functional definition of self-study is we study practice to improve it. One assumption is improved understanding of practice leads to improvement. A second assumption is improvement is always a goal - no practice arrives at perfection. Self study produces two kinds of knowledge: embodied knowledge residing in the inquirer's practice and research knowledge that contributes to the field.

Interactive

Self-study requires collaboration with others in the practice, with researchers (including research texts), with data sets, etc. It is grounded in a process of knowing that can be characterized as dialogue (Pinnegar & Hamilton, 2009).

Multiple, Primarily Qualitative, Methods

Self-study of inquiry requires multiple means for defining, discovering, developing, and articulating knowledge of practice, thus self study of practice researchers use whatever methods will provide needed evidence and context for understanding practice.

Exemplar-based Validation

For the self-study inquirer the authority of their own experience provides a warrant for their knowing. The validity of its claims is established through an exemplar approach to validation articulated by Mishler (1990, cited in LaBoskey, 2004). A study receives validation when other investigators use it in their work.

INQUIRY CYCLE

Design for self-study inquiry projects usually proceeds through consideration of sets of questions that begin by focusing the inquiry, uncover what is already known, indicate appropriate data collection and selection of method, and connect to the research literature as a whole (Pinnegar & Hamilton, 2009).

- The first set of questions help the inquirer narrow the study by identifying what it is they want to study further: What am I interested in exploring? What are your living contradictions? What issues do I want to further understand? What do I want to learn about these interests, issues, and concerns?
- The second set of questions support the inquirer in deciding practice or context to explore and who to involve: How could I explore these concerns and issues? What contexts might be most fitting? Who are the most appropriate participants - you? Your students?
- The third set of questions engages the inquirer in deciding what methods to use and what evidence to collect: What methods might I use? What would count as evidence?
- The forth set of questions orients the inquirer theoretically, philosophically and personally: What work in teacher education research (or other research fields) will guide my inquiry? What beliefs are embedded in my questions? What values do I embody in my practice and research? How will I hold myself accountable? What do I expect to contribute to the knowledge base?

CONCLUSION

Zeichner (1999) argues for a "new scholarship in teacher education" where such scholarship provides "a deep and critical look at practices and structures in teacher education in order to "contribute to knowledge and understanding for the larger community" (p. 11). He encourages those enacting this scholarship "to be sensitive to the personal and social complexities of the work" (p. 11). Those who use selfstudy inquiry practices embark on such a quest.

REFERENCES

Carnegie Foundation. Website. Retrieved July 29, 2009, from http://www.carnegiefoundation.org/

Clandinin, D. J. (2006). *Handbook of narrative inquiry: Mapping a methodology.* Thousand Oaks, CA: Sage Publications.

Cochran-Smith, M., & Lytle, S. (2009). *Inquiry as stance: Practitioner research for the next generation.* New York: Teachers' College Press.

Ellis, C. (2004). *The ethnographic I: A methodological novel about autoethnography.* Walnut Creek, CA: Alta Mira Press.

Goodson, I., & Sikes, P. (2001). *Life history in educational settings: Learning from lives.* Buckingham: Open University Press.

Lieberman, A. (1992). The meaning of scholarly activity and the building of community. *Educational researcher, 21*(6), 5–12.

LaBoskey, V. K. (2004). The methodology of self-study and its theoretical underpinnings. (99 817–871). In J. J. Loughran, M. L. Hamilton, V. K. LaBoskey, & T. Russell (Eds.), *International handbook of self-study of teaching and teacher education practices* (pp. 817–871). Dordrecht, The Netherlands: Kluwer Academic Publishers.

McNiff, J., & Whitehead, J. (2009). *Doing and writing action research.* Thousand Oaks, CA: Sage Publications.

Pinnegar, S., & Hamilton, M. L. (2009). *Self-study of practice as a genre of qualitative research: Theory, methodology, and practice.* Dordrecht, The Netherlands: Springer.

Zeichner, K. (1999). The new scholarship in teacher education. *Educational Researcher, 28*(9), 4–15.

Stefinee Pinnegar, a teacher educator at Brigham Young University, inquires into teachers' and teacher educator's tacit knowledge using self-study of practice methodologies.

Mary Lynn Hamilton, Professor in Curriculum & Teaching at the University of Kansas, combines teachers' professional knowledge, social justice, and self-study of practices in her research.

CLOSING

GAVIN BOLTON

57. FROM A DISTANCE

Keywords: personal history, changes, practice/theory, caution

No, I am not referring to Brecht's *Verfremdung* or Shklovsky's *Ostrananie*, both concepts usefully summarised by Stig Eriksson in his lucid analysis of 'distancing' in drama education (pp. 65–71), but to the distance of time since I gave up full-time employment at Durham University over 20 years ago. As someone who has for many years been out of touch with what is now going on in education (still an active theatre-goer however) I realised, as I began reading the contributions to this publication that I am experiencing another kind of distance: a sense of detachment. I no longer have a vested interest in any particular direction the academic field might be taking. I am just curious, open-minded (I hope!) and looking for new horizons.

As I started reading the 'attachments' piling into my computer, I appreciated a difference in tone, for now the genre of 'drama education' is much more firmly established than in my day. When I started putting pen to paper or rather, 'fingers to typewriter', there were only two UK University lecturers in the subject – Dorothy Heathcote and me. And, of course, I was not really an academic. I was a drama *teacher*, experimenting in new practices, desperately trying to find the right words to describe what I was doing, relying heavily on all sorts of sources such as philosophers of aesthetics, approved educationists, psychologists and sociologists. The post second world-war image of drama education shared three contrasted contexts: the stage (training kids to put on a show); the classroom (speech-training); and, seen as the most exciting, the school hall (the children stripped off in their P.E. gear for self-expression – in a space on their own). So, underlining my early attempts at writing, was my continuing determination to establish alternative practices to these. But of course that was not as single-minded as it sounds, for throughout my career I found myself also trying to absorb into my theorising other peoples' innovations, for example, two contrasting American themes of Spolin's *Theatre Games* and Moreno's *Psychodrama*[1] along with the amazing developments in Heathcote's practice. On reflection, I would (reluctantly!) suggest that although the centre of my theoretical arguments remained rooted in drama as an art form, perhaps the edges at times have been somewhat blurred by my dual role of fighting to replace the 1950s' image described above and embracing the innovations pouring in from many different directions. Along with others my main concern was to open doors for drama teachers and for teachers using drama, inviting them to experiment with new ideas.

But on reading the entries in this book I appreciate that things are different now. The tone has changed. Contributors, secure in an established academia of drama educators, know that they have a virtual library of publications on the subject to refer to and more importantly, know they can rely on an audience of readers who are ready to make an informed response to their texts, a captive audience, as it were! It is clear, however, that although there now exists a supportive collegiate of experts, the public at large remain relatively ignorant of the value of educational drama. As John O'Toole writes, we need to "get visible" (p. 17).

I was not surprised that *research* features as a key topic in current writings. In my day research in the arts was treated with suspicion. Even today Liora Bresler (p. 325) warns us that Arts-Based Research (ABR) is still in its adolescence, but what has surprised and excited me is the notion put forward by Kathleen Gallagher (pp. 327–331), Lynn Fels (pp. 339–343), George Belliveau and Lea Graham (pp. 333–338) that the very structure of theatre form is in itself a possible framework for research, so that that moment of **grandfather's sweater being thrust "into the startled hands of the business tycoon"** (p. 341), a moment of sheer theatre, is convincingly explained by Lynn Fels as also a moment of "performative enquiry".

After I retired I heard about 'Applied Theatre', but have never been sure in what context it should be used, although I have been tempted, when asked by a casual acquaintance "What was your work, Gavin?" to offer "Oh, I worked in Applied Theatre" as a way of frustrating the usual assumptions that 'working in drama' means 'an acting career'. Helen Nicholson's contribution (pp. 241–245) clarifies the concept, not with a view to severely limiting its application, but to extending our understanding of the political context from which it derived. For me one of the most openly politically motivated pioneers of the 20th century was Augusto Boal whose first workshop in Europe, following his exile from Brazil, I was lucky enough to attend[2]. I learnt about empowering the spectators into taking action. Nicholson favours broadening the concept beyond any political route but accepts that its purpose may well be to bring about 'social change' while warning us that "more work needs to be done" (p. 244) in defining its context and purpose. This notion of empowering participants to make change is not, of course, confined to Applied Theatre. Bethany Nelson's *Power and the Community* (pp. 81–85), focusing on school students, advocates the use of Process Drama, in-role drama and playmaking as a means of engaging "in a collective struggle against the status quo" (p. 81).

Of course some of the current concerns relating to drama education are essentially covering the ground I struggled with throughout my career. Julie Dunn's (pp. 29–33) careful examination of the teacher's function in promoting child- structured dramatic play brought back memories of trying to persuade teachers that 'play' did not mean 'free play'. Her reference (p. 31) to John O'Toole's image of the necessary tension as 'boulders in a stream' reminded me of the workshops I used to run on the various categories of tension a teacher might usefully insert into the creative action. Turning to Cheela F K Chilala's writing (pp. 159–162), I was intrigued by his account of the African Narrative Tale, not something I have had the privilege of experiencing, although my first ever drama teaching abroad was during a brief visit to Lesotho in the late '60s. Carole Miller and Juliana Saxton (pp. 147–151) also promote Storydrama, actually giving us the first steps of a lesson plan so that we enter the classroom as we read - and their Storydrama experience becomes 'real'.

Perhaps there is a danger sometimes that in taking an overdose of academically pitched argument we become distanced from practice. I suppose it is inevitable that we become so absorbed in clarifying concepts, categories, objectives, labels, means of assessment, issues etc that we provide insufficient illustrations of practice, of teacher/student actions and dialogue that have actually taken place. And is there another danger, that in writing *about* the art form we *lose* it? Not, however, when we read Kathryn Ricketts' contribution (pp. 135–139): "**I have a suitcase in hand, donning my oversize overcoat and hat**" (p. 138) Thus she thrusts a theatrical image (a signifier) at us when we are in the middle of absorbing her scholarly explanation of 'Embodied Poetic Narrative' – and we are momentarily held by the on-stage picture in our heads. She later in her entry writes of 'fractured signifiers' (p. 138) using the example of a man's hockey stick to ask new questions. Such manipulation of objects reminds me of the playwright Edward Bond (I don't think he is referred to in any of the entries) whose TIE scripts focus on the meaning of and the revaluing of objects.[3]

Rickett's notion of making the familiar unfamiliar is also close to the heart of Dorothy Heathcote's artistry. Heathcote, whom I can only describe as an artist/educator of genius whose influence will be more appreciated as future generations of teachers – all teachers, not just drama teachers - understand and accept the significance of her work, is referred to or quoted in many entries. An example of a rich absorption of Heathcotian methodology, in this instance the use of 'double-framing', can be seen in Alistair Martin-Smith's *Looking for Shakespeare* (pp. 191–195) in which Martin-Smith gives a vivid account of his work with adolescent groups. It is Heathcote's *practice* and not necessarily her early attempts to codify that practice into handy guidance charts for teachers that must be the source of inspiration for future generations. As for all of us, her occasional ventures into formalising her approach need continual revising. There is a good example of such revision in this publication by Kari Mjaaland Heggstad (pp. 259–264) who re-examines and refines Heathcote's use of the 'framing' concept.

In describing his Shakespeare journey Martin-Smith refers, in passing, to Heathcote's 'Mantle of the Expert'. I think I had been hoping for more such references in this book, but overall there is a silence on the subject. However, Bogusia Matusiak-Varley (pp. 35–38) makes up for this. She paints a compelling background to this relatively unrecognised educational strategy. And, such is its nature, that if you have not seen it in action, reading Matusiak-Varley's account may leave you simply bewildered, as it is very difficult to explain on paper: it aims at changing the very culture of the classroom as a context for learning. Dorothy Heathcote began inventing this method some 30 years ago. It was not until 1995 that I offered to co-author her in a publication[4] on the subject. Not that I was any good at teaching it! – I lacked the patience needed to prepare the materials and tasks required for the gradual opening up of knowledge - but I just saw huge possibilities in its usage by all teachers who believe that education of children is about wanting to learn, personal well-being, leadership and, as Matusiak-Varley puts it: "developing responsible and ethical practices" (p. 36).

GAVIN BOLTON

A project I have been interested in reading about, but of course have no first- hand experience of, is the formation of DRACON here written about by Margret Lepp (pp. 99–104). This scheme, dealing with 'conflict management', extended into partnership with Malaysia and Australia and then, as its viability became respected, to other countries of the world. The methodology employed appears to link with what Eva Österlind (pp. 247–251) refers to as Forum *Play* a sophisticated extension of Forum Theatre that colleagues in Sweden have been developing over many years.

Another topic in this book that I have not ever read about before is *Drama Education for Individuals on the Autism Spectrum* by Parasuram Ramamoorthi and Andrew Nelson (pp. 177–181). Here we are given a fascinating picture of a highly specialised area in which the authors conclude that, overall, it is the "artist within" (p. 180) that should be given priority over a mere set of skills and behaviours. One can see that the use of role-play and scripts to try out social situations could also be effective, but I would be wary of following some of the recommended techniques detailed in the entry in case I, as an amateur, failed to recognise the complex range of needs which I understand may be present even within a small group. This reminds me of a strand of my own work which I enjoyed immensely: For many years I worked once a week in term time in a Psychiatric hospital with adult patients using what I called 'sitting down' drama in which we improvised fictitious events relating to a problem with which one or more of the small circle of patients was connected. The consultant (always present) used the material as a shared reference point in meeting up with each patient a day or so later. We seemed to have some success, but I often wondered whether there were occasions when more harm than good was done because of the complexity of some patients' illness. (Crying out for research!) I think perhaps I am disappointed that Drama Therapy barely gets a mention in this publication.

An important strand of the book is 'Theatre for Young Audiences' (even as young as babies![5]). There seems to be a shared concern among the contributors to this aspect of drama education that gauging what kind and content of theatre is appropriate for children may well be problematical. Roger Bedard (pp. 283–287) reminds us of the historical distrust of theatre; Annie Giannini (pp. 301–305) records some of the pitfalls experienced in trying to change a cultural attitude to sexuality; Persephone Sextou (pp. 313–318) writes of the desperate need 'to draw smiles on sick children's faces' (p. 313) when the hospital patients are victims of war. Amy Petersen Jensen's entry (pp. 227–232), on the other hand, bursts with enthusiasm for the use of digital technology in TYA (p. 228), a concept that leaves my generation far behind!

Tony Jackson raises important issues in his authoritative entry on participatory forms of educational theatre (pp. 235–240). Using John O'Toole's three levels of participation, he indicates for the reader both the degree of engagement involved in each category and the range of conventions most commonly utilised. And then he challenges us to consider whether the term 'participation' is itself adequate, a concept, he suggests, that does not necessarily imply a 'moving forward'. In the wrong hands it could be "…just one more ornamental, illusionistic device: a treachery perpetrated on the audience while disguised as being on behalf of the audience"

(p. 239). Although Jackson's paper is focused on T.I.E., his warning could well apply to classroom drama and Applied Theatre. I am sure I am guilty of using the term 'participation' too loosely at times in the past, rather like the popular 'free expression' of the 1950s, as though it was sufficient in itself. Jackson is right to replace it with words such as 'transaction' and 'interactivity', both implying negotiation on equal terms.

I have enjoyed pondering on these important changes of emphasis in our shared field of drama education. Some things have not changed: for instance, pioneers today still seem to rely on John Dewey and Paulo Freire as sources of educational wisdom! The contribution to this publication that I just cannot get out of my mind, however, is the one that challenges us all to recognise the conflicting dimensions of our individual and cultural identities. Dan Baron Cohen, President of IDEA, using the very language of theatre to confront us with the nature of our humanity, reminds us all of our responsibility in choosing to work within this art form of drama (pp. 87–91).

This whole book is about individual and cultural identities! Sixty people from around the world have contributed to this tapestry of theatre/drama education, using a remarkable variety of colours and textures to portray a field of study, scholarship, classroom enterprise, artistry and adventure. I do not know of any other publication that so clearly says: "We are a community of artists/teachers/ students and this is the frame we share". And within that frame, of course, the newcomer is welcomed to experiment in weaving his/her own thread. The way in which this book has evolved is remarkable. The gradual growth of interdependence and intercommunication between the contributors gives the publication a special place in our scholarly resources. We thank Shifra for her inspiration, her dedication and for her sheer hard work in taking on this responsibility. I believe she has created something unique, a new way of perceiving how professional people might comfortably share their experiences and aspirations.

NOTES

[1] Interestingly, these barely get a mention in the preceding 57 entries.
[2] Manon van de Water's *Framing Children's Theatre: Historiography, Material Content and Cultural Perception* (pp. 277–281) gives an interesting historical account of the political control over Soviet children's theatre.
[3] Davis, D. (Ed) (2005). *Edward Bond and the Dramatic Child*. Stoke on Trent, UK: Trentham Books.
[4] Heathcote, D. & Bolton G. (1995). *Drama for Learning: Dorothy Heathcote's Mantle of the Expert Approach to Education*. Portsmouth, NH: Heinemann.
[5] Evelyn Goldfinger's *Theatre for babies: a new kind of theatre?* (pp. 295–299)

Gavin Bolton, PhD, is Reader Emeritus of the University of Durham, UK, retired visiting Professor of Victoria University, Canada and of New York University.

INDEX